WATCHING DARKNESS FALL

Also by David McKean

Suspected of Independence: The Life of Thomas McKean,
America's First Power Broker

The Great Decision: Jefferson, Adams, Marshall, and the
Battle for the Supreme Court (with Cliff Sloan)

Tommy the Cork: Washington's Ultimate Insider from
Roosevelt to Reagan

Friends in High Places: The Rise and Fall
of Clark Clifford (with Douglas Frantz)

Partners of First Resort: America, Europe, and the Future
of the West (with Bart M. Szewczyk)

WATCHING
DARKNESS
FALL

FDR, HIS AMBASSADORS, AND THE RISE OF
ADOLF HITLER

David McKean

ST. MARTIN'S PRESS
NEW YORK

First published in the United States by St. Martin's Press, an imprint of
St. Martin's Publishing Group

WATCHING DARKNESS FALL. Copyright © 2021 by David McKean.
All rights reserved. Printed in the United States of America.
For information, address St. Martin's Publishing Group,
120 Broadway, New York, NY 10271.

www.stmartins.com

Library of Congress Cataloging-in-Publication Data

Names: McKean, David, 1956- author.
Title: Watching darkness fall : FDR, his ambassadors, and the rise of Adolf Hitler /
David McKean.
Other titles: FDR, his ambassadors, and the rise of Adolf Hitler
Description: First edition. | New York : St. Martin's Press, 2021. | Includes
bibliographical references and index.
Identifiers: LCCN 2021027073 | ISBN 9781250206961 (hardcover) |
ISBN 9781250206985 (ebook)
Subjects: LCSH: United States—Foreign relations—1933-1945. | Roosevelt, Franklin
D. (Franklin Delano), 1882-1945. | Ambassadors—United States—History—20th
century. | Germany—Foreign public opinion, American—History—20th century. |
United States—Foreign relations—Europe. | Europe—Foreign relations—United
States. | World War, 1939-1945—Diplomatic history.
Classification: LCC E806 .M465 2021 | DDC 940.53/2573094—dc23
LC record available at https://lccn.loc.gov/2021027073

Our books may be purchased in bulk for promotional, educational,
or business use. Please contact your local bookseller or the
Macmillan Corporate and Premium Sales Department at
1-800-221-7945, extension 5442, or by email at
MacmillanSpecialMarkets@macmillan.com.

First Edition: 2021

10 9 8 7 6 5 4 3 2 1

Dedicated to the memories of my father, Shaw, who came of age during the 1930s and, according to family lore, never voted for Roosevelt; my brother, John, who came of age during the 1960s and considered Roosevelt an American hero; and my mother, Katherine, an independent woman, who loved both her husband and her sons

CONTENTS

AUTHOR'S NOTE

In 2004, I published a book about one of President Roosevelt's most important, yet little-known political advisers: Thomas Corcoran, known by the president as "Tommy the Cork." Corcoran was a brilliant lawyer, an energetic operative, and a vibrant personality who played an important role in the New Deal. Roosevelt never had a chief of staff, but for a period of time, no one had more influence on domestic policy and access to the president than Tommy the Cork.

A decade after writing about Corcoran, I served as United States ambassador to Luxembourg—one of the first countries overrun by the Nazis in 1940. I remember on Veterans Day walking among the marble headstones marking the graves of fallen American heroes at Hamm cemetery, the second-largest American military cemetery in Europe, and wondering how President Roosevelt had navigated the events leading up to World War II. Later, after returning to the United States, I wondered who had advised Roosevelt during this critical period? How did the president make decisions when confronted with the rise of fascism? Who was his Tommy Corcoran in foreign policy? I decided to investigate the role of United States ambassadors in Europe in the run-up to the war, believing that whatever role they played would also reveal something about Roosevelt and his leadership.

John Gunther, a journalist in the 1930s and one of Roosevelt's earliest biographers, maintained, "Sometimes Roosevelt made terrible appointments. He shopped for ambassadors, it seemed, like a housewife choosing among apples over the telephone."[1] I discovered that, in fact, there was a great disparity in both the abilities and competencies of many of Roosevelt's ambassadors—something that could probably be said of the ambassador corps, comprised of both political and Foreign Service appointees, during every administration in the twentieth century, and continuing to this day.

I decided not to write about the events—or the ambassadors—in Asia or Latin America, which, of course, would be critical to gaining a more complete picture of American foreign policy during this period. Nevertheless, the story of Roosevelt and his ambassadors in Europe between 1933 and 1941 provides a new perspective on the president and his principal advisers as they struggled to deal with the rise of fascism.

I could never really understand what was going on in Roosevelt's heavily forested interior . . . His character was not only multiplex, it was contradictory to a bewildering degree.

—ROBERT SHERWOOD

[Roosevelt] believed in his own ability, so long as he was at the controls to stem this terrible tide. He had all the character and energy and skill of the dictators, and he was on our side.

—ISAIAH BERLIN

WATCHING DARKNESS FALL

INTRODUCTION

After the bugle sounded, followed by the ceremonial music of the Marine Band, Franklin Roosevelt, his arm locked to that of his eldest son, James, walked slowly to the lectern on the Capitol's East Portico. As he stood hatless and coatless, tens of thousands of eager supporters who had long waited in the cold on the Capitol's grounds cheered loudly. Roosevelt raised his right hand and placed his left hand on a Dutch family Bible brought to the New World by his ancestors. Chief Justice Charles Evans Hughes administered the oath of office, ending with the president's promise to "preserve, protect and defend the Constitution of the United States. So help me God." The more than 150,000 spectators who huddled together on the grounds of the U.S. Capitol roared their approval.

When Roosevelt was sworn in as thirty-second president of the United States in March 1933, during the throes of an unprecedented economic crisis, he most assuredly never anticipated that by the end of the decade he would be preoccupied with foreign policy. And yet by 1940, Roosevelt found his presidency increasingly consumed with the march of fascism and widening conflict in Europe. Although it was ultimately the Japanese who precipitated America's entry into World War II, during his third term in office, Roosevelt had grown increasingly concerned that the war already raging in Europe threatened democracy everywhere, including in the United States.

Roosevelt came to the presidency with a particular appreciation for European customs and culture. French and German governesses tutored him until he was fourteen, and he accompanied his parents on their frequent travels to Europe during the summer months. He also knew something of Europe's turbulent history and bitter rivalries. As a young man, he served in the Wilson administration and knew well the impact of the Great War in which ten million soldiers were killed, and an equal number of civilians perished.

As president, Roosevelt's views, and ultimately his policies, concerning Europe were shaped by his own experiences, but he also gleaned information about international developments from many sources—newspapers, diplomatic cables, former diplomats, and friends who traveled abroad. However, nothing was more important to his understanding of the foreign landscape than the information and analysis he received from his ambassadors.

The president wanted to know what his ambassadors were seeing at post, to whom they were talking, and what they thought. Stricken by polio, which limited his ability to travel, and in an age before today's instant communication, he was a voracious reader of cables and an inveterate letter-writer. Whenever his ambassadors were in Washington, D.C., he nearly always met with them. Sometimes the ambassadors provided prescient advice; other times they were terribly mistaken. A born skeptic, Roosevelt understood the value of information collected on the ground and had an uncanny ability to sift through the often-contradictory data and opinions he received.

Roosevelt's direct communication with his ambassadors was atypical, but he didn't especially care about protocol; in fact, he had little respect for the Department of State as an institution of government. In part, his disdain stemmed from his view that most diplomats were entitled bureaucrats marking time during a grave economic crisis. He was partially correct; after decades of American isolation in the world, diplomats didn't have a lot to do, but neither did they show much initiative.

In fairness, it wasn't entirely their fault; there was no overarching conception of America's role in the world around which to focus the work of diplomacy.

Roosevelt's criteria for choosing ambassadors varied from man to man depending on the country. He doled out embassies to friends, campaign contributors, and the occasional professional. Although many of Roosevelt's ambassadors were from a similar social background, it is difficult to find common denominators in the choices he made for those who served him in key positions except for two consistent traits: He appeared to value loyalty and trustworthiness above all else.

While he didn't necessarily choose the most capable individuals, he sized up men better than any politician of his era and built each of his personal and political relationships on a set of commonalities, distinct for each man. With William Dodd, his ambassador to Germany, Roosevelt appealed to their shared admiration for the international idealism of Woodrow Wilson. With Breckinridge Long, appointed to Italy, Roosevelt shared a cultural and class affinity, not to mention the love of political battle. With William Bullitt, ambassador to the Soviet Union and later to France, he shared a sense of humor, bonhomie, and an unabashed optimism. Then there was his ambassador to the United Kingdom, Joseph P. Kennedy, with whom Roosevelt had little in common. They did not enjoy a personal chemistry and were more competitors than friends. But Roosevelt did respect Kennedy's drive and ambition, though he felt constantly compelled to check it.

After World War I, during his political career in New York, Roosevelt had observed Americans turn inward, become skeptical of foreign entanglements, and grow suspicious of European governments that couldn't seem to resolve their differences or pay their international debts. Yet almost from the moment he became president, Roosevelt sensed that the futures of America and Europe were intertwined. Two of his ambassadors, Dodd and Bullitt, generally shared the president's worldview. Ambassador Long somewhat admired European fascism, and Kennedy, like most Americans at the time, was an avowed isolationist. Dodd and Bullitt, Long and Kennedy, personified the different approaches to foreign policy, and their advice was often emblematic of the tensions pulling Roosevelt in opposite directions.

These four ambassadors, some of whose diplomatic service overlapped with one another, served in the most important posts in Europe during the 1930s. *Watching Darkness Fall* is their story—the story of a fascinating though problematic team of men who had little in common except that they witnessed, and interpreted for the president, many of the most tumultuous events leading up to World War II. It is also the story as well of a president who weighed their advice and ultimately made the fateful decision to take the country to war. And, finally, it is the story of America's struggle to define its role in a changing world.

HAPPY DAYS ARE HERE AGAIN

Inspired by his older fifth cousin President Theodore Roosevelt, Franklin Roosevelt's political career began in 1910 at the age of twenty-eight when he was elected to the New York State Senate. Tall, good-looking, with a square jaw and gray-blue eyes, Franklin was charismatic and a gifted orator. He sported a pince-nez like his cousin, but in contrast to the high-pitched, nasal timber of "TR," his voice was clear, strong, and melodic. And when the young senator smiled, his face lit up, projecting a warmth and friendliness that enveloped those around him.

Franklin followed in the footsteps of his cousin TR when after only three years in state government, newly elected president Woodrow Wilson appointed the thirty-one-year-old state senator with a famous name to be assistant secretary of the navy. As the second-most powerful man in the navy, Roosevelt was responsible for civilian personnel as well as administration of naval bases and the operations and contracting at shipyards. It gave him exposure to the workings of the federal government, and because he was responsible for upgrading and expanding the navy during the Great War, he received an education in international relations as well.

By 1920, Roosevelt was viewed as a rising star in the Democratic Party and was nominated for vice president on the ticket with Governor James

M. Cox. Although Republicans Warren Harding and Calvin Coolidge soundly defeated the Democrats, the experience gave Roosevelt a political education in running for higher office and an appreciation for the vastness and diversity of the nation. Retreating to New York after the election, Roosevelt joined a law firm, but was stricken with polio during the summer of 1921 while on vacation at Campobello Island in New Brunswick, Canada.

In January 1922, Roosevelt was fitted with braces that locked in at the knee and continued the length of his leg. By the spring of that year, he could stand with assistance, and he returned to his law practice. In 1924, at the Democratic National Convention, he gave presidential nominating speeches for Governor Al Smith. The speech marked a return to public life for Roosevelt, and four years later, he ran successfully for governor of New York, succeeding Smith in office. After the stock market crash of 1929 and President Hoover's failure to effectively address the deepening economic crisis, Roosevelt, with encouragement from his wife, Eleanor, ran for president.

In 1932, Franklin Roosevelt campaigned on ending the Great Depression and restoring American prosperity. He focused almost exclusively on the domestic economy, broadly laying out his vision for a "New Deal." While the concept was rooted in a political realignment toward progressivism, Roosevelt offered few specifics about what he would actually do if elected, leading some to question his commitment to making his vision a reality. Walter Lippmann, one of the era's leading journalists and pundits, observed, "Franklin D. Roosevelt is no crusader. He is no tribune to the people. He is no enemy of entrenched privilege. He is a pleasant man who, without any important qualifications for the office, would very much like to be President."[1]

Like so many political observers at the time, Lippmann vastly underestimated Roosevelt, but correctly characterized the governor's campaign to be based more on personal charisma than any blueprint for the future. Roosevelt loved interacting with people, and his magnetism translated to votes. During the 1932 campaign, he projected a warmth and confidence that communicated genuine concern for the people and assured voters that he would use the highest office in the land to fight for them.

Because the economy was the most important issue on voters' minds, candidate Roosevelt almost never mentioned foreign policy. When he did, his message conformed to the isolationist mood that was sweeping the country, articulated most clearly by newspaper publishing magnate William Randolph Hearst. Hearst, a nemesis of Theodore Roosevelt and a onetime presidential candidate himself in 1904, paid for a nationwide radio address in early 1932 to blast "the disciples of Woodrow Wilson . . . fatuously following his visionary politics of intermeddling in European politics." Hearst declared, "We should see to it that a man is elected to the presidency whose guiding principle is 'America First.'"[2] Unwilling to challenge Hearst, Roosevelt publicly opposed American membership in the League of Nations and vowed that, if he were elected president, debtor nations would pay the bills they owed to the United States. In a speech before the New York State Grange on February 2, 1932, he declared, "The League of Nations today is not the League conceived by Woodrow Wilson." Roosevelt claimed that the nations of Europe had not demonstrated "a disposition to divert the huge sums spent on armament into the channels of legitimate trade, balanced budgets and payment of obligations," and concluded the organization no longer served "the highest purpose of the prevention of war and a settlement of international difficulties in accordance with fundamental American ideals."[3]

Notwithstanding his campaign rhetoric, Roosevelt was at heart an internationalist. He had traveled widely, understood the value of international trade, and perhaps most importantly, abhorred war as a waste of human life and resources. Privately, Roosevelt continued to embrace the Wilsonian view that global diplomacy could bring about a more peaceful world.

The 1932 Democratic Convention was held in Chicago at the end of June. Roosevelt campaigned throughout the country and won a majority of the seventeen state primaries, and arrived in Chicago with the firm commitment of 600 delegates. However, he needed 770 votes to secure the two-thirds majority required by party rules at the time, and there were a number of potential aspirants to the White House, including John Nance Garner, the Speaker of the House, as well as his onetime mentor, former governor Al Smith of New York. Garner had won the important primaries of his home state of Texas and, with the support of William Randolph Hearst, had trounced Roosevelt in California. Smith, an undeclared candidate, posed perhaps the biggest threat to Roosevelt's nomination. He and Roosevelt had once been close friends but now were bitter rivals.

For two days before the balloting began, delegates haggled and horse-traded over chairmanship of the party, convention rules, and the party platform in efforts to gain an advantage for their preferred candidates. The balloting process finally began on July 1 but the convention soon deadlocked. After the third ballot, the delegates adjourned, promising to reconvene in the evening for the fourth ballot. Back in his hotel room, Roosevelt's campaign manager, Louis Howe, assessed the situation and decided that there was no way to persuade Al Smith's delegates to support Roosevelt. The Ohio and Illinois blocs pledged their respective "favorite sons" would "hang on grimly in hopes of a 'dark horse' nomination." That left the California and Texas delegations, at the time pledged to Speaker Garner. Approaching Garner through two separate Texas allies, the Roosevelt camp offered the Speaker the vice presidential nomination if he would withdraw. Garner wanted to think it over.

While Garner equivocated, Hearst, monitoring the proceedings from the comfort of his California estate at San Simeon, began to question whether or not the Speaker could win the nomination. Roosevelt's operatives tried to reach Hearst by telephone but were unsuccessful. However, early in the morning on July 2, Hearst accepted a call from Joseph P. Kennedy, an early Roosevelt supporter whom Hearst had gotten to know during the late 1920s, when Kennedy lived in Los Angeles and was making millions in the movie industry. Kennedy persuaded Hearst that Garner could not win and that if the convention remained deadlocked, then a potential dark horse—perhaps an internationalist—might carry the day. For Hearst, internationalism was an anathema and disqualified any candidate who embraced it; because Roosevelt had walked back his Wilson-era belief in the League of Nations, Hearst favored him over other remaining prospects, like Wilson's former secretary of war Newton Baker, another undeclared candidate waiting in the wings.

Hearst telephoned Garner and advised him to fall in behind Roosevelt and release his delegates. Other political bosses put pressure on Garner as well. The Speaker acquiesced, and after some internal debate within the delegations, both California and Texas lined up behind Roosevelt. The next day, Franklin Roosevelt was officially nominated as the 1932 Democratic candidate for president. At the time, few people understood that Roosevelt's statements on America's role in the world—carefully crafted to satisfy William Randolph Hearst—helped him secure his party's nomination.

Following the convention, Roosevelt's sons Franklin Jr., James, and John joined him for a two-week vacation aboard a forty-foot yawl that set sail from Long Island up the Atlantic coast to Portsmouth, New Hampshire. Afterward, during the remaining weeks of the summer and into the fall, Roosevelt crisscrossed the country by train. In September, he traveled to Los Angeles, which had hosted the summer Olympics the previous month. *The Boston Globe* reported that Joe Kennedy joined the trip as a member of the candidate's "inner circle," and that Kennedy was consulting on policy as well as discussing "political tactics" and "business matters" with Roosevelt.[4] Kennedy also contributed $10,000 directly to the campaign and lent it another $50,000.[5]

Roosevelt and Kennedy had known each other for a number of years, beginning when Roosevelt served as assistant secretary of the navy in the Wilson administration and Kennedy, six years his junior, was the assistant manager of the Fore River Shipyard in Quincy, Massachusetts. As Kennedy remembered years later, "We never got along then."[6] Their first encounter was not an auspicious beginning.

In early 1917, Roosevelt summoned Kennedy to the Navy Department. The assistant secretary appealed to the shipyard manager to release two Argentinian-built battleships that were docked at Quincy and badly needed for service in the Atlantic. The only problem was that the government needed the ships delivered immediately—and wanted them on credit. "Don't worry," Roosevelt assured Kennedy, "the State Department will collect the money for you." However, Kennedy refused the assistant secretary's request and argued that the ships could only be delivered after they were fully paid for. Roosevelt rose from his desk, smiled, and put his arm around Kennedy, and then quietly informed him that if the ships were not delivered immediately, he would use the power of the government to expropriate them. An indignant Kennedy returned to Boston and ignored Roosevelt. A week later, four tugboats carrying armed soldiers arrived at the shipyard and seized the battleships. Kennedy would later remember Roosevelt as "the toughest trader I'd ever run up against."[7]

In October, Roosevelt set off on a second whistle-stop tour through the Midwest, South and mid-Atlantic. Kennedy was not invited on this trip, likely because Louis Howe, the campaign manager, neither liked nor trusted him. Howe thought Kennedy too close to Wall Street and likely heard the rumors that Kennedy had voted for Herbert Hoover in 1928.[8] But other financial backers were along for the ride. Breckinridge Long, a friend from their days serving in the Wilson administration, was on board and occasionally introduced the candidate at events. Long had supported Roosevelt from the beginning of the campaign and was a member of a small group of political supporters who referred to themselves as "WRBC"—"With Roosevelt Before Chicago."

Some of President Hoover's advisers had been eager to confront Roosevelt in the election of 1932, believing that the New York governor's paralysis would make it impossible for him to wage an effective campaign, much less fulfill the duties of the presidency. "What is he, himself, thinking about when he allows himself to aspire to that office?" Hoover's congressional liaison, James MacLafferty, sneered. During the fall campaign, President Hoover never talked about Roosevelt's disability, instead attacking his "social philosophy," which he called "very different from the traditional philosophies of the American people." Hoover warned that these "so-called new deals" would "destroy the very foundations" of American society.

Louis Howe concluded that because President Hoover was so unpopular, Roosevelt's main strategy should be not to commit any gaffes that might divert the public's attention. Foreign policy was barely mentioned. While Roosevelt didn't offer specific programs or policies to address the economic crisis at home, in a famous speech to the Commonwealth Club in San Francisco on September 23, he talked about the need to redress the balance between corporate and individual economic rights. The capitalist marketplace had failed, and in his view, only the federal government could resuscitate the economy and put people back to work. As he put it, "Every man has a right to life; and this means that he also has a right to make a comfortable living."[9]

While many Americans came to know Roosevelt via newsreels and the radio, he was never filmed in his wheelchair, and the vast majority of Americans were unaware of his physical disability. During the fall of 1932, he waged an energetic campaign, traveling around the country, attacking Hoover and promising better days ahead. Whenever Roosevelt spoke before a crowd, he pulled himself to an upright position, standing at a podium, or at the rear of a train, as a band or orchestra played "Happy Days Are Here Again." His campaign song and ever-present smile lent an air of optimism and hope to every campaign appearance.

The outcome of the election was never really in doubt. The American people wanted change.

On November 8, Franklin Roosevelt won forty-two states and nearly twenty-three million votes, crushing the incumbent president who managed to win only six states and fewer than sixteen million votes. Roosevelt was elected president of the United States with a lopsided electoral vote victory of 472–59.

Soon after his election, Roosevelt asked a wealthy former diplomat named William Bullitt if he would travel to Europe to investigate the issue of World War I debts owed by Germany to the United States under the

Treaty of Versailles. Roosevelt was concerned that Germany was not adhering to the treaty. He also recognized that Europe had its own economic crisis and wanted a report on the general state of European affairs.

Bullitt had been working on the campaign at the headquarters in Albany through the fall, editing speeches and preparing a daily digest of the news. Roosevelt first met Bullitt in early October, but undoubtedly already knew him by reputation. Though only forty-one years old, Bullitt had been something of a controversial figure in Democratic Party circles for many years. As a young man, during World War I, Bullitt had been a diplomatic prodigy, sent to Moscow to negotiate in 1917 with Lenin on behalf of President Wilson. Bullitt later became disillusioned with President Wilson for his failure to stand by "the fourteen points" laid out in a speech before Congress in January 1918 as the foundation for a lasting peace. Bullitt testified before Congress that Wilson had betrayed the Allies in the Treaty of Versailles, and his widely reported testimony was a contributing factor to the congressional defeat of American participation in the League of Nations in 1919. Many Democrats in Congress at the time were angered by what they viewed as Bullitt's disloyalty to the president.

Bullitt was handsome, quick-witted, and extremely knowledgeable. Educated at Yale and Harvard Law School, he hailed from Philadelphia and was a descendent of Founding Father Patrick Henry. He had been married and divorced twice: first to socialite Aimee Ernesta Drinker and then to Louise Bryant, a free-spirited feminist and writer, whom he had asked on a date after reading her exclusive interview with Prime Minister Benito Mussolini of Italy. Bryant had previously been married to John Reed, a Harvard-educated American journalist turned Russian revolutionary, who was buried in the Kremlin. Bullitt also had something of a reputation as novelist; he published a novel in 1926 entitled *It's Not Done*, which sold over 150,000 copies. By contrast, F. Scott Fitzgerald published *The Great Gatsby* the same year but sold only 20,000 copies.

Bullitt and the president-elect were immediately drawn to one another. Roosevelt, who had an eye for talent, wanted the former diplomat on his team; Bullitt was intrigued with the idea of undertaking a secret mission for the next president of the United States. Privately, Bullitt wondered if he might be able to secure an ambassadorship, perhaps even the coveted embassy in Paris. To avoid running afoul of the Logan Act, which prohibited private citizens from negotiating on behalf of the United States, punishable by a fine of up to $5,000 and three years in prison, Bullitt agreed to pay for the trip himself. To add a layer of secrecy, he and Roosevelt agreed that they would correspond with one another through an intermediary using coded language. For instance, the head of the French government at the time was Édouard Marie Herriot, whom Bullitt code-named Valentine. In a December 2 cable, Bullitt informed the president-elect that while Valentine favored debt repayment, he faced "almost unanimous opposition" in the French Chamber of Deputies.[10]

In December 1932, Bullitt traveled to many of the major European capitals, meeting with high-ranking officials to discuss both the general state of European affairs and the ability of individual countries to pay their debts. One of his most important meetings was in Berlin with Konstantin von Neurath, a banker who would become Germany's foreign minister. He outlined for Bullitt Germany's grievances with other European nations as well as its balance-of-trade problems with America.

Bullitt returned to the United States before Christmas and briefed the president-elect in Albany over dinner a few days later. Roosevelt found Bullitt's information and observations integral to his thinking about foreign policy in the context of the American economic crisis, specifically, whether Europe's democracies would help or hinder America's recovery. He would learn in the coming months that the problems abroad were much more sinister and the solutions much more elusive than he or anyone else had imagined.

1

THIS IS A DAY OF NATIONAL CONSECRATION

Daybreak on March 4, 1933, brought clear weather, but by the time the black limousine carrying President-elect Roosevelt and his wife, Eleanor, reached the White House for the traditional, pre-inauguration meeting with outgoing president Herbert Hoover and his wife, the sky had turned overcast and gray. The winter in Washington, D.C., had been cold and dreary, and Inauguration Day would be no different.

Roosevelt had begun the morning with a prayer service at St. John's Episcopal Church just across from the White House. The Reverend Dr. Endicott Peabody, the seventy-five-year-old rector of Roosevelt's prep school alma mater, the elite Groton School in Massachusetts, conducted the service with Roosevelt seated in the front row. All of the president-elect's future cabinet attended the service as well. Though the reverend had voted for President Hoover, whom he deemed more "capable," he was nevertheless proud of his former student.

After the service, Roosevelt returned to the Mayflower Hotel, changed into his morning suit, and was driven to the White House, where President Hoover and his wife greeted him and Eleanor formally, though somewhat icily. For the two-mile drive to the Capitol, the president and the president-elect were seated next to each other with a blanket spread across their laps in an open-air Packard automobile.

The motorcade exited the metal gates of the North Portico of the White House, past the Treasury Department, turned left, and proceeded down Pennsylvania Avenue. As President Hoover sat glumly and silently, Roosevelt, animated by the cheering crowd that lined Pennsylvania Avenue, smiled and waved his silk top hat in the air.

Hoover and Roosevelt had once been on friendly terms, but the outgoing president deeply resented his younger successor, whom he believed had intentionally mischaracterized his policies during the campaign and whose vague bromides he predicted would have little effect. Hoover believed the economic crisis had its roots in the intransigence and incompetence of European governments in the aftermath of the Great War. He considered Roosevelt wholly unprepared and ill equipped to be president.

Hoover was not alone. Many in the political elite, including a number of Roosevelt's fellow Democrats, considered the president-elect an intellectual lightweight. It was true that Roosevelt didn't yet know what he would do to end the worst economic depression since the Civil War. He didn't have a plan. Still, at fifty-one years old, he had already shown himself as governor of New York to be a master politician as well as a gifted and inspirational leader. Most important perhaps, he had confidence in himself, and in the American people, that together they could rise to the challenge and meet the moment.

Upon arriving at the Capitol, Roosevelt was wheeled into an anteroom where he made a few last-minute additions to the inaugural address that he is generally credited with having written himself. On the first page, he wrote across the top a new opening: "This is a day of consecration."

After being sworn in, the new president delivered a speech of approximately fifteen minutes in length. He further added to his opening line, calling the day one of "*national* consecration." He then used the metaphor of a foreign invader to insist that if Congress did not quickly approve his domestic recovery program, he would ask for "broad executive authority to wage war against the emergency." His choice of words was not arbitrary; while he never mentioned President Wilson, Roosevelt undoubtedly recalled that the twenty-eighth president had used the war to increase his executive authority. The only other reference to foreign policy was a brief paragraph in which he dedicated the "Nation to the policy of the good neighbor . . . the Neighbor who respects his obligations and respects the sanctity of his agreements in and with a world of neighbors."

President Roosevelt's most memorable line in his inaugural address was "the only thing we have to fear is fear itself," a reformulation of a phrase originally penned by Henry David Thoreau.[1] The line was widely quoted in the nation's newspapers the following day, and the speech received generally favorable reviews, with most newspapers printing a headline similar to that in *The New York Times*: ROOSEVELT INAUGURATED, ACTS TO END THE NATIONAL BANKING CRISIS QUICKLY; WILL ASK FOR WAR-TIME POWERS IF NEEDED.[2]

That same day, *The Times* also ran a shorter story on its front page with a smaller headline below the fold: VICTORY IS EXPECTED FOR HITLER TODAY.[3] The story reported that German chancellor Adolf Hitler had persuaded the elderly president, Paul von Hindenburg, to dissolve the Reichstag, Germany's parliament, and to call for new elections. While Hitler would fall short of his goal to establish a dictatorship by consent of the parliament, it would turn out to be only a temporary setback in his rise to power.

After bidding President Hoover farewell on the marble steps of the Capitol, the Roosevelts returned to an unoccupied White House with only the portraits of past presidents staring at them from the white plaster walls. The emptiness would not last for long. President Roosevelt's closest advisers were the same people he had counted on for his entire political life, and they would soon surround him in the White House as well.

His wife, Eleanor, was in many respects his most important confidante, although their marriage was an unconventional one. In 1918, Eleanor discovered that Franklin had been carrying on a romantic affair with Lucy Mercer, a refined and beautiful young woman who had been serving as Eleanor's social secretary. Eleanor was emotionally crushed, but did not divorce Franklin. Instead, her marriage to him evolved into more of a partnership, and she became increasingly interested and involved in politics, often serving as his surrogate at campaign events and official functions. Once in the White House, her activism only increased as she championed worker's rights and human rights, developing a political following of her own.

Roosevelt had a more intimate (and possibly romantic) relationship with his longtime secretary Missy LeHand, who had come to work for him in 1920 during the campaign for vice president. Fourteen years younger than Roosevelt, LeHand had deep blue eyes, prematurely gray-streaked hair, and a warm smile. She was also extremely well organized and possessed of keen political instincts. But her greatest value to Roosevelt was that she understood him perhaps better than anyone, including Eleanor. She helped the president navigate social occasions as his hostess, served as an effective gatekeeper, and could also be an empathetic friend. She knew when her boss needed to relax—often mixing his drinks in the evening—and knew when situations demanded his full attention. She devoted herself completely to Roosevelt's success and happiness. As Roosevelt historian Jonathan Alter put it, she "clearly loved him."[4]

The president's other close adviser was his longtime political aide and campaign manager Louis Howe. Howe had started his career as a newspaper reporter, but went to work for Roosevelt when he ran for the New York State Senate. Short and wiry, the chain-smoking, dark-eyed Howe looked more like a down-and-out racehorse jockey than a presidential adviser. But Roosevelt saw in Howe a capacity to understand what the average voter was thinking. Roosevelt was by nature a humanitarian, but also an aristocrat. Howe had been born into a wealthy midwestern family, but was street-smart and pragmatic; he was not impressed by money, fame, or social class. Most importantly, he knew how to translate Roosevelt's political instincts into concrete action.

Missy LeHand and Louis Howe would have their own bedrooms in the White House. Harry Hopkins, also a Roosevelt favorite, would move into the executive mansion more than a half dozen years later. None of them had any particular foreign policy experience or expertise, but due to their proximity to the president, they would play important, albeit supporting roles as Roosevelt's focus gradually shifted during the 1930s from domestic to international affairs.

2

A SMALL, OBSCURE AUSTRIAN
HOUSE PAINTER

While Franklin Roosevelt was sailing off the coast of New England, basking in his party's nomination and largely oblivious to European politics, forty-three-year-old Adolf Hitler, leader of the German National Socialist Party, innovated German political campaigns by barnstorming Germany in a chartered Junkers passenger plane. He crisscrossed the country, using the slogan "Hitler über Deutschland" ("Hitler over Germany") as he campaigned for a Nazi majority in the Reichstag. A mesmerizing speaker, Hitler addressed rallies in as many as four cities a day.[1] He spoke before massive crowds: fifty thousand in Potsdam, sixty thousand in Brandenburg, and more than one hundred thousand in Berlin on July 27.[2] His "appeal to the nation" stump speech promised "honor and freedom—work and bread!"

Earlier in the year, Hitler had lost his campaign for German president, running against eighty-five-year-old World War I hero Paul von Hindenburg, but he learned a lesson about how to connect with the German people in the process. When President Hindenburg failed to capture a majority at the polls in March, a runoff election was scheduled for April. In the first leg of the campaign, Hitler often spoke about a declining economy and inveighed against entrenched interests. In the second leg, during the runoff election, he spoke more about positive change, vowing that his leadership would bring about a bright future for all Germans: He promised jobs, higher wages, a stronger military, and a renewed sense of German pride.[3] Hitler generated great excitement among his supporters, but in the end, it was not enough. He received a larger percentage of the vote than in the March election, but many fewer Germans turned out at the polls. Hindenburg once again prevailed, leading to an ultimately premature headline in *The New York Times*: HITLER DICTATORSHIP IN REICH HELD UNLIKELY.[4] However, in the summer of 1932, Hitler was already on the rebound, campaigning to build the support he needed in the Reichstag to finally take the reins of power.

Hitler also used the rise of communism to whip up support in his homeland. As Joseph Stalin consolidated power in the Soviet Union, the international Communist movement was perceived as a growing threat in Germany and throughout Europe. Hitler's storm troopers, a small private army of Nazi sympathizers, swarmed the streets of Germany's largest cities and fought pitched battles with Communists and anyone else who dared to oppose them. Many Germans viewed the Nazis as defending their nation against Communist infiltration.

The rise of Adolf Hitler had been well documented in the American press, although few could have predicted the extent of his demented and relentless thirst for power. During the spring of 1932, *The Atlantic Monthly* magazine published a comprehensive two-part series of articles that chronicled Hitler's unremarkable youth as well as the evolution of his political philosophy, which the author, Nicolas Fairweather, likened to "a kind of religion, based on pseudo science and tribal psychology."[5] After studying Hitler's speeches and writings, Fairweather observed that Hitler possessed a "violent hatred of Jews as the racial enemies of all Aryans."[6] He noted Hitler had contempt for "parliamentary institutions as the organs of . . . democracy," that he insisted "Germany must acquire more land in Europe as a vital requirement for national expansion and progress," and that he declared, "France is the archenemy."[7]

Months after the German election, with growing political unrest in the streets, Hitler persuaded President Hindenburg that he could not govern effectively without Nazi support. Hindenburg agreed to form a coalition in the Reichstag with members of the Nationalist Socialist Party, which is how on January 30, 1933—President Roosevelt's birthday—Adolf Hitler became chancellor of the German Republic.

Hitler's move was viewed as a compromise and something of a concession by *The New York Times*, which declared in a headline, HITLER PUTS ASIDE AIM TO BE DICTATOR. Of course, Hitler's quest for complete power had only suffered a temporary setback, and among the German populace, attraction to his message was growing while organized opposition fractured. As William Shirer, correspondent for CBS news in Berlin, later wrote, "No class or group or party in Germany could escape its share of responsibility for the abandonment of the democratic Republic and the advent of Adolf Hitler. The cardinal error of the Germans who opposed Nazism was their failure to unite against it."[8]

President-elect Franklin Roosevelt knew he would soon inherit an economy that had likely hit bottom; more than 25 percent of American workers couldn't find employment; gross domestic product had sunk to a third of what it had been only three years earlier; average income had cratered to turn-of-the-century levels; and the banking system was in crisis—every day, another bank closed its doors, and those depositors who hadn't already withdrawn their money and stuffed it under a mattress were wiped out.

The dire effects of the economic depression were not limited to the United States. After the stock market crash of 1929, foreign lending was curtailed, commodity prices plummeted, and the economies of other countries that depended on exporting raw materials, including Germany, spiraled downward. By 1931, World War I reparations payments to the United States, totaling billions of dollars, had stalled. The collapse of trade and debt payments created havoc with European banks and finance ministries. The nations of Europe, which had never really recovered from the Great War fought only thirteen years earlier, were once again bickering with one another as they confronted economic catastrophe. Roosevelt knew that once in office, he would be consumed by the nation's economic crisis. With foreign policy expected to be an afterthought in the middle of an economic storm, he wanted to gain a better understanding of the issues while he had the time before inauguration.

Early in 1933, Roosevelt wrote to President Hoover, asking to "have the privilege of discussing with the Secretary of State certain matters relating to the State Department." Roosevelt wanted to meet with Secretary of State Henry Stimson to obtain "first-hand information" on U.S. foreign policy. Although Stimson was a Republican, Roosevelt respected his long career of public service.[9] Stimson had served as secretary of war at the outbreak of World War I, and again nearly twenty years later, as secretary of state, when he negotiated the London Naval Treaty, limiting a worldwide naval buildup. Similar to Roosevelt's request that William Bullitt bring him inside information directly from European leaders, it was another indication that the president-elect considered America's international relations critical to America's economic recovery.

President Hoover complied with his soon-to-be successor's request, and Stimson traveled to Roosevelt's home in Hyde Park, New York, to spend several hours with Roosevelt discussing such varied issues as war debts, disarmament, and the upcoming World Economic Conference scheduled for the summer.

After meeting with Stimson, Roosevelt asked Bullitt to undertake a second trip to Europe and update him on the challenges Stimson described. This time, the president-elect wanted Bullitt to send reports directly to him. Bullitt, once again nervous about the perception that he might be seen as violating the Logan Act, called Missy LeHand shortly before sailing on January 14, 1933, to ask her "to please be sure that no word about my present trip escapes to the public."[10]

Bullitt arrived in London on January 20 and met the following day with Prime Minister Ramsay MacDonald. A few days later, as Bullitt had feared, word of his mission leaked when a news agency reported that he was in London acting as an "emissary" of President-elect Roosevelt. Roosevelt publicly—and falsely—denied that Bullitt was engaged on his behalf, but Senator Joseph Robinson of Arkansas, a Democrat, demanded that Bullitt be investigated and potentially prosecuted for violations of the Logan Act.

Despite the controversy, Bullitt continued his trip, traveling to Paris for conversations with French premier Joseph Paul-Boncour. On January 26, Bullitt wrote Roosevelt that he was leaving France for Germany.[11] Anxious to learn more about the new and relatively unknown chancellor Adolf Hitler, Bullitt looked up an old acquaintance, Ernst "Putzi" Hanfstaengl in Berlin. Hanfstaengl was a wealthy German and a social gadfly who had graduated from Harvard about the same time that Bullitt had graduated from Yale. A former newspaper publisher, Hanfstaengl served Hitler as a liaison with the American and British press. "What kind of man is Hitler?" Bullitt asked his old friend. Hanfstaengl took Bullitt by the arm and whispered to him surreptitiously, as though fearing someone might be eavesdropping on their conversation, "He is a small, obscure Austrian house painter with the ability to speak to crowds."[12]

Upon his return to the United States, Bullitt found a letter from Colonel Edward House waiting for him. Following the public disclosure of his meetings in Europe allegedly on behalf of Roosevelt, Bullitt apparently had written to House, a former adviser to President Wilson, asking if he thought the controversy might jeopardize his chances for an ambassador post. Colonel House replied, "On the contrary, I believe it would be helpful . . . it shows the American public how wide your acquaintance is in Europe, and how many of the leading statesman who are now in power are your friends."[13]

The uproar over Bullitt's trip faded, and in February, he briefed the president-elect once again, describing his meetings with Europe's leaders and emphasizing how difficult it would be to persuade them to pay off their debts from the Great War. While many of his observations were sound, Bullitt apparently made one enormous mistake in judgment: He declared that Adolf Hitler, who had gained notoriety disrupting German politics throughout the summer and fall of 1932, was nothing more than an erratic and ineffectual politician whose influence and appeal would be ephemeral.

3

THE STRIPED-PANTS BOYS

By 1933, the U.S. Department of State occupied the largest share of the State, War, and Navy Building adjacent to the west wing of the White House. The elegant five-story Second Empire–style building, constructed during the administration of Ulysses S. Grant, had a distinctly European feel to it and seemed somewhat out of place in the nation's capital whose architecture more resembled "southern Georgian." In many ways the building symbolized the growth of the executive branch over the years; from a two-story clapboard house with two dozen employees under Secretary of State Thomas Jefferson—three of whom were ambassadors, called "ministers" at the time—the State Department had mushroomed to more than 700 Foreign Service officers and over 2,500 civil service and support staff.[1] The vast majority of Foreign Service officers and staff worked abroad in one of the nearly 60 missions and 300 consular offices around the world, with just under 900 staff working in Washington, D.C. The department was also a men's club; internal memoranda made the distinction between "gentlemen" (presumably diplomats) and "clerks" (usually women). Most of the high-level diplomats had been educated at Harvard, Yale, or Princeton. The question for President Roosevelt as he began to put together his government was, who would manage the "boys in striped pants?"[2]

Although Roosevelt respected former secretary Stimson and various other members of the Foreign Service, he generally considered the State Department to be populated by a coterie of wealthy, effete, Republican-leaning dilettantes. He complained of too much bureaucracy and "dead wood," impressions informed to a large degree by his observations of the department during World War I.[3]

In 1917, President Wilson and his top foreign policy adviser, Colonel House, viewed the State Department as a provincial, ineffective club for a bunch of Eastern socialites. When World War I broke out, they established a kind of shadow Department of State—mainly historians, geographers, and demographers—called "the inquiry," which produced 2,000 reports and 1,200 maps. Given Wilson's circumvention of the State Department, it was unsurprising that at the Paris Peace Conference in 1919, the department seemed poorly prepared and professional diplomats found themselves ultimately marginalized. President Wilson called for a "New Diplomacy" to reform the way in which America conducted its international relations.

Consistent with Wilson's vision, the foreign policy bureaucracy grew both in size and complexity. Within the State Department the division of European Affairs quadrupled in size, and a separate Russia division was established. While the scope of work expanded and its quality improved, most of the high-level diplomacy still rested in the hands of the president. "It is difficult to explain exactly how business is conducted here," wrote the British ambassador, Cecil Spring-Rice, to his superior, Foreign Secretary Arthur Balfour, noting that "the president rarely sees anybody . . . Mr. [Robert] Lansing [the Secretary of State] is treated as a clerk who receives orders which he has to obey at once and without question." The opinion was evidently shared by Lansing himself. Upon resigning in February 1920, Lansing summed up both his job and relationship to President Wilson in a quip written to his nephew John Foster Dulles: "The question is 'where is he to find a rubber stamp?'"[4]

After conferring with his political adviser Louis Howe, Roosevelt chose Senator Cordell Hull from Tennessee to be his secretary of state. Hull had privately hoped to be chosen the year before as Roosevelt's running mate and may have come close to being selected. Had Roosevelt not needed California and Texas delegates to break the convention logjam, he might have preferred Hull to John Nance Garner.[5] Like Garner, Hull was a veteran of Congress, having served in both the House and the Senate. And like Garner, Hull was conservative and a Southerner. However, the similarities ended there. While Garner was a large, portly man, folksy, and known for his earthy language, Hull was more often described as courtly, dignified, and a true gentleman. With his white hair, erect posture, and high-collared white shirts, Hull looked the part of a statesman.

Roosevelt and Howe likely wanted Hull at the State Department for reasons beyond the fact that it was a consolation prize for his fervent support in the campaign. Tennessee was a safe Democratic seat, so Democrats would maintain their majority of 59–36 in the Senate if Senator Hull left to become secretary of state. The president also viewed trade as an essential component to the nation's economic recovery, and Hull had become one of the Senate's experts on trade.

After some resistance to his nomination from a handful of senators who believed Hull did not have the requisite diplomatic experience, he was confirmed. Ordinarily, the new secretary's first order of business would have been to recommend to the president candidates to fill senior diplomatic posts. Roosevelt worked a little differently, however. Even before Hull had arranged the furniture in his office, the president handed him a piece of paper on which he had jotted down the names of Sumner Welles, William Bullitt, William Phillips, and Breckinridge Long. Hull didn't personally know any of them, although he recognized a few of the names. Roosevelt told Hull that he wanted these men serving in prominent positions in the department.[6] The lack of consultation was perhaps an early sign that the president would assume many of the responsibilities traditionally reserved for the secretary of state, including direct communication with U.S. ambassadors around the world. Hull briefed the president during weekly cabinet meetings and often attended meetings with the president, but Roosevelt never developed the close personal relationship with the secretary that he had with other members of his cabinet and senior staff.

With the exception of Bullitt, the men Roosevelt recommended to Hull had all known Roosevelt for decades. Sumner Welles, a descendant of Massachusetts abolitionist Civil War senator Charles Sumner, was actually closer to the First Lady, Eleanor Roosevelt, than he was to the president; Welles's parents were friends of her family's, and when only ten years old, Welles had been a page in Franklin and Eleanor's wedding. Roosevelt had known William Phillips since they had both served in the Wilson administration; their offices had been in the same hallway. They came from similar backgrounds, and their wives were friendly with one another as well. The president also knew Breckinridge Long from the Wilson administration. Long's mother hailed from the politically famous Breckinridge family of Kentucky, and he was married to the very wealthy granddaughter of Francis Preston Blair, who built Blair House, the president's guesthouse located across the street from the White House.[7] Long also worked on Roosevelt's presidential campaign. William Bullitt, for his part, did not have a long personal relationship with Roosevelt, but Bullitt came from wealth, had political connections, and had impressed Roosevelt with his two missions to Europe.

Roosevelt also had another priority for the Department of State. He needed a prominent person to serve as his ambassador to Germany.

4

I WANT YOU TO GO TO GERMANY
AS AN AMBASSADOR

President Roosevelt rewarded his friends and campaign contributors with ambassadorships. He appointed Jesse Straus, the president of R. H. Macy & Co., and a longtime political ally and financial backer, to France. For the Court of St. James's, the president chose Robert Worth Bingham, a former mayor of Louisville, Kentucky, who later became a judge and, after inheriting $5 million, left the bench to serve as publisher of *The Courier-Journal* and *The Louisville Times*. Both newspapers endorsed Roosevelt's candidacy. Straus and Bingham were not foreign policy experts, but they were well-known business leaders and loyal Democrats.

However, with increasing concerns over the rise of Hitler in Germany, Roosevelt wanted someone with national stature and deep political experience to take over the embassy in Berlin. Within a week of his inauguration, he wrote to former presidential candidate James M. Cox and asked him to serve as his ambassador to Germany. Roosevelt had joined Cox as his running mate on the unsuccessful Democratic national ticket in 1920, and he respected the former governor of Ohio turned newspaper publisher. President Roosevelt wrote Cox, "I regard Berlin as of special importance at this time, for many reasons which you will understand." He added, "The future of the League of Nations and our cooperation with the League are also very definitely linked to German action."[1] Cox declined the president's offer. He was done with politics and intent on expanding his media empire. Roosevelt would need to look elsewhere.[2] In the meantime, there were other ambassadors to appoint.

James Michael Curley, the flamboyant mayor of Boston, had been an early supporter of Roosevelt. As a Catholic, he had taken a political risk by endorsing Roosevelt, a New York Episcopalian, over former governor Al Smith, a fellow Catholic. It wasn't enough; notwithstanding Curley's support, Smith trounced Roosevelt in the Massachusetts primary. Still, after Roosevelt captured the Democratic nomination and then the presidency, Curley felt he deserved to be rewarded. Initially, he told Jim Farley, Roosevelt's point person on patronage, that he hoped to be appointed secretary of the navy. While grateful for Curley's endorsement, Roosevelt knew of the mayor's reputation for unpredictability—not to mention graft—and had no intention of appointing him to such a powerful position. Curley's recollection is that the president's son James had also floated the possibility of ambassador to Italy, but Curley turned it down. However, after learning that the navy secretary position was beyond his reach, Curley changed his mind about Italy. Here, too, there was a problem.[3] For many years, there had been an unwritten rule in American diplomacy that the ambassador to Italy would be a non-Catholic so as to create neither the appearance nor the reality that the pope exercised undue influence over diplomatic relations. Farley told the mayor that the president had decided on someone else. Ultimately, Curley was offered the post of ambassador to Poland, a consolation prize that Farley, and presumably Roosevelt, calculated the mayor would not accept. They were correct.[4]

The man Roosevelt wanted for his ambassador to Italy was his friend from the Wilson administration, Breckinridge Long. During the Wilson presidency, Long had served as a third assistant secretary of state overseeing Asian affairs, but it was his political pedigree and fundraising prowess that impressed Roosevelt more. Long was credited with

President Wilson's "He Kept Us Out of War" slogan, which helped secure Wilson's reelection in 1916. Long, a scion of wealth born in Kentucky, had graduated from Princeton and twice run unsuccessfully for the U.S. Senate in his adopted home state of Missouri. Though unsuccessful in elective politics, Long was a tireless political organizer and had been one of Roosevelt's most effective floor managers during the 1932 Chicago convention. Tall, with a sallow face and dark eyes, Long had impeccable manners, and Roosevelt liked him. Eleanor thought him shallow, but her disapproval didn't stop the president from making the appointment; Long was easily confirmed and, by the late spring, had departed for Rome.

Both Sumner Welles and William Phillips, whose names Roosevelt had given to Hull, also received significant State Department assignments. Forty-year-old Welles was appointed the assistant secretary of Latin American affairs. He had aspired to be undersecretary, the second-most important position in the department, but that post went to Phillips.[5] Welles and Phillips actually had much in common. They were both wealthy graduates of Ivy League colleges, but at age fifty-four, Phillips was older and far more experienced. He had previously served in the undersecretary position, as well as ambassador to Belgium and ambassador to Canada.

With the dogwood trees in bloom, spring came early to the nation's capital in 1933, but the president still could not find the right man for Germany. Roosevelt had written the French ambassador to the United States, Paul Claudel, that he considered Hitler "a madman."[6] The president's view of Germany's young chancellor undoubtedly had been influenced by what he was both reading in newspapers and hearing from those who had firsthand accounts of Hitler's increasingly erratic behavior and the unsavory characters who surrounded him. On Tuesday, March 21, *The New York Times* reported in a front-page story that one of those underlings, chief of the German police Heinrich Himmler, announced that "the first of several concentration camps will be established . . . for the detention of Communists, Marxists and leaders of the Reichsbanner organization."[7] Himmler was also head of the paramilitary Schutzstaffel, or SS, and would ultimately direct the killing of more than six million Jews.

Underneath the article on the formation of concentration camps in Germany was another story with the headline JEWS HERE DEMAND WASHINGTON ACTION. It reported on the American Jewish Committee request that the U.S. government "make proper representations to the government of Germany" against the discrimination and detention of German Jews.[8] The president may have also seen a cable from the consul general in Berlin, George Messersmith, warning his superiors in the Department of State that the persecution of the Jews was "one of the most serious and one of the saddest problems that has arisen in a civilized society in modern times." Messersmith, a career foreign service officer, offered a dire prediction: "I personally can see no hope for the Jews in Germany for years to come and all those who can possibly get out of the country, will wish to do so."[9]

On April 20, 1933, President Roosevelt sent a memorandum to Secretary of State Hull: "What would you think of asking Newton Baker to go as Ambassador to Germany?" Baker had distinguished himself as President Wilson's capable secretary of war. Although he was never an official candidate for president in 1932, he was considered a viable prospect and at the convention had worked behind the scenes to secure the nomination for himself. Afterward, he returned to his very successful law practice. Baker also declined Roosevelt's offer, telling the president he had no interest in returning to government.[10]

A few weeks after Messersmith's cable, Roosevelt would have learned from press reports how Nazi students organized a rally in front of the Munich opera house. Erecting a speaker's platform illuminated by giant klieg lights, a throng of some seventy thousand, many carrying torches, gathered in the square as young, brown-shirted students unloaded from trucks hundreds of crates filled with books and threw them onto a giant bonfire. Some twenty thousand books, deemed to be against the "German spirit," had been removed from libraries and academic institutes across Germany. Among the volumes incinerated that evening were those by internationally celebrated authors Thomas Mann, H. G. Wells, and Albert Einstein. One of the young organizers threw a book written by Sigmund Freud into the fire, shrieking that it glorified "the instinctual urges that destroy the soul!"[11]

While the president continued to focus his energy on the domestic economic crisis, on May 7, in a radio address to the nation—his second fireside chat—he made certain to emphasize the importance of international relations. He framed American foreign policy as critical not only to American prosperity but to world peace. In his distinctive, confident voice, Roosevelt declared, "Hand in hand with the domestic situation which, of course, is our first concern is the world situation."[12] The president then briefly discussed his objectives in foreign policy: a reduction in armaments, an increase in international trade, and greater cooperation between nations. Although he had rejected American participation in the League of Nations, Roosevelt had enormous respect for Woodrow Wilson's vision of global peace. In a letter that spring to Joseph Tumulty, President Wilson's former personal secretary, the president wrote, "I wonder if you realize how often I think of our old Chief when I go about my daily tasks. Perhaps what we are doing will go a little way toward fulfillment of his ideals."[13]

One thing President Roosevelt didn't mention in his radio address was the growing unrest and tension gripping Germany. But it was undoubtedly on his mind. In addition to the stories describing concentration camps and book burnings, the president had received reports of attacks upon American citizens, accounts of discriminatory actions against U.S. businesses, and rumors that the German government would soon refuse to honor its wartime debts. This made his search for someone to represent the United States in Berlin all the more urgent. A few days after the address, Roosevelt met with Undersecretary Phillips and suggested four possible candidates—none of them with prior diplomatic experience—and asked Phillips to run the names by Secretary Hull. The next day, Phillips wrote a short note to the president reporting, "Mr. Hull did not know any of the names personally, and he was therefore unable to express any opinion, other than he was under the impression that Glenn Frank was of Jewish extraction and, for that reason, would be unsuitable for the post." In fact, Mr. Frank, president of the University of Wisconsin, was not Jewish, although ironically, Hull's own wife was.[14]

On June 7, 1933, at a meeting with a number of cabinet officials in the White House, the president complained that he could not find the right man for Germany. He was especially concerned about further delay because the Senate, which was responsible for confirming ambassadors, was preparing to adjourn for the summer recess and leave town. Daniel Roper, the secretary of commerce, tossed out an idea: "How about William E. Dodd?" According to Roper, Roosevelt paused, then nodded and said, "Not a bad idea. I'll consider it." Roosevelt had met Dodd once before—in Chicago, when Roper arranged for them to speak with one another in the president's suite the day after Roosevelt had secured the Democratic nomination.[15] While Dodd was not the prominent politician that Roosevelt had initially wanted, he was a well-respected professor—the chair of the History Department at the University of Chicago. He had studied in Germany as a young man and spoke the language competently. Roosevelt was also aware that Dodd had written a complimentary book about Woodrow Wilson. While sharing Dodd's admiration for the twenty-eighth president, the president understood that many in Congress were strongly isolationist, and Americans overwhelmingly wanted to avoid involvement in another foreign war. Dodd would need his marching orders, but he was an acceptable choice.

The next day, just before lunch, Roosevelt telephoned the professor: "Hello, this is Franklin Roosevelt," the president announced to a very surprised Dodd on the other end of the line. "I want to know if you will render the government a distinct service," the president first asked, and then declared, "I want you to go to Germany as an ambassador." Dodd was deeply honored, but he immediately raised the issue of his past writing: "I hope you will ascertain whether the German government takes exception to my Woodrow Wilson book." As Dodd later recalled, Roosevelt brushed aside his concern. "I'm sure they will not . . . That book, your work as a liberal and as a scholar, and your study at a German university are the main reasons for my wishing to appoint you. It is a difficult post and you have cultural approaches that will help. I want an American liberal in Germany as a standing example."[16]

Three days later, Roosevelt sent Dodd's nomination to the Senate, which confirmed him on a voice vote that day. Secretary Hull had not even been consulted.[17] There was barely a mention in the press about the appointment. The president, however, was greatly relieved and invited Dodd to come to the White House as soon as possible.

On June 16, 1933, at approximately 1:00 p.m., William Dodd was ushered into the Oval Office and warmly greeted by President Roosevelt sitting behind the same desk that President Hoover had used. The sixty-three-year-old professor was slightly built, only five feet eight inches tall. He had neatly combed light brown hair, and his blue eyes imparted intensity in his otherwise expressionless face. Dodd sat rigidly opposite the president as Roosevelt reclined in his chair and launched into a humorous story about how he and Secretary Hull had recently played a joke on Hjalmar Schacht, the head of Germany's Reichsbank and the man ultimately responsible for honoring Germany's war debts to American creditors. A few weeks earlier, Schacht had visited Washington to meet with administration officials, including Secretary of State Hull. After inviting Schacht into his office, Hull, sitting at his desk, ignored the arrogant and impatient bank director for several minutes while he pretended to look for an important document. Eventually, Hull handed Schacht a letter from the president: a demand that Germany honor its debts. Hull then smiled and thanked Schacht for coming to see him. Much to the president's amusement, Schacht was apparently completely flustered by the meeting.[18] Roosevelt delighted in telling the story, but Dodd, deeply earnest and a political naïf, undoubtedly found it strange for a secretary of state to be engaged in such behavior.

After a White House butler carefully placed luncheon trays on the president's cluttered desk, Roosevelt got down to business. Germany owed American banks and businesses approximately $1.2 billion. Roosevelt knew Germany was facing its own economic crisis and unable to pay even the interest on the loans. Technically, the issue involved private parties, not the government, and Roosevelt disdained what he viewed as greedy bankers who "had made exorbitant profits" off the war, but the president wanted Dodd to do all he could to encourage payment because a moratorium would only slow America's recovery.[19]

The president then raised the issue of Hitler's treatment of the Jews in Germany. He told Dodd, "The German authorities are treating the Jews shamefully, and the Jews in this country are greatly excited." The president then explained his view that because it was not "governmental affairs," the Department of State could do nothing "except for the American citizens who are made victims." Still, Roosevelt said, "We must protect them," and encouraged Dodd to do whatever possible "to moderate the persecution by unofficial and personal influence."[20]

Lastly, Roosevelt asked Dodd to work on the issue of bilateral trade. Roosevelt knew generally that German trade had plummeted but wondered if perhaps there were opportunities to help Germany find new markets that could in turn help them in their debt payments. At the same time, Roosevelt recognized that economic nationalism was a global phenomenon, and Europe needed to make trade concessions. Dodd, sounding more like a professor than a diplomat, worried that economic nationalism in America "would tend to make peasants and day laborers of farmers, and proletariats of all unorganized city workers."[21]

When the president finished going over his agenda, he asked Dodd if he had any questions or concerns about the job. Dodd had recently read that some ambassadors abroad were spending vast sums of their own money on residences, servants, and entertainment. Dodd was not a wealthy man. He worried that he could not afford the job on an ambassador's salary and that ostentatious displays of wealth sent the wrong message about American values, especially during such difficult economic times. Roosevelt responded, "You are quite right." The president sidestepped the issue of the ambassador corps and focused on Dodd's personal situation: "Aside from two or three general dinners and entertainments, you need not indulge in any expensive social affairs . . . I think you can manage to live within your income and not sacrifice any essential parts of the service."[22] Reassured, Dodd left the White House ready to assume his new post. He had little concept of the great challenges that awaited him.

5

THE VEHICLE OCCUPIED BY
GREAT CAESAR'S GHOST

While Dodd prepared to leave the United States for Germany, Ambassador Breckinridge Long was already comfortably ensconced in his palatial home in Rome, Italy. Having arrived in mid-May, Long immediately decided the embassy's built-in living quarters were "dingy" and unsuitable for the United States ambassador. He arranged to rent the Villa Taverna, a pink stucco manor house that had been commissioned by Cardinal Consalvi in the fifteenth century. It had been renovated in the nineteenth century and had multiple bedrooms on the second floor, as well as large rooms for entertaining on the ground floor. Situated on seven acres in one of Rome's most central and exclusive neighborhoods, the residence was surrounded by lovely gardens that included a Roman sarcophagus dating to the third century and ancient Egyptian granite columns.[1]

On June 1, 1933, Long presented his credentials to the king of Italy, Victor Emmanuel III. Long breathlessly described the event in a letter to Roosevelt, addressing the president as "My dear Frank" and gushing, "Your ambassador to Italy has been part of a big show." Long went on to recount how "a regular procession of coaches with footmen in gorgeous uniform . . . four coaches, an empty carriage like a spare tire and one outrider on horseback at the head of the procession" arrived in front of Villa Taverna to escort him to the Quirinal Palace.[2]

The following day, Long met with Italy's prime minister, Benito Mussolini in his cavernous office at the Chigi Palace. At the time, fascist Italy was considered neither a threat to the United States nor to any of its neighbors in Europe. Though Il Duce, as Mussolini was known, had transformed Italy into a police state, Soviet Russia and Communism were more widely regarded as the primary challenge to a free and democratic Europe.

The leader of Italy's National Fascist Party, Mussolini was appointed prime minister in 1922. By 1927, he had systematically dismantled virtually all of Italy's prevailing constitutional restraints on his power to create a dictatorship. Mussolini's political success relied on his support from the military, his extensive use of propaganda, and the personality cult that he created to surround himself. He presented himself as a skilled sportsman and was often photographed without his shirt on. Whether fishing by a stream or skiing in the mountains, the bare and barrel-chested Il Duce used his body as a political tool and symbol of machismo. A boxing club in Florence underscored his appeal to Italy's yearning for a strong leader when it plastered his words in large letters on its walls around the ring: "I don't want a population of mandolin players, I want a population of fighters."[3]

Long provided the president with a detailed account of his meeting with Mussolini: "He is a man of comparatively short stature with a very soft well-modulated voice and an air of quiet and dignified elegance." The ambassador presented the prime minister with a specially bound, autographed copy of Roosevelt's inaugural address. Mussolini, according to Long, was grateful and spoke of Roosevelt in a complimentary manner. Long insisted Mussolini had "expressed very great personal admiration."[4]

After about fifteen minutes of conversation, with Mussolini doing most of the talking, Il Duce stood up from behind his desk, and he and Long "walked the whole length of the enormous room." At the double doors, Mussolini assured the ambassador, "You can count on me." Long then boasted to the prime minister that he had "the complete confidence" of the president and that he looked forward to drawing the United States and Italy closer together. Mussolini had both flattered and charmed the ambassador, and in his letter to Roosevelt, Long wrote admiringly of Il Duce, declaring that he was "conscious of having been in the presence of a really unusual person."[5]

If Long was inordinately impressed by Mussolini, so too was Roosevelt, who after receiving Long's report, wrote to him. "There seems no question that he is really interested in what we are doing [in the New Deal] . . . I am much interested and deeply impressed with what he has accomplished and by his evidenced honest purpose of restoring Italy to prevent general European trouble."[6] In the same letter, Roosevelt, who genuinely liked Long, couldn't resist a slight dig at his ambassador's pomposity. The president claimed to have greatly enjoyed Long's "description of the visit to the palace. You are, however, saying that there was one empty carriage. That was the vehicle occupied by Great Caesar's ghost."[7]

In late June, two transatlantic messages arrived in Washington, D.C., within days of one another: a second letter from Ambassador Long to the president, and the latest cable from George Messersmith, the consul general and highest-ranking embassy official in Berlin pending the arrival of Ambassador Dodd, addressed to Undersecretary Phillips.

Having already informed Roosevelt how he had been honored at his accreditation, Long wanted to also provide the president with his initial impressions of Italian society. In a breezy, conversational style, Long wrote, "I was here twenty odd years ago and formed the most distinct and lasting impressions . . . but the landscape, a few donkey wagons and bullocks are the only things to remind one of the Italy that was." He went on to describe how "Rome is not to be recognized . . . Great avenues run through the city. The streets are clean. The people are well dressed. They move with alacrity. In the country the houses are all painted and clean. The farms are all teeming with people, just now reaping wheat by hand . . . The whole temper and attitude of the people have changed. They all seem happy. They seem busy."[8]

Long attributed the improvements in the everyday lives of Italians to the "organized activities" of Mussolini and the fascists. "The Fascists in their black shirts," wrote Long "are apparent in every community. They are dapper and well-dressed and standing straight and lend an atmosphere of individuality and importance to their surroundings . . . The trains are punctual, well-equipped and fast." According to Long, "Mussolini is an astounding character."[9]

Messersmith, who managed the ten American consuls in Germany, was not your typical Foreign Service officer. Born in 1883 in southeastern Pennsylvania, Messersmith's father was an insurance salesman who died when Messersmith was only six years old. His mother homeschooled him until he was eleven, and he then attended the local high school. Highly motivated but lacking the funds to afford a four-year college, Messersmith earned a teaching certificate from the Kutztown Normal School in two years. At age eighteen, Messersmith went to work in a one-room schoolhouse, but was quickly promoted to principal of a school in a neighboring town. In 1914, with the outbreak of World War I, Messersmith joined the Foreign Service. He was known by his colleagues as a tireless worker and by his superiors as a highly opinionated and somewhat tedious writer who produced long and dense dispatches.

Just as Long had been startled by the changes in Italy, so, too, Messersmith believed life had changed in Germany since his arrival in 1930. In his June 26 cable, he opined, "I wish it were really possible to make our people at home understand." Unlike Long's sunny appraisal of Italian life, however, Messersmith painted a deeply pessimistic portrait of Germany's future: "If this government remains in power for another year and carries on in the same measure in this direction, it will go far towards making Germany a danger to world peace for years to come . . . With few exceptions, the men who are running this Government are of a mentality that you and I cannot understand. Some of them are psychopathic cases and would ordinarily be receiving treatment somewhere."[10]

This was not the first warning that Messersmith had conveyed to his colleagues in the Department of State. Earlier in the month, he sent a cable describing how Germany's democratic republic was in danger of becoming a Nazi dictatorship.[11] There is no record of who read Messersmith's cable, but it seems to have had little impact, likely because the official policy of the United States was not to interfere in the internal affairs of another sovereign nation. At the time, all that mattered to the United States concerning U.S.-German relations was that Germany honor its debts.

Consul General Messersmith was waiting beside the tracks at the Berlin Hauptbahnhof when the train carrying Ambassador Dodd and his family arrived. It had been a long journey for the ambassador, his wife, and two grown children, who left New York on July 6, bound for Hamburg aboard the SS *Washington*—the same luxury liner that had carried President Woodrow Wilson to the Versailles Conference in 1919.[12] Aboard the ship, Dodd met Rabbi Stephen Wise, the prominent Jewish leader who was already warning the public about Adolf Hitler. Wise and Dodd had several conversations during the weeklong voyage. Wise worried that Dodd, who for the moment reserved judgment on Hitler, did not really understand what he was getting into. He wondered what the ambassador would do "with the truth when he learns it about Hitler."[13]

In a way, Dodd felt that he already knew Messersmith. Before his departure, Dodd had visited the Department of State, where he met with Undersecretary Phillips and Assistant Secretary for European Affairs Jay Pierrepont Moffat. To give the ambassador a better sense of the challenges he faced, they suggested he read the cable traffic from Berlin. Dodd had been especially impressed by the series of dispatches written by Messersmith that painted a deeply depressing picture of Hitler's use of bigotry and brutality to consolidate his power. Now in Berlin, meeting the five-foot-six-inch Messersmith for the first time, Dodd felt buoyed that he had found a kindred spirit in the State Department—an intelligent, serious-minded diplomat. The ambassador would make his own appraisal of Hitler, but at least there was someone in the embassy who could be counted on to speak his mind. Perhaps even more important to Dodd, he and Messersmith shared a common distinction in the State Department: They did not come from the usual stock of wealth, privilege, and the Ivy League.

Only days after Dodd's arrival, Chancellor Hitler decreed that henceforth the Nationalist Socialists were the only political party in Germany. The chancellor's cabinet then enacted new laws regarding the Prevention of Offspring with Hereditary Diseases, which authorized sterilization of individuals suffering physical or mental handicaps, and the Army Law, which abolished the jurisdiction of civil courts over the military, a change that had been favored by many in the German officer corps.[14] Ambassador Dodd was already getting a taste of what life would be like under Nazi rule, yet in his first letter to Roosevelt, he equivocated:

> It is impossible as yet to say whether the new regime here is going to take a more liberal or a more ruthless direction. From conversations with Neurath, the head of the Foreign Office, and Luther [the German ambassador to the United States]. . . . it is my guess they are to take a more moderate course. One must remember that German statesmen . . . are quite adolescent in their analysis of international problems. The people have never learned the give-and-take group compromises, which English and Americans always apply. They are much here concerned about United States attitudes, but hardly know how to ease down off their dangerous position. This applies especially to the Jewish persecutions.[15]

Before Dodd sent his letter to Roosevelt, Messersmith informed the new ambassador that it was necessary to take extraordinary precautions with diplomatic cables because Nazi spies were almost certainly intercepting them. Messersmith had no reservations about criticism of the Nazis, and from the beginning of Dodd's tenure in Berlin, he did all he could to educate the ambassador about what he viewed to be the limitless depth of Hitler's evil.

Back in Washington, Roosevelt's first one hundred days had produced a whirlwind of reform, economic stimulus, and new governmental institutions. He had signed into law the Federal Emergency Relief Act to fund public works projects around the nation; the Agricultural Adjustment Act to raise farm income by limiting agricultural production; and the Emergency Farm Mortgage Act to extend repayment schedules and offer emergency financing for those behind on loan payments. He created the Civilian Conservation Corps, a public relief work program, and secured enactment of the Securities Act to promote better disclosure by companies and rein in speculative investing. Notwithstanding his frenetic schedule, the president still took time out to read the letters and cables from his ambassadors and to reply to them personally. He thanked Breckinridge Long and praised his "description of modern life in Italy" as "splendid" and for providing him with "a very clear picture of the changes which have taken place."[16] Roosevelt wrote Dodd that it was "good to get your letter . . . and I am glad to note that you do not seem quite as pessimistic as some other people."[17]

For Roosevelt, any good news from abroad was welcome. Aware that Europe was suffering its own version of the Great Depression, Roosevelt had nevertheless declared during his inaugural speech, "I shall spare no effort to restore world trade by international economic readjustment, but the emergency at home cannot wait on that accomplishment." Reading the cables from Long and Dodd, the president was also mindful that representatives from sixty-six nations were currently gathered at the Geological Museum in London for a multilateral conference to reduce tariffs, discuss repayment of World War I debts, and stabilize prices internationally. The London Economic Conference, as it was known, had been the brainchild of President Hoover and was billed as an effort to resuscitate the world economy. Hoover believed the depression in America was rooted in the global depression that, in turn, had its origins in Europe after the Great War. The conference had been convened to consider financial issues ranging from currency stabilization to war debts to international exchange.[18]

Roosevelt appointed Secretary Hull to lead the large U.S. delegation and asked William Bullitt, whose earlier missions to Europe had impressed him, to be a part of the team. The president was extremely wary of any multilateral panacea and gave very little direction to Hull. The secretary of state, though well versed in international trade, knew next to nothing about international finance. This became all too apparent once the delegates arrived at the conference. The Americans, often arguing among themselves, didn't seem to have a considered opinion of what could or should be accomplished.

In the middle of the conference, as Hull beseeched Roosevelt for instructions, the president went for a relaxing cruise off the coast of New England. He returned to find a proposed draft compromise related to the issue of currency stabilization that had been worked out by the United States, Britain, and France after many hours and late nights of tedious discussion. Roosevelt rejected the plan because it proposed tying the dollar to the world currencies. He felt such an arrangement might hurt the recovery at home.[19] The president's decision raised concerns in Europe. In the aftermath of the conference, Breckinridge Long reported, "A good many criticisms have been leveled against the American policy." Hull, who had been somewhat sidelined in the negotiations because he lacked financial expertise, had been humiliated before his European counterparts. In a lengthy letter to the president, Long remarked on the unpopularity of the U.S. in "all the capitals of Europe."[20]

William Bullitt also reported to the president on the London conference. Bullitt, who opined to Roosevelt about anything that was on his mind, inserted an observation on diplomatic recognition of the Soviet Union. Aware of the Japanese government's growing imperialism, Bullitt proposed having "a diplomatic representative not only in China but also in Russia since the two countries will henceforth be intimately related in their priority toward Japan." Bullitt recommended the appointment of "first-rate men in both countries" and noted that Maxim Litvinov, the Soviet commissar for foreign affairs, had suggested that he, Bullitt, would be an excellent choice for ambassador to Russia. With false modesty, Bullitt informed the president that he could not think "of a worse" person for the job. "I have no idea that you would contemplate such a thing but I should like to argue with you if by chance someone should suggest an appointment to you."[21] In fact, in addition to Litvinov, Bullitt almost certainly knew that even before Roosevelt had taken office, someone close to the president-elect had already recommended Bullitt to Roosevelt as an ideal candidate to serve as the first United States ambassador to the Soviet Union.

6

SOME CHANGES ARE IN ORDER

In early August 1933, after living out of suitcases in a hotel suite for nearly a month, Ambassador Dodd and his family moved into a luxurious three-story town house on Tiergartenstrasse, rented to them by a wealthy Jewish banker for $150 a month. The owner, hoping that the protective cover of the top United States diplomat might shield him from Nazi persecution, vacated the first two floors and lived with his elderly mother on the third. The thrifty ambassador was uncomfortable with displays of wealth, disapproving of the ostentatious lifestyle of many in the Foreign Service. Nevertheless, he had reconciled himself to living in a grand, well-appointed house in Berlin, understanding that he would need to entertain prominent Germans from time to time. Moreover, the arrangement was made more palatable to him since he had been able to negotiate a very good deal for the rental.[1] However, Dodd seemed not to have seriously considered the circumstances under which he had obtained such favorable terms from the Jewish owner. His twenty-four-year-old daughter, Martha, remembered that during those early days, her father was "slightly pro-German," and that the Dodd family didn't much "like the Jews anyway."[2]

Because President Hindenburg was unwell and convalescing at his country retreat, Dodd was not able to present his credentials immediately and therefore could not be officially recognized as ambassador. With time on his hands, he set himself the task of better understanding how the embassy functioned and learning about the work ethic and habits of the embassy's officers.[3]

From the beginning of his ambassadorship, Dodd bristled at State Department protocol and disdained the lax work ethic and lifestyle of many of his colleagues in the embassy. When a U.S. congressman visited in late July, Dodd joined the meeting in Messersmith's office instead of hosting the representative in the ambassador's office; George Gordon, a buttoned-down aristocrat who served as counselor in the embassy, thought the ambassador showed very poor judgment in allowing staff to conduct a meeting that ordinarily would be led by the ambassador.[4] While Dodd didn't much care about protocol, he did care about a frugally managed embassy. The ambassador conveyed in a letter to President Roosevelt his view that "some changes are in order" for the "diplomatic and consular service." He observed that the budget could be "considerably reduced" because "many of the men are engaged in duplicating each other."[5]

Dodd was well aware of Hitler's treatment of Jews in Germany. Not only had he discussed the issue with President Roosevelt during their Oval Office luncheon and with Rabbi Wise aboard the SS *Washington*, but before leaving for Berlin, Dodd had met with a number of prominent bankers, politicians, and former high-ranking government officials who offered a wide range of advice on how he should approach Hitler's persecution of Jews. Colonel House—who also advised William Bullitt about obtaining an ambassadorship—urged Dodd to do everything possible "to ameliorate Jewish sufferings," but added that he did not believe Jews should be allowed to "dominate intellectual and economic life in Berlin as they have done for a long time."[6] Charles R. Crane, the extremely wealthy son of a bathroom-fixtures mogul, told Dodd, "Let Hitler have his way."[7]

After his first month as ambassador, Dodd wrote to President Roosevelt, declaring that while he did not approve of Germany's treatment of Jews or Hitler's drive to restore the country's military power, "Fundamentally, I believe a people has a right to govern itself and the other peoples must exercise patience even when cruelties and injustices are done. Give men a chance to try their schemes."[8] That view, consistent with State Department policy, would be tested in mid-August when Dodd and his family embarked on a sightseeing trip around Germany.

Two days after they began their journey, Dodd received a disturbing report that an American surgeon, a Jew, had been brutally attacked by Hitler's storm trooper detachment, the Nazi Party's paramilitary unit. Three days later, Dodd's two children, Martha and Bill, and a friend took a side trip to Nuremberg. After checking into a small hotel, they took a stroll before dinner. Wandering onto the Koenigstrasse, the city's main thoroughfare, they came upon a large crowd of boisterous, brown-shirted Nazis parading a young woman in a white smock; her head shaved, face smeared with white powder, and wearing a sign that read "I have offered myself to a Jew."[9]

Martha Dodd described the incident to her father, who was appalled and later wrote that he had accepted his ambassadorship with the view that he "could have some influence in moderating the policies of the Nazi regime."[10] A Wilsonian Democrat and an idealist, he believed there would be "a chance to bring them back to reason, to recall forcefully to them their recent democratic past."[11] Now, after only a month, the ambassador was beginning to question whether it was possible, but decided that he needed to try.

Dodd cabled the State Department for advice about attending the Nazi Party rally in Nuremberg at the beginning of September. He was inclined to skip it. The rally was not an official governmental event, but Dodd knew his absence would be noted and he hoped that it would send a message to those in German society not yet enthralled by Hitler. The State Department responded that they would support whatever he decided, and Dodd did not attend. However, privately, Undersecretary Phillips and Assistant Secretary for European Affairs Moffat believed the ambassador's decision had been needlessly provocative. They felt Dodd had missed an opportunity to build goodwill and make a favorable first impression on Nazi officials.

It would not be the last time Dodd would disappoint his superiors in the Department of State. And while President Roosevelt respected Dodd, they barely knew one another. The president, preoccupied with his domestic agenda, gave his inexperienced ambassador little direction.

Like Dodd, William Bullitt hadn't known Franklin Roosevelt before the 1932 campaign. However, after listening to one of Roosevelt's campaign speeches on the radio that year, Bullitt had written the candidate an enthusiastic letter: "It was the most inspiring address that I have heard since Wilson's speeches in 1918. You not only said the right things, but said them with a 1776 spirit."[12] Bullitt, of course, knew that Roosevelt had loyally served Woodrow Wilson as assistant secretary of the navy, but Roosevelt apparently didn't completely register that Bullitt, who had served as a young diplomat during World War I, had ultimately betrayed Wilson. In any event, Bullitt immediately started a correspondence with Roosevelt and donated $1,000 to the campaign. This led to a meeting with Roosevelt in Albany arranged by Louis Brandeis Wehle, the nephew of U.S. Supreme Court Justice Louis Brandeis, and a friend of both men. Roosevelt and Bullitt were immediately drawn to one another: "There was a certain community of social background as well as temperamental congeniality," Wehle observed. "Roosevelt was apt to absorb only what he could grasp quickly; Bullitt has the capacity for prodigious, and sustained toil . . . Yet he could swiftly and vividly make available to Roosevelt his scholarship in history and also his familiarity with Europe and the current leaders. They made an ideal team."[13] Bullitt joined the campaign in Albany, working on speeches and occasionally contributing thoughts on foreign policy.

A few months after their first meeting, Roosevelt, Bullitt, and Wehle met again for dinner. At some point, after coffee had been served, Bullitt briefly excused himself from the room to make a phone call. Wehle turned to Roosevelt and said, "There is your man for Paris." Roosevelt, however, already had identified Jesse I. Straus, the president of Macy & Co., who had made a sizable campaign contribution, for that position.

"Well," said Wehle, "if we should recognize Russia, he would by all odds be your best man as our first ambassador."[14] Roosevelt nodded, although given that he had yet to be inaugurated, it's doubtful that the appointment was something to which he had given much thought. Moreover, as Wehle noted, the U.S. and the Soviet Union did not have diplomatic relations at the time.

After Roosevelt's inauguration, Bullitt had continued to ingratiate himself with the president and expanded his charm offensive to others surrounding the president in the White House. In August 1933, Eleanor Roosevelt made a visit to Appalachia to see for herself the deep poverty that afflicted the region. Upon her return, at a White House dinner, she told a story about meeting a little boy who clung to his pet white rabbit because his sister said the family was hungry and desperate for food. Bullitt immediately promised to send the family a check for one hundred dollars in the hopes of keeping the rabbit alive.[15]

The president increasingly sought Bullitt's views on foreign policy, especially on the multitude of issues related to Europe. During his visits to the White House, Bullitt struck up a friendship with the president's personal assistant, Missy LeHand. Before long, the two were involved romantically. One Monday morning, after a Sunday drive in the country, LeHand received an official looking envelope from the "Special Assistant to the Secretary of State." Inside the envelope were LeHand's pearl earrings, which Bullitt informed her "had turned up on the floor of the car."[16] The president was aware of the relationship, and as long as LeHand was happy, Roosevelt approved.

Bullitt was also popular in the State Department with those who counted. During the London conference, he stayed at the Carlton Hotel, where Secretary Hull was also staying. During the nearly month-long conference, the two men often conferred over drinks after a full day of meetings.[17] In his memoirs, Hull referred to Bullitt as "an intimate friend of the president's" who was "a brilliant person, well versed in international affairs . . . particularly friendly toward Russia and an ardent proponent of recognition."

President Roosevelt had listened to Bullitt's advocacy for diplomatic relations with the Soviet Union and agreed that it should be given serious consideration. However, there were a number of obstacles. In a memorandum to Secretary Hull, Bullitt advised the secretary "by negotiation" to "attempt to obtain an agreement in regard to repayment of the loans of the Government of the United States." Bullitt then recommended a "prohibition of communist propaganda in the United States by the Soviet Government" and "the protection of civil and religious rights for Americans in Russia." Over the next month, Hull and Bullitt managed to negotiate successfully with their Russian counterparts, reaching a breakthrough compromise on the issue of the more than $600 million debt owed by the Russian government.[18]

There was, of course, political opposition within the United States to recognition of the Soviet Union. Isolationists and political conservatives in Congress felt strongly that there should be no diplomatic relations with a country that served as the bedrock of Communism, an ideology that directly targeted America's model of capitalist democracy.[19] The president, however, believed that the negatives were outweighed by potential strategic benefits that included opening Russia to American investment, curbing Japanese expansionism, and eventual repayment of czarist debts.

On November 17, 1933, President Roosevelt signed documents extending diplomatic recognition to the Soviet Union. Afterward, in his West Wing study near the Oval Office, an elated Roosevelt celebrated with drafts of beer, raising a toast with Russian ambassador Maxim Litvinov, Secretary of the Treasury William Woodin, Undersecretary of the Treasury Morgenthau, and Undersecretary of State William Phillips (Cordell Hull was traveling in South America). According to Phillips, as everyone was leaving, the president asked him to stay for a minute. Both graduates of the Groton School, Roosevelt trusted Phillips and wanted to know what he thought of Bullitt. As Phillips remembered the conversation, "I praised [Bullitt's] help and left the President with the impression that [Bullitt] would receive the appointment as Ambassador to Russia, which did occur a few days later."

The New York Times reported on November 19, 1933, that diplomatic relations between Washington, D.C., and Moscow had been established and that William Bullitt would be the first American ambassador to the Soviet Union. In a rare interview with *The Times,* Joseph Stalin, the Soviet ruler, complimented Roosevelt as a "realist" and thanked him for appointing Bullitt, whom Lenin had "liked" and who he understood to be "a direct man who says what he thinks."[20]

Eleanor Roosevelt viewed Bullitt's appointment with a somewhat jaundiced eye, writing to her close friend Lorena Hickok, "Well, Russia is recognized. Bullitt goes as ambassador. I wonder if that is why FDR has been content to let Missy play with him?" She then added, with evident sarcasm, "She'll have another embassy to visit next summer, anyway."[21]

Ambassador Dodd was experiencing frequent headaches and stomach discomfort. He wrote a friend in the United States after only a few months in Berlin that his job was a "disagreeable and difficult business."[22] Attacks on Americans by Nazi thugs had continued unabated, and no one was ever arrested, much less charged for assault. The German press was being increasingly manipulated by the state, and creative material such as plays and books had to be submitted to Ministry of Public Enlightenment and Propaganda for approval to be produced or published.[23] Newspaper editors, by law, were required to be German citizens of Aryan descent and not married to a Jew.[24] Indeed, the persecution of German Jews by the government had increased markedly by the late summer of 1933; Hitler and his minister of propaganda, Joseph Goebbels, had publicly declared that Jews needed to be wiped off the face of the earth. American Jews visiting Germany pleaded with Dodd to do something. Dodd was increasingly disgusted by Germany's treatment of Jews, but he was still not officially accredited as ambassador and felt powerless.

In mid-September, Dodd decided to make his grievances known to the German government and arranged to meet for the first time with Konstantin von Neurath, the German foreign minister. Like Dodd, the sixty-year-old Neurath had once been a gentleman farmer. Short, overweight, and bald, Neurath had previously served in posts in London and

Rome. While not known for his intellectual prowess, he was considered a wily and effective diplomat. Before Dodd could levy a formal protest, Neurath told Dodd that he had already met with Hitler and Hermann Goering to discuss how best to deter attacks against Americans. He then addressed the issue of the Jews, reporting that he had recently been in the company of three prominent Jews at the races in Baden-Baden and "there were no unfriendly expressions." Neurath acknowledged the government's persecution of Jews was wrong and that he was working behind the scenes to change the policy. Most importantly, he assured the American ambassador that Germany did not want another war in Europe.[25]

Dodd was not altogether assuaged, but he did not challenge Neurath's explanations and even somewhat sympathized with the Nazi perception of a Jewish problem. In fact, Dodd told the foreign minister, "You know, of course, that we have had difficulty now and then in the United States with Jews who had gotten too much of a hold on intellectual and business life." He added that some of his "peers in Washington . . . appreciated the difficulties of the Germans . . . but that they did not for a moment agree with the method of solving the problem which so often ran into utter ruthlessness."[26]

Perhaps because he did not yet have official ambassador status, or perhaps because he felt he needed further confirmation, Dodd failed to raise an important issue with Neurath. Dodd had received a disturbing report from his consul in Stuttgart that Germany was rearming: "No doubt can be entertained any longer that large scale preparation for a renewal of aggression against other countries is being planned in Germany."[27]

On October 12, Ambassador Dodd entered the ornate banquet room at the Hotel Adlon, just beyond the Brandenburg Gate in Berlin. He was scheduled to deliver his first public address to a group of businessmen. He had anticipated a small crowd and so was surprised to see that the room was packed with more than two hundred guests. As he made his way to the head table, he shook hands with a number of fellow diplomats and acknowledged a few of the foreign journalists and businessmen who were also present. He also observed a number of Nazi officials from the Foreign Ministry and the Propaganda Ministry sitting at tables near the front.[28]

At the podium, Dodd unfolded a typewritten speech from his coat pocket and for the next half hour read in an even tone a 2,500-word indictment of economic nationalism as the cynical ploy of autocratic rulers. He used several historical allusions, which he hoped the audience would understand as a veiled criticism of the Nazi regime. When he had finished, the audience erupted in sustained applause. As he would later recall, "When the thing was over about every German present showed and expressed a kind of approval which revealed the thought, 'you have said what all of us have been denied the right to say.'" Dodd was greatly encouraged by the response, writing to President Roosevelt, "My interpretation of this is that all liberal Germany is with us—and more than half of Germany is at heart liberal."[29]

In his report to the Department of State, George Messersmith praised his ambassador for having delivered a timely and substantive address that had been widely reported in the German press. However, Messersmith's positive view of Ambassador Dodd's outspokenness was not uniformly shared in the department. After ignoring some of the ambassador's earlier letters, Undersecretary of State Phillips wrote Dodd, expressing his opinion that "an Ambassador, who is a privileged guest of the country to which he is accredited, should be careful not to give public expression to anything in the nature of criticism of his adopted country, because in so doing, he loses ipso facto the confidence of those very public officials whose good-will is so important to him in the success of his mission."[30] In fact, Phillips was not alone—other senior officials in the State Department, including the secretary, were losing confidence in Dodd as well.

Precisely at noon, only five days after his speech at the chamber of commerce, Ambassador Dodd, dressed in top hat and tails, arrived at No. 77 Wilhelmstrasse. The address was for the city palace of the late Prince Radziwiłł, where President Hindenburg had once lived and worked and which was now occupied by Chancellor Hitler. Only a few days earlier,

Hitler had announced that Germany was "immediately withdrawing from the disarmament conference and from the League of Nations."[31] In his diary, the ambassador blamed the "autocratic methods" of Hitler for the withdrawal, but he also held responsible the "French politicians" who "for ten years violated the spirit of disarmament clauses of the Versailles Treaty."[32] Up to that point, it was the French who had built the largest air force in Europe after World War I.

Dodd climbed the broad marble stairway, guarded by jackbooted soldiers with right arms raised in the Nazi salute. After being ushered into an anteroom, he waited briefly before Foreign Minister Neurath opened another door and welcomed the ambassador into the chancellor's opulent office, "a great room some fifty feet square with tables and chairs placed all around for group conferences." Dodd later noted that Hitler, "in simple work-a-day suit neat-and erect," walked across the room to greet him. According to the ambassador, the chancellor "looks somewhat better than the pictures that appear in the papers."[33]

The three men sat down. Dodd immediately raised the issue of the growing number of assaults upon Americans—primarily Jewish Americans. "The Chancellor assured me personally," Dodd recorded in his diary, "that he would see that any future attack was punished to the limit and that publicity would be given to decrees warning everyone that foreigners were not to be expected to give the Hitler salute." Next, Dodd discussed what he viewed as discrimination against American creditors. Again, Hitler assured him that he would do everything in his power to see that legitimate claims were honored. Lastly, Dodd alluded to the chancellor's recent decision to withdraw from the League of Nations. The ambassador acknowledged to Hitler that defeat in war is often followed by injustice, and he pointed to the example of the aftermath of the American Civil War and the North's "terrible" treatment of the South. However, Hitler was unmoved by Dodd's attempt at empathy. He grew angry, railed against France and Britain, and declared that Germany would fulfill its destiny and would not be subjugated by its neighbors.[34] The meeting lasted approximately forty-five minutes, and

Dodd's overwhelming impression of Hitler "was of his belligerence and self-confidence."[35]

Dodd was unfailingly polite and gentlemanly—an academic who operated by marshaling facts to make an argument much the way he would approach an essay on history. While he had adhered to his talking points with Hitler, his total unfamiliarity with international politics left him ill equipped to engage in serious negotiations and confounded by Hitler's furious outbursts. It was likely the first instance that the ambassador recognized the magnitude of the diplomatic challenges he confronted.

7

I WONDER IF YOU WOULD TRY TO GET THE PRESIDENT MORE INTERESTED IN FOREIGN AFFAIRS

I n the weeks before his departure for the Soviet Union, newly minted Ambassador Bullitt, who knew he would not return to the United States for several months, was busy visiting friends and arranging his personal affairs and business interests. As testament to their friendship, President Roosevelt invited him to spend a few days in Warm Springs, Georgia, where the president often retreated to soak his atrophied legs in the town's therapeutic hot springs. There, at the "Little White House," Bullitt spent a happy week with the president and with Missy LeHand. In a farewell letter to Missy, he implored her to visit him in Moscow, joking that he hoped "to have some sort of embassy in which to entertain you."[1]

Once back in Washington, Bullitt was cleaning out his desk in the State Department when a young Foreign Service officer introduced himself. George Kennan, thirty years old, had been serving in Latvia as an observer, monitoring developments in the Soviet Union. Bullitt asked him if he spoke Russian. Kennan did, and Bullitt immediately offered him a job in the embassy. The young man eagerly accepted.

Kennan left for Europe a few days earlier than Bullitt, who made the transatlantic voyage with his young daughter, Anne. The two men met in Paris and boarded a train at the Gare de L'Est. As the train started to pull away from the station, Kennan observed a woman standing alone on the platform. He was told it was Louise Bryant, Bullitt's second wife and the former wife of John Reed, the renowned American Communist and revolutionary. Kennan surmised that Louise came to say goodbye to her daughter, who was sitting in the next car with her father.[2] Bullitt had divorced Louise in 1930, accusing her of being an alcoholic and an unfit mother.

The voyage to Russia took nearly a day and a half and covered over two thousand miles by rail. The train made a brief stop in Berlin, where Bullitt introduce himself to Ambassador Dodd. The two men, barely acquainted with one another, were a study in contrasts: Dodd, the slightly built, somewhat reserved and modest professor, and Bullitt, the ebullient, dashing, Ivy League–educated Brahmin. Bullitt liked to remind folks of his close relationship with Roosevelt and blithely told Dodd that the president sent his "cordial regards" and "thanked him for his service." Then, according to Dodd, Bullitt launched into a self-congratulatory soliloquy about how recognition of Russia had been delayed too long and about his success in getting the Russians to agree to open their markets to American industrial goods and to make a down payment of $100 million on their debt to American creditors. In his diary, Dodd noted that "Germans owe Americans over a billion dollars," and he wondered how those debts would be paid "if German markets are closed . . . if the United States monopolizes Russian markets and still further isolates the Germans." Dodd privately did the math, which suggested that Russia should not be a priority; and in his diary lamented, "Collect one hundred million from Moscow and lose one billion in Berlin."[3]

The next day, December 10, the train carrying Bullitt crossed the Polish-Soviet border at twilight and arrived at the border town of Negoreloe. In his diary, George Kennan vividly described passing from the relative freedom of western and central Europe into the Soviet police state. He recalled how:

The deserted forests of the border zone crowded the single track on either side; silent, snow-covered and forbidding. At the barbed wire stood a lone sentry, in a clearing, and on top of him was a dim figure of a Polish soldier with gun and fixed bayonet, and his great coat turned up against the intense cold. A short distance beyond the border, the train slowed down to a little cottage beside the tracks, and Soviet border guards, with their long snug overcoats and blue caps of the OGPU, the Soviet uniformed force [secret police], came on board. A few minutes later there were lights and voices outside the windows and the train pulled up to the station.[4]

Russia in 1933 was a very different country from the one that Bullitt had promoted during the Paris talks of 1918. The Communist Party, OGPU, and People's Commissariat had consolidated power and established a rigid bureaucratic system of governing. At the top of the pyramid stood Joseph Stalin, a doctrinaire Marxist-Leninist. Stalin had implemented a five-year plan to eliminate the last vestiges of capitalism in Russian society. A great influx of Russian peasants from the villages poured into the cities as the factories and mines became the engines of the nation's industrial revolution. Stalin made routine use of violence to silence his detractors and expanded the gulag, a network of labor camps, to eradicate political opposition. In the throes of this political, social, and economic upheaval, the Soviet Union experienced a major famine. Millions were starving to death—largely as a result of Stalin's policies.

Bullitt and the American entourage left the train and entered the empty station at Negoreloe, where a long banquet table and chairs had been set out for a welcome dinner. Bullitt wrote President Roosevelt: "The air stank of sheepskin coats, sawdust, disinfectant, tobacco, and human sweat." No one ate very much, and soon thereafter, they boarded a different train—a Russian train—which Kennan likened to "wooden ships on wheels," because the passenger cars were "roomy vehicles" and "comparably cozy and comfortable."

Only days after his arrival in Moscow, Ambassador Bullitt was invited by the senior Soviet military officer, Marshal Klementi Voroshilov, to a gala dinner at his apartment in the Kremlin. All of the senior Soviet government officials were in attendance. Voroshilov introduced Bullitt to the general secretary, Joseph Stalin, whom Bullitt recalled was dressed "in a common soldier's uniform." They shook hands formally and Stalin welcomed Bullitt to the Soviet Union.

During dinner, Stalin arose from his chair, lifted his glass of vodka, and proposed a toast to President Roosevelt. Bullitt, in turn, rose to toast Mikhail Kalinin, the chairman of the Central Executive Committee. Vyacheslav Molotov, chairman of the Council of People's Commissars, drank to Bullitt "who comes to us as a new ambassador but as an old friend." Stalin stood again: "To the health and prosperity and happiness and triumphs of the American Army and Navy and the President of the United States." As soon as Stalin sat down, Bullitt once again raised his glass "to the memory of Lenin and the continued success of the Soviet Union." Bullitt later speculated that there might have been as many as fifty toasts.[5]

After hours of eating and drinking, Bullitt and Stalin sat down and talked through an interpreter. Bullitt later reported to President Roosevelt that Stalin told him, "In spite of being a leader of a capitalist nation," Roosevelt was "one of the most popular people in the Soviet Union." The Soviet leader, in an ebullient mood, wanted Bullitt to feel welcome. "If you want to see me at any time, day or night," he stated, "you only have to let me know, and I will see you at once." As the evening came to a close, the two men stood to say good night to one another. Stalin asked the ambassador for help procuring 250,000 tons of steel rail to complete strategic double tracking for the Trans-Siberian Railway. Bullitt said he would do what he could. Stalin then asked the ambassador if there was "anything at all in the Soviet Union" that Bullitt wanted.[6]

Bullitt may have been taken aback by Stalin's magnanimity, or perhaps he had drunk too much and wasn't thinking clearly. The Soviet leader had made a significant request of the United States, and this was the new ambassador's opportunity to make a similarly important request of the Soviet Union—perhaps a meaningful down payment on its debt obligation to the United States. However, Bullitt replied that the United States needed to find a suitable building for an embassy as well as a residence for the ambassador; he had his eye on a neoclassical mansion that had been built by one of the richest men in pre-revolutionary Russia. Stalin threw his head back and laughed, and then, according to Bullitt, "took my head in his two hands and gave me a large kiss." Astonished, Bullitt nevertheless kissed him back.

A few days later, Bullitt wrote the president a long letter describing the evening and his encounter with Stalin. The Soviet leader impressed Bullitt as a man of "great shrewdness and inflexible will," someone with "intuition in extraordinary measure." Lastly, Bullitt praised Stalin as having "the quality of being able to treat the most serious things with a joke and a twinkle in his eye." Bullitt added, "Lenin had the same quality. You have it."

Bullitt had missed an important opportunity to advance American interests in the Soviet Union, choosing instead to lobby for an opulent residence. In his letter to the president, Bullitt engaged in saccharine flattery of the president, while seeming oblivious to his own vanity. Roosevelt liked Bullitt, but adulation didn't impress him. He didn't respond to Bullitt's letter.

Like Bullitt, Breckinridge Long adopted a personal and familiar tone when corresponding with the president, often beginning his letters, "My dear Frank." And like Bullitt, Long was also smitten with the country to which he had been posted, as well as with its leader, Benito Mussolini.[7]

Besides praising Il Duce to Roosevelt during his first months as ambassador, Long shared his approbation with others. In a letter to his home-state senator Bennett Clark of Missouri, Long called Mussolini "an earnest peace advocate, duly committed to the pacific resolution of international questions." He also declared Mussolini to be "building his influence as well as he can to be used in the interests of a peaceful Europe and to try to coordinate the industrial and commercial activities of European countries to bring an end to the panicky situation, to promote normal trade relations, and secure development."

Two weeks later, Long wrote his friend Joseph Davies, future ambassador to the Soviet Union, calling Mussolini "an astounding character . . . one of the most remarkable persons." Long characterized Fascist Italy as "the most interesting experiment in government to come above the horizon since the formulation of our Constitution 150 years ago."[8] Long had access to the highest levels of government in Rome and led a very active social life. "I am enjoying it all," he told Davies.[9] Long seemed oblivious to the fact that Mussolini was a dictator who had stifled democracy in Italy. The ambassador was not alone. After receiving a handwritten letter from Mussolini in June 1933, Roosevelt expressed interest in meeting with him to discuss "the outstanding world problems in which the United States and the Italians are mutually interested."

Long's upbeat letters and cables initially gave Roosevelt and those around him a sense of optimism and hope that Italy could play a constructive role in Europe, perhaps even a leadership role. The United States would soon participate in a multilateral disarmament conference, and unlike the London Economic Conference, Roosevelt pressed for a specific, successful outcome whereby the nations of Europe would agree not to rearm. The president asked Long to encourage Mussolini to play a significant role, writing that Il Duce "had a wonderful chance to force an agreement," and that "frankly, I feel he can achieve more than anyone else."[10]

As his first nine months in office came to a close, President Roosevelt could point to significant accomplishments on the domestic front. He had pushed nearly twenty major pieces of legislation through Congress, reshaping every aspect of the economy, from banking and industry to agriculture and social welfare. However, in the area of foreign policy as it related to western Europe, his record was decidedly mixed. The London conference, in which the United States had participated, had largely failed. The president had managed to normalize diplomatic relations with the Soviet Union, but relations with Germany had become increasingly strained. Roosevelt, of course, was not entirely focused on events in Europe—he also kept an eye on Asia and the rise of Imperial Japan. Yet, notwithstanding the growing list of international challenges, Roosevelt made few public statements on foreign policy and plainly was much more focused on domestic issues. When *New York Times* reporter Anne O'Hare McCormick joined Eleanor Roosevelt in the White House for dinner one evening late in 1933, the First Lady suggested, "I wonder if you would try to get the president more interested in foreign affairs."[11]

8

I AM MUCH TOO FOND OF YOU ALL

After Roosevelt's victory in the 1932 election, Joe Kennedy let it be known that he would be interested in serving as the secretary of the treasury. Roosevelt genuinely appreciated Kennedy's support during the campaign but had no intention of appointing the headstrong Irish American to such a critical position at such a crucial time. The president really didn't know what to do with Kennedy, but he knew he needed to do something. Louis Howe, who advised Roosevelt on political appointments, wanted to keep Kennedy as far away from the president's inner circle as possible. Howe was aware that the Boston financier had a well-deserved reputation for arrogance and unsavory business practices and that Roosevelt's son James had helped Kennedy start his liquor business after Prohibition. Nevertheless, in the spring of 1934, James, acting on instructions from his father, approached Kennedy and asked if he would be interested in being the ambassador to Uruguay, the small South American country over five thousand miles away from Washington. Kennedy listened carefully to James, but politely declined the offer. A few days later, James suggested that perhaps Kennedy would like to be ambassador to Ireland. Although Kennedy was deeply proud of his Irish heritage, he didn't believe the position was important enough and, again, refused the offer.[1]

After the president finished his vacation, he asked Kennedy to come see him in Washington. Kennedy later remembered being ushered into the Oval Office to meet with Roosevelt and, to his surprise, seeing Louis Howe there as well. The president was his usual cheerful self, but Howe, according to Kennedy, "looked at me as though he were looking at the devil himself."[2] After some small talk, Kennedy recalled the president suggested "it might be a very great idea to have me come down as in charge of the Securities and Exchange Commission." This appealed to Kennedy.

Roosevelt's choice of Kennedy to be chairman of the Securities and Exchange Commission was controversial and a powerful example of how Roosevelt wielded power to keep friends and foes alike off balance. Kennedy had amassed a personal fortune in the stock market and had a reputation as a stock manipulator. He had added to his already enormous wealth through shrewd investments in Hollywood when film was still a fledgling industry. The president decided that if anyone knew how to rein in Wall Street, it was someone like Kennedy, who had profited so handsomely from it.

Kennedy cared for nothing more than his nine children and their futures. He was both aggressive and strategic in seeking out ways to groom them for future success. At the top of Kennedy's plans for his offspring was for his oldest son, Joseph Jr., to be the first Catholic president of the United States. In September 1933, Kennedy wrote to George St. John, the headmaster at Choate School, the Connecticut preparatory from which his son had graduated in June, to tell him that he was "taking Joe to Europe with me tomorrow night, to put him in school there for a year to study German and French, and to get a tremendous appreciation of the problems facing the world, by getting first hand information of the foreign problems."[3] He wanted his son to have some worldly experience before entering Harvard College.

Several weeks later, Kennedy reported on his son's progress to St. John: "I have left him in London at the branch of the University of London, a school of economics and political science, and he is doing a remarkable job." In the same letter, Kennedy revealed plans for his second-oldest son, Jack, also a student at Choate. "I would very much like to have Jack follow in [Joe's] footsteps and he can only do that if he senses his own responsibilities."[4]

Joe Jr. enjoyed a heady experience in London, mixing with high society and the elite of academia. He wrote his father in late November that he went to "Laski's for tea," referring to one of the most prominent political theorists at the London School of Economics. Active in the British Labour Party, Harold Laski was a strong advocate for British socialism. Young Joe reported that also attending the tea "there were two Nazis there who were attacked by Laski and another German, a Socialist. Thought the Nazis answered them very well, they have certainly got a lot of faith in Hitler."[5] Though Kennedy didn't describe the substance of the conversation to his father, it was an early indication that he saw merit in the Nazi cause.

Joe Kennedy was delighted with his son's burgeoning interest in international affairs. He wanted him to use London as "a launching pad for the exploration of the European continent," to personally observe "the French and Italian situations" because they would be "the most interesting." He noted, "I can arrange for you to meet Mussolini through Breckinridge Long, the American Ambassador to Italy and also arrange an audience with the Pope." Kennedy also suggested that his son "see something of Russia," which he could arrange with the help of Ambassador William Bullitt. Finally, while his father didn't mention Hitler or the Nazis, he offered that it would be "highly educational and instructive" for Joe Jr. "to go into Germany."[6]

President Roosevelt and members of his administration were hearing from American Jews stories of Hitler's savage discrimination in Germany. The president was also getting an earful from his diplomats. From Germany, Ambassador Dodd continued to report on Hitler's persecution of Jews. Next door in Austria, United States ambassador George Earle wrote the president that "Hitler is a paranoiac with a gift of eloquence of a kind about half way between [William Jennings] Bryan and Billy

Sunday . . . [who] stirs up latent racial antipathy of the Germans to the Jews, a thing easy to do since the Jews still have a little left, in contrast to the utter impoverishment of the Germans."[7] Earle worried that Hitler's hatred of Jews had deep roots in Austria as well.

In late 1933, Ambassador Earle toured nine Austrian provinces, visiting cities and towns and talking to local officials, merchants, and religious leaders. Upon his return to Vienna, he held a press conference to denounce the rising level of anti-Semitism that he had heard of during his travels. Earle's comments were relayed to his superiors in the State Department, who made it clear that meddling in the internal affairs of other countries was not looked upon favorably. However, President Roosevelt, in a letter to Earle just before Christmas, applauded his ambassador: "Strictly between ourselves, I am glad you committed what some have suggested was a diplomatic blunder, I can assure you it did not embarrass me at all!"[8]

Roosevelt may have been content to allow his ambassadors in Europe to condemn anti-Semitism—the American press barely covered Ambassador Earle's remarks—but the president did not speak out publicly on the issue at home. When Senator Millard Tydings of Maryland introduced a resolution communicating "to the government of the German Reich an unequivocal statement of the profound feelings of surprise and pain . . . upon learning of discriminations and oppression imposed by the Reich on its Jewish citizens," Secretary of State Hull used his influence with his old friends on the Foreign Relations Committee to make sure that the resolution never reached the Senate floor for a vote. Hull—and presumably Roosevelt—feared that the resolution not only represented a usurpation of executive power but risked comparison to America's treatment of black Americans.[9] Moreover, the president still held out hope that either Hitler would moderate his policies or his government would collapse.

The hope that Hitler might temper his militancy was reinforced in January 1934, when Germany and Poland announced a ten-year non-aggression pact. Weeks later, Anthony Eden, Britain's Lord Privy Seal, traveled to Berlin to meet with the German chancellor and came away impressed with the führer's sincerity in "wanting peace."[10]

It was, of course, wishful thinking. Hitler had only been chancellor for a year, but in that short time, as correspondent William Shirer would later write, had "overthrown the Weimar Republic, substituted his personal dictatorship for its democracy, destroyed all the political parties but his own, smashed the state governments and their parliaments and unified and defederalized the Reich, wiped out the labor unions, stamped out democratic associations of any kind, driven the Jews out of public and professional life, abolished freedom of speech and of the press, stifled the independence of the courts and 'coordinated' under Nazi rule the political, economic and social life of an ancient and cultivated people."[11] All of this had been previewed in Hitler's book *Mein Kampf,* as had his view that Germany's destiny included the unification of all German-speaking peoples in Europe and therefore expansion of its territory. Hitler continued consolidating power, and his professions of peaceful coexistence would soon enough be exposed as the gross deceptions that they were.

Missy LeHand pined for William Bullitt after his departure for Moscow. In the early months of 1934, she wrote to him frequently, once revealing her "love—much more of it than I like to confess." In one letter in January, she gushed, "You really are an angel and I miss you so much."[12] And then a few months later, after "five miserable days in bed," she confided, "I am sure that Moscow cannot be as lonely as Washington even though this place has lots of people I know."[13] Missy also described to the ambassador what was going on in Washington and, more importantly, passed on the gossip from inside the White House. For his part, Bullitt wrote to Missy regularly, but the new ambassador was also preoccupied with getting his embassy in Moscow up and running.

Bullitt filled out his staff by hiring Charles "Chip" Bohlen and Loy Henderson, both of whom had been colleagues of George Kennan's in Latvia, and like Kennan, spoke Russian. He also brought on Carmel

Offie as his private secretary. Offie did not speak Russian but was an enormously capable and intelligent Foreign Service officer; Kennan would later describe him as a "Renaissance man."[14] The ambassador hired a young navy officer, Roscoe Hillenkoetter, as his chief of security. More than a decade later, President Truman would appoint Hillenkoetter the first director of the Central Intelligence Agency. It was an extraordinary team of talented young Americans assembled to serve in Moscow in 1934. Years later, Kennan recalled that Bullitt infused the embassy with his "blitheness of spirit, this insistence that life could be at all times animated and interesting and moving ahead."

At first, Bullitt lived at the Hotel National near the Kremlin. After meeting with Stalin, he had been granted the opportunity for the United States to purchase the neoclassical mansion on No. 10 Spasopeskovskaya Square for the ambassador's residence. The domed house had a dark history: In 1913, Princess Lobanova-Rostovaya sold the house to the family of industrialist Nikolay Vtorov, who owned the largest textile-manufacturing firm in imperial Russia. One evening, after a violent argument, Vtorov was shot to death by his son in the ballroom of the house. Anne Bullitt, the ambassador's daughter, later described the house that was her home for three years as an example of "Russian Victorian pomposity, badly proportioned and cold, enormous with no room for anything. It was built around the central ballroom with a glass dome like the capitol, so I could crawl from my bedroom and lie on the floor upstairs and watch between the marble balustrade what was going on below."

The Vtorov House—it would later become known by the hybrid Russian-English name Spaso House—appealed to Bullitt because it had a large space for entertaining and an American-style heating system, installed by the Soviet government in 1928. George Kennan negotiated a three-year lease for the modest sum of $20,000. Bullitt did not ask for a longer lease, because he had plans to build a new, grand residence. He had in mind a version of Thomas Jefferson's Monticello, an incongruous vision given both the Great Depression in the United States and the famine in the Soviet Union. However, the Soviet government never granted the land for a new house, so Spaso House eventually became the ambassador's permanent residence.

Almost immediately, Bullitt impressed the Soviets with his lavish entertaining, inviting to Spaso House not only government officials but writers and artists as well. One evening, the Moscow ballet company gave a private performance at the embassy for Bullitt and his colleagues. Bohlen later recalled that for months after the performance, "there were usually two or three ballerinas running around the embassy." Bohlen's memory is likely accurate given that one of the ballerinas, who often stayed over in one of the guest bedrooms, was alleged to have had an affair with him and with Bullitt as well.[15] Although he omitted any salacious details, Bullitt titillated President Roosevelt with tales of entertaining the Communist elite. The president teased his ambassador in one letter, writing, "After this wild-eyed Congress goes home I will be able to pay more attention to dispatches and you might also write me the real low-down on what happens at your parties with the Russian foreign office at 3 a.m."[16]

After a few months in Moscow, however, Bullitt had soured on the Soviet regime and his post as ambassador. At Easter, he wrote President Roosevelt a long and personal letter, beginning with an admission that "Moscow has turned out to be just as disagreeable as I anticipated." In fact, Bullitt had arrived with very high hopes for the diplomatic relationship, but now complained about the inability of the Russians to negotiate anything in good faith. He noted, sardonically, "misunderstandings" about "extra interest on credits," and grumbled about the "property on which we expect to build our Embassy, the obtaining of paper roubles, the payment of consular fees in paper roubles, repairs to the Embassy residence, and apartments in the office building." He told the president that the next time he discussed the payment of debts and claims with Litvinov, the Soviet commissar for foreign affairs, he would give his Russian counterpart the impression that "if the Soviet Union does not wish to use the credits of the Import-Export the Japanese Government will be eager to use the facilities of the Bank to finance large purchases from certain American heavy industries." Bullitt knew that the Russians feared the growing military might of their East Asian neighbor more than almost anything.

Bullitt ended his letter to the president on a saccharine note, confessing, "[I] am a bit homesick."[17] He explained, "In many years I have not had the sensation that I had a home, but in this past year you and Mrs. Roosevelt and Miss LeHand have made me feel that I was a member of the family, and the thing I miss so much is the afternoons and evenings with you in the White House. I am much too fond of you all."[18]

9

JUST THINK WHAT THE CAREER BOYS WILL SAY!

Sunday, March 4, 1934, marked the first anniversary of Franklin Roosevelt's inauguration. While the president's remarkable first year in office was noted in the press, most of the newspapers in the United States splashed photographs of the notorious bank robber John Dillinger across their front pages. Dillinger had escaped from prison using a fake pistol carved out of wood.

Sitting at his desk in the large study of his residence in Berlin, Ambassador Dodd wrote in his diary a personal reflection on the historical significance of Roosevelt's presidency "at a moment when all social-economic relations of the so-called western world were undergoing drastic reform. It was a decisive moment . . . like the beginning of the American Revolution in 1774." Dodd praised the president as a champion of social and economic equality "in spite of the fact that his training at Groton and Harvard was faulty." Dodd feared that if "Roosevelt does not succeed, or if he should die before the greater part of his work is accepted, there will be a dictatorship, which would be ruinous to the United States."[1] When he wrote of American dictatorship, Dodd likely had in mind Senator Huey Long of Louisiana, the firebrand populist who, while a Democrat like Roosevelt, was increasingly outspoken in opposition to the president. A few months later, in June 1934, Long split with Roosevelt because he didn't believe the president was sufficiently committed to redistribution of the wealth in the United States.

Dodd was headed back to the United States for home leave later that month. He looked forward to seeing the president and discussing in person the challenges ahead. He especially wanted to share with the president his ideas about reforming the Department of State.

The next morning, March 5, Dodd was unexpectedly summoned to meet with German foreign minister Neurath. The first time he had met the foreign minister, Dodd was kept waiting for several minutes, but this time was shown into Neurath's office at the appointed time. The minister got right to the point. He had become aware of a planned mock trial of Chancellor Hitler scheduled to take place in New York's Madison Square Garden. Neurath expressed outrage that the United States government would allow the American Jewish Congress and the American Federation of Labor, sponsors of the event, to engage in the public vilification of an elected leader of a foreign, sovereign nation. He pressed Dodd to appeal to his superiors in Washington to cancel the event. Unknown to Dodd, Hans Luther, the German ambassador to the United States, had met with Secretary of State Cordell Hull that day and made a similar appeal. Hull expressed sympathy for the German position but explained to the German ambassador that it was the constitutional right of the organizers to proceed with their event and that the government was powerless to stop them.[2]

Two days later, over 20,000 people, under the protection of 320 police officers and 40 plainclothes detectives, packed into New York's Madison Square Garden to attend "The Case of Civilization Against Hitler."

The proceedings were called to order with the words "Hear ye, hear ye . . . All those who have business before this court of civilization, give your attention and ye shall be heard." Bainbridge Colby, President Wilson's last secretary of state, gave the opening remarks, followed by twenty prominent Americans who provided testimony about the atrocities being committed by the Hitler regime. Among those bearing witness were

New York mayor Fiorello La Guardia and Rabbi Stephen Wise, who had befriended Dodd on their transatlantic voyage. No one from the Department of State or the Roosevelt administration participated.

Meanwhile, in Berlin, Ambassador Dodd had been granted a second meeting with Chancellor Hitler. While he mostly listened to the führer during their first meeting, this time Dodd felt emboldened to raise specific issues. Once again, meeting in the führer's office, the ambassador complained that pamphlets had been circulating in the United States with an appeal to Germans in other countries to think of themselves always as Germans owing political allegiance to the fatherland. Hitler at first feigned surprise at Dodd's claims, dismissing them as nothing but Jewish propaganda.[3] This opened the door for Dodd to turn the conversation to Germany's treatment of Jews, and he told Hitler that his "current approach was doing great harm to the country's reputation in America." Hitler stared at him stone-faced, and then exploded. "Damn the Jews!" he shrieked. Dodd tried to calm the situation by calling Hitler's attention to incipient efforts to relocate Jews under international protection "without too much suffering."[4] Hitler was unmoved, insisting that such schemes were bound to fail.

Dodd then raised the issue of German rearmament. He explained that "public opinion in the United States" was "firmly convinced that the German people, if not their government, are militaristic, if not actually warlike" and that "most people of the United States have the feeling Germany is one day aiming to go to war." According to Dodd, Hitler responded sternly, declaring, "Germany wants peace and will do everything in her power to keep the peace; but Germany demands and will have equality of rights in the matter of armaments." Germany had been violating the Treaty of Versailles by rearming for many years; Hitler made it clear to Dodd that the Third Reich would continue its buildup of military forces.

That evening, Dodd noted in his diary "general impressions" of Hitler and other high-ranking Nazi officials. He labeled the führer "a strict imitator of Mussolini . . . romantic-minded and half-informed about great historical events and men in Germany." Dodd wrote, "In the back of [Hitler's] mind is the old German idea of dominating Europe through warfare."[5] Dodd characterized Joseph Goebbels, minister of propaganda, as "far cleverer than Hitler, much more belligerent." He described Hermann Goering, minister without portfolio, as representing "a more clearly aristocratic and Prussian Germanism."[6]

Dodd's initial optimism for what he might accomplish as ambassador had given way to gloom. He felt Hitler and his ministers were depraved and dangerous. Even more discouraging, he sensed he had little support from his colleagues in the U.S. State Department whom he considered for the most part to be passive, lazy, and entitled. Dodd believed only President Roosevelt grasped the gravity of the situation in Europe, but domestic issues burdened the president. Dodd doubted the president was engaged with foreign policy on a daily basis, accurately perceiving him to be preoccupied with the economic crisis. Dodd would have known, for instance, that on the same day the he had met with Neurath in Berlin, Roosevelt had addressed an overflowing crowd of three thousand in Constitution Hall in Washington, D.C., on the National Recovery Act, urging businesses to raise wages by 10 percent and cut hours by 10 percent so as to create jobs for another million Americans. But it wasn't just a matter of competing priorities. Though it was true that President Roosevelt did not fully share Dodd's urgency about Hitler, more significantly, he also believed that America should not interfere in the internal affairs of another nation.

Dodd left Germany on March 13, 1934, for the United States. While Dodd sailed across the ocean, the German Foreign Ministry scrambled to find a response to the "mock" trial, ultimately engaging in a kind of schizophrenic diplomacy. First, the German ambassador to the U.S. angrily complained to Secretary Hull about "insulting" language used to describe Germany's government during the trial. Then, the very next day, Neurath sent a cable to his consul general in New York and asked that it be delivered to Dodd upon his arrival. Dodd was asked to extend on behalf of the "Chancellor of the Reich" his congratulations to "President Roosevelt for his heroic efforts in the interests of the American people." The cable then declared, "The Chancellor is in accord with the president that the virtues of duty, readiness for sacrifice, and discipline should dominate the entire people. These moral demands which the President places before every individual citizen of the United States, are also the quintessence of the German state philosophy, which finds expression in the slogan 'The Public Weal transcends the Interests of the Individual.'"[7] The strategy was unsuccessful. If Hitler hoped to flatter Roosevelt, perhaps hoping to mitigate the negative publicity Germany had received following the mock trial, his awkward attempt to find common ground fell on deaf ears.

After arriving in New York on March 23, Ambassador Dodd released a press statement explaining that he had returned to the United States "on a short leave . . . in order to get some rest from the tense European atmosphere." Dodd then included a curious addendum: "Contrary to the predictions of many students of international problems, I feel fairly certain that we shall not have war in the near future."[8] There was, however, no doubt in Dodd's mind, as he had expressed more than once in his diary, that Hitler was preparing for war on the European continent; but Dodd made a distinction between the German people and the German government. He continued to believe that Germans were fundamentally a civilized people, and notwithstanding Hitler's irrational behavior and treacherous agenda, Dodd did not believe the people would engage once again in the folly of a continental war.

Dodd took the train from New York to Washington, D.C., and checked into the exclusive Cosmos Club on Lafayette Square. The following day he went to the State Department, where he huddled with Secretary Hull and Undersecretary Phillips, discussing how the president should respond to Hitler's letter. Phillips did not want the president too receptive or responsive to Hitler's flattery, writing in his diary, "We sought to sidestep the impression that the President was becoming a Fascist." Before a reply letter could be drafted for the president's signature, the German ambassador to the U.S. informed Hull that his government would not be able to make the approximately $50 million payment due under the debt agreement signed at the Paris Peace Conference in 1919.

Hull told the president that the German government "desired to find ways of arranging some adjustment which would have the effect of postponing payment and added that the entire debt would have to be readjusted."[9] While Hitler had lavished praise on the president in the cable sent through Dodd, the führer had no intention of honoring his nation's obligations to the United States.

On March 26, 1934, Dodd met with Roosevelt for lunch. They talked of Hitler's tightening grip on German political life and the overall deterioration in relations between the United States and Germany. Roosevelt seemed most concerned about the reaction to the mock trial that had taken place in New York a few weeks earlier. A similar trial was scheduled in Chicago in mid-April—when the president planned to be on vacation. Roosevelt worried that Americans were being further divided by the mock trials at a time when everyone needed to come together to overcome the nation's domestic problems. Recalling that Dodd had taught at the University of Chicago, the president asked his ambassador to do whatever he could do to "get the Chicago Jews to call off their mock trial."

Although there is no record of other issues Roosevelt and Dodd discussed that day, it's likely that the ambassador also raised the issue over which he obsessed—his contempt for what he viewed as the culture of snobbery and inefficiency in the Foreign Service. It is equally likely that the president, who from time to time flared up about the department's arrogance and ineffectiveness himself, could have raised the issue as well.

Only a few days earlier, Roosevelt made the one and only visit of his presidency to the Department of State. According to one of Roosevelt's earliest biographers, John Gunther, the president decided "in person to check up on reports that the building was so crowded with archives that nobody could get proper work done." As Gunther tells it, the president never contacted Hull or Phillips, but instead "wheeled himself over at five in the afternoon and made his way to the office he had used as Assistant Secretary of the Navy." Once there, according to Gunther:

He asked a young (and startled) aide to let him in, and then amiably demanded to know what the filing cabinets contained. Pointing to one of the cabinets, the President said, "Pull that one open." The aide hesitated and Roosevelt opened it himself. The drawer contained archives on China dating back many years; after perusing a sheaf of documents, the President observed they had no possible relevance and should be discarded. Later, Roosevelt cheerfully asked his staff, "Don't you think my popping over there served a very useful purpose? By nine o'clock tomorrow morning every man in Washington will think I may come rolling in at any moment."[10]

Another subject of conversation at the luncheon between Roosevelt and Dodd might have been George Messersmith, the consul general in Berlin. While Dodd had initially found Messersmith's honesty about the Nazis refreshing, he felt increasingly uneasy about his outspoken subordinate. Messersmith pushed Dodd to be more vocal and critical of Hitler, but the ambassador had resisted. Dodd wrote Undersecretary Phillips that Messersmith "has developed a sensitiveness, and perhaps even an ambition, which tend to make him restless and discontented."[11] The fussy ambassador also objected to Messersmith's lengthy cables back to Washington. He complained to Phillips that "Hitler could not have left his hat in a flying machine"[12] without Messersmith providing a tedious account of it. Finally, Dodd exhibited a streak of bigotry about Messersmith that he rarely revealed elsewhere in his public or private writings. In a letter to Secretary Hull, Dodd relayed that "German officials have said to one of the staff here: '[Messersmith] is also a Hebrew.'" Dodd declared, "I am no race antagonist, but we have a large number here and it affects the service and adds to my load."[13] Messersmith, in fact, was not Jewish, and Dodd, apparently, was not entirely the "liberal" that Roosevelt had hoped for.

Less than two weeks after the president's lunched with Dodd, President Roosevelt appointed George Messersmith as the new United States ambassador to Austria. According to Gunther, who interviewed the president in the Oval Office shortly after Messersmith's confirmation by the U.S. Senate, "Roosevelt was leaning back, relaxed, with the look of an officer who had just won a minor skirmish." Gunther, who lived in Vienna, told the president he both knew and admired Messersmith: "The president suddenly broke out into laughter, 'Ha, ha! That was a good joke on the State Department, wasn't it! Just think what the career boys will say! I put a lowly consul into a diplomatic post. Ha, ha, ha!'" However, by appointing Messersmith, a fervent anti-Nazi, to the country of Hitler's birthplace, the president was doing more than simply tweaking the striped-pants boys in the State Department; he was also sending a message of the seriousness with which he viewed the Nazi threat both in Austria and in Germany. Gunther was impressed with the apparent ease with which Roosevelt made such tactical decisions. After leaving the White House that day, Gunther recalled his first thought was, "Obviously that man has never had indigestion in his life."[14]

Around the same time as Messersmith's appointment, Roosevelt asked Harry Hopkins to make a trip abroad. The forty-three-year-old Hopkins had grown up in Sioux City, Iowa, moving to New York City after college where he became a social worker. In 1931, he was appointed by then governor Roosevelt to be his relief administrator. When Roosevelt became president, Hopkins presented a state-federal jobs plan to Secretary of Labor Frances Perkins, who in turn recommended it to the president. Although Hopkins had worked for Roosevelt in New York, the president didn't know him particularly well. However, after a meeting with Hopkins in the Oval Office, the president felt he had new insight into the man, considering Hopkins to be not only a capable administrator but a visionary as well. Roosevelt appointed him as director of the Federal Emergency Relief Administration. Hopkins immediately threw himself into the job, working eighteen-hour days. Within months, he established a program that created jobs for hundreds of thousands of out-of-work Americans. One colleague later described the chain-smoking Hopkins "looking as though he had spent the previous night sleeping in a hayloft. He would wear the same shirt three or four days at a time."[15] Although foreign policy was outside Hopkins's government bailiwick, being a favorite of Eleanor Roosevelt's and increasingly of the president himself, he was increasingly called on to offer his opinions on these issues as well.

It wasn't long before the president ordered Hopkins to "make a trip as soon as you can possibly get away and look over the housing and social insurance schemes in England, Germany, Austria and Italy." The president also asked Hopkins confidentially to meet with U.S. ambassadors in Europe and to evaluate America's Foreign Service personnel in the embassies. Hopkins spent the following month traveling from country to country and, upon his return, reportedly told Eleanor that in his view most American diplomats seemed to be living in a sort of elite bubble. He said that they gathered information from economic and social elites but had little idea of what was actually happening at street level in the countries to which they were posted. Even worse, they didn't seem to care. Their indifference extended to what was going on in the United States. According to Hopkins, very few members of the Foreign Service had any substantive knowledge of the New Deal or even bothered to ask him what was happening in America.[16]

Ambassador Dodd, for his part, was very much aware of the New Deal and the great inequality of wealth in the United States. For the remainder of his stay in Washington, Dodd worked in the State Department offices across from the White House, and took particular pleasure in attending a conference of personnel officers, where he railed against the excesses of the Foreign Service. As he recalled in his diary, "I then talked of American staff officials who shipped furniture enough for twenty-room houses at the cost of $3,000, with only two persons in the family." Dodd described one of his assistants in Berlin who had "a chauffeur, a porter, a butler, a valet, two cooks and two maids. All for two persons!" He suggested that the Department of State should only hire "ambassadors and assistants who knew the history and traditions of the countries to which they were sent, men who think of their own country's interest, not so much about a new suit of clothes each day or sitting up at gay but silly dinners every night until 1 o'clock." Dodd noticed that Sumner Welles, the very wealthy acting assistant secretary of Latin American affairs, "winced a little."[17]

Dodd wasn't the only ambassador critical of the Department of State. Breckinridge Long told the president that ambassadors didn't receive information in a timely way, and agreed with Dodd's consistent refrain that there were too many Foreign Service officers who frittered away their time. He also claimed that they were uninformed. After hearing the complaints, the president sent a memo to Secretary Hull: "I am still disturbed about the inadequacy of American news for our Embassies and Legations, especially in Europe. Every returning ambassador or Minister complains that they have insufficient means of knowing what is going on here." Hull's response was to suggest that the navy broadcast a daily digest of news over short wave radio to "receiving sets manned by navy personnel . . . in our missions in Berlin, Rome, Paris, and Geneva." When the president inquired about reducing the number of diplomats in U.S. embassies and consular offices, Secretary Hull wrote in a memo that he felt it would be unwise. Roosevelt acquiesced, but scribbled at the top of the memo, "A rule compelling everybody, in all Embassies and Legations, to work eight hours a day—five days a week—would create the kind of cyclone which would be heard round the world!"

Beyond complaining to Hull, Roosevelt did little to actually change the culture of the Department of State. Only weeks after his meeting with Dodd, the president nominated Sumner Welles to be U.S. ambassador to Cuba. Old school ties, money, and family connections still mattered to Roosevelt. Just as he valued family connections with Welles, Roosevelt enjoyed the back-and-forth repartee with the aristocratic William Bullitt and trusted the judgment of Undersecretary of State William Phillips—who, after all, had attended his prep school alma mater, Groton.

10

AMBASSADOR LONG WAS SWELL TO US

Because Ambassador Dodd was on leave in the United States, he missed the visit of young Joe Kennedy Jr. to Berlin in the spring of 1934. Eighteen-year-old Joe Jr. had already visited Italy, where, he reported to his father, "Ambassador Long was swell to us." Joe Jr. observed that Long didn't "seem like the ambassador type, at least not on the English lines, but seems more the 'regular guy' type. Had quite a long talk with him."[1]

Joe Jr. also met a German businessman in Pisa. While he didn't identify the gentleman, Joe Jr. informed his father that he "was quite a learned man, did a lot of business in the States, and was pretty well informed all around." Young Kennedy reported he was very much "impressed by the enthusiasm and confidence which this German businessman had in the policies of Hitler." Joe Jr. explained to his father that his acquaintance "agreed that it was regrettable that the Jews had to be driven out, but he said that the methods they employed in business were appalling."

On arriving in Munich, Kennedy remarked on "the quietness of the city. . . . The only signs of Nazi Germany were the brown shirts, who were very numerous, parading the streets. They have snappy brown open touring cars, and they get quite a kick out of driving through the streets

at a high speed. They are very nice and polite, however, at least to foreigners, and one sees no signs of brutality." The young globetrotter was
struck "by the number of people marching. They march to their celebrations, the children march to school. They seem to love it. The troops
seem to have a great spirit, and they sing songs as they march. Just to
watch them one feels he would like to join them, so it is not strange
that the small boy wants to be a soldier." Kennedy also observed the
outward similarities between German and Italian fascism: "In all parts of
the country, as in Italy, the children give you the Hitler salute as you pass,
thus showing the appeal even to children. No one is required to salute,
but nearly everyone does, and I'm sure if I was a German and valued my
health I would expound [sic] that slight effort which is required to raise
my arm. It is almost comical the number of times the two words 'Heil
Hitler' are used. . . . The Germans are not allowed to forget him for a
minute."[2]

Kennedy tried to explain to his father why the German experiment in
fascism was necessary and worthy of respect:

> In talking with the Germans, both inside and out, they wish to
> impress on you their feeling before the coming of Hitler. They
> had tried liberalism, and it had severely failed. They had no
> leader, and as time went on Germany was sinking lower and
> lower. The German people were scattered, despondent, and
> were divorced from hope. Hitler came in. He saw the need of a
> common enemy. Someone of whom to make the goat. Someone,
> by whose riddance the Germans would feel they had cast out
> the cause of their predicament. It was excellent psychology and
> it was too bad that it had to be done to the Jews. This dislike of
> the Jews, however was well founded. They were the heads of all
> big business, in law, etc. It is all to their credit for them to get
> so far, but their methods had been quite unscrupulous . . . As far
> as the brutality is concerned, it must have been necessary to use
> some, to secure the whole hearted support of people, which was
> necessary to put through this present program. I can see how a

great deal of brutality was on private lines, as those supporters of Hitler felt so strongly that they lost their heads over the non-supporters. It was a horrible thing, but in every revolution you have to expect some bloodshed.

Kennedy closed his long letter to his father with an expression of deep admiration for Hitler, whom he declared "is building a spirit in his men that could be envied in any country." Kennedy did not view Germans to be "thinking of war, but of Germany through Hitler." He gushed that the German people "know [Hitler] is doing his best for Germany, they have tremendous faith in him, and they will do whatever he wishes. The spirit could very quickly be turned into a war spirit, but Hitler has things well under control." Kennedy offered his father a final, bizarre, and chilling example of Hitler's leadership: "As you know he has passed the sterilization law which I think is a great thing. I don't know how the church feels about it, but it will do away with many of the disgusting specimens of men which inhabit the earth ... In all, I think it is a remarkable spirit which can do tremendous good or harm, whose fate rests with one man alone."[3]

Joseph Kennedy wrote back to his oldest son on May 4, 1934, expressing his delight "to see how much you got out of the trip through the Continent." He told Joe Jr., "I was very pleased and gratified at your observations of the German situation. I think they show a very keen sense of perception, and I think your conclusions are very sound." However, Kennedy cautioned that "it is still possible that Hitler went far beyond his necessary requirements in his attitude towards the Jews, the evidence which may very well be well covered up from the observer who goes in there at this time."[4]

Dodd had been back in Berlin a little more than a month when he described the atmosphere as "more tense than at any time since I have been in Germany."[5] On June 17, 1934, Vice Chancellor Franz von Papen, a loyal supporter of President Hindenburg, delivered an anti-Nazi speech to students at the University of Marburg. Papen, an aristocratic Catholic who served as chancellor prior to Hitler, hatched a plan with President Hindenburg to neutralize Hitler and the Nazis. Back in 1933, Papen stepped aside from the chancellorship, agreeing to become vice chancellor. Hindenburg replaced him with Hitler in the belief that it would be easier to control the Nazis if they were inside the government and not plotting from the outside to bring it down. However, Nazi storm troopers, under the direction of Ernst Röhm, continued to terrorize citizens throughout the country, especially Jews. It was clear that Hitler had no intention of working collaboratively with Hindenburg and Papen and, in fact, only sought greater power for himself. Papen decided to take his case to the German people.

Before hundreds of students at the University of Marburg, Papen denounced the Nazis for "the selfishness, the lack of principle, the insincerity, the unchivalrous behavior, [and] the arrogance which is on the increase under the guise of the German revolution."[6] As the students cheered their approval, Papen called on Germans "to join together in fraternal friendship and respect . . . to avoid disturbing the labors of serious men and to silence fanatics."[7]

When Hitler learned of Papen's address, he was apoplectic. He contacted Joseph Goebbels and ordered him to do everything possible to suppress reporting on the speech. Goebbels immediately threatened a number of the leading newspapers, ordering them to halt publishing or excerpting any part of the address. Upon learning of Goebbels's efforts to censor him, Papen confronted Hitler and threatened to resign his post as vice chancellor in protest. He also declared his intention to "advise Hindenburg of this immediately." Hitler knew Hindenburg was increasingly displeased with the Nazis and worried the vice chancellor might persuade the president to declare martial law and turn the government over to the military. Hitler needed to act quickly.[8]

The next day, Hitler flew to Nuremberg to visit Hindenburg at his country estate. The president confirmed to Hitler that he was "concerned about the rising tension" and reminded the chancellor that he had made a pact with the army to suppress the storm troopers and put an end to their "revolution." Hitler promised Hindenburg that he would take care of the situation. He immediately contacted Heinrich Himmler, head of the SS bodyguards, an elite branch of the storm troopers (SA), and ordered him to develop a plan of action. Himmler viewed it as an opportunity to eliminate his competitors within the Nazi Party. He convinced Hitler that the storm trooper chief of staff, Ernst Röhm, once a stalwart ally of Hitler, was a liability to the chancellor. Hitler demanded Himmler do something about Röhm.

Ambassador Long heard from his sources in the Italian government of the political turmoil enveloping Germany around the Papen speech. On Saturday, June 23, Long called Ambassador Dodd in Berlin "very anxious to know the state of things." Long was well meaning, but he approached the conversation as though he were engaging in idle chit-chat at a cocktail party at his mansion in Maryland. Dodd recorded in his diary that he "was surprised at [Long's] indiscretion . . . No wires in Europe, England excepted, are ever free of eavesdroppers when such talk is indulged in." Nevertheless, Dodd told Long, "all is quiet" in Berlin and there "is no disturbance in Germany that I know of as yet." Dodd considered Long's call to be reckless and was being circumspect in his conversation with his colleague from Rome, whom he didn't know.[9] In fact, Dodd had expressed a number of times in his diary that he feared Hitler was a madman. He would soon bear witness to Hitler's next step in his murderous grab for power.

11

DOWNHEARTED ABOUT EUROPE

On Sunday, July 1, 1934, *The New York Times* front page included a story about the infamous bank robber John Dillinger, who had been wounded in a bank robbery in South Bend, Indiana, that netted $28,000, and another article about the wedding of the extremely wealthy John Jacob Astor, who married the very rich Ellen French, a Vanderbilt relation. And then there was a story about political disruption and violence in Germany: HITLER CRUSHES REVOLT BY NAZI RADICALS; ... LOYAL FORCES HOLD BERLIN IN AN IRON GRIP.[1] The episode would later be known as the "Night of the Long Knives."

As *The Times* recounted, at 2:00 a.m. the previous day, Adolf Hitler had flown from Berlin to Munich with members of his elite SS armed force to put down an "alleged rebellion" by Chief Ernst Röhm, with whom he had cofounded the paramilitary storm troopers. The storm troopers had played an important role in Hitler's rise to power, but after Himmler's warning about Röhm, the paranoid chancellor worried that his onetime collaborator was preparing to turn against him.

Hitler and a coterie of his elite troops sped from the Munich airport to the SA barracks just outside the city. Rohm and his men were sleeping when Hitler's troops arrived and dragged the SA lieutenants out of their cots, shooting many of them on the spot.

Röhm was seized, thrown into prison, and shot, reportedly after having been given a gun so that he might take his own life. His death was ruled a suicide, but he was executed by Hitler's henchmen. While Röhm had made it clear that he hoped to become the head of the German army, there was never evidence that he had plotted against the chancellor. Hitler reportedly justified the purge because Röhm had failed to deliver "blind obedience and unquestioning discipline."

Back in Berlin, Hitler's allies Goering and Himmler rounded up 150 SA leaders and, according to reporting by William Shirer, stood them "against a wall at the Cadet School at Lichterfelde and shot them by firing squads." Although it was never firmly established how many men Hitler's troops killed that day, it was estimated to be in the hundreds. Many more were arrested and thrown into prisons. His targets were not just the storm troopers under Röhm's command. Hitler also used the occasion to silence dozens of real and perceived political enemies.[2]

Notwithstanding the outrage from around the world that greeted Hitler's savagery, President Hindenburg congratulated the chancellor for his "determined action and gallant personal intervention." The aged hero of World War I, who would die only weeks later, concluded, "You have saved the German nation from serious danger."[3]

Twelve days after the purge, Hitler addressed the German people in a speech to the Reichstag and, not surprisingly, made no apologies for the brutal crackdown. "Only a ferocious and bloody repression could nip the revolt in the bud," Hitler screamed, and then, raising his fist, continued, "If someone asks me why we did not use the regular courts, I would reply: At the moment I was responsible for the German nation; consequently it was *I alone* during those twenty-four hours who was the Supreme Court of Justice for the German people."[4]

Dodd sent a cable to Secretary Hull the day after the speech, saying, "Nothing more repulsive than to watch the country of Goethe and Beethoven revert to the barbarism of Stuart England and Bourbon France." Dodd's outrage had little impact. President Roosevelt, cruising in the Pacific aboard the SS *Houston* on his way to Hawaii, refrained from comment and left the matter to the Department of State. Secretary Hull apparently felt this was an internal German matter and continued to view repayment of debt as the overriding American priority. Neither the United States nor any other country recalled its ambassador as a sign of protest or took any other meaningful step to express their outrage.[5]

Ambassador Dodd was horrified by Hitler's cold-blooded murders and disgusted by reports that Röhm allegedly killed himself. Dozens of Germans, some of whom Dodd had known and had been guests at the U.S. ambassador's residence, had simply disappeared. While Dodd had previously referred to Hitler in private as insane, the führer's actions on the night of June 30, 1934, went beyond his comprehension and signaled a watershed moment. He felt as though he were trapped in a nightmare populated by bloodthirsty megalomaniacs, and making matters worse, his own government seemingly lacked the capacity to understand the implications of what was happening. He considered resigning, but convinced himself that he had been sent to Germany "to work for peace and better relations." He would not abandon his post, deciding instead that as long as he was ambassador, he would live his remaining days in Berlin according to his own moral code. As long as Hitler, Goering, and Goebbels were in control of the government, Dodd vowed in his diary to henceforth refuse hosting any of the German leadership at the residence. He also declared that he would "never again attend an address of the Chancellor or seek an interview . . . except upon official grounds."[6]

It was an odd and not entirely logical compromise that Dodd made with himself; from the beginning, he had disdained attending the kind of social functions that most other ambassadors participated in to gain greater access to the country's leadership. Dodd was never an extrovert— someone who put his guests at ease and enjoyed small talk. He wanted to be an ambassador who made an impact—the liberal model that Roosevelt had described—but he really didn't know how to do it. Of course, even if he had mastered the art of diplomacy, he undoubtedly would have had little chance to influence the horror that Hitler had planned for Germany and the Continent. Ambassador Dodd was a serious man,

a man of rectitude. He understood in July 1934 that Western civilization might be on the edge of madness, but no one was listening to his
warnings.

"I am back again after a perfectly heavenly cruise . . . It was too lovely."[7]
President Roosevelt wrote his ambassador in Moscow, William Bullitt,
in early August 1934 after returning to Washington, D.C., from sailing
around the Hawaiian Islands. However, Roosevelt's breezy note to Bullitt
belied his growing concern about recent events in Europe.

President Roosevelt had been cruising in the Pacific in late July when
he received word that a group of Austrian storm troopers, dressed in
Austrian army uniforms, had broken into the Federal Chancellery in
Vienna and murdered Austria's dictator, Engelbert Dollfuss. A fervent
nationalist, Dollfuss was friendly with Mussolini, but rejected Hitler and
his vision for unification of German-speaking peoples in Europe. For
months, Austrian Nazis, with covert support from Germany, had been
using terror tactics to bring down the Dollfuss fascist government. His
assassination on July 25, 1934, marked the first step toward the reunifi-
cation of Austria and Germany, fulfilling the vision that Hitler had laid
out in his blueprint for Germany's future, written nearly a decade earlier
in *Mein Kampf*.

On August 1, as President Roosevelt continued his vacation, German
president Hindenburg died at the age of eighty-six. Three hours after
Hindenburg's death was confirmed, Hitler announced the offices of the
chancellor and the president had been combined, and that he had assumed
the additional title of commander in chief of the armed forces. From that
point on, all members of the military took a different oath of loyalty—not
to the fatherland but to the führer.[9]

In the wake of Hitler's consolidation of power, Ambassador Dodd
wrote President Roosevelt a deeply pessimistic letter. Dodd recalled that
eight months earlier, Hitler promised him that Germany would not rearm militarily, but that now "more men are trained, uniformed and armed
than in 1914, at least a million and a half . . . So, it seems to me that war
and not peace is the objective, and the Hitler enthusiasts think they can

beat Italy and France in a month." Dodd also recalled that after his complaining to Hitler about the government's treatment of Jews, the führer had "issued an order that no man must be arrested and held in restraint more than 23 hours without a warrant." Dodd's letter claimed the order had apparently been a sham from the start; Hitler's ministers, men such as Goebbels who called Jews "the syphilis of European peoples," never enforced it. Dodd closed his letter to the president on a final dispirited note: "It all looks bad . . . Perhaps you can see a way out."[10] He was referring to the deteriorating situation in Germany, but at this point, his plea to Roosevelt might just as well have been for himself.

The president wrote back to Dodd an equally somber personal letter. He thanked Dodd for his candor "even though your situation cannot exactly be called a rosy one." Roosevelt told the ambassador his assessment of Germany's political and military situation "confirms my fear that the drift in Germany, and perhaps in other countries in Europe is definitely downward and that something must break within the next six months or a year." The president admitted that he, too, was "downhearted about Europe." He said he "looked for any ray of hope or opening to lend a helping hand." But, he confessed, "there is nothing in sight at present."[11] It was clear that President Roosevelt wanted to help Europe's democracies, but did not believe that the United States was in a position to do anything actively to stop Hitler's brutality. The United States was still in the midst of a serious economic depression, and the president had no intention of involving the United States in the affairs of Europe. Moreover, Roosevelt knew that isolationists largely controlled the United States Congress, and that the American people favored isolationism as well. He would need to go slowly, biding his time while he watched the gathering storm.

12

WHAT A MESS IT ALL IS!

Ambassador Dodd returned again to the United States for home leave on December 23, 1934. A week later, he joined President Roosevelt for lunch at the White House in his second-floor study. Although the president enjoyed none of the good-natured banter with Dodd that he had with Bullitt and Long, they talked for over an hour about the deteriorating conditions in Europe, including "German militancy, Italian aggressiveness and British fear of another depression." Dodd recommended the United States join the League of Nations to force "Germany and Italy into co-operation with England and France for peace and reduction of armaments."[1] It was a totally unrealistic proposal, revealing Dodd's lack of knowledge about politics and how Congress worked. The president politely told his ambassador that he was "skeptical of public opinion."[2]

The president explained that a joint resolution to join the league could not gain enough votes in Congress. Roosevelt, however, reassured the ambassador that he had asked the Senate to approve United States membership on the World Court, an arm of the league dedicated to solving international disputes. The United States had played an important role in establishing the court in the aftermath of World

War I. More than fifty other countries were members, but Congress had never ratified American participation. In Roosevelt's view, participation in the court seemed like a practical way to exercise some influence in Europe and elsewhere while avoiding the sticky controversy over sovereignty issues that had prevented American participation in the League of Nations.

President Roosevelt's domestic legislation had been strongly supported by the overwhelmingly Democratic Congress during 1934. Since he had an equally bold agenda for 1935, a number of his political advisers cautioned him against any attempt to involve the United States in an international tribunal. The country was still reeling from the economic crisis. Some blamed outsiders for having contributed to America's problems, while others simply felt the United States had no business involving itself in the problems of other nations until it sorted out its own affairs.

However, President Roosevelt increasingly had one eye on international events and worried that America's emergence from nearly a decade of economic woes could be jeopardized by global instability. In his January 4, 1935, State of the Union address, the president declared, "The maintenance of international peace is a matter in which we are deeply and unselfishly concerned." At this juncture, Roosevelt was not interested in restoring America's military might to ensure peace—it had significantly atrophied in the aftermath of World War I—rather he wanted the United States to serve as a symbol for the international rule of law in order to prevent wars from starting in the first place. On January 16, he sent his proposal to Capitol Hill for the United States to become a member of the World Court.

There was immediate and vociferous opposition to the proposal. Radio evangelist Father Charles Coughlin whipped up the estimated thirty million listeners to his weekly broadcasts, warning them hyperbolically that joining the court would "destroy our way of life." Conservative publisher William Randolph Hearst, who had supported Roosevelt in 1932, felt he had been betrayed. In Hearst's view, the World Court was a back door into the League of Nations, meaning that the president, just like his cousin Theodore Roosevelt, was an internationalist willing to cede the sovereignty of the United States to other nations. Hearst's newspapers denounced the measure and pressured wavering senators. The Senate, where Roosevelt had enjoyed near-unanimous support for his domestic legislation, suddenly became a fraught political battleground. Offices were flooded with telegrams opposing U.S. membership, and senators lined up on the Senate floor to voice their opposition to the measure. Roosevelt needed two-thirds of the Senate to approve the proposal. In the end, it received only fifty-two votes.

The day after the Senate defeated his proposal, Roosevelt wrote to Senator Joseph T. Robinson, a Democrat and the Senate majority leader, and thanked him for "the splendid fight you have made." The president was not used to losing; in his letter, he derided "the thirty-six senators who placed themselves on the record against the principle of a world court." Roosevelt wrote that he was "inclined to think that if they ever get to Heaven they will be doing a great deal of apologizing for a very long time—that is if God is against war—and I think He is."[3] Roosevelt, however, refused to engage in any public recriminations against those senators who had voted against the resolution. Some of them had supported his domestic agenda. He knew he would need their votes again for future New Deal measures.

The president and Ambassador Dodd lunched again in the White House on February 6, little more than a month after their last meeting. After spending time on his farm in Virginia, Dodd felt somewhat rejuvenated, but was disheartened by the Senate's defeat of the World Court proposal. He considered resigning in protest. As he noted in his diary, "It would create a sensation, but it would give me the chance to say to the country how foolish it seemed to me for our people to denounce minority dictatorships in Europe and then allow a minority of men, largely under Hearst and Coughlin influence, to rule the U.S. in such an important matter."[4] He expected to find the president equally deflated by the defeat.

Dodd was surprised to discover that Roosevelt was "far more cheerful and optimistic" than he had expected. Roosevelt was in a mood to talk about politics, specifically his reelection. The president conjectured that in 1936, Huey Long of Louisiana would be "a candidate to the Hitler type" and would "have a hundred votes in the Democratic convention and will set up an independent run with Southern and midwestern progressives." Long, a colorful personality and fiery orator, had stepped up his populist attacks on the president, accusing him of being secretly in the pocket of big business. Now, sitting across the desk from his ambassador, Roosevelt smiled and sketched out for Dodd how "by 1940 . . . Long thinks he [will] be made a dictator."[5] It was vintage Roosevelt. He didn't dwell on the past and looked forward to the next political battle.

Dodd then criticized William Randolph Hearst for the role he played in defeating the court proposal, alleging that the newspaper publisher was "close to Nazi Germany" and had provided "help [to] the Italian dictatorship." He and Roosevelt also commiserated about the "waste of American diplomats." According to Dodd, the president complained, "Since Theodore Roosevelt's time, rich men have injured the service by enormous personal expenditures."[6] Of course, Roosevelt had appointed numerous "rich men" as ambassadors, but he wanted Dodd to know that he was sympathetic to his viewpoint.

After an absence of over two months, Dodd returned to Germany on February 23, 1935. Although he retained the title of ambassador, he was essentially persona non grata with the Hitler government. And he had no intention of doing anything to ingratiate himself with what he viewed as Hitler's loathsome entourage. In his diary he declared, "Never . . . has a great people been guided by a less sensible group. Hitler knows nothing of history, Goering is even less informed, Goebbels is utterly incompetent except in his German propaganda."[7] Most distressing to Dodd, many of the Germans he had befriended during his first year at post had been killed, incarcerated, or fled the country. He sourly scribbled in his diary, "I am not happy." The ambassador felt impotent in his job and resigned to "the delicate work of watching and carefully doing nothing."[8]

Like Dodd, Breckinridge Long had returned from a vacation in the United States, but unlike his sullen counterpart in Berlin, Long continued to be on good terms with the Italian government and was negotiating a reduction of trade barriers on olive oil and cheese in exchange for a commitment to buy more American cotton. In a letter to the president, Long relayed Mussolini's "interest" in the trade arrangement and included a brief update "on the question of European politics." Long cited Mussolini's "definite and ineradicable impression" that there would be "war with Germany within a comparatively short time." According to Long, Mussolini felt that peace would hold for another year or so because "of the agreement between France and Italy" and because "Germany was not quite ready" but Il Duce was "very, very doubtful about the future." Sounding a dramatic note, Long made a definitive prediction about the possibility of war: "The prospect is not good. It must come. We have known it must come. It is only that the day is actually approaching. We must be realists." And while Long was easily taken in by Mussolini's bravado and charm, he ended his letter to the president with a prescient warning and a sound recommendation: "You might consider giving instructions to somebody that a good equipment for your diplomatic and consular offices in Europe would be gas masks, because when it comes it will come over night and come from the air."[9]

In late February 1935, Long reiterated his prediction "that Europe will be at war within two years." He wrote the president, "Italy is preparing what she thinks is a certain eventuality. While no responsible statesman in Europe will admit it, I am just as certain of it as I am sitting in this chair."[10] Long's view was shared by a number of his colleagues. Ambassador Messersmith in Austria seconded Long's warning and declared that the Nazis could not be trusted and that Hitler's aim was "unlimited territorial expansion."[11] Ambassador Bingham in England told Roosevelt he believed war was inevitable due to Nazi expansionism and worried that it would be extremely difficult for the United States to keep itself out of a major European war.[12] In the Soviet Union, Ambassador Bullitt was also fatalistic: "No one in Europe is any longer thinking of peace but everyone is thinking furiously about obtaining as many allies as possible for the next war."[13]

Hearing from his ambassadors, President Roosevelt was growing increasingly concerned about the prospect of war in Europe and what, if anything, America should do about it. Ambassador Dodd appeared to want Roosevelt to take unspecified action, but he understood that he was in the minority. He brooded in a letter to the president, "If Woodrow Wilson's bones do not turn in the Cathedral grave, then bones never turn in graves. Possibly you can do something, but from reports of Congressional attitudes, I have grave doubts. So many men . . . think absolute isolation a coming paradise."[14] Ambassador Bullitt had a very different view of the United States role: "As each day passes I become more convinced that our only sane policy is to stay just as far as possible outside of the mess."

Of all the U.S. ambassadors in Europe, Breckinridge Long provided the most trenchant analysis to the president: "Germany is not going to change her characteristics or her nature . . . The German infusion is of blood and race. It runs all through Poland, Czechoslovakia, Hungary, Jugoslavia, and Austria." Long recommended that America stay on the sidelines while the Europeans fought each other. Long's assessment of Germany might have been accurate, but his conclusions were not only illogical but deeply callous; he essentially advised the president to accept a Europe ruled by Hitler. As he put it in his letter to the president, "War is the only cure for the malady with which Europe is afflicted . . . There are only two governments in Europe capable of being a real victor. One is Germany, and the other is Russia . . . I shudder to think of a Russian domination of Europe. While a German domination would be hard and cruel—at least in the beginning—it would be an intensification of a culture which is more akin to ours than would be that of Russia."[15] Long's view of a "culture more akin to ours" was not just based on an abhorrence of Communism. As became evident later, it was also rooted in bigotry and anti-Semitism.

President Roosevelt summed up his quandary in a letter to Ambassador Bullitt, "What a mess it all is!"[16]

13

WITHOUT DOUBT THE MOST
HAIR-TRIGGER TIMES

As part of Europe's mad scramble to carve up the African continent in the 1890s, Italy had unsuccessfully attempted to conquer and colonize Ethiopia. Italy's humiliation from its failure simmered for nearly forty years, until December 5, 1934, when a border incident between Ethiopian and Italian Somaliland soldiers reignited tensions between the two countries. Mussolini decided that the border incident gave him the cover needed to again attempt subjugation of Ethiopia. Indeed, Il Duce's reasons for coveting this impoverished country with few significant natural resources were never entirely clear beyond the symbolic restoration of the Italian empire and an appeal to Italian nationalistic and imperialistic sentiment. To lay the groundwork for an invasion, on January 7, 1935, Mussolini and French foreign minister Pierre Laval signed an agreement in Rome essentially giving Italy carte blanche to pursue its goals in the Horn of Africa. In his confidential personal letters to the president, Ambassador Long surmised that France had likely agreed to support Italy's Africa policy for fear of losing Mussolini's aid in checking Hitler.

In a letter dated February 8, 1935, Long described the shifting alliances in Europe, acknowledging that he was not sure why Mussolini was advancing the Italian campaign against the small, impoverished North African country. He wrote, "I don't know what [Mussolini] is thinking of in spending so much money . . . and preparing to engage in warfare there, unless he thinks it would be good training for his men." The ambassador went on to note that the Italians and the French had formed their alliance—the Mussolini-Laval Accord—because, as he put it, they feared Hitler "emboldened now to pursue his pan-Germanic ideas into fields of former German territories and Austria." On that issue, Long was exactly right. Mussolini had strong ties to the Austrian government and wanted to deter Hitler from annexing Austria while his army prepared to deploy to the Horn of Africa. An alliance with the French, who also were worried about Germany's expansionist goals, provided both countries with a potential deterrent.

Long was less sure where the British stood concerning Ethiopia, but noted that "the growth of air forces in Europe has brought England to the realization that the Channel no longer separates her from the Continent . . . on that basis England seems to be now expected to participate on the side of Italy and France and against a possible aggressive move on the part of Germany."[1]

On February 21, 1935, Long sent the president yet another lengthy and substantive letter, his third in as many weeks. He explained that he wrote so frequently because he was "in such close contact with the rumors of war and with the actual preparations to engage in war." Long began his letter bluntly: "There is no doubt in my mind that Europe is headed straight for war." Long told Roosevelt that he hoped "with every fervent wish that we can stay out of the devastating show and fulfill our real destiny as trustee for the future of the civilization which we have in America and with which we can subsequently revive the world."

President Roosevelt thanked Long for his "extraordinarily interesting" correspondence, even though "pessimistic in tone."[2] Still smarting from his defeat in Congress over the World Court, the president added, "We, too, are going through a bad case of Huey Long and Father Coughlin influenza—the whole country aching in every bone. It is an internal disease, not external as it seems to be in Europe." Roosevelt concluded his short letter by noting, "These are without doubt the most hair-trigger times the world has gone through in your lifetime or mine."[3] It was only the beginning.

Over the next few months, a number of events left President Roosevelt feeling "much discouraged." Disarmament talks in Geneva broke down when the British refused to agree to international inspections. This gave cover to Hitler, who announced on March 9, 1935, that Germany would establish an air force. One week later, the führer proclaimed a law mandating universal military service to create a peacetime army of twelve corps and thirty-six divisions—approximately one million men. There was little anyone could do to stop him. Germany was rebuilding its armed forces in flagrant contravention of its commitment to the League of Nations. The league registered strong opposition to Hitler's announcements, but its only follow-on action was to appoint a committee to make recommendations on preventing further militarization of the Continent.[4]

Recognizing that the Treaty of Versailles was no longer relevant, Britain, France, and Italy decided to take matters into their own hands. They sent diplomats to a conference in Stresa, Italy, in April 1935 to discuss "a complete blockade of Germany." While the representatives of the three nations at Stresa condemned Hitler's actions, they failed to agree on concrete proposals to stop Germany from militarizing. Instead, each country found it in its self-interest to use vague, noncommittal language in the conference's final declaration to resist further efforts by Germany to circumvent the League of Nations. President Roosevelt wrote Ambassador Dodd, "We are naturally much concerned here over the results at Stresa . . . I feel very helpless to render any particular service to immediate or permanent peace at this time."[5]

Yet another important shift in the politics of Europe occurred on June 18, 1935, when Britain and Germany entered into a naval agreement, which allowed for equivalency in the building and deployment of warships. The two governments presented the accord as a sign of improved relations. In private, the Germans hoped the agreement represented a first step toward an alliance with Britain against France and the Soviet Union, while the British viewed it as an initial step toward limiting German expansionism. However, as Ambassador Bingham explained in a letter to President Roosevelt, the agreement was controversial—even in Britain. Bingham wrote, "The clause permitting Germany to build up 100% of British submarine strength whenever Germany thought it desirable to do so, has been severely criticized by many influential people here." One of those influential people, Winston Churchill, a former First Lord of the Admiralty, called it "the acme of gullibility." In his letter, Bingham also accurately described the reaction in the rest of Europe: "In addition, the method pursued, apart from the agreement itself, has undoubtedly aroused bitter resentment in France, and I think in Italy as well . . . they were not informed of an actual agreement until it was an accomplished fact."[6]

Writing from Berlin, Ambassador Dodd told President Roosevelt that the naval agreement had been "unexpected" and "unprecedented." He maintained that it marked "the first time in modern history that England has sided with a threatening imperialist power." Dodd attributed England's decision "to the hope that she can moderate Hitler's conduct . . . the English people are more pacifist than ever before."[7] Only months earlier, the Oxford Union, the debating society of England's premier university, had considered the motion: "This house will under no circumstances fight for its king and country." The motion was approved by a nearly two-to-one margin, an indication that Britain's younger generation, painfully aware of the still-recent loss of life in World War I, were steadfast in opposing future wars.[8]

Roosevelt was not entirely sure he could trust the British, and the naval agreement did not reassure him. In responding to Ambassador Bingham, he commented on his experience in dealing with the United Kingdom, "Many years ago I came to the reluctant conclusion that it is a mistake to make advances to the British Government; practical results can be accomplished when they make the advances themselves. They are a funny people and, though always polite, can be counted on when things are going well with them to show a national selfishness towards other nations which makes mutual helpfulness very difficult to accomplish. Their average conception of mutuality differs from mine."[9]

The president expressed his fear that "the British have . . . let themselves in for real resentment on the continent, and for much trouble to themselves in the days to come." At this point, while Roosevelt was still assessing the British intentions, he was now convinced that Germany bent towards war. He maintained that the agreement was irreparably flawed. Noting that "Germany began to violate her . . . obligations from two or three years ago," he then asked rhetorically, "What is to prevent Germany from violating this new agreement and calmly announcing the violation after she had doubled her new allowance of submarines, cruisers, etc., etc.?"[10]

During the spring and summer of 1935, amid a swirl of rumors about war and the rising tensions in nearly every country in Europe, American diplomats continued to attend lavish social events and to host parties of their own. Socializing was part of an ambassador's job, but it was also likely their attempt to maintain some sense of normalcy during decidedly abnormal times.

In Germany, William Dodd, the perennially dour ambassador, gave a party for his daughter, Martha, attended by "twenty young people . . . some were interesting persons," among them, Prince Louis Ferdinand, the grandson of the exiled kaiser.[11] A few weeks later, Martha hosted her own party, a gathering at the embassy to welcome Thomas Wolfe, the author of the bestselling novel, *Look Homeward, Angel,* who had recently arrived in Berlin. Wolfe was greatly honored by the occasion and instantly smitten with Martha. The two would later have a brief, torrid affair.[12] Wolfe also admired the ambassador, whom he described in a letter to his literary agent, Maxwell Perkins, as having instilled in him "a renewed pride and faith in America."[13]

In Britain, Ambassador Bingham represented the United States during a month of celebrations for King George V's silver jubilee. There were parties all over London and, indeed in every town and hamlet in

Britain. Bingham also attended Queen Charlotte's Ball, where select American debutantes were presented to society along with British socialites from the high echelons of English society.

Perhaps the most original—and outlandish—party was hosted by Ambassador Bullitt in Moscow to celebrate the coming of spring. Bullitt, who had attended more than a few hedonistic parties in Paris during the 1920s, instructed his aides to design a party "that would compete with anything Moscow had yet experienced, before or after the Revolution." The ambassador and his team worked with Alexander Tairov, an acclaimed theater director, to transform the embassy into an ethereal dreamscape. They imported hundreds of white tulips from Finland, placed birch trees in giant urns around the ballroom, hung huge fishing nets soaked in gold dust on the marble walls, and released hundreds of chirping zebra finches that flew around the inside of the dome in the ballroom. They also used light projectors to illuminate images of stars and a bright moon on the ceiling and of flowers on the walls. In the dining room of the embassy, they created a "collective farm," complete with pens holding goats, sheep, roosters, and even bear cubs. At midnight, nearly five hundred guests, many arriving in costume, were greeted by Ambassador Bullitt and his fellow diplomats, who were decked out in white tie and tailcoats.

Bullitt reported on the success of his flamboyant production to President Roosevelt, "It was an astonishingly successful party, thoroughly dignified yet gay. Everyone happy and no one drunk. In fact, . . . it was the best party in Moscow since the revolution."[14] The president would have appreciated Bullitt's sense of fun; the year before, on his fifty-second birthday, his close friends and political advisers organized a toga party at the White House. Roosevelt mocked his critics, who increasingly compared him to a dictator, by dressing as Caesar.

14

IF MEN WERE CHRISTIAN, THERE WOULD BE NO WAR

On May 12, 1935, one of Europe's most esteemed, albeit author-itarian, statesmen, Poland's Józef Piłsudski, died from stomach cancer at the age of sixty-seven. Piłsudski, a hero of World War I, had served as Poland's chief of state after the war and then as Po-land's minister of military affairs, which made him the de facto leader of the Polish government. A significant force in European politics, he tried to navigate an independent course for his country. Piłsudski sought support for Poland in alliances with Western powers, including France and the United Kingdom. However, the French and British signing of the Locarno treaties (post–World War I agreements establishing Euro-pean borders) frustrated Piłsudski, who viewed them as appeasement. Without the possibility of strong alliances with Britain and France, it was even more critical to ensure sound relations with Poland's power-ful neighbors, the Soviet Union and Germany. In 1932, Poland signed the Soviet-Polish Nonaggression Pact, and in 1934, the German-Polish Nonaggression Pact. Notwithstanding his diplomatic efforts, Piłsudski recognized the still-precarious position of Poland: "Having these pacts," he wrote, "we are straddling two stools. This cannot last long. We have to know from which stool we will tumble first, and when that will be."[1]

There would be two funeral services for Piłsudski in two different countries, attended by two American ambassadors: Dodd and Bullitt. Their descriptions of the memorials and how they conveyed them to President Roosevelt revealed a great deal about them as well as the challenges confronting Europe.

The year before Piłsudski's death, Hitler sent Goering to Poland to sound out the Polish leader about a possible alliance against the Soviet Union. Piłsudski had rejected the idea, but Hitler continued to hope for an eventual pact with Poland against Russia. To honor the memory of Piłsudski, Hitler ordered a memorial service at St. Hedwig's Cathedral in Berlin. As soldiers with raised swords stood in front of the Catholic cathedral, a symbolic coffin with a Polish flag and eagle was carried into the nave and placed before the altar. Seated to the right of the coffin was Hitler. Neurath, Goebbels, and generals of the Reichswehr were seated behind him in the first row, with Dodd seated a few rows behind them. This was the only time that the führer attended a holy mass as leader of the Third Reich and one of the last times he was seen in a church.

At 11:00 a.m., the papal nuncio, the pope's permanent representative in Germany, wearing a long red robe that extended twelve feet and trailed by twelve priests, walked slowly up the center aisle of St. Hedwig's. The nuncio took his seat on a gilded throne to the right of the great altar where candles were burning. The elaborate mass, over an hour in length, was performed in Latin.

Dodd wrote down his impressions of the funeral in his diary. He was deeply cynical of the entire event, commenting that "no one understood" Latin, and acknowledging that he "did not know much about Pilsudski, except that he was a dictator who put people to death when they opposed him." Dodd doubted there was "one follower of Jesus in the whole congregation" and wondered how Germans would "honor Hitler, a professed Catholic, if he should die. . . . He has murdered or caused to be murdered hundreds of innocent people." Dodd left the service a little after noon, "relieved to be free from so much hypocrisy."[2] That evening, the ambassador recorded in his diary that he felt "compelled out of honesty to cease attending church services, save on official occasions," because "if men were Christian there would be no war, also none of the terrible exploitations which our business men have applied to our people."[3] As a historian, it was an odd comment for Dodd, who would have been familiar with Europe's long and bloody history of religious wars.

As Hitler was paying homage to Piłsudski in Berlin, leaders and dignitaries from all over Europe attended the Polish leader's funeral at the St. John's Archcathedral in Warsaw. President Roosevelt had designated Ambassador Bullitt as his special representative to attend the service. Bullitt subsequently wrote a long letter to the president, beginning with a detailed description of Reichsmarschall Hermann Goering, who had been sent by Hitler to represent the German government:

> Goering swept into Warsaw cathedral late as if he were a German tenor playing Siegfried. He has the usual German tenor proportions. He is at least a yard across the bottom as the crow flies! In an attempt to get his shoulders out as far as his hips he wears two inches of padding extending each one. It is useless. The shoulders just won't go that far. He is nearly a yard from rear to umbilicus, and as he is not even as tall as I am and encases himself in a glove-tight uniform, the effect is novel. He must carry with him a personal beauty attendant, as his fingers are almost as thick as they are short, carry long-pointed, carefully enameled nails and his pink complexion shows every sign of daily attention. His eyes pop wildly as if they were either suffering from a glandular derangement or still taking cocaine. His lips are as thin as those of an infant. When he was 250 pounds lighter he must have been a blond beauty of the most unpleasant sort. He really is the most appalling representative of a nation I have ever laid eyes on.[4]

Bullitt then provided Roosevelt with his views on the impact of Piłsudski's death on the future of European politics: "I am more convinced than ever that there is no secret agreement between Poland and Germany. The Polish army is definitely anti-German . . . [The] whole policy is based on the determination never to allow the foot of a German or Russian soldier to be placed on Polish soil and never to permit airplanes of either power to fly over Polish territory. That is not pro-Germanism but plain common sense."

Finally, Bullitt ended his missive to the president with his usual unctuous flattery, "I wish I could transfer myself to Washington by radio for an evening talk with you . . . And I would like to hear your voice again."[5]

The passing of Piłsudski was just one more indication that the world order was crumbling and that Europe was descending into turmoil. Poland's future was uncertain. Hitler had torn up the Versailles Treaty. Mussolini was girding for war in Ethiopia. Japan was becoming more belligerent, and there was fighting in northern China. While the United States was at peace and its economy had improved, many Americans were barely getting by. There was still widespread unemployment and countless families uprooted, no longer able to pay rent or afford a home.

Given the continuing economic malaise in the United States, the American public had a palpable and deep distrust of foreign entanglements. In part, the distrust stemmed from the nearly two-year congressional investigation by the Nye Committee into the nexus between bankers, financiers, and the munitions industry in the run-up to U.S. entry into World War I. Led by forty-three-year-old Senator Gerald Nye of North Dakota, the committee held ninety-three hearings in the third-floor Senate Building Caucus Room. After the hearings ended in February 1936, the committee produced a report that offered little evidence to support the widespread public belief that the greedy profiteers had been a significant factor in America's decision to enter the war. It didn't matter—the public was not persuaded.[6]

With American popular opinion overwhelmingly opposed to involvement in another European war, on August 31, 1935, Congress passed the Neutrality Act, prohibiting the export of "arms, ammunition, and implements of war" to foreign nations at war and requiring U.S. arms manufacturers to apply for an export license. American citizens traveling in war zones were also advised that they did so at their own risk. President

Roosevelt originally opposed the legislation, but likely felt that after his defeat over joining the World Court, he didn't want to risk another foreign policy embarrassment. Moreover, if he was going to expend political capital, his domestic agenda took priority. The president relented and signed the legislation into law.

A few months later, President Roosevelt wrote Ambassador Dodd defending his decision on the neutrality bill: "If you had been here I do not think that you would have felt the Senate Bill last August was an unmitigated disaster."[7] The ever-pragmatic president reassured his ambassador in Berlin, "Complete stoppage of all arms material in the broadest sense in the case of a European conflict can be attained, and last summer's law tends in that direction." Roosevelt believed he knew the mood of the public; he explained to Dodd, "The country is being fairly well educated, and I hope that next January I can get an even stronger law, leaving, however, some authority to the President."[8]

15

HYPNOTIZED BY MUSSOLINI

On October 3, 1935, Italian troops, supported by their air force, invaded Ethiopia. Emperor Haile Selassie's soldiers fought back valiantly with all they had, but they didn't have an air force of their own or antiaircraft weapons to protect against Italian bombers. One of the Italian pilots was Mussolini's son Vittorio, who compared the bombing of lance-carrying horsemen—as their bodies were blown apart—to the blooming of "red roses." He declared it to be "exceptionally good fun."[1]

President Roosevelt was cruising on the SS *Houston* off the coast of California when he received a radiogram informing him of the Italian incursion. Roosevelt wanted to issue a declaration of neutrality, but then follow up with the imposition of sanctions on both countries. The president knew that sanctions against Italy, especially on oil, would have a much greater impact than on impoverished Ethiopia, which imported very few commodities. According to his son Elliott, the president said, "They are dropping bombs—and that is war." During the remainder of the cruise, the president "eagerly waited reports on the progress of the fighting, jubilant if it seemed to swing in favor of Haile Selassie's pathetic forces, gloomy over the Italian's [Mussolini's] every success."[2]

Italy and Ethiopia were both members of the League of Nations. Italy's invasion was a clear violation of the League's covenant. The league, straining to maintain its relevance, imposed a range of economic sanctions on Italy the day after the invasion, but then undercut itself by omitting oil from the list of prohibited goods.

On October 5, President Roosevelt declared an embargo on the export of weapons and munitions to both Italy and Ethiopia. *The New York Times,* noting the act "represents the clear resolution of the American people to stay out of the next war," reported that the president "was following the very letter" of the legislation passed by Congress earlier in the year.[3] However, not everyone in Congress or the State Department agreed.

Ambassador Dodd encouraged the president to hold firm against Italian aggression, linking it to future German adventurism: "One thing is certain: the early defeat or forced withdrawal of Italy from Ethiopia would be considered a serious set-back for German autocratic military procedures." Dodd predicted dire consequences "if Italy succeeds," telling the president, "The two dictatorships [German and Italy] would unite upon a common feeling of aggression." One of the first American officials to envision a potential alliance of the future Axis powers, Dodd warned the president, "If Italy, Germany and Japan at some critical moment move at the same time in their spheres, I cannot see any way to stop dictatorships."[4] Roosevelt never responded to Dodd's letter. Perhaps the president still held out hope that Mussolini could be encouraged to play a more positive role in Europe, or perhaps he simply didn't have a useful response to Dodd's gloomy forecast.

From his perch in Rome, Ambassador Long applauded the president's stated neutrality in the Italian-Ethiopian conflict, though he didn't see the embargo as consistent with neutrality. Seemingly unaware of how Roosevelt felt privately about Mussolini's invasion, Long supported Il Duce in his quest to subjugate Ethiopia. Louis Howe, Roosevelt's chief political adviser, complained about Long in a radiogram to Roosevelt, who was still cruising in the Pacific on October 18. Howe derided Long for having been "hypnotized by Mussolini," and reported that Long was "sending five or six cables a day little short of Italian propaganda." Howe had conferred with Secretary Hull on the subject as well. They both worried that Long was not only unpredictable and uncontrollable but that his judgment was unsound. "Knowing Long as we do," Howe radioed the president, "we see danger if this goes unchecked."[5]

Long, however, had direct access to the president and continued to send him personal letters on the Italian-Ethiopian conflict. He warned the president that sanctions "may be neutral from the American point of view, but it is not consonant with the status of neutrality as fixed in the principles of international law." Long claimed to be "motivated entirely by the desire to see the United States out of this war," and he advised the president "to continue the policy of allowing Italy—and Ethiopia—to buy the same quantities [of oil] they have bought in normal times."[6] Long, of course, was fully aware that only Italy relied on oil imports to perpetuate its mechanized war; Ethiopia had no tanks, armored vehicles, or airplanes. Members of Congress held the same view and argued that selling oil to Italy would help the American economy.

A few weeks after the invasion, Long again wrote the president, noting that "under the conditions in the world as now organized and mechanized, nobody can make war unless he has an oil well." Long pointed out, "On that thesis there are only three governments in the world that can successfully wage war—The United States, England, and Russia," and he declared, "There is no doubt that English companies are preparing to sell oil to Italy through Germany . . . The British do not miss one chance to 'earn an honest penny.'"[7] After the League of Nations' tepid response to Italy's invasion, Roosevelt finally accepted Long's advice, and the United States continued to sell oil to both Italy and Ethiopia. Roosevelt knew selling the oil would only prolong the war and inure to the benefit of Italy, but under the Neutrality Act, he now felt he had no choice. Even though members of Congress praised him for following the act—a law he signed—Roosevelt felt the constraints unhelpful.

Back on dry land in early November, the president held a press conference at his residence in Hyde Park. Asked about the Italian invasion, Roosevelt commented, "It is not encouraging. That is why I am spending such an awful lot of time on the foreign situation." Roosevelt saw fascism on the rise in both Italy and Germany, and for the first time in his presidency, he publicly declared Europe's troubles to be "a good deal more worrying than the domestic situation."

It's not clear what Roosevelt actually planned to do about "the foreign situation."[8] There wasn't a lot he could do. He wrote wearily to Ambassador Dodd that to his great dismay, Hitler's policies "were succeeding admirably." The president felt hamstrung by the neutrality legislation, by an isolationist American public, and by developments on the European continent over which he had no control. As he put it in his December 2, 1935, letter to Dodd, "I do not know that the United States can save civilization, but at least by our example we can make people think and give them the opportunity of saving themselves. The trouble is the people of Germany, Italy and Japan are not given the privilege of thinking."[9]

As the year 1935 came to a close, President Roosevelt had a final cabinet meeting. Only a few days earlier, he had received a letter from Ambassador Dodd. The ambassador had been warning about the possibility of war in Europe for more than a year. Now, seated around the large, oval wooden table, the president told his cabinet that Dodd predicted "such horrors that one can hardly imagine the consequences." Secretary of the Interior Harold Ickes recalled the president telling his cabinet that Dodd's letter "was the most pessimistic letter he had ever read." Roosevelt reported that Dodd "thinks nothing can restrain Hitler." According to Ickes, "The President remarked that, of course, some allowance should be made for Dodd's intense prejudice against Hitler, but there seems to be no question that the international situation is very grave indeed."[10]

For his part, Ambassador Dodd felt relieved to have had "some free time" during the holidays. He wrote in his diary, "My wife and daughter were busy half the time filling the house with Christmas decorations, a tall tree, flowers and little lights to make the house look joyful. Everything was beautiful enough, but restful hours were of chief importance to me."[11] The ambassador's respite would be short-lived.

16

PACK UP YOUR FURNITURE, THE DOG, AND THE SERVANTS

It was the first time that the State of the Union message had been delivered in the evening. President Roosevelt made the last-minute decision hoping to attract greater media attention. At 9:00 p.m. on Friday, January 3, 1936, an election year, Roosevelt delivered his annual message to Congress. Eleanor Roosevelt, who that afternoon had taken the grandchildren to the Smithsonian, where they had viewed Charles Lindbergh's *Spirit of St. Louis* hanging in the entrance hall, listened to the speech on the radio in the White House.

With Vice President Garner and Speaker of the House Joseph Byrns of Tennessee sitting on the dais behind him, the president reaffirmed the neutrality of the United States in foreign conflicts. But he also noted that the American people "must take cognizance of growing ill-will, of marked trends towards aggression, of increasing armaments, of short-ened tempers—a situation which has in it many of the elements that lead to the tragedy of general war."[1] The president's ambassadors in Europe shared his grim assessment of the international landscape, and several wanted to vacate their posts.

Ambassador William Bullitt was lonely and unhappy. His residence had become a refuge for anti-Communist sympathizers, and he felt increasingly alienated from a Soviet government that tapped his phones and watched his every move.[2] Adding to his despondency, in early January, Bullitt learned that Louise Bryant, his second wife and the mother of his daughter, had fallen down a flight of stairs in her Paris apartment, suffered a cerebral hemorrhage, and died. He had divorced Bryant, claiming she was an alcoholic and an unfit mother, but he nevertheless mourned her death, and it contributed to his malaise in Moscow.[3] Although he would wait several months before telling the president, Bullitt wanted to leave the Soviet Union.

Ambassador Breckinridge Long was experiencing constant stomach discomfort and, in April, left Rome stopping briefly in Berlin before returning to the United States. Once back, he checked into a hospital for tests and learned that his stomach pains were not cancer—which he had feared—but an aggravated ulcer that would require an operation. While he admired Mussolini's autocratic style of governance and credited Il Duce with energizing the Italian economy and managing to maintain decent relations with Italy's neighbors, Long nevertheless was eager to leave his post for good. The ambassador told the president that his health would not allow him "to continue working in Rome."[4]

Ambassador Jesse Straus in Paris wrote the president a lengthy letter in late January in which he painted a deeply pessimistic picture of the state of affairs in France. He described a growing anti-intellectualism and wrote of moral decay and venality, describing a nation riven by fear. Straus was deeply critical of French politicians and felt he was having little impact as ambassador. Privately, he pondered returning to the United States, for he, too, was not a well man.

Not surprisingly, perhaps no ambassador despaired of his situation so much as William Dodd in Germany. Roosevelt credited Dodd for influencing his comments on foreign policy in the State of the Union, noting in a letter to the ambassador that he had confirmed his "previous feeling of extreme disquiet in regard to European and Asiatic affairs. Hence the serious and, at the same time, clear note of my Message to the Congress."[5] Sharing once again his high regard for President Wilson, Roosevelt noted, "I tried to bring out that in the countries you and I are thinking about the theory of Woodrow Wilson that one can appeal to the citizens over the heads of their government is no longer tenable, for the reason that the dissemination of news—real news— such for instance of my Message—is no longer possible . . . I do not anticipate much of a response within the autocratic nations—but at least enough of the thought behind what I said may seep through to make peace a slightly greater probability during the coming year."[6]

Ambassador Dodd revered President Roosevelt, but was depressed by the worsening situation in Germany and resentful of what he viewed as an ineffectual and unsupportive State Department. In his diary, he groused about the department, his fellow ambassadors, and even the officers in his own embassy. He continued to complain that the department was a refuge for the "sons of rich men," who were "graduates of Harvard, Princeton and one or two other universities."[7] He was contemptuous of his fellow ambassadors in Europe, noting on one occasion that Bulgaria's ambassador to Germany displayed "a breadth of view and appreciation of the international situation which surpassed the American ambassadors I have met." He specifically mentioned "Long in Italy" and "Bullitt in Russia."[8] Dodd was especially critical of Bullitt, falsely characterizing him as "heir to a great fortune and . . . known as a liberal contributor to the Roosevelt campaign in 1932."[9] He derided Bullitt as "an emotional friend of the President but not one whose judgment can be relied upon."[10] Dodd didn't elaborate, but he was undoubtedly referring to Bullitt's lack of success in getting the Soviet Union to pay its debts. Within the embassy in Berlin, Dodd complained about his staff, noting the extravagance of one Foreign Service officer who "sent long, detailed, even unimportant cables, the cost of some of them being over $100." He described other staff arriving at "their offices at 10 or 11 in the morning," remaining "two hours . . . and go[ing] away to some luncheon and remain[ing] until 4 o'clock."[11] Dodd simply couldn't understand how anyone in the American embassy could justify such frivolity in the midst of the Nazis' barbarity.

Ambassador Dodd relieved the tension of his job by taking evening strolls in the Tiergarten, Berlin's large, beautiful public park in the heart of the city. One evening, he noticed that yellow stars had been crudely painted on a number of the benches along the paths; those benches had been set aside for Jews.[12] Around the same time, he learned that an American journalist had been imprisoned at Dachau, "the terrible . . . concentration camp near Munich," as he described it in his diary.[13] There were now dozens of concentration camps in Germany, and the persecution of anyone Hitler deemed undesirable was increasing day by day. Dodd wanted nothing to do with a government dominated by Hitler, Goering, and Goebbels, again noting in his diary the humiliation he felt "shaking hands with known and confessed murderers."[14] Moreover, like Bullitt in Moscow, secret police followed him everywhere he went and his residence, and the embassy telephones were tapped. Dodd had previously considered resignation as a sign of protest to Congress for its failure to approve the proposal for joining the World Court. Now he wanted to resign because he no longer felt that he was making a difference and certainly no longer enjoyed the job.

In addition to the various ambassadors in Europe, Secretary of State Hull thought about leaving government at the end of the first term. He found the travel physically draining, and at sixty-five years old, he wanted to make some money while he still could. His wife, Frances, worried about the constant stress her husband faced serving as the nation's top diplomat, told a friend, "I often fear for his continued strength to cope with the many problems which increasingly come up."[15]

Louis Howe had been a chain-smoker all his life. Now, at age sixty-five, he suffered from what was likely emphysema. He had moved into a bedroom on the second floor of the White House, keeping an oxygen tank by his bedside. Although very ill and bedridden most of the time, he continued to exude a cantankerous energy, pestering the White House chef, Henrietta Nesbitt, to prepare his favorite foods. Elliott Roosevelt, the president's son, recalled that on one evening Howe telephoned Mrs. Nesbitt and in his weakened voice asked for "two hot and two cold codfish balls, and after that I want some corned-beef hash, with a poached egg and chow chow."[16] Despite his illness, his facile mind functioned brilliantly; he kept busy developing strategies for the president's reelection campaign in 1936. No one knew who Roosevelt's opponent would be, though the president speculated to Ambassador Long that it would likely be former president Hoover facing him again in the general election.

President Roosevelt, presumably concerned about Howe's declining health, wanted a number of ambassadors to return to the United States and join the campaign. Breckinridge Long immediately offered his services. When Long visited Washington the previous year, he had heard rumors that Roosevelt might want him to head up his reelection campaign. In February, Roosevelt wrote to Long, and while not offering the job of manager, he stated very clearly, "I want you here during the whole of the campaign." The president mentioned to Long the names of a few other ambassadors that he wanted involved, including Bill Bullitt, and "two or three among the ministers who will do likewise."[17]

That same month, Ambassador Bullitt stopped in Berlin on his way back to Russia. Bullitt told Dodd that he anticipated returning to the United States sometime later in the summer, explaining that his home state of Pennsylvania would be "a crucial state" for Roosevelt. In his diary, Dodd wrote, "Bullitt seems to think he will have to go back . . . perhaps to become an intimate advisor to take the place of poor Howe who is about to die." Dodd thought Bullitt was a big self-promoter and was skeptical that the president would put him in charge of the presidential campaign: "I doubt if these hopes will be realized."[18]

Bullitt was plainly positioning himself for a major role in the campaign, which, assuming the president's reelection, might be leveraged for a more important role in the government, perhaps even secretary of state if Hull were to leave. Bullitt wrote the assistant secretary of state, "Judge" R. Walton Moore, "I am ready to go anywhere and do anything that the President wants me to do: but I would honestly prefer to take a leave of absence without pay this summer and work in the campaign, rather than be appointed to Italy, with the prospect of moving on later to Paris." Moore, seventy-seven years old, was a former congressman from

Virginia whom Secretary Hull had recruited to oversee the department when Hull was traveling. With their shared Virginia heritage, Moore had become a mentor to Bullitt; the ambassador felt comfortable confiding in him:

> I know Italy well and I have talked over intimately with Breckinridge Long the diplomatic work in Rome. It doesn't seem to differ greatly from the work in Moscow. There are infrequent meetings with Mussolini. Long has, I think, talked with him only twice in three years. There are no negotiations of importance and there is a great deal of the sort of social life that I participated in with pleasure at the age of 17, and from which I have attempted to escape every day since ... London and Paris are the only two ports in Europe at which can make one's contacts mean something. What I would like beyond anything else at the present time is to work and to work hard.[19]

At daybreak on March 5, 1936, thirty-two thousand heavily armed German troops marched across the Rhine River and occupied the demilitarized Rhineland, a region in western Germany that borders France, Belgium, and a section of the Netherlands. The demilitarization of the Rhineland occurred after World War I pursuant to the 1919 Treaty of Versailles, and the 1925 Locarno Pact, which stipulated that Germany would keep political control of the area, but not be permitted to station military forces. Germany had been steadily rearming since 1933, but still did not have the strength to hold the Rhineland if France or Britain counterattacked. Hitler later acknowledged, "The forty-eight hours after the march into the Rhineland were the most nerve-racking in my life. If the French had then marched into the Rhineland we would have had to withdraw with our tails between our legs."[20]

Only weeks after Germany's move into the Rhineland, Roosevelt's European ambassadors began making their way back to the United States. Dodd sounded gleeful as he wrote in his diary about driving to Hamburg with his family to board an ocean liner for the voyage home:

"The country looked beautiful . . . wheat, barley, rye everywhere and quite green for the season."[21] Long also left his post, happy to be away from Rome, but somewhat apprehensive about the operation that he needed to have on his stomach. Before leaving, Long wrote in his diary an appraisal of Hitler's occupation of the Rhineland, declaring that he saw no evidence "of a pathological conditions in Hitler's recent speeches and actions, which would indicate that he was not acting in a very sane and able manner."[22] Long still planned to join the campaign, but he would first need to check into the Mayo Clinic for an unspecified period of time.

Back in February, President Roosevelt had told William Bullitt that he would find him another assignment—presumably after the campaign: "When the change is made you will pack up your furniture, the dog, and the servants—where you will deposit them, we will have to tell you later."[23] Now in April, Judge Moore, acting at the behest of the president, wrote Bullitt that he should return to the United States as soon as possible. Bullitt replied that he would leave Moscow the following week, but indicated that he hoped to make several "one night stops" along the way: in Warsaw, Berlin, and Brussels, with longer stays in Paris to sort out "the belongings of my late wife," and in London where he wanted to "spend a few days with the Astors." Lady Astor, née Nancy Langhorne, was born in Virginia and was a distant cousin of Bullitt's. She had married Waldorf Astor, one of the richest men in the world, and had won election as Britain's first female member of Parliament. Though she championed women's rights and the poor, she was also an anti-Semite and a conservative Tory who admired ironfisted leadership. As it was the horse-racing season in London, Bullitt informed Judge Moore that he planned to accompany Lord Astor and cousin Nancy "to the Derby" at Epsom Downs Racecourse.[24]

Bullitt's itinerary revealed his desire to live as a bon vivant, yet be viewed as Roosevelt's most trusted European ambassador. His ability to compartmentalize the different and contradictory parts of his life matched that of his boss, the president.

By the time Bullitt arrived in Berlin, Dodd had already sailed for the

United States, but that didn't prevent Bullitt from paying a courtesy call on Hitler's foreign minister, Neurath. According to Bullitt, in their meeting, Neurath assured him that Germany would do "everything possible to prevent rather than encourage an outbreak by the Nazis in Austria, and would pursue a quiet line with regard to Czechoslovakia."[25] A few months later, in July, Germany would sign an agreement with Austria pledging "its recognition of Austria's sovereignty and the promise not to interfere in [its] internal affairs." Both actions were outright lies, part of a committed pattern of deception intended to buy Germany the time it needed to finish preparing for war.

In early May 1936, President Roosevelt wrote his ambassador to France, Jesse Straus, to update him on his plans for the campaign: "Breck Long is here and, as you know, he has not been at all well. Strictly between ourselves, I am not at all certain that he will go back. Dodd arranged with the Department months ago to get here at this time and deliver a series of lectures, returning to Berlin in the early summer." Roosevelt also wanted his ambassador to the United Kingdom, Bob Bingham, to return in June. Roosevelt told Straus that he had asked Bingham "to undertake special work of seeing that the Associated Press maintains a thoroughly neutral position." However, in France there was a new prime minister, Léon Blum, and a half a million French workers were on strike, leading Roosevelt to suggest to Straus that "it would perhaps be best if you could come back here a little later than the others, in order that you would not all be away at the same time. Also, so far as the campaign goes, I think you would find it more interesting to be here in August or September."[26]

The 1936 Democratic National Convention opened in Philadelphia on June 23. The president looked forward to rousing the delegates and to the campaign that would follow, but he knew the challenge would be difficult for him; it was going to be his first political campaign without Louis Howe, who had died two months earlier. Howe's death had not been unexpected, but it deeply saddened the members of the First Family, who were devoted to him. Howe had not only directed Roosevelt's campaigns, he had helped the president govern, providing strategic advice on issues and helping to choose personnel. While no one could replace Howe, the president managed over time to find people to fill the many roles that his trusted aide had once played.

At the convention, Roosevelt's mastery of politics was on full display. According to historian James MacGregor Burns, President Roosevelt "dominated the proceedings throughout. He drafted the platform, reviewed and approved the major speeches, made the main convention decisions, and brought the affair to a stunning climax with his acceptance speech."[27] On June 25, delegates voted for a platform that included a section on foreign policy, likely authored by William Bullitt, affirming "opposition to war as an instrument of national policy" and declaring, "Disputes between nations should be settled by peaceful means."[28] In addition to such anodyne language, Bullitt included a statement that perfectly melded the country's isolationist foreign policy with its populist mood: "We shall continue to observe a true neutrality in the disputes of others; to be prepared, resolutely to resist aggression against ourselves; to work for peace and to take the profits out of war; to guard against being drawn, by political commitments, international banking or private banking, into any war that may develop elsewhere."[29] As in many of Roosevelt's speeches, there was something for everyone.

On Saturday, June 27, 1936, the weather in Philadelphia was overcast; early in the afternoon, two thunderstorms passed through the city. At Franklin Field, more than one hundred thousand people gathered to hear Franklin Roosevelt accept his party's nomination for a second term. Near the front of the stage, in the VIP section, William Bullitt took his seat next to Secretary of the Interior Harold Ickes. Ickes both liked and admired Bullitt, and as they waited under a darkening sky for the president to arrive, Ickes asked the ambassador "about the chances of any serious disturbances in Europe this summer." Ickes recorded in his diary that Bullitt told him "things will probably be kept quiet." Bullitt explained to Ickes that Germany was biding its time, confident that "Austria will fall into its lap sooner or later and that it is only a matter of time and patience," but that "[Mussolini] may precipitate some trouble." Bullitt was less sanguine about the future beyond 1936, telling Ickes, "The chances were better than sixty-five percent out of a hundred that during the term of the next President there would be a war in Europe." Bullitt felt Roosevelt was "firmly set on peace" and that he could "keep the country out of war." But the ambassador expressed a lack of confidence in the British who had neither "the competency nor the experience, nor the ability to bring the country through such a crisis."[30] The question Ickes did not ask, and that Bullitt did not address, was whether the United States would accept a Europe ruled by Hitler.

17

I HATE WAR

The fireworks "almost made the ground shake," according to Ambassador Dodd, who attended a lavish dinner party given by Joseph Goebbels to honor the athletes participating in the 1936 Olympic games in Berlin. Goebbels chose the site of a "former Jewish Mansion" on Pfaueninsel, an island fifteen miles outside of Berlin, to entertain an estimated two thousand guests to a sumptuous dinner, followed by dancing, and then a fireworks display. According to Dodd, the fireworks began "about 10 o'clock" and "continued for a half hour [and] people at our table trembled when the bombing made such a terrible noise." In his diary, Dodd characterized the dinner as ostentatious and complained that the "explosions" were a "form of war propaganda." Though Dodd had vowed to never again host Nazi leaders at the American embassy, he nevertheless felt obligated to attend some of the events, including Goebbels's party. With the party being held during the second week of the olympiad, Dodd knew as the U.S. ambassador he needed to show support for the more than three hundred American athletes who had traveled to Berlin to participate.[1]

The following day, August 16, Dodd walked out of his residence at 1:00 p.m. with his wife and daughter and climbed into the rear seat of the black embassy limousine. Dodd had little interest in sports and was not looking forward to attending closing ceremonies that he regarded as nothing more than the capstone of a two-week Nazi propaganda extravaganza.

It was a seven-mile trip from the Tiergarten to the stadium. As the limousine rolled through the central city, Dodd noticed the changes that had taken place for the games. All the signs reading "Juden Unerwuenscht"—"Jews Not Welcome"—had been removed from the stores, hotels, and restaurants.[2] Instead, along the route to the stadium, he saw numerous German flags displayed, as well as the flags of the nations whose athletes were participating in the games. While changes like these were intended to convey a false narrative of tolerance, other changes were not. Most striking to Dodd, the route to the stadium that day was lined with thousands upon thousands of jackbooted storm troopers who stood shoulder to shoulder at attention.[3] Along with the pageantry of the sporting event, Hitler wanted to impress upon his international guests the military might of Germany.

The Dodd family entered the packed Olympic coliseum and took their seats in the diplomatic box. At approximately 3:00 p.m., the crowd stood and roared: the führer had entered the stadium.[4] Hitler had attended several of the events during the games, including earlier that week when he watched United States sprinter Jesse Owens claim the title to the fastest man in the world. Martha Dodd, the ambassador's daughter, had been in the box watching the race with Thomas Wolfe, who let out a "war whoop" when Owens crossed the finish line. Martha noticed that Hitler "twisted in his seat, looked down, attempting to locate the miscreant, and frowned angrily." In her diary, Martha wrote, "It was the Nazi attitude . . . to consider Negroes as animals and utterly unqualified to enter the Games."[5] There is no evidence that Martha found it even a little ironic that Wolfe had been known for racial insensitivity in his youth, and that her own father, the ambassador, could hardly have been considered a progressive on race relations.

In early August 1936, the president received a letter from his ambassador to France, Jesse Straus, who told him, "Upon arriving at home my physicians informed me that I was in a very run-down condition and that I must have a complete rest for six months."[6] Straus resigned. He was certainly much sicker than he let on to Roosevelt. Only two months later, he died of pneumonia in his Park Avenue apartment in New York City.

Roosevelt moved quickly to fill the post in Paris, informing Missy LeHand that she could "tell Bullitt you know that he is going to Paris."[7] Bullitt was thrilled with the news. In the back of his mind he had hoped that he might be secretary of state in Roosevelt's second term, but when it became clear that Hull would not be retiring, the embassy in Paris held great allure. Bullitt had spent significant time in Paris during the 1920s, had many friends there, and appreciated its culture. During one summer he had traveled the length of the country with a friend, the painter Henri Matisse. Bullitt also spoke French fluently, enjoyed fine wine, and had studied the country's history. More importantly, he understood French politics in the context of Europe. He recognized the increasing potential for war and believed a French and German rapprochement was needed to prevent a conflict that could engulf the Continent.

Bullitt's appointment to Paris was met with mixed reaction at the Department of State. A number of colleagues and Foreign Service officers recognized Bullitt's deep experience, intelligence, and leadership qualities, while others, like Dodd, thought Bullitt was pompous and potentially a dangerous self-promoter. Some still remembered Bullitt's betrayal of Woodrow Wilson when he testified in opposition to the Treaty of Versailles. Upon hearing the news, Eleanor Roosevelt reportedly exclaimed, "Damn it!" Eleanor knew Democratic Party chairman Jim Farley had wanted the job, and she felt he deserved it. "That's just like Franklin," she told Farley, irritated that the president seemed to value camaraderie over political loyalty.[8]

Bullitt remained in Washington until the end of September, working on the campaign and organizing his affairs before leaving for Paris. On September 13, he attended Missy's birthday party in the White House and gave her a puppy.[9] Missy still had feelings for Bullitt, apparently having forgiven him for his romantic dalliances in Moscow, but she had no illusions that they would ever be anything more than close friends. Bullitt had been the "one big romance" in Missy's life, according to James Roosevelt, who later claimed, "Bill treated her badly."[10] While Bullitt was certainly attracted to Missy, undoubtedly part of that attraction had always been her proximity to the president.

The day after the birthday party, September 14, Bullitt paid a visit to the director of the Federal Bureau of Investigation, J. Edgar Hoover. The forty-one-year-old Hoover had gained renown for cracking down on notorious bank robbers, notably John Dillinger. Bullitt wanted to make Hoover aware of Soviet diplomats in the United States who were being sent to Washington to enlist Communist sympathizers to become spies. Afterward, the director wrote a memorandum to the file recording Bullitt's warning: "Communist leaders in Russia make every effort to put spies in all foreign government agencies." Hoover initiated an internal security program, instructing the FBI to begin checking on the activities of Soviet diplomats and known Communists in the United States.[11] By the end of the decade, he would expand the program to include German diplomats and those suspected of being part of the Third Reich's "fifth column" of German sympathizers in the United States. Breckinridge Long, an admirer of Hoover, later seized upon the fifth column scare to limit Jewish immigration to the United States.

By the election campaign of 1936, Franklin Roosevelt understood that Europe was likely on the brink of war. His ambassadors on the Continent, especially Dodd, had been issuing warnings about Hitler for months. Italy was at war with Ethiopia, and over the summer, civil war had engulfed Spain when General Francisco Franco, having failed in an attempt to overthrow the recently elected Popular Front government, staged an armed rebellion, supported militarily by both Hitler and Mussolini. There was political turmoil in France, while Britain, seemingly aloof and adrift, struggled to prop up its sagging economy.

However, only occasionally during his campaign for reelection did

President Roosevelt mention foreign policy, and only once at length—in his address at Chautauqua, New York, on August 14, a speech for which Bullitt is generally credited with having developed the themes and much of the language.[12]

Standing before a crowd of twelve thousand in the amphitheater at Chautauqua, the president struck an isolationist note when he vowed to "shun political commitments which might entangle us in foreign wars" and "to avoid connection with the political activities of the League of Nations." His tone then bordered on pacifist when he decried the "production for a war market which may give immense fortunes to a few men" and promised that "no act of the United States" would help "to produce or promote war."

The most arresting part of the speech came when Roosevelt vividly described the human toll and misery of battle: "I have seen war. I have seen war on land and sea. I have seen blood running from the wounded. I have seen men coughing out their gassed lungs. I have seen the dead in the mud. I have seen cities destroyed. I have seen 200 limping, exhausted men come out of line—the survivors of a regiment of 1,000 that went forward 48 hours before. I have seen children starving. I have seen the agony of mothers and wives. I *hate war*."[13]

In fact, neither Roosevelt nor Bullitt had actually served in the military. In contrast to Bullitt, however, the president had at least "seen war." After the United States entered World War I, former president Theodore Roosevelt advised his much-younger fifth cousin that he needed to resign his civilian post as assistant navy secretary, join the armed forces, and fight for his country. Young Roosevelt was ready to do so. However, President Wilson told Franklin that no man had "the right to select his place of service" and ordered him to remain right where he was. But Roosevelt, who even then had presidential aspirations, decided that if he couldn't enlist, he needed at least to witness firsthand the devastation of war, and so in the summer of 1918, he toured the French battlefields.

In Bullitt's novel, *It's Not Done,* published in 1926, a fictional Woodrow

Wilson tells a young diplomat, "I hate this war . . . I hate all war."[14] Although Bullitt had lifted the the phrase from his novel, it was the Roosevelt's dramatic oration that day had such a profound impact on the crowd in Chautauqua—and on the millions of Americans listening to their radios; they heard their president's heartfelt commitment to keep the United States out of conflict.

The speech was clearly a politically motivated attempt to curry favor with isolationists, but Roosevelt recognized the need to preserve his future options as well. He also used the address to warn the American people that the United States could not remain detached and indifferent to events abroad. The president skillfully expressed skepticism about the efficacy of the neutrality laws. Historian Edward Nixon later wrote that internationalists as well as isolationists "were able to applaud the speech and, despite FDR's concern with reelection, there is little evidence that the campaign caused him to yield anything of substance" to the isolationists.[15]

Since the outcome of the election was never really in doubt, President Roosevelt didn't need to travel the country campaigning as he had four years earlier. However, Roosevelt loved receiving the adoration of his supporters around the country, so it wasn't a lack of enthusiasm for campaigning that kept him in Washington that September. He acknowledged in an off-the-record gathering of reporters that he had been thinking about making a campaign trip to the West Coast, but was not sure whether it would be advisable for him "to be so far away from first base for four days." The president, who enjoyed cozy relations with the press corps, confided, "Now, don't say there is a European situation—a war scare—in this but the fact remains . . . I ought not to be away, at the present time . . . I probably ought not to be four days away from Washington."[16]

By October, however, Roosevelt felt comfortable enough to leave the nation's capital. Little had changed in Europe, but the talk of war seemed to have subsided enough for the president to embark on a two-week whistle-stop campaign aboard the *Ferdinand Magellan*, the presidential railway car. Roosevelt preferred campaigning by train, and this trip would take him through the Midwest and the South, two regions where he was especially popular. Recently discharged from the Mayo Clinic after successfully completing surgery for his ulcer, Breckinridge Long joined Roosevelt's campaign train. It was an exhilarating experience for Long, who marveled at the huge crowds Roosevelt attracted wherever the train stopped. In Bloomington, Indiana, twenty thousand people gathered for a ten-minute visit. Long estimated, likely with some exaggeration, that one million people showed up in Chicago and an even bigger crowd in Detroit. In Long's hometown of Saint Louis, the attendance was "very large." Near the end of the trip, at a rally in Rochester, New York, Long noted the "wildness of the crowd."[17]

"It was an astonishing experience to travel through much of the territory we had travelled through four years ago when I was also on the President's train," Long recalled. Then the crowds had been big "but quiet and undemonstrative, glum, and even sullen," but now in 1936, the president was greeted like a conquering hero. Long remarked on the "excellent speeches," written mostly by Judge Samuel Rosenman, but was quick to add that he had contributed "ideas, paragraphs and other suggestions."

Long rode in car number four, which was furnished with "a very comfortable drawing room," while the Roosevelt family occupied the rear car. Long lunched twice with the president and Mrs. Roosevelt. He also dined with them twice, including once when the train rumbled through Missouri and freshman senator Harry Truman joined the first family. Long recorded in his diary that he had an "intimate" talk with the president just before they reached Albany. He wrote that he told the president he wished all Americans could have been on the train to experience firsthand the hope that he engendered with so many people across the country. Roosevelt replied that he wished "every Republican chairman of the boards of big corporations could have been on hand to see something of the human side of America."[18] Roosevelt later thanked Long for the "splendid help you gave me on our western trip."[19]

Throughout the fall, references to foreign policy were confined to two or three statements on the importance of foreign trade and of friendly relations with Canada. Roosevelt delivered a speech in Saint Paul, Minnesota, part of which was devoted to international affairs. According to Edward Nixon, "The emphasis throughout the campaign was upon the close connection between reciprocal trade and world peace."[20]

On November 3, nearly forty-five million Americans went to the polls. In a landslide victory, President Roosevelt crushed Kansas governor Alf Landon, winning over 60 percent of the popular vote, and 98 percent of electoral college votes. Landon won only two states: Maine and Vermont. Although unemployment remained high, and many Americans still struggled, the results were an overwhelming endorsement of both Roosevelt's leadership and the New Deal, which had provided the American people with a highly popular economic safety net in the form of Social Security and unemployment benefits.

Writing from his new home in Paris, Ambassador Bullitt gushed to the newly reelected president, "I am as happy as a proud father about the election!" He added, "The wave of enthusiasm in France which greeted your election was really phenomenal. No American president has ever received such a tornado of praise . . . [T]he French regard you as a national leader who has succeeded in giving the lower classes a greater proportion of the national income without disturbing any of the ancient liberties." However, the ambassador also sounded a note of caution about the euphoria surrounding Roosevelt:

> The French all feel that somehow you will keep Europe from plunging again into war. . . . Every minister of a small European state who has yet called on me has expressed the hope that you might intervene, saying that if you do not, his country would certainly be destroyed by the inevitable conflict . . . [N]o one in Europe can think of any way you can intervene effectively—but

you might be able to think of some way yourself. You are, in other words beginning to occupy the miracle man position. And I am strongly reminded of the sort of hope that for a time was reposed in Woodrow Wilson.[21]

Given that Bullitt felt Wilson had failed miserably with the League of Nations, his comparison of Roosevelt to the former president was likely meant to warn the president that he should make his intentions toward Europe very clear.

18

I STILL DON'T LIKE THE EUROPEAN OUTLOOK

A mbassador Bullitt's residence at 2 Avenue d'Iéna looked out over the manicured gardens of the Trocadéro, with the Eiffel Tower looming in the background. Bullitt's brother, Orville, described the house as an "ostentatious, ugly and uncomfortable dwelling." It was nevertheless well suited for entertaining, with three drawing rooms and a large dining room for formal dinners.[1]

Relieved to be gone from dreary Moscow, Bullitt relished his new role as ambassador at the largest, most glamorous U.S. embassy in the world. He quickly gained a reputation not only as a seasoned and savvy diplomat but as a charming and charismatic host as well. As he had in Russia, Bullitt enjoyed throwing large parties at the residence that sometimes lasted until the early-morning hours. He hired an excellent chef, served only the finest wines, dressed immaculately, and flirted in flawless French with his female guests. Known as the "Champagne ambassador," according to CBS foreign correspondent Eric Sevareid, Bullitt once had cartons of caviar shipped from Moscow "that broke all the records."[2] After dinner, guests were often treated to chamber music in the central drawing room, or to the latest American movies projected on a screen in the spacious hall on the second floor at the end of the grand staircase. The house was filled with vases of brightly colored flowers, which his butler purchased each morning at the flower market in Les Halles.[3]

In addition to his embassy residence, Bullitt rented the Château de Vineuil-Saint-Firmin at Chantilly, an eighteenth-century limestone manor house with a wine cellar that he reportedly stocked with eighteen thousand bottles of wine. On weekends, Bullitt often entertained foreign visitors as well as France's senior politicians at the château. Chantilly was horse country, and Bullitt enjoyed early morning rides in the countryside. Ernest Hemingway, who had left Paris in 1929 but remained in Europe working as a journalist covering the Spanish Civil War from 1936 to 1939, often visited Paris and came out occasionally to shoot clay pigeons with the ambassador.[4]

Bullitt also leased a small apartment on the Rue de Ponthieu, near the Rond-Point of the Champs-Élysées. According to his brother, Orville, "he loved it and I thought it was dreadful: a small living/dining room with an alcove for a bed, a tiny kitchen, and a small room for his Chinese manservant."[5] It was rumored that Bullitt used the apartment to avoid being seen with his numerous female liaisons.

As in Moscow, rumors of female conquests swirled around him. According to one account, when *Washington Herald* publisher Eleanor "Cissy" Patterson visited Bullitt, he tried to persuade her to marry him. Missy LeHand had friends in the embassy, and she heard the gossip. "Incidentally," she teased Bullitt, "Marguerite [Missy] would like to know if she should stop thinking about you, and just save her pennies to buy a station wagon for your wedding present."[6]

The ambassador's annual salary was $17,500, and he received an entertainment allowance of $4,800, but his expenses in Paris—the parties, the wine cellar, the château, the apartment—far exceeded his salary and the budget he received from the Department of State. While Bullitt had inherited money from his parents, in Paris he was living far beyond his means. He was not anywhere near as rich as some of his fellow ambassadors in the State Department, but he blithely paid most of the entertainment expenses from his own pocket.

President Roosevelt reveled in his landslide victory. There remained an enormous amount of work to do to right America's economic ship, but Roosevelt was confident his approach was succeeding. The year before, he had appointed Harry Hopkins as head of the Works Progress Administration (WPA), the agency responsible for public works such as the building of roads and bridges. Secretary of the Interior Harold Ickes had hoped to lead the WPA, arguing that money should be spent on heavy capital expenditures. But the president ultimately chose Hopkins, who advocated instead for a focus on reducing the number of Americans on relief.

In Hopkins, the president had found his most trusted domestic policy adviser. Under Hopkins's leadership the WPA spent nearly $5 billion, building hospitals, schools, public buildings, and airports, and providing paid jobs for hundreds of thousands of unemployed people. Yet despite the now positive trajectory in the employment numbers, the president's concern over international events weighed on him. He wrote Eleanor in November 1936 that his greatest worry was the situation abroad: "I still don't like the European outlook."[7]

Roosevelt's concern was both fed and echoed by his ambassadors in Europe, who continued to lament rising tensions on the Continent and raise the specter of war. Ambassador Bullitt, paraphrasing Benjamin Franklin, wrote to the president, "There is beginning to be a feeling that if the nations of Western Europe do not hang together, they will hang separately." Bullitt believed that the civil war in Spain had been a wake-up call for the democracies of Europe. As he put it, "Most people in most European countries realize that there is such a thing as European civilization which reposes in certain very old civilized principles that may be destroyed by war or Bolshevism." Bullitt thought there might be a solution, and he added, "If we can assist diplomatically in laying the basis for reconciliation between France and Germany, I think we should help." At this point, Bullitt's notion of a grand bargain between France and Germany was naive at best, and totally unrealistic. At least he had the good sense to tamp down expectations: "If we should get anywhere diplomatically and see a fair chance of success, you could then come forward with some stupendous public announcement. But I feel emphatically that you should not let yourself be persuaded to make some grand gesture until you have prepared the ground with great care."[8]

Bullitt was extremely vague as to how to "prepare the ground" between France and Germany, but it seems clear that once again he hoped Roosevelt would view him as the key intermediary.[9] Of course, Bullitt's proposal hinged on having a like-minded United States counterpart in Germany to work with and he recommended that Roosevelt remove Ambassador Dodd and appoint someone else. In his letter to the president, Bullitt was blunt: "Dodd has many admirable and likable qualities, but . . . he hates the Nazis too much to be able to do anything with them or get anything out of them. We need someone in Berlin who can at least be civil to the Nazis and speaks German perfectly."[10] Dodd spoke German well enough, but it was true that he despised the Nazis. He also understood the Nazi mindset better than almost everyone in the Department of State, perhaps with the exception of his former deputy, George Messersmith, who was now ambassador to Austria. Nonetheless, Bullitt knew the man he thought the president should appoint to replace Dodd: Hugh Wilson, a fifty-one-year-old career Foreign Service officer who was then serving as the American envoy to Switzerland. It was highly unusual for one U.S. ambassador to be advocating for the dismissal of another and then attempting to hand pick his successor. Bullitt's doing so demonstrated both his unbridled ambition and the confidence he had in his relationship with the president.

A few weeks later, Bullitt sent the president another letter; his message this time was even more direct. Bullitt recounted how Jim Farley, who had directed the president's successful reelection campaign, had visited him in Paris. The ambassador began his letter on a light note: "I took him to the dog races but did not lead him any further into the paths on iniquity so that, if he returns to you a changed man, you must [not] blame . . . the result on me."[11] Then, Bullitt got to the point: "In talking to Jim, I tried to convince him (and believe I did) that the situation in Europe was too serious to suggest the planting of duds in diplomatic posts in order to repay them for contributions to the campaign fund. Jim said that he agreed with me, and we went on to discuss how it might be possible for you to get rid of some of the men who are not fit to hold their present jobs as chiefs of mission in the present world crisis." Bullitt suggested that all chiefs of mission should hand in their resignations a few weeks after the president was inaugurated for a second term. Roosevelt could then replace certain weak ambassadors—"misfits," as he called them. As he often did with the president, Bullitt laced his prose with humor: "As a result of this letter I am likely to receive the only one of such instructions issued. Anyhow, I hereby submit my resignation."[12]

But Bullitt was not kidding when he returned to his idea of a grand bargain between Germany and France proposed in his earlier letter. "If there is a chance to maintain peace in Europe during your next Administration," Bullitt wrote, "that chance lies in the small possibility that it may be possible to draw the French and German Government closer together." He went on to describe his close relationship with the French prime minister, Léon Blum, noting that he had "managed to establish entirely confidential relations" and had the ability to arrange a "private meeting" whenever he wished. He then twisted the knife into Ambassador Dodd, writing, "If we had an Ambassador who could do that in Berlin, he and I could at least be of some assistance in bringing France and Germany together—nothing much is needed except some verbal assistance in erasing the lies that each believes about the other—and in any event we should be able to keep you fully informed with regard to the most intimate inner details of the European situation."[13]

Around the same time as the president received Bullitt's letters, a number of unflattering articles about Dodd appeared in the American press. Dodd wrote in his diary, "Yesterday I saw a clipping from the front page of a Washington paper attacking me violently as a complete failure here and pretending that the President is of the same opinion. This is news to me. The man who wrote the article on the Foreign Service pretends that the Department has given him the information." The article went on to suggest that, as Dodd put it, "The President and the Department are planning to have Ambassador Bullitt sent here to deal with the Nazis because he favors their politics."[14]

The author of the piece was Drew Pearson, who wrote a syndicated column, "Washington Merry-Go-Round," that appeared regularly in *The Washington Herald,* which was owned by William Bullitt's good friend Cissy Patterson. It seems highly likely Bullitt was Pearson's source for the story.

While it's not clear that Dodd understood Bullitt was trying to undermine him—Dodd knew he had a number of detractors in the Foreign Service—he neither respected nor trusted his colleague in Paris. Instead of writing to the president, Dodd kept his distress and irritation to himself, and only criticized Bullitt in the privacy of his diary. He described how Bullitt, had taken "a large staff and many consuls" to Moscow "in spite of the fact that little real work could be done in Russia" and how Bullitt "also spent huge sums building an Embassy palace." Dodd wrote that Bullitt, "having not succeeded very well at the end of his first year" in Moscow, "became angry." Dodd thought Bullitt "had made a good beginning" in Paris, but that he was now "on the reactionary side," meaning that Bullitt didn't understand the threat posed by Hitler.

Apparently, Bullitt's machinations did not stop with the American press. Ambassador Dodd noted in his diary that the editor and owner of one of France's leading newspapers, *Le Matin,* had been asked by Bullitt to pay a courtesy call on Dodd "to advise the President [Roosevelt] to lend a hand in . . . working for an alliance between France and Germany." Dodd was not used to such political tactics. In his diary, he wondered whether "this means the United States is intermeddling, or that Bullitt is moving in . . . without official instructions?" Dodd didn't know what to do. He had planned to resign in the spring of 1937, but he felt "to give up my work here under these circumstances would put me in a defensive and positively false position at home." As his biographer, Erik Larson, put it, Dodd was "deeply wounded." The ambassador "had spent the better part of four years seeking to fulfill Roosevelt's mandate to serve as a model of American values and believed he had done as well as any man could have been expected to do."[15] An acolyte of Woodrow Wilson, Dodd had been sabotaged by one of Wilson's fiercest critics: Bill Bullitt.

Ambassador Bullitt sent the president a letter just before Christmas, reiterating his view that "the only chance of preserving peace in Europe lies in the possibility that the French and the Germans may reach some basis of understanding." Bullitt noted that due to the "bombing plane," the "French Government knows the Germans can destroy the city of Paris within 24 hours and the French can destroy the German city of Essen and all the towns of the Ruhr in 24 hours." Bullitt argued there was "a general realization, therefore, that war will mean; horrible suffering . . . that it will end in general revolution and the only winners will be Stalin and Company."[16] Bullitt was convinced that Stalin, like Hitler, had territorial ambitions.

Bullitt closed his letter in his typically intimate style, telling the president, "I wish to Heaven I could swim with you today. There is so much to talk about and all of it interesting—tragically interesting. My love to you and a Merry Christmas and Happy New Year to Mrs. Roosevelt and all the family."[17] No other ambassador at the time was sending his "love" to the president and the First Family.

As the tumultuous year of 1936 came to a close, Franklin Roosevelt took note of Bullitt's warnings, but was reluctant to convert Bullitt's ambassador designation into that of special envoy for purposes of seeking French and German rapprochement. Neither did the president ask for the resignations of his other ambassadors in Europe—as Bullitt had suggested. He had, after all, only months before made a number of changes in U.S. embassies around the world, including significant changes in Europe, a fact that Bullitt chose to ignore because he was primarily focused on getting rid of Ambassador Dodd. Joseph Davies, a flamboyant millionaire and the husband of General Foods heiress Marjorie Merriweather Post, had been sent to Moscow only a few weeks earlier as Bullitt's replacement. Besides the appointments of Davies in Moscow, and Bullitt in France, Roosevelt had appointed Undersecretary of State William Phillips as ambassador to Italy. However, the president was contemplating additional moves, including at the Court of St. James's. Indeed, 1937 would bring a significant changing of the guard in the Department of State.

Roosevelt celebrated New Year's Eve, according to his son Elliott, "in the style he liked best—with Mother and others of the family in his oval study, comfortable in his big chair, listening to the radio tell how the rest of the country was seeing that in another twelve months the president would put the United States well along the road to renewed prosperity." The eggnog that night was "laced with some of the most excellent examples of Dominican manufacture—rum sent from Moscow by our new ambassador there."[18]

President Roosevelt's second term was to begin in January, rather than in March as it had four years earlier, due to the passage of the Twentieth Amendment to the Constitution that shortened the period between the election and the inauguration. Although the president looked forward to his second term, a number of issues weighed on him. While he was greatly concerned about the crisis building in Europe, he was even more focused on what he believed was a deepening emergency at home: the hostility of the United States Supreme Court to the New Deal. Beginning in May 1935, the court issued a series of landmark opinions striking down key components of Roosevelt's domestic program, including the National Industrial Recovery Act and the Agricultural Adjustment Act. With his reelection landslide victory, Roosevelt felt he had been given a mandate to govern. When in December Attorney General Homer Cummings suggested that it might be possible to increase the number of justices on the Supreme Court, thereby giving the president the ability to appoint a slate of jurists favorable to his agenda, Roosevelt reportedly exclaimed, "The answer to a maiden's prayer."[19]

19

WHAT A GRAND FIGHT IT IS GOING TO BE!

On January 20, 1937, Chief Justice Charles Evan Hughes swore in President Roosevelt for a second term. As rained poured down on the tens of thousands of onlookers who huddled under umbrellas on the Capitol grounds, President Roosevelt stood on the west front portico, right hand raised, left hand on the family Dutch Bible, and repeated the oath of office.[1] He then delivered his second inaugural address, and much like the first one in 1933, it made scant reference to America's role in the world. Instead, the president focused on the unfinished business at home, using a refrain to describe the challenges ahead and punctuated by the memorable words, "I see one-third of a nation ill-housed, ill-clad, ill-nourished. It is not in despair that I paint you that picture. I paint it for you in hope."[2]

Only two weeks later, Roosevelt stunned the nation when he revealed a plan for the reorganization of the judiciary based on a drastic altering of the Supreme Court.[3] On February 5, the president called an emergency meeting at 10:00 a.m. at the White House; wheeled into the Cabinet Room at the appointed hour, Roosevelt greeted the members of his cabinet and key members of Congress he had invited. Declaring that within the next hour he would send his plan to Congress, Roosevelt highlighted its principal components, including the key provision that whenever a Supreme Court justice who had served for at least ten years did not retire upon reaching the age of seventy, the president could appoint a new additional justice.

The president had greatly underestimated the resistance to his plan from within Congress. Not only were Republicans outraged by what they viewed as a blatant usurpation of power by the president, many Democrats on Capitol Hill, including some of the New Deal's staunchest supporters, also opposed the plan. Even Roosevelt's liberal friends on the court, including Louis Brandeis, disapproved. In newspapers across the country, editorial boards blasted the president. Notwithstanding opposition from political elites, Roosevelt felt confident that he had the support of the American people, refusing to either yield or scale back his proposal. "What a grand fight it is going to be!" an animated president exclaimed to one friend.[4]

President Roosevelt never publicly criticized his ambassadors in Europe nor his State Department advisers in Washington. However, he was growing increasingly concerned not only about the possibility of conflict in Europe but about America's capacity to wage war should it be necessary. He needed the right foreign policy team in place. He had made important personnel changes the previous year, but now he contemplated other moves.

Fully recovered from his stomach ulcer, Breckinridge Long was angling for a big position following his loyal service on the campaign and stint as U.S. ambassador to Italy. Even before the president was sworn in for a second term, Long approached Senator Key Pittman of Nevada, the chairman of the Foreign Relations Committee, to ask him to lobby Roosevelt on his behalf for a significant post, either ambassador to England—it was rumored that Ambassador Bingham would soon resign—or perhaps undersecretary of state, the job recently vacated by veteran Foreign Service officer William Phillips, who replaced Long as ambassador to Italy. Senator Pittman reported back that Roosevelt "very promptly" told him "that he had other ideas about London" and that Cordell Hull would choose the next undersecretary.[5]

Three days after the inauguration, Long pursued another track, meeting with Jim Farley, the manager of the president's sucessful reelection campaign. Farley checked with the boss and gave Long the impression that Roosevelt would consider him "in connection with the Cabinet or some other high post." Long speculated that it might be in the War Department because "Farley had dwelt so long on that position."[6]

Roosevelt liked Long but didn't see him in any of the roles Long pined for. Perhaps he recalled the view of his late political adviser, Louis Howe, who had a poor opinion of Long. Perhaps he wanted someone with more experience for such critical positions.

The president was focused on finding a prominent American to serve as the next ambassador to London because, as his son Elliott put it, "Father's opinion of the British was at a low ebb and still descending." To represent the United States at the Court of St. James's, the president wanted someone who could prod the British to exhibit "a little more unselfish spine."[7] Long had been too easily taken in by Mussolini's charm and promises of peace. Roosevelt had time to think it over because Bingham would not resign his post in London until the fall. Breckinridge Long would have to wait for another appointment.

William Bullitt was apparently briefly considered for undersecretary of state, but he had been in Paris for only six months and, during that short time, had incurred the disdain of many in the Department of State for his freelance style of diplomacy. One of Bullitt's detractors, Norman Davis, a former undersecretary of state whom Roosevelt had designated as a "roving ambassador," wrote in his diary, "While Bullitt is a very brilliant and able man in so many ways, I fear that his feelings are so strong on certain subjects as to prejudice and becloud his judgment." Davis claimed that "several responsible persons" told him "that for the past year" Bullitt "has been quietly conveying the impression that he is the spokesman for the president in Europe and that he deals directly with the president, without going through the secretary of state. It is a tragedy and a disgrace that American representatives abroad do not pull together as a team for their country. We always seem to have some prima donna trying to play a personal role which can be done only to the detriment of the United States."[8] Bullitt certainly aspired to be the spokesman for Roosevelt in Europe, but, in fact, did deal directly with the president and only rarely engaged with the secretary of state.

In April, contrary to what he reportedly told Secretary Hull about leaving to him the choice for the next undersecretary of state, the president appointed Sumner Welles. Roosevelt had briefly considered "Judge" Walton Moore for the position, but the president had been impressed with Welles's tenure as assistant secretary of state for Latin American affairs, and later as ambassador to Cuba: Welles successfully engineered the removal of the Cuban president in favor of the opposition leader more favorable to United States interests. The foundation for the president's Good Neighbor policy was his view that Latin America should serve as an increasingly important bulwark against the spread of Nazism to the Americas.

The president had known Welles for many years and trusted his judgment, especially since Welles, like he, was a graduate of Groton and Harvard. As Eleanor explained in her diary, "Sumner's mother and mine were great friends and he went to school with my brother." She noted, "Franklin never knew him as well as I did but appointed him because of his abilities . . . I think Sumner was very much in sympathy with what Franklin wanted to do."[9]

Welles, however, was not a natural diplomat. He allegedly greeted visitors and colleagues who came to his office in the Department of State by standing, placing his fingers on the edge of his desk and bowing. Dean Acheson, a young lawyer at the time and future secretary of state, had been a class behind Welles at Groton and observed that Welles's "manner was formal to the point of stiffness. His voice, pitched much lower than would seem natural, though it had been so since he was a boy, lent a suggestion of pomposity."[10]

In Berlin, Ambassador Dodd greeted Welles's appointment with reflexive disdain. Though Dodd barely knew the new undersecretary, he nevertheless had contempt for the "owner of a mansion in Washington which outshines the White House in some respects and is about as large." Dodd had a similar view of Breckinridge Long, and noted in his diary that he had been "a little surprised to read a day or two ago in the press that

Roosevelt had spent a Sunday with Long in his Maryland mansion." He opined, "Politics is a strange game, even with a real man like Roosevelt."[11] Around the same time, Dodd heard from Judge Moore that he was going to be replaced in Berlin by Joseph Davies, the wealthy United States ambassador to the Soviet Union. Dodd considered Davies to be a wealthy dilettante and in his diary, scoffed that Davies was probably in London, spending "large sums to see the Coronation ceremony" of George VI.[12]

In actuality, there is no evidence Roosevelt ever considered moving Ambassador Davies from Moscow to Berlin, and it's not clear why Judge Moore passed on this misinformation to Ambassador Dodd. Nevertheless, Dodd railed against Davies, "The idea of having a man here who speaks no German, is insufficiently versed in European history or the background of the present situation and is preparing to spend $100,000 a year! At any rate, I shall postpone my return to the United States and also give the President my judgment of such a man in so important a position."[13]

The dissatisfaction with Dodd within the Department of State, fanned by Bullitt, had increased, and Dodd himself mentioned to a number of people that he was considering resigning. *New York Times* columnist Arthur Krock reported that Dodd had "long been one of the Department's worries . . . it is no secret in those generally discreet corridors that a change at Berlin has long been desired and would be welcomed at any time." According to Krock, Dodd had "impressed his diplomatic associates as a man inclined to forget his responsibilities as an envoy in his zeal as an historian and in his views as a contemporary observer of governing trends."[14]

Dodd was unhappy in Berlin, but could not bear the thought of being replaced by either Bullitt or Davies. The more he felt pressured to resign, the more he resisted leaving his post, and the more he felt emboldened to make his views known. He wrote Secretary Hull an ill-conceived letter complaining about "millionaires who speak no language but their own and know little of the history of the country to which they were appointed." Dodd made the arbitrary—and totally unrealistic—suggestion that the department should employ no more than two millionaires at any one time.[15] Although Cordell Hull was not a rich man, Dodd's continuous carping about the wealth of men like Welles and Davies, about the habits of Foreign Service officers, and about the budget of the department, undoubtedly grated on the secretary, especially when there were more important issues confronting the world.

Dodd made his position even more precarious in May when he wrote a letter to several United States senators, copied to the *Richmond Times-Dispatch,* in which he weighed in on the debate over the president's proposal to enlarge the Supreme Court. Dodd supported the president's plan and warned against "individuals of great wealth who wish a dictatorship and are ready to help a Huey Long."[16] Former senator Long had been assassinated in 1935, but Dodd used him as the American archetype of "politicians who think they may gain powers like those exercised in Europe." Finally, he made the wild claim that "one man I have been told by friends, who owns nearly a billion dollars, is ready to support such a program and, of course, control it." Dodd was likely referring to William Randolph Hearst, who at 74 years old was still very much alive and despised Roosevelt. A number of senators who opposed Roosevelt's court-packing plan took issue with Dodd's letter. Senator William Borah called the ambassador an "irresponsible scandalmonger," and "a disgrace to the country." Senator Gerald Nye wanted him subpoenaed by Congress and forced to testify publicly as to the name of the secret billionaire. Others asked Roosevelt to recall him from Berlin.[17]

Dodd's eccentric cables and irritable letters led some in the State Department to believe that he was not well. There was something to the beliefs: Dodd was experiencing severe "nervous headaches." Although he had only been back in Germany for less than eight months, his wife urged him to request another home leave to rest. Ambassador George Messersmith, who had left his post in Austria to be an assistant secretary of state back in Washington, worried about his former boss. Some years later, Messersmith wrote in an unpublished memoir, "It was quite obvious that something had happened to Dodd." According to Messersmith, "He was suffering from some form of mental deterioration."[18]

President Roosevelt, however, wasn't quite ready to give up on Dodd. He wrote his ambassador a reassuring letter, telling him that he was "frankly . . . delighted" with his letters to the senators supporting the court packing plan. Roosevelt absolved Dodd as "too honest and sincere to be a publicity expert" who "did not realize that one sentence about the billionaire would be the one thing in the whole letter seized on by the press and a certain type of false liberal like Borah." Reassured by the president, Dodd wrote Secretary Hull and once again asked for home leave.

When Dodd returned to the United States in July 1937, he told the press "the basic objective of some powers in Europe is to frighten and even destroy democracies everywhere."[19] Hans Dieckhoff, the Third Reich's ambassador to the United States, seized upon the statement and made a formal protest to Hull and to Welles, though he advised his foreign office in Berlin to let the matter drop, "so as not to cool the inclination to recall Dodd from Berlin, which has existed in various quarters for some time."[20] However, when Dodd met with President Roosevelt a few days later, the president asked him to remain at his post for a few more months and encouraged him to give as many lectures as possible and speak "the truth" about what was happening in Europe. Notwithstanding Dodd's eccentricities, the president knew his ambassador understood the threat that Hitler posed, while the American people did not.

By all accounts Joseph Kennedy had done a very good job as the chairman of the Securities and Exchange Commission. He had hired a young cadre of extraordinarily capable lawyers to assist him, and together, they had restored investor confidence in the financial markets by cracking down on insider trading and requiring that companies register and provide transparency about their finances and operations. After serving for just over a year, Kennedy, confident in his success, left the agency to return to the private sector. However, he still harbored dreams of serving in Roosevelt's cabinet as secretary of the treasury. In the summer of 1936, he published at his own expense a book entitled *I'm for Roosevelt*, in which he defended the New Deal as "founded upon a basic belief in the efficacy of the capitalist system." Roosevelt thanked Kennedy and called the book "splendid and . . . of real service, not only from a campaign point of view but also as a distinct step in sane education of the country."

While he appreciated Kennedy's work and loyalty, President Roosevelt had no intention of replacing Henry Morgenthau Jr. at the Treasury Department. Instead of a cabinet position, the president offered Kennedy the opportunity to be the first head of the Maritime Commission, which would build on his experience during World War I running a shipyard. It was an important position—though not nearly as significant as the chairmanship of the Securities and Exchange Commission—but it was certainly not what Kennedy had hoped for. Nevertheless, Kennedy set aside his higher ambition, responded to the president's call, and agreed to serve in the new position.

Now, five months later, Joseph Kennedy relaxed in the living room of his palatial estate, Marwood, on the banks of the Potomac River in Maryland. Kennedy poured a drink for his guest, James Roosevelt, the president's twenty-eight-year-old son. Though of different generations, the two men were friends and had done business together in the past. Jimmy, as he was known, praised Kennedy's return to government and thanked him for serving once again in his father's administration. Kennedy smiled and said, "I've been thinking about it." And then he landed a bombshell: "I'm intrigued by the thought of being the first Irishman to be Ambassador from the US to the Court of St. James's." Jimmy, taken aback, replied, "It certainly would set quite a precedent." Still, he promised to talk to his father.[21]

"He laughed so hard he almost toppled from his wheelchair," Jimmy wrote later in his memoirs.[22] The president had offered ambassadorships to Kennedy before, but they had been for relatively insignificant countries. In Roosevelt's mind, appointing Kennedy to be ambassador to the United Kingdom, especially during such a critical time in Europe, was out of the question. Kennedy was too coarse, too manipulative, and too untrustworthy. Yet only months later, the president would revise his opinion.

After the July 4 recess, the Senate reconvened to consider the president's court-packing plan. Roosevelt and his supporters in Congress believed they still held a slim majority in favor of the legislation. Then, following a week of rancorous floor debate, the president's most trusted and most powerful ally, Senate majority leader Joseph T. Robinson, fell dead in a hotel room, clutching a copy of the congressional record in one hand. After Robinson's death, momentum for the plan faltered. Vice President Garner told the president, "You are beat. You haven't got the votes." On July 22, the bill was remanded to committee and never reemerged for consideration. It was a colossal defeat for a president who until this point had enjoyed an almost free hand with legislation before Congress. Although rulings by the Supreme Court had not directly impacted Roosevelt's foreign policy, the president now knew his previously bulletproof coalition on Capitol Hill could no longer be counted on in any sphere of policy, whether domestic or foreign.

20

JOE, JUST LOOK AT YOUR LEGS

Adolf Hitler wanted to impress Benito Mussolini on the Italian dictator's first state visit to Germany. The führer greeted Il Duce at the station in Munich when his private train arrived on September 25, 1937. Over the next few days, Hitler and his guest attended army maneuvers in Mecklenburg, visited the Krupp Works factory in Essen, and inspected a chemical plant in Hanover. When they arrived by automobile in Berlin on September 27, Mussolini delighted in seeing that the boulevards had been decorated with both fascist and Nazi symbols illuminated by floodlights. The following day, Hitler and Mussolini addressed a mass rally, estimated at more than eight hundred thousand, at the Maifield, which had been constructed as part of the Olympic complex. Hitler referred to Il Duce as one of the rare leaders who "are not made by history, but make history themselves." Mussolini in turn pledged to support Hitler "to the very end."[1]

Earlier in the year, the führer had dispatched emissaries to Rome to cultivate Mussolini and "smooth some ruffled Italian feathers on the question of Austria." According to William Shirer, Mussolini's September visit "was the go ahead for which Hitler had been waiting."[2] In addition to pledging their allegiance to each other, the two leaders agreed to support General Franco in Spain.

President Roosevelt viewed the meeting of the fascist dictators as a particularly ominous sign. At one time, he believed Mussolini might act as a positive force in Europe, a hope once fortified by reports that Mussolini disliked Hitler. But Il Duce had failed to respond to Roosevelt's request for disarmament, and his invasion of Ethiopia revealed the strutting, totalitarian bully behind the façade of statesman. Now in Berlin, Mussolini and Hitler were photographed smiling broadly at one another. Roosevelt understood that a fascist alliance on the European continent—something both Bullitt and Dodd had warned him about a year earlier—was growing increasingly likely.

A week later, President Roosevelt delivered a speech in Chicago in which he called for "a quarantine" against the "epidemic of world lawlessness" perpetrated by authoritarian nations. Convinced that war in Europe (and Asia) was now inevitable unless the United States could somehow forestall it, Roosevelt had hoped to gauge public opinion. He proposed that America use its economic power to isolate countries such as Japan, Italy, and Germany. Secretary of the Interior Harold Ickes had suggested the use of the word *quarantine,* and Roosevelt thought it brilliant because it provided an alternative to the threat of military force on the one hand, and to strict American neutrality on the other, instead offering something of a middle ground.[3] Nevertheless, the press framed the speech as a radical departure from the neutrality legislation that Roosevelt had signed in 1936 and what Congress had updated only months earlier. The reaction was swift, and overwhelmingly negative. Not surprisingly, William Randolph Hearst used his newspapers to whip up public opposition to interference in the affairs of other nations. Several Republican congressmen suggested Roosevelt should be impeached. The president told Sam Rosenman, his speechwriter, "It's a terrible thing to look over your shoulder when you are trying to lead—and find no one there."[4]

Seeking other ways to rein in aggressor nations, the president asked Undersecretary Sumner Welles for his thoughts. Welles produced a memorandum, which he first sent to Secretary Hull, calling for an international disarmament conference. The undersecretary suggested that on Armistice Day, November 11, the president should invite the international diplomatic corps to the East Room of the White House, make the case for disarmament as critical to world peace, and then formally call for a conference. The proposal would have undoubtedly appealed to the president, who had floated a similar idea the year before. However, Secretary Hull pointed out to Welles that Hitler, and others before him, had violated peace treaties already in force and were unlikely to participate in a conference, and even if they did attend, any commitment they might make would probably be meaningless. Hull vetoed Welles's plan.[5]

Still determined to find a way to confront the increasingly bellicose behavior of Hitler and Mussolini, Roosevelt decided in late 1937 that it was time to make changes among the ambassador corps. Robert Bingham, ambassador to the United Kingdom, returned to the United States in late August and, after a series of meetings at the State Department, visited the president at Hyde Park. The press had picked up rumors that Bingham might resign. While he publicly denied that he was relinquishing his post, Bingham was experiencing frequent recurrences of malaria that he had contracted as a young man. The ambassador likely told Roosevelt that he would leave his post as soon as the president picked a new ambassador. As it turned out, Bingham had a much more serious illness than malaria. He went back to the United Kingdom in October, but returned to the United States only weeks later. His doctors then diagnosed a malignant tumor. Bingham died the following month.

Roosevelt still harbored serious reservations about Joseph Kennedy, but he was beginning to reconsider appointing him ambassador to the Court of St. James's. While the president continued to bristle at Kennedy's arrogance, at the same time, he admired Kennedy's energy, toughness, and independent-mindedness. Above all, Kennedy had demonstrated loyalty even when Roosevelt had repeatedly denied him a preferred appointment. The president invited Kennedy to the White House to discuss the ambassadorship in what turned out to be one of the most bizarre job interviews in history.

James Roosevelt accompanied Kennedy to the meeting. When they entered the Oval Office, President Roosevelt was seated behind his desk.

After exchanging pleasantries, the president reportedly asked in a deadpan tone, "Would you mind taking your pants down?" A stunned Kennedy asked if he had heard the president correctly and if he was serious. "Yes, indeed," replied Roosevelt. Kennedy looked bewildered but, after several seconds of awkward silence, loosened his suspenders, dropped his trousers, and stood self-consciously before the president in his underwear. Roosevelt smiled and said, "Someone who saw you in a bathing suit once told me something I now know to be true. Joe, just look at your legs. You are about the most bow-legged man I have ever seen. Don't you know that the Ambassador to the Court of St. James's has to go through an induction ceremony in which he wears knee breeches and silk stockings? Can you imagine how you will look? When photos of our new ambassador appear all over the world we'll be a laughingstock. You are just not right for the job, Joe."[6]

A humiliated Kennedy asked if it might be possible to wear a cutaway coat and long striped pants to the ceremony. The president, clearly enjoying himself, shook his head. "Well, Joe, you know how the British are about tradition. There's no way you are going to get permission and I must name an Ambassador soon."[7] However, Roosevelt agreed to give Kennedy a few weeks to see what could be worked out.

After Kennedy left the White House, the president and his son James had a long laugh. If Roosevelt wanted someone else to be his ambassador in London, there was obviously no need for the meeting, much less the extraordinary exchange over what Kennedy should wear at his induction ceremony. In all likelihood, Roosevelt already intended to nominate Kennedy when he invited him to the Oval Office, but wanted to humble him and to let him know who was boss. Roosevelt had started to like the idea that the appointment might raise eyebrows in Great Britain. He told his son that sending an Irish Catholic to the Court of St. James's was "a great joke, the greatest joke in the world."

The president also decided that it was finally time to replace his ambassador in Berlin. He knew that Ambassador Dodd had flirted with resigning on several occasions.

Only days before his scheduled departure for Berlin, Dodd met once more with President Roosevelt. According to Dodd, they had a wide-ranging conversation in which "the President revealed his anxiety about foreign affairs."[8] Dodd told the president that he planned to leave his post the following March. Roosevelt did not try to dissuade him.

Dodd then turned the conversation to the question of his successor. He had seen Ambassador Bullitt's name mentioned as his possible replacement and thought this would be a mistake. Ambassador Dodd urged Roosevelt to instead appoint Professor James T. Shotwell of Columbia University. Shotwell was president of the League of Nations Association, and Dodd knew him from academia. Most important to Dodd, Shotwell was ideologically grounded in the Wilsonian tradition. The president commended Dodd's service and assured the ambassador that he would consider Shotwell. Roosevelt then casually remarked that he might also consider Hugh Wilson, the current ambassador to Switzerland. The president didn't tell Dodd that Bullitt had recommended Wilson for the job.[9]

As Dodd stood up to leave, Roosevelt said to him, "Write me personally about things in Europe. I can read your handwriting very well."[10] Dodd may have thought this an innocent remark by the president, but Secretary Hull had likely informed the president that Dodd's letters, increasingly written in longhand, had become notorious within the Department of State. Apparently, Dodd had ceased to trust the stenographers, and wrote long, rambling letters and memoranda in cursive. The problem was that no one in the Department could decipher his handwriting, so Assistant Secretary George Messersmith, who had served with Dodd, was often called in to read and translate the missives.[11] It was another indication that Dodd was not an altogether well man.

Dodd returned to Berlin on October 29, 1937, with mixed emotions. He was content that the next few months would be his last ones in Germany, but felt despondent about and helpless to deal with the steadily worsening situation. The Nazis were plainly preparing for war. Nothing had changed, except perhaps that Hitler had stepped up his persecution of the Jews. Dodd wearily scrawled in his diary, "In Berlin once more.

What more can I do."[12] A few days later, he wrote, "I feel I must go because of the unbearable tension of Nazi Germany."[13]

Ambassador Bullitt continued to view himself not only as the United States ambassador to France but increasingly as a kind of United States ambassador-at-large in Europe. He spent three days in Warsaw in mid-November, where he was assured that the Poles would do everything possible for peace and not align themselves with any nation. Next, Bullitt visited Germany, arriving on November 18. That evening, the French ambassador, André François-Poncet, gave a dinner party for Bullitt, attended by forty guests. The next day, Dodd hosted a luncheon for Bullitt with twenty-four guests, including Dr. Hjalmar Schacht, the German financier. In the afternoon, Bullitt paid a call on Reichsmarschall Goering. Never a fan of Bullitt, but perhaps feeling that it wasn't worth his time anymore, Dodd didn't elaborate in his diary on his colleague's visit.

Bullitt, however, wrote extensively about his trip to Berlin. In a lengthy letter to President Roosevelt, he recounted his meeting with Goering, which he characterized as "a source of amusement to say nothing of instruction. It was really an amazing conversation and I hated to have to put it into respectable form for the Department." Bullitt visited Goering at his private residence, "a house in the middle of a huge block of public buildings." Bullitt described Goering's office as "a big room with a huge oak table at one end; a table about fifteen feet long, six feet broad, and at least four inches thick. There were three chairs, all built in mammoth proportions and covered with cerise velvet, trimmed with gold. The chairs were so big that Goering looked rather less than the size of a normal man and, as you know, he strongly resembles the hind end on an elephant. In my chair I must have looked like some sort of animated flea." After his humorous depiction of Goering, Bullitt took direct aim at Ambassador Dodd. "For any man who spoke good German and had some brains and bluntness it would, I think, be the easiest thing in the world to have a direct relationship with him [Goering]."[14]

Notwithstanding his pointed barbs, Bullitt did not want the president to think he was a troublemaker, so he noted:

In the account of the conversation which I am sending to the Department, I have left out, for obvious reasons, his [Goering's] reference to Dodd. After he [Goering] expressed to me his desire to have better relations with the US, he then said that he desired to say something to me, which he hoped I would not resent. The matter was a delicate one. But he considered it simply disastrous that there should be no American Ambassador in Berlin. Neither he nor anyone else in the German Government could recognize Dodd as an American Ambassador. Dodd was too filled with venomous hatred of Germany to have any relations with members of the Government, and in fact did not exist.[15]

In his letter to the president, Ambassador Bullitt was not yet done with Dodd. He also recounted his conversation with the German foreign minister: "Most of my conversation with Neurath was taken up by Neurath's remarks on the subject of Dodd which were far more violent than Goering's . . . Neurath said that he desired to have better relations with the United States instead of worse relations and, therefore, did not wish to be compelled to ask for Dodd's withdrawal; but the fact was that the German Government could no longer tolerate his presence in Berlin and would in the near future ask for his withdrawal unless the American Government should withdraw him." According to Bullitt, Neurath concluded their meeting by remarking "I want to impress upon you once more that Dodd's presence in Berlin is intolerable."[16]

Finally, Bullitt told the president that he had engaged in conversations with both the Italian and French ambassadors to Germany. He claimed the Italian ambassador "felt . . . a great opportunity was being lost by keeping Dodd in Berlin." Bullitt noted his surprise when the French ambassador, François-Poncet, told him:

Bullitt, for God's sake, get Dodd moved out of Berlin. He used to be bad as an Ambassador, but now he is impossible. He even scolds me because I invite members of the German Government to my Embassy. And he embarrasses all of us ambassadors by taking the line that we should not be ambassadors to the Government to which we are accredited but should carry on a sort of holy crusade against National Socialism. He is conducting a personal crusade against the Nazi Government and has no patience with anyone who will not join him in that crusade, forgetting that a crusader against a particular government should be anything in the world except an ambassador accredited to that government.

According to Bullitt, François-Poncet went on to say, "He felt that at the present time it might be possible for the U.S. to exercise great influence in Berlin in the direction of European peace, provided we had a really first-rate ambassador, and that he hoped ardently he would soon have an American colleague with whom he could work."[17] There is no way of knowing, of course, if François-Poncet actually said all of this to Bullitt—the French ambassador did not memorialize the conversation— though it is worth noting that François-Poncet's "advice" to Bullitt hewed exactly to that of Bullitt's previous advice to Roosevelt.

Bullitt closed his letter to the president by providing a broad assessment of the threat posed by Hitler and the Third Reich. Bullitt wrote:

The situation today is the following: Germany is increasing in military strength more rapidly than France and England combined . . . The British, so nearly as I can discover, are at the moment on the following line: They will finally, deviously, by silences and tacit approvals, as the lesser evil, permit Hitler to take Austria; take the Germans of Czechoslovakia, and dominate Central Europe and the Balkans . . . I am less sure than I was a few weeks ago that France will actually go to the support of Czechoslovakia in case of a German attack . . . The only way that I can see halting that growth of German strength, which I regard as inevitable . . . is by a general effort to make the giving of these concessions to Germany a part of a general plan of unification of Europe.

Bullitt tried to end his letter on a somewhat hopeful note: "I believe that we can have a considerable influence in bringing about such a result . . . I realize that all of this may sound as if I had become a Polly-anna. I don't think I have. I admit that the chances are against peace and in favor of war, and I believe that the year 1938 will be decisive, but I think we ought to make the effort to preserve peace—just as quietly as possible . . . Love and Good luck."[18]

Although Bullitt's hopes for Europe proved illusory—his view that giving concessions to Hitler was frighteningly naive—his prediction that 1938 would be a decisive year proved correct. His criticisms of Ambassador Dodd were not new, and more importantly, President Roosevelt had already made the decision to remove Dodd ahead of schedule. The same day that Bullitt wrote his letter, Ambassador Dodd received a curt telegram from Secretary Hull marked "Strictly Confidential." The ambassador was surprised and confused when he read, "Much as the President regrets any personal inconvenience which may be occasioned to you, he desires me to request you arrange to leave Berlin if possible by December 15 and in any event not later than Christmas, because of the complications with which you are familiar and which threaten to increase."[19] Dodd was crestfallen; he wanted to leave Germany, but to do so on his own terms. He appealed the decision, promising to leave in March 1938, as had been originally planned. His request was denied. Interestingly, Dodd didn't blame Hull, or Roosevelt, or even Bullitt. Writing in his diary, Dodd accused Undersecretary Sumner Welles "for this violation of my understanding with the President." Dodd claimed to "have recently seen signs of [Welles's] opposition to everything I have recommended" and asserted, "It is well known to me that he is violently opposed to my policies in regard to public service."[20]

In the brief time that he had been undersecretary, Welles had accrued significant influence within the Department of State, and more importantly, his views held sway with President Roosevelt. The president usually opened his cabinet meetings by turning first to his secretary of state and asking, "Cordell, what's the news from abroad?" Hull seemed invariably to reply, "Mr. President, the reports are not very encouraging."

Historian John Gunther observed, "If Sumner Welles were present in place of Mr. Hull, the reply would be swift, precise and comprehensive. FDR must have wished at least ten thousand times that Welles, not Hull, was the actual secretary."[21] The president admired his secretary of state, even if he found him somewhat dull and plodding. He had no intention of replacing him. Hull continued to serve a useful purpose for the administration as an expert on trade and a liaison to the Senate on critical issues such as neutrality. Job titles weren't all that important to Roosevelt; he tended to seek out the people like Welles, whom he felt offered him the best advice, no matter where they were situated in the bureaucracy. Roosevelt had been hearing from many quarters that Ambassador Dodd needed to be replaced. Bullitt, of course, had made his views known to the president, but as Dodd presumed, it was likely Welles who ultimately precipitated his dismissal.

While Roosevelt refused to reconsider Ambassador Dodd's plea to remain in Germany another four months, James Roosevelt informed Joseph Kennedy that the president had indeed decided to appoint Kennedy to the Court of St. James's in London. Kennedy was elated and looked forward to hearing personally from the president. A few days later, however, James telephoned Kennedy, who was having dinner with *New York Times* columnist Arthur Krock at Kennedy's rented estate, Marwood, on the banks of the Potomac, to ask if he could drop by. James arrived at Marwood a little later in the evening, and Krock recalled that Kennedy and young Roosevelt "retired to another room for a half hour or so," after which James Roosevelt departed and Kennedy returned. Joe was angry. "You know what Jimmy proposed?" Kennedy asked Krock. "That instead of going to London, I become Secretary of Commerce! Well, I'm not going to. FDR promised me London, and I told Jimmy to tell his father that's the job, and the only one, I'll accept.'"[22]

President Roosevelt was earnest in his desire to reward Kennedy for the loyalty shown in both of his presidential campaigns, as well as for the good work he had done at the Securities and Exchange Commission and more recently at the Maritime Commission. He knew appointing Kennedy as ambassador to the Court of St. James's would be controversial, but decided to move ahead after Kennedy's ironclad refusal to accept anything else. Kennedy, however, did not entirely trust the president, given that Roosevelt had clearly tried to back away from the original offer, so Kennedy shared the news of his impending nomination with Krock. On December 9, 1937, Krock wrote a front-page story in *The New York Times*, revealing that President Roosevelt would soon publicly nominate Kennedy as ambassador, asserting that it was a "complete surprise" to Kennedy. Roosevelt, annoyed by the story, telephoned Krock, who would only say that his source had come from within the Department of State.

Henry Morgenthau Jr. was both surprised and aghast after reading the news of the president's impending appointment, but Roosevelt assured his secretary of the treasury that while he, too, considered Kennedy "a very dangerous man," he had "made arrangements to have Joe Kennedy watched hourly." The president declared, "The first time he opens his mouth and criticizes me, I will fire him."[23] It's not entirely clear what Roosevelt meant in reference to the "arrangements" he had made, but there is evidence to suggest that Roosevelt asked FBI director J. Edgar Hoover to keep an eye on Kennedy. From time to time, Hoover sent the president newspaper stories from the British press as well as occasional reports from sources in London.

It is also not clear why Roosevelt moved ahead with Kennedy's appointment if he had such serious misgivings. Roosevelt was now considering the possibility of running for a third term and knew he would again need Kennedy's support. Or he may have worried that Kennedy himself might run for president—there were certainly rumors that Kennedy harbored ambitions for it—and the president wanted to remove him from the playing field. More likely, Roosevelt wanted to shake up a British government that he found opportunist yet weak in the face of rising fascism in Europe.

Months earlier, Neville Chamberlain, Chancellor of the Exchequer, had become prime minister. Roosevelt didn't personally know the new prime minister, but after Chamberlain's victory in May 1937, Roosevelt had invited him to visit the White House. However, the invitation had been declined, contributing to Roosevelt's previously held view of British arrogance. Regardless of the slight, the president was more concerned than ever that Britain would fail to deal with an impending European crisis.

His concern was heightened in November 1937 when Lord Halifax, a leader in the House of Lords and a future foreign secretary, met with Hitler in Berlin. Driven from the airport to Hitler's offices, Halifax, sitting in the back seat, had opened the car door and initially mistaken Hitler for a footman, nearly handing him his overcoat before recognizing that it was the führer standing before him. Despite the initial awkwardness, Halifax believed the meeting had been constructive as Hitler laid out his vision in a general way for the peaceful creation of a greater Germany to include Austria and other German-speaking enclaves in Europe. Halifax reported to the prime minister and his cabinet, "We ought to get on good terms with Germany." Also anxious for a settlement with Germany, Chamberlain proposed continuing the talks and appeared willing to offer significant concessions to Hitler.[24]

Even before being considered as ambassador to the United Kingdom, Kennedy had made it clear to anyone who would listen that America should not involve itself in another European war. Roosevelt knew Kennedy was unpredictable and anything but diplomatic, but if war did come to Europe, the president believed someone as pugnacious and outspoken as Kennedy could be useful in communicating American interests. Just before Christmas in 1937, Roosevelt publicly announced Kennedy's appointment in a press conference.

The official announcement was met with decidedly mixed reviews. Eleanor Roosevelt privately referred to the ambassador-designate as "that awful Joe Kennedy."[25] Boake Carter, a British American news commentator, one of the most popular radio personalities in the United States, and a friend of Kennedy's, warned him that he would soon tire of acting as a liaison between the U.S. State Department and the British Foreign Office. Kennedy assured Carter that he had an agreement with the president that he would have significant input into developing policy. Carter was unimpressed: "My dear lad, agreements mean nothing in [Roosevelt's] life. They never have. They never will." Carter told Kennedy, "The job of Ambassador to London needs not only honesty, sincerity, faith and an abounding courage—it needs skill brought by years of training. And that, Joe, you simply don't possess . . . Joe, in so complicated a job, there is simply no place for amateurs."[26] While others shared concerns similar to Boake Carter's, Kennedy had one constituency firmly on his side: Kennedy's wife and children were thrilled with the appointment.

Four days after Christmas, Dodd and his wife left Berlin and drove to Hamburg, where they boarded the *Manhattan*, an American ocean liner. Dodd recorded in his diary, "When we walked about the boat, we found that more than half of the second-class passengers were Germans hoping to locate in the United States. More than half of these were Jews. But at our table in the dining room were several Nazis or Nazi sympathizers, one a West Virginia woman, the wife of the Yugoslav Minister to London. She described to us the London situation where there are apparently many aristocratic Fascists or Nazis now."[27]

The *Manhattan* arrived in New York on January 6, 1938. Interviewed shortly after his arrival by an Associated Press reporter, Dodd stated that he "doubted if any American envoy who held his ideals of democracy could represent his country successfully among the Germans at the present time." He was tired and worn down, which only added to his pessimism about Europe's future.

A few days later, Dodd made his way to Washington for exit interviews at the Department of State and a final meeting with the president. Dodd wrote in his diary, "When I saw the President and told him a little of what I thought of Undersecretary Welles and his method, no reply was made. When I talked with Secretary Hull, he confirmed in part what I thought had been done to recall me when it had been understood that I was to retire in March, 1938."[28]

Dodd was bitter, especially resentful that he had been required to needlessly spend his own money at the embassy: "For me to have gone back to Berlin on November 1, and for my wife to have spent over $1,000 on furniture, became a disgrace when I received a notice on November 23 to return in January." Somewhat sanctimoniously, he declared, "There were and are still officials in the State Department who do not like me or the thing I tried to stand for. . . . I have been four and a half years in Europe with the hope of serving my country. How much one could do is an open question."[29]

However, in the end, Dodd, perhaps more than any of his ambassadorial colleagues, grasped the historical context of Europe's growing crisis. In his diary he reflected on the failure to prevent senseless conflict:

> The present-day world has learned nothing from the World War. Instead of keeping the treaties of 1919–1923, nearly all peoples have violated them. Twice as much money is being spent now each year in preparation for another war as we spent in 1913, in spite of the fact that nearly all peoples are bearing the greatest debts known to history. Shall we be confronted by another world war? And would isolation be possible for any great industrial country? . . . So many influential men have failed to see that inventions, industrial revolution and financial relations have brought mankind to a point where cooperation and peace are the fit conditions of prosperity for the masses of men everywhere.[30]

Dodd's remaining ray of hope when he left the State Department was a still unshaken confidence in President Roosevelt's leadership. He continued to hope that somehow the president who had shied away from rearmament in the United States, fought for workers in their quest to earn a living wage, and confronted the nation's financial institutions to make them accountable to the public, would find a peaceful way to avoid the horror of another world war.

As 1937 came to a close, President Roosevelt shared Dodd's hope of avoiding war, but as he took the measure of Hitler in Germany and Mussolini in Italy, he increasingly felt—as his ambassadors had warned—that conflict seemed unavoidable and that the United States might not be able to remain neutral. Complicating matters, the economy had once again stalled. While unemployment had been halved during his first term, largely through government spending, the president, spurred on by conservatives in Congress, decided to suspend deficit spending and work toward balancing the federal budget in 1937. The approach backfired when a deep recession and rising unemployment immediately followed.

Elliott Roosevelt described Christmas in the White House in 1937 as "subdued." He later wrote, "There was a tree, of course, and a turkey, which Father carefully carved into paper-thin slices as a matter of pride in the skill, and economical besides." Notwithstanding the challenges he faced as president, for Roosevelt, "it was a day for an extra drink in celebration." As Elliott recalled, his ever-optimistic father offered a toast to mark the occasion: "'How about another little sippy?' he would say as he stirred the martinis or his own special formula for rum punch. 'Love thy neighbor and thine enemy, too.'"[31]

21

EVERYBODY DOWN THE LINE
WILL BE SENT TO SIAM

O n March 8, 1938, U.S. Justice Stanley Reed administered the oath
of office to Joseph Kennedy in a brief ceremony in the Oval Office, as the president looked on, and a gaggle of reporters snapped
photographs. A few days later, Kennedy traveled to Springwood, the
Roosevelt estate in Hyde Park, New York, for a final meeting with the
president before departing for London. Roosevelt returned from Sunday
church service and greeted Kennedy in the wood-paneled library of the
Italianate-style house. The two men engaged in an hour-long discussion of European affairs. As Kennedy stood to bid Roosevelt farewell, a
relaxed president could not resist teasing his newly minted ambassador
one last time, "You'll be a knock out in knee britches."[1] Kennedy forced
a smile.

President Roosevelt gave Kennedy few instructions and no concrete
expectations for his ambassadorship. Kennedy would later claim that the
president only told him, "Don't forget that this country is determined to
be neutral in the event of any war." However, it seems unlikely Roosevelt
actually promoted neutrality to Kennedy; the president was always one
to keep his options open. The claim also contradicts Kennedy's stated

frustration with the Department of State, and particularly with Secretary of State Hull, for the failure to provide him with a clear statement of American foreign policy toward Britain. Of course for his part, Kennedy had an interest in being remembered as having worked diligently to fulfill the president's agenda.[2]

Whatever the president's parting words had been, once in London, Ambassador Kennedy got off to an auspicious beginning. He met with Prime Minister Neville Chamberlain, and the two men immediately established a bond. Both were former businessmen who viewed international relations through what they believed was a pragmatic lens; they were in complete agreement that war with Germany should be avoided at all costs. Chamberlain hoped Kennedy could persuade President Roosevelt to support a policy of accommodation toward Germany. Others in the British government echoed the prime minister's view to Kennedy, including the new foreign secretary, Lord Halifax, and Ambassador Bullitt's cousin, Lady Astor.

In his first letter to the president, Ambassador Kennedy reported that, after making the official rounds in government, he believed the British were most interested in having the United States "stay prosperous and build a strong navy." According to Kennedy, everyone he talked to felt the United States would be "very foolish" to mix in European affairs; he also included in his letter some advice for the president: "The time is going to come, after Chamberlain has made the political offers necessary, for you to make a worldwide gesture and base it completely on an economic standard."[3] It was an early indication that the ambassador believed he had been sent to London not just to implement directives from the State Department but also to make foreign policy.

Kennedy's large, photogenic family contributed to the warm reception he received in London. The British tabloid newspapers gushed about "America's nine-child envoy." His popularity was reinforced back in the United States when *Life* magazine ran two pages of photographs featuring all the Kennedy children, with the caption "The most politically ingratiating family since Theodore Roosevelt's." President Roosevelt was surprised—but pleased—with the favorable publicity his ambassador received.[4] Missy LeHand wrote Bullitt, "Joe is a different human being, completely released." She added playfully, "And of course the country is saved again for a time."[5]

Now that he was no longer ambassador, William Dodd felt liberated to talk openly about the threat of Nazi Germany. At a dinner given in his honor in January 1938, Dodd declared, "Mankind is in grave danger, but democratic governments seem not to know what to do." Dodd predicted, "If they do nothing, Western civilization, religious, personal and economic freedom are in grave danger."[6] After reading a report of Dodd's speech the following day, the German ambassador to the United States, Hans Luther, stormed into Secretary Hull's office to demand the State Department silence the former ambassador. Hull reminded the German envoy that Dodd was now a private citizen, his views were his own, and the department had no power to prevent him from speaking. A month later in Rochester, New York, in a speech before a Jewish audience, Dodd warned that if Hitler gained control of Austria, he would continue to seize territory wherever he could in Europe. He predicted, for the most part with accuracy, that Czechoslovakia would be next, then Poland, then Romania. He worried that Europe's democracies were blind to the threat of Hitler and noted that Great Britain was "terribly exasperated but also terribly desirous of peace," suggesting Chamberlain's government was supine in the face of impending disaster.[7]

Speaking at gatherings of academics, religious congregations, and business clubs around the country, Dodd hoped to raise awareness of the Nazi threat. His quest was an uphill battle, not only because the country remained fervently isolationist but also because there was a disturbing amount of support for Hitler and Mussolini in the United States. American fascists and anti-Semites joined organizations like William Dudley Pelley's Silver Shirts. Modeled after Hitler's Brownshirts and Mussolini's Blackshirts, Pelley's membership claimed to represent "the cream, the head and flower of our Protestant Christian manhood." In Kansas, evangelist Gerald Winrod ran for the United States Senate on a platform blaming "the international Jew" for "the scourge of communism."

Although Winrod lost the Republican primary race, he received fifty-three thousand votes.[8]

A few months later, twenty-two thousand supporters of the German American Federation attended a boisterous rally in Madison Square Garden in New York, where they listened to a number of speeches praising Hitler and denigrating Jews. At one point, a Jewish protester rushed the podium where the federation's German-born leader, Fritz Kuhn, was speaking. Kuhn's brown-shirted bodyguards sized the man and beat him mercilessly while the crowd repeatedly gave the Nazi salute and shouted, "Free America!" Outside the arena, an even larger crowd of counter-demonstrators, estimated at close to one hundred thousand, filled the surrounding midtown Manhattan streets, chanting anti-Nazi slogans. Hoping to avoid a clash between the two sides, New York City mayor Fiorello La Guardia and Police Commissioner Lewis Valentine encircled the Garden with a security cordon of seventeen hundred police, including mounted officers.

In early March 1938, President Roosevelt formally announced that Hugh Wilson would be Dodd's replacement in Germany. The former ambassador to Switzerland had been serving as an assistant secretary of state in Washington, and both Ambassador Bullitt and Undersecretary Welles championed the nomination. His appointment was not a complete surprise; news of Wilson's nomination had been leaked to *The New York Times* two months earlier, leading the president to send a memorandum to Undersecretary Welles declaring, "We must stop the leaks in regard to the diplomatic appointments. It is becoming a positive scandal." Only half jokingly, Roosevelt threatened, "I think the time has come to announce if in the future there is any leak, everybody down the line will be sent to Siam!"[9]

Ambassador Bullitt wrote President Roosevelt, congratulating him on choosing Wilson: "I do believe the chances for peace in Europe are increased definitely by your appointment of Hugh to Berlin, and I thank you profoundly."[10]

Bullitt's optimism turned out to be misplaced; only a week after

Roosevelt's announcement, and before Wilson arrived in Berlin, Adolf Hitler set in motion a plan to annex neighboring Austria, the first of several countries that Germany would occupy on the European continent.

Austrian chancellor Kurt von Schuschnigg, a member of the right-wing Christian Socialist Party, had assumed power in 1934 after the Nazis murdered his predecessor, Engelbert Dollfuss. Schuschnigg considered Austrians to be Germans by heritage, but he strongly opposed Hitler's plans to absorb Austria into the Third Reich. Angered by Schuschnigg's obstinacy, Hitler summoned him to his fortified retreat, the Berghof in the Bavarian Alps, where he berated him for continuing to promote Austrian independence. After a tense lunch, during which the führer did most of the talking, Hitler's new foreign minister, Joachim von Ribbentrop, handed Schuschnigg a document memorializing the führer's demand that the Austrian chancellor turn over his government to the Nazis. Schuschnigg reluctantly signed the document, but a few weeks later made one last desperate attempt to maintain Austria's independence, announcing a plebiscite to be held on March 13 to allow the Austrian people to vote for a united and sovereign country.[11]

Furious with Schuschnigg, Hitler was adamant the plebiscite should not take place but hesitated to order German military intervention to stop it. He worried about jeopardizing relations with his fellow fascist, Mussolini, who had long supported Austria; worried that neighboring Czechoslovakia might ally with Austria; and worried about the inevitable condemnation, and perhaps armed resistance, from the more democratic countries on the Continent, not to mention his archenemy, Russia. Nevertheless, Hitler gambled and demanded that Schuschnigg include Nazis in his cabinet, or confront a German military invasion. It was enough to persuade Schuschnigg to call off the impending plebiscite. Schuschnigg undoubtedly considered the fate of his predecessor, Dollfuss, and meekly submitted his resignation. The führer then arranged for one of the high-ranking Austrian Nazis loyal to him to send a telegram imploring Germany to invade Austria to save it from catastrophe. Instead of the plebiscite on March 13, Hitler's troops marched into Vienna, cheered by thousands of Austrians lining the streets. The Nazis immediately took control of the government and proclaimed the success of the Anschluss: the annexation of Austria by Germany.[12] Three hundred miles away, Hitler announced the news to the Reichstag whose members stood and gave the führer a lengthy, standing ovation with the Nazi salute.

The international response to the Anschluss was decidedly muted. Mussolini did nothing. Neither did Chamberlain in Great Britain, nor Blum in France. Officials in Czechoslovakia referred to Germany's annexation as "nothing more than a family affair." Secretary of State Hull conferred with senior officials in the Department of State, but the United States did little to protest the Anschluss, subsequently withdrawing embassy personnel from Vienna in acknowledgment that the Austrian government no longer had any decision-making authority. Breckinridge Long wrote in his diary that Hitler's speech to the Reichstag had been "a very able presentation of the German point of view." He claimed somewhat bizarrely that Hitler "desires an extension of German influence to the east and southeast, but that does not mean military or political control or domination or annexation."[13]

At a press conference two days after the Anschluss, asked if the events in Austria would have any impact on the United States' "defense situation," Roosevelt responded, "None at all—as recommended by me."[14] However, William Shirer succinctly summed up the significance of Hitler's bloodless conquest: "Without firing a shot . . . Hitler had added seven million subjects to the Reich and gained a strategic position of immense value to his future plans."[15]

Some of Hitler's new subjects, Austrian Jews, now found themselves in extreme peril. Among them was Sigmund Freud, whom the Nazis considered a heretic. The American consul in Vienna, John C. Wiley, had worked for Ambassador Bullitt in Russia and knew that the ambassador and Freud had coauthored an unpublished biography of Woodrow Wilson. The day after the Anschluss, Wiley telegraphed his former boss in Paris: "Fear Freud, despite age and illness, in danger." Bullitt immediately telephoned President Roosevelt, who directed Secretary Hull to call Wiley.[16] Roosevelt told Hull he wanted the consul to raise the possibility of Freud's emigration with Viennese authorities, but not to divulge that anyone in a position of power in Washington, D.C., was interested in the doctor's case because it could result in Freud becoming a bargaining chip.

A few days later, Nazi authorities visited Freud's apartment and demanded to search the premises. Consul Wiley had wisely sent his wife, Irena, and two officials from the embassy to provide diplomatic protection to the doctor. As the Americans looked on, the Nazis ransacked the apartment and confiscated Freud's passport and all the money he had on the premises. However, they neither harmed nor arrested the doctor or his family.

Bullitt knew that the Nazis in both Austria and Germany were extorting vast sums of money from Jews to allow them to leave the country. Freud was not an especially wealthy man, but hoped that his entire extended family—sixteen people in all—would be permitted to leave Austria. Bullitt offered to help financially, but told Freud that there was no time to spare and that he could only pay the expenses for him, his wife, and daughter Anna. Only a few days later, the Gestapo arrested Anna. Wiley protested to the authorities, and she was released the same day. Fearing that Freud would soon be arrested, Wiley telegraphed Bullitt in Paris, who arranged with French authorities to have visas issued to the doctor and his immediate family. It would take nearly another three months, but eventually, Austrian authorities allowed Freud, his wife, and his daughter to leave Vienna. They boarded the Orient Express for the fourteen-hour trip to Paris, where Ambassador Bullitt met them at the train station. After a few hours of rest, Freud and his family continued their journey to London, where he had been granted political asylum.[17]

Thousands of other Austrian Jews, who, unlike Freud, were not famous, were not so fortunate and suffered under the brutal reign of the Third Reich.

22

MAY GOD . . . PROVE THAT YOU ARE WRONG

Joseph Kennedy was scheduled to deliver his first speech in London as the American ambassador on March 18, 1938, to the Pilgrims Society, an organization founded decades earlier "to promote good-will, good-fellowship, and everlasting peace between the United States and Great Britain." Adhering to protocol, Kennedy submitted his remarks in advance to the Department of State for clearance. A few days after receiving the draft, Secretary Hull sent back his comments, indicating the president had approved the edits he made. Hull praised Kennedy's address but, in light of the Anschluss, declared the speech too isolationist in tone. Hull offered "suggestions for your consideration," asking Kennedy to omit sections in which the ambassador remarked on the general lack of interest in foreign policy on the part of the American people and their overwhelming desire to avoid war at all costs. As Hull put it, Kennedy's version would be "subject to misinterpretation." Finally, Hull informed the ambassador that he intended to give his own speech on the subject of Europe.[1] Certain that Hull's objective was to preempt him; Kennedy felt what he often described as his "true Irish anger." President Roosevelt had given him assurances that he would have an important role in making policy, and the Pilgrims Society speech was the perfect opportunity for him to curry favor with Prime Minister Chamberlain and perhaps to increase American influence with the British government.

A defiant Kennedy placed a call to Jay Pierrepont Moffat, the State Department's assistant secretary of European affairs. After vigorously arguing that Hull should postpone his speech, the ambassador asked to speak directly to President Roosevelt. At this point, Secretary Hull, who had been listening in on the conversation, interjected and explained to Kennedy in his soothing Southern drawl he intended only to reiterate administration policy and would break no new ground. Kennedy fired back, "Why say anything when there is nothing you can say or do which will help the situation? Why not keep quiet?"[2] The call ended when Assistant Secretary Moffat informed the ambassador that the president was at the dentist and therefore unavailable.

The Pilgrims dinner, a white-tie affair, was held in the ballroom at Claridge's, one of London's most luxurious hotels. Lord Halifax, the foreign secretary, lightheartedly introduced Kennedy, remarking that the ambassador had already scored a hole in one golfing on British links and giving him credit for Britain's unseasonably good weather. Amid applause, Kennedy strode to the podium, thanked Halifax for his introduction, and then abruptly changed the tone, telling his audience that instead of the "usual diplomatic niceties," he intended to "speak plainly" about "certain factors in American life which have a greater influence than some of you may realize on my countrymen's attitudes towards the outside world." Despite Hull's edits, much of Kennedy's original speech remained unchanged. He noted, "The average American has little interest in the details of foreign affairs . . . [and] today has two great worries. He fears that he may lose his job and he fears that the country may get into war." Borrowing a famous phrase from George Washington, Kennedy continued, "It must be realized that the great majority of Americans oppose any entangling alliances." He summed up American isolationism by alluding to the terrible price Britain had paid in the Great War: "We cannot see how armed conflict can be expected to settle any problem or to bring happiness or contentment to any nation. There certainly was no winner in the World War, we can all see now."

In deference to Secretary Hull and President Roosevelt, Kennedy made clear to the audience at Claridge's that there were circumstances under which "the United States could never remain neutral." If "a general war should break out, Americans," he insisted, would be prepared to "fight" if directly threatened. In the end, what distinguished Kennedy's speech from the administration's position was that he viewed Europe's problems primarily through an economic lens, not a political one. He declared, "We regard the economic rapprochement of the nations as imperative," because "a higher standard of living for the workers of the world" would lead to a "reduction in those internal pressures which all too frequently lead to war."[3] A few days after his speech, Kennedy wrote his friend, financier Bernard Baruch, expanding on the economic theme, "An unemployed man with a hungry family is the same fellow whether the swastika or some other flag floats over his head."[4] Kennedy was undoubtedly correct about what motivated an "unemployed man," but he seemingly failed to understand what motivated Hitler. The führer wanted nothing short of world domination.

Hitler decided to make official the merger of Austria with Germany by calling for plebiscites in both countries. The führer had previously quashed former Austrian chancellor Schuschnigg's plan for a plebiscite, but now that the Third Reich controlled the Austrian government, the outcome was not in doubt. The Nazis had no intention of permitting a fair election. Fortunately for Hitler, the rest of Europe had moved on, with speculation already turning to the question of whether Germany's next conquest would be Czechoslovakia.

Located in the heart of Europe, Czechoslovakia had a strong industrial base and the most sophisticated weapons production facilities in all of Europe. Yet in many respects, it lacked a national identity, having been created through a patchwork of peace treaties in the aftermath of World War I. There were more than three million German Bohemians, ethnic Germans, living in the Sudetenland, and its overall population of fifteen millions citizens was also comprised of several other minorities, including Russians and ethnic Hungarians. Hitler wanted both to subjugate

Czechoslovakia and to plunder its resources. Just as he had invented a rationale for occupation of Austria, Hitler intended to use Czechoslovakia's Sudeten Germans as a pretext for his next move. Recognizing that he had cowed Britain and France during the Anschluss, Hitler hoped to capitalize on his momentum to "convince foreign powers of the hopelessness of military intervention." The führer found a receptive audience in Prime Minister Chamberlain, who merely expressed his hope for a settlement between Czechoslovakia and Germany and offered no support for resisting German incursion. Chamberlain's eagerness for accommodation led Prague's ambassador in London to complain that the prime minister has "yet to find out that Czechoslovakia was a country, not a disease."⁵

In late March 1938, Ambassador Kennedy attended a major address by Prime Minister Chamberlain in the House of Commons. Standing over the podium, Chamberlain stated emphatically that Great Britain would not pledge to come to the rescue of Czechoslovakia if she were attacked by Germany. Seated in the gallery, Kennedy later recalled in his diary that he was "spellbound." The prime minister's refusal to be drawn into a European conflict struck Kennedy as shrewd: "As I size it up, there will be no war if Chamberlain stays in power with strong public backing, which he seems to be acquiring day by day." Kennedy didn't seem to worry much about the fate of Czechoslovakia, which he claimed would "solve itself without interference." Somewhat incongruously, he predicted, "Germany will get whatever it wants in Czechoslovakia without sending a single soldier across the border."⁶

Kennedy had at least one ally in the Department of State: William Bullitt. Kennedy and Bullitt were not close friends, though Kennedy, a graduate of Harvard in 1912, and Bullitt, a graduate of Yale that same year, had undoubtedly become acquainted with one another years earlier in the rarified society of wealthy, Ivy League graduates living in the northeast. After visiting Paris in May 1938, Secretary of the Interior Ickes recorded in his diary Bullitt's assessment of the European situation:

He [Bullitt] looks for German subjugation of Czechoslovakia. He commented on the fact that Hitler's timing had always been perfect; that he had moved from one objective to another and so far obtained his ends without having to fire a gun. He thinks that Hitler will have his will in Czechoslovakia, not by invading it by armed forces, but by working through the very large German population in Czechoslovakia. The deed will be done in such a way that Russia and others will claim justification for not going to the aid of Czechoslovakia.[7]

Like Kennedy, Bullitt felt strongly that the United States should stay out of any European conflict, because, as he explained to Ickes, the war would likely last for a very long time. In his view, the United States should focus on building up its economy and its democratic institutions, and then, in the aftermath of the conflict, salvage whatever was left of Western civilization.

Some of Kennedy's friends were not as smitten with Chamberlain. Bob Allen, who partnered with Drew Pearson in writing the "Washington Merry-Go-Round" syndicated column, warned the ambassador about giving his public support to the prime minister. "I wouldn't think of advising you," he wrote Kennedy, "but just as a friend, Joe, I'd keep my fingers crossed on Chamberlain and his Tory crew." Allen, who like Pearson had excellent sources within the Department of State, characterized the Chamberlain government as "about as competent as [former president] Hoover's and is rapidly becoming as unpopular."[8]

Before conquering Czechoslovakia, Hitler wanted to take care of unfinished business with Il Duce in Rome. The two men had improved their relationship after Mussolini's visit to Berlin, and to follow up, Il Duce invited Hitler to visit him in Italy. Now it was Hitler's chance to be feted in Rome and to perhaps form an alliance with his fellow fascist. In early May 1938, with an entourage of 120 men, Hitler made an official visit to Italy, where he was given the red-carpet treatment. King Victor Emmanuel squired the führer around in a horse-drawn carriage. At a banquet at the Palazzo Venezia, Hitler and Mussolini exchanged what they described as blood oaths with each other. He visited the monuments of imperial Rome, and as a sign of Il Duce's growing admiration for the Nazis, Italian soldiers now paraded using a version of the German goose step.[9]

While Mussolini entertained Hitler in Rome, the American aviator Charles Lindbergh and his wife were the guests of honor at a dinner party given by Lord and Lady Astor at their Cliveden estate near London. Besides the Lindberghs, guests included Mr. and Mrs. George Bernard Shaw, as well as Ambassador Kennedy, and Ambassador Bullitt who had flown from Paris for the occasion. Shaw, a revered playwright, was eighty-one years old at the time and a member of Lady Astor's Unionist Party. A few years earlier, he had referred to Hitler as "a very able man. A very remarkable man." The conversation that evening was not about literature but rather aviation and military issues. Lindbergh was greatly impressed by Kennedy, whose plainspoken style—and admiration for Germany—appealed to the aviator, now also a German sympathizer. Bullitt did not admire Hitler and worried about the rise of Germany, but was somewhat fatalistic. Rather than argue with the other guests, he peppered Lindbergh with questions about German war preparations. Not surprisingly, the dinner guests also discussed rumors that Hitler was preparing to invade Czechoslovakia, and as they sipped wine, the consensus was the invasion seemed inevitable. No one at the table seemed especially concerned.[10]

On Thursday, May 19, 1938, Czechoslovakian intelligence sources intercepted Hitler's plans for an attack on their country. Soon after, there were unverified accounts that German troops were on the move and that invasion was imminent. President Edvard Beneš ordered the four-hundred-thousand-man Czech army put on high alert, and reservists were sent to border areas to fortify defenses. Czechoslovakia's fierce determination to defend itself motivated the governments of Russia and France, which had treaty obligations with the Beneš government, to declare that, in the event of German aggression, they would come to the country's defense. In an awkwardly worded, cautionary statement, the

British informed Berlin "that they could not guarantee that they could not be forced by circumstances to become involved also."[11] Notwithstanding the confusing "double negative" diplomacy of the Foreign Office, Britain and all of Europe were now on edge, finally recognizing that for the first time in two decades, the Continent had moved dangerously close to once again being consumed by war.

President Roosevelt offered no immediate response. Although he understood that the situation in Czechoslovakia could lead to war—he trusted neither the British nor the French to honor their commitments to safeguard the Czechs—he also knew that the United States did not have the leverage to prevent Germany from invading. It didn't help that his ambassadors in Europe were offering somewhat contradictory advice.

The new U.S. ambassador to Germany, Hugh Wilson, suggested President Roosevelt send "representatives" to both Prague and Berlin to seek a "peace settlement." Ambassador Bullitt offered a variation of Wilson's approach, recommending that the president summon to the White House the German, Italian, French, and British ambassadors and urge that the heads of their governments meet in The Hague to hammer out a lasting peace. Bullitt even scripted for Roosevelt a somewhat pedantic appeal to the European ambassadors: "[We] are the children of the civilization of Europe; that we cannot stand by and watch the beginning of the end of European civilization without making one last effort to stop the destruction . . . the only result of European war today would be an Asiatic despotism established on fields of dead." Notably, Bullitt didn't include either Russia or Czechoslovakia in his proposed peace conference. As far as Russia was concerned, Bullitt felt that the one thing European democracies agreed on was their hatred of Communism. Bullitt excluded Czechoslovakia because he speculated, "The conference in the Hague would probably have to recommend a plebiscite," whereby Czechoslovakia would be forced to give up the Sudeten region, the part of the country where most German-speaking Czechoslovakians lived. Bullitt acknowledged that Roosevelt would be "accused of selling out a small nation in order to produce another Hitler triumph. [But] I should not hesitate to take a brick on my head and I don't think you should either, if, thereby, you could avoid a general European war."[12]

At the time, Ambassador Kennedy made no recommendation to the president regarding the Czech crisis. A few days later, however, he wrote the president's son James, "The momentary lull in Central Europe has not caused anyone here to think that Czechoslovakian business is settled . . . We seem to be living through one crisis after another these days, and no one appears to have any idea how long this fumbling can go on without getting out of hand. The British certainly wish someone would tell them. Living dangerously is all very well in its place, but it can get on the nerves of placid British bureaucracy."[13] Kennedy's opinion was that the collapse of Czechoslovakia was inevitable, and the United States should break the tension by acknowledging as much.

In the end, Hitler's generals persuaded him that Germany would pay a steep price for invading Czechoslovakia. Not only did the Czechs have a well-trained army and state-of-the-art armaments, the Beneš government had erected an estimated ten thousand heavily fortified bunkers that ringed the country. The generals also feared possible retaliation from Britain, France, and Russia. Reluctantly, Hitler opted to declare publicly that Germany had no aggressive design on Czechoslovakia and wanted peace. However, he was infuriated by the growing perception that he had backed down, and privately vowed that the day was not far off when he would seize Czechoslovakia and make it part of his empire.[14]

Ambassador Bullitt had a number of visitors during the summer of 1938. Secretary of the Interior Harold Ickes and his second wife, Jane Dahlman, along with Secretary of Labor Frances Perkins—the only woman in Roosevelt's cabinet—dined with the ambassador at his Paris residence. In a letter to President Roosevelt, Bullitt referred to Mrs. Ickes, as the secretary's "little wife" but also called her "charming" and wondered, "How Ickes accomplished this is beyond me."[15]

Bullitt wrote the president that Secretary Perkins "seemed well and lively and I kept her smothered in orchids the day she was here."[16] Before arriving in Paris, Perkins had visited England, Belgium, and Austria, where she not only met with high-ranking government officials but also engaged laborers, housewives, shopkeepers, and people on the street, something she did everywhere she went. Though not a foreign policy expert, she sensed a general malaise among people across the Continent.

In France, Perkins spent several days traveling around the country, visiting military installations, and meeting with top French officials, including General Henri-Philippe Pétain, a hero of the Great War. Pétain told her, "We have the most magnificent defenses . . . You have heard of the Maginot Line . . . It is stronger than you or anyone knows. Everything is fine."[17] During the 1930s, the French built a series of concrete fortifications on its borders with Germany, Italy, Switzerland, and Luxembourg. With its state-of-the-art weapons installations, French military experts were confident they could repel any German aerial or tank attack.

Besides meeting with French generals and government officials, Perkins also engaged with ordinary citizens. From them she gained a very different perspective; she concluded that the French people had little faith in their leaders, saw only fear and resignation and the possibility of war, and showed nothing of the resolve or determination necessary to prevail.

Once back in Paris, she expressed serious doubts to Bullitt about France's political will to take on Germany. Bullitt told her, "Oh, Frances, that's crazy." But Perkins remained skeptical. On the voyage home, she decided to share her concerns with the president. When they met in the Oval Office, the president listened with interest, "Hmmm. Hmmm. That is not Bullitt's story," he said, but acknowledged that "there are whole areas of human life that are never taken into account by diplomats. They just don't think about it."[18] Perkins's observations were impressionistic and lacked both detail and analysis, but the president did not dismiss them, filing them away in the back of his mind.

Only a week after the visits of Secretaries Ickes and Perkins, Charles Lindbergh, a guest at the Hôtel de Crillon adjacent to the embassy in Paris, dropped by to see Ambassador Bullitt. They had first met at the dinner hosted by Lord and Lady Astor in England earlier in the spring.

In the intervening weeks, the celebrated American aviator had taken it upon himself "to see as much of the European situation as possible" and was extremely critical of French air defenses. "There are not enough modern military planes in this country to even put up a show in case of war," he declared. "In a conflict between France, England, and Russia on one side, against Germany on the other," Lindbergh predicted, "Germany would immediately have supremacy of the air . . . Germany has developed a huge air force while England has slept and France has deluded herself with a Russian alliance."[19]

At the end of June, Bullitt received two more American visitors: Joseph P. Kennedy Jr. and his twenty-one year-old younger brother, Jack. They stayed for a week in the ambassador's residence on Avenue d'Iéna, and with assistance provided by Carmel Offie, Bullit's secretary, moved into an apartment on Rue de Rivoli, which they rented for several weeks. Offie later recalled that "they did not learn much French but they had a good time because we got them invited to various parties in the diplomatic corps where they could meet young ladies . . . No one took them very seriously but just being around the Embassy for a time each day they sat in with various officers of the Embassy and thereby learned a lot of what was going on." Offie liked the Kennedy boys: "I remember Jack sitting in my office and listening to telegrams being read or even reading various things that were actually none of his business but because he was who he was we didn't throw him out." After he left, Jack wrote the ambassador a thank-you letter: "You were awfully kind to put me up and that month ranks as just about the best I've ever put in."[20]

Bullitt was a gracious host and always appeared positive in public. But the ambassador's pessimism about Europe was finally deepening. In June, he wrote President Roosevelt a long letter, declaring he felt "like a participant in the last days of Pompeii." He was convinced that war was coming to Europe and that most Europeans believed the United States "will be drawn in . . . after a comparatively brief period. This conviction is helpful in so far as it may tend to diminish the readiness of Germany to go to war, but we shall find ourselves violently unpopular in both

France and England when it becomes clear that we intend to maintain our neutrality."[21]

Bullitt told the president that he had conferred with the chief of the French general staff and the commander of the French army, both of whom remained concerned about a possible attack by Germany along the Siegfried Line, the sector between Strasbourg, the largest city in northeastern France, and Luxembourg, the small duchy in the north that bordered both France and Germany, as well as Belgium and the Netherlands. However, Czechoslovakia remained the more immediate concern, and Bullitt offered essentially the same advice he had previously provided to the president: "If I cable you that the Germans are about to cross the Czech frontier, I hope that you will issue an immediate appeal to the British, French and Germans to meet at once at the Hague." Bullitt made one important amendment to his previous recommendation, suggesting the president include in the meeting "a representative of the United States." He speculated that an American envoy might "be able to get a settlement on the basis of autonomy for the various minorities in Czechoslovakia as an independent state by England, France and Germany. That might be the beginning of something like peace in Europe."[22] Bullitt didn't offer himself as a potential envoy, but it was an appointment he would have relished.

Bullitt had begun his letter to Roosevelt by painting a serene picture of his Chantilly country retreat in the evening "with the nightingales singing and the river pouring its white cascade below the still woods." After filling several pages with his views on the coming military conflict, he ended the letter on a more wistful note: "I wish you could be here with me tonight. This place is so beautiful that you would forget even your stamps for an evening."[23] Bullitt knew that the president had been a stamp collector since childhood. A onetime novelist, the ambassador seemed captivated by his own poetic prose and inexplicably overly confident of his relationship with Roosevelt. There was no other ambassador or official in the Department of State who so often appealed to the president's romanticism.

President Roosevelt was in no mood to engage in lighthearted correspondence with his ambassador. On June 25, 1938, he responded to Bullitt's letter, "May God in His infinite wisdom prove that you are wrong."[24] Roosevelt wouldn't allow that the United States could be drawn into a world war, but his curt reply also indicated that he was once again deferring the declaration of a policy related to the deteriorating situation in Europe. The president was likely still mulling over reaction to the fireside chat he had delivered the night before. In his thirteenth radio address since becoming president, Roosevelt told the American people, "The Seventy-Fifth Congress, elected in November, 1936, on a platform uncompromisingly liberal, has adjourned," leaving "many things undone," but having "achieved more for the future good of the country than any Congress did between the end of the World War and the spring of 1933." The president only made one oblique reference to international relations, declaring, "We believe that we can solve our problems through continuing effort, through democratic processes instead of Fascism or Communism." The main purpose of his radio address was to prepare the American people for the midterm elections in which "as the head of the Democratic Party," he would "speak in those few instances where there may be a clear-cut issue between candidates for a Democratic nomination involving [liberal] principles, or involving a clear misuse of my own name." Roosevelt's announcement of his intention to campaign against Democrats who opposed his policies was the beginning of what came to be known as the "Democratic purge."[25] It was also a clear sign of his continuing prioritization of national politics and his domestic agenda over foreign policy.

23

RESISTANCE AND WAR WILL FOLLOW

Every summer, London seemed to empty in August, as much of the population went on holiday. In 1938, Ambassador Kennedy spent the vacation period in the south of France with his family. He played golf, swam in the ocean, entertained visitors, and doted on his children. Joe Jr. had graduated from Harvard and had plans to attend law school. But his father decided it might be a good idea for his son to spend a year working and traveling, so the ambassador wrote George Messersmith, now the assistant secretary for administration at the State Department in Washington, and asked to have young Joe "added to my staff as my private secretary at a dollar a year." Kennedy justified the proposed nepotism "because of the tremendous amount of personal work I find myself called upon to perform here . . . The reason I am asking for diplomatic status for him is that I can use him on a lot of small events where they want members of the family, and to build up good-will." When after several days Messersmith failed to respond, an irritated Kennedy sent the assistant secretary a telegram demanding an answer. Shortly thereafter, Messersmith replied with a terse cable informing Kennedy that department rules prohibited ambassadors from appointing family members to their staffs. The ambassador reluctantly accepted the decision and decided that young Joe would spend the entire year traveling the

Continent and relaying information to the ambassador about what was happening on the ground in Europe.[1]

Ambassador Kennedy enjoyed himself while on the French Riviera, but he didn't leave his work altogether behind. Without approval from the Department of State, Kennedy granted an exclusive interview to the Hearst newspapers in which he trumpeted his belief that the United States should stay on the sidelines if war came to Europe; he advised Americans not "to lose" their "heads."[2] It was an implicit rebuke of Roosevelt's attempt to straddle the neutrality issue. Making matters worse, Kennedy had provided the interview to the newspaper chain owned by one of the president's most vociferous critics.

A few weeks later, Kennedy met with Lord Halifax, the British foreign secretary. Halifax wanted to know whether Congress might amend the neutrality laws if Britain were to go to war with Germany. Kennedy told him it was unlikely and encouraged him to promote accommodation with the Third Reich even though he knew it was not official U.S. policy. The substance of the meeting was then leaked to the press. When asked, Kennedy refused to comment but did not refute any details in the story. Once again, Kennedy's willingness to use the press to publicize his personal views angered the president. Roosevelt did not directly confront his ambassador but complained instead to Secretary Hull, "Frankly, I think Joe Kennedy's attention should be called to this . . . If all of our fifty-five or sixty Ambassadors and Ministers were to send exclusive stories to specially chosen newspapers in the United States, your Department might just as well close shop."[3] Secretary Hull reprimanded Kennedy, but the ambassador defended himself, arguing that talking to the press was part of his job. Roosevelt became angrier, and personally wrote Kennedy, declaring that he had been "greatly disturbed" by the interview given to the Hearst papers. The president made it clear that Kennedy should not be providing a "special message of advice" to the American public. He closed his note with "I know you will understand."[4] If Kennedy did understand, he plainly didn't care.

Secretary of the Treasury Henry Morgenthau visited Kennedy at his vacation home in Cannes that summer. On his return to Washington,

Morgenthau met with Roosevelt in the Oval Office and fed the president's irritation by suggesting that the ambassador's "popularity with the English"—meaning Chamberlain and Halifax—stemmed from his inclination to argue for a strategy of appeasing Hitler. Roosevelt agreed. He didn't want his ambassadors making foreign policy during such an unsettled period. With Morgenthau sitting across from him, Roosevelt then made a startling accusation: "I don't think there is much question but what Kennedy is disloyal to his country."[5]

However, the president had a political problem: The Catholic vote would be important in the next presidential election, and Kennedy was one of America's best-known and most respected Catholics. In his diary, Secretary Ickes wrote about the prospect of a future presidential ticket consisting of Vice President Garner and Postmaster General Farley. He noted they were both prominent Democrats, but whereas Garner was a Methodist, Farley was a Catholic. Ickes suggested that the "President might have to turn to Joe Kennedy as a candidate for Vice President. This would match a Roman Catholic against a Roman Catholic."[6] There was nothing to suggest that Roosevelt had yet seriously considered a third term, but if he were contemplating running again, he was not thinking of putting Kennedy on the ticket. After all, Kennedy had never been a candidate for elective office and was totally untested; more importantly, Roosevelt neither entirely trusted nor especially liked him.

Kennedy was ambitious, wealthy, and very well connected—especially with influential members of the press. While Roosevelt knew he could not afford to incur the wrath of American Catholics by firing Kennedy, the only other position that Kennedy would accept was treasury secretary, which the president had no intention of giving him. Roosevelt knew Kennedy was not happy in his current job and hoped he might resign sometime in the near future. He told Morgenthau, "If Kennedy wants to resign when he comes back [for leave], I will accept it on the spot." Once back in "private life," without the platform of a prominent ambassadorial post, Roosevelt believed Kennedy's political influence would be greatly diminished; "He is through," the president confidently predicted to Morgenthau.[7]

Kennedy was not the only ambassador causing problems for the president in 1938. On September 4, Ambassador Bullitt attended a dedication ceremony at Pointe de Grave to unveil a plaque celebrating Franco-American relations. In his speech, Bullitt declared that "France and the United States are united in war and peace." Bullitt had been telling Roosevelt for months that the United States should avoid a European conflict at all costs, and neutrality remained the official position of the White House. However, Bullitt's remarks at Pointe de Grave led the press to speculate about a change in policy. If Hitler's army invaded Czechoslovakia, would the United States join the war in opposition to Germany? Four days later, during a press conference at Hyde Park, President Roosevelt made certain to note to reporters that Bullitt was "110% wrong [in suggesting] that the United States is allied morally with the democracies of Europe in a sort of 'stop-Hitler' movement."[8] Although it is almost certain the president privately agreed with Bullitt, he did not want his ambassador speaking in public and out in front of him on any issue. The president's comments were not only a clear rebuke of Bullitt but also a clear indication that he was not prepared to deviate from America's stated position of neutrality.

In Berlin, Ambassador Hugh Wilson wrestled with the same issue that had confounded his predecessor, William Dodd. In June he had written Undersecretary Welles asking if he should attend Hitler's Nuremberg rally in September.[9] Welles kicked the decision upstairs to the president, who replied in a memo, "The first question for determination is this: Is the Nuremberg Rally an official government celebration or a Party Convention? If the answer is that it is the first, our Ambassador can and should attend."[10] Given that the only political party in Germany was the Nazi Party and it controlled the government, the answer to the question was technically that the rally was both. Secretary Hull urged Wilson to attend the rally, and the ambassador accepted the invitation.

Nuremberg, the second-largest city in Bavaria, located in the heart of Germany, had a rich history dating back to the Holy Roman Empire. The Nazi party rallies were held at Zeppelinfeld, a four-square-mile expanse located to the southeast of the city. Nineteen thirty-eight marked the Tenth Party Congress, and like the previous gatherings, it had a name: Rally of Greater Germany, in honor of Germany's annexation of Austria. The stadium consisted of a large grandstand backed by a line of columns. Behind the central grandstand stood a giant, gilded stone swastika. On the left and right of the grandstand were two massive wing towers topped by flaming cauldrons, and in between them rose a double row of stone columns.[11]

Tens of thousands of Germans had poured into Nuremberg over the weekend of September 3, and now on Saturday evening, as dozens of drummers beat a low but steady cadence, they waited patiently for the arrival of Hitler at Zeppelinfeld. Suddenly, the beat of drums grew louder, and a fleet of black Mercedes-Benz cars carrying the führer and his entourage rolled into the arena, parking near the stage. Nazi architect Albert Speer had designed the field to accommodate more than 150 floodlights, and according to one visitor, "the stadium looked like a simmering sea of swastikas."[12] As twenty thousand Nazi flags fluttered in the night air, Hitler strode to the podium and began to speak. The crowd hushed in silence, but the drums continued their steady beat. Hitler started slowly, but before long he was shrieking about the supposed injustice and suffering of the Sudeten Germans in Czechoslovakia. As Hitler gesticulated wildly, the crowd broke into a roar of cheers, and thousands swayed back and forth, chanting, "Sieg Heil!" over and over again. One woman recalled that she "looked into the faces around me and saw tears streaming down people's cheeks. The drums had grown louder and I suddenly felt frightened."[13] Hitler did not declare war on Czechoslovakia that night but made it clear that the Third Reich would no longer tolerate what he viewed as the indignity and insolence directed toward Germany by its European neighbors. Three months after his "May crisis" threatened Czechoslovakia, Hitler once again appeared ready to plunge the Continent into war.

Aboard the presidential train, *Ferdinand Magellan*, in Rochester, Minnesota, where the president was making a campaign appearance later that day, he and Harry Hopkins listened to Hitler's speech over the radio. After the speech, Hopkins later recalled, the president "was sure then that we were going to get into the war." Roosevelt had flirted with involving America in Europe's troubles before and had always backed away, but Hitler's fanatical tone convinced him that he needed to prepare the United States for possible conflict. The following day, he discussed with Hopkins the sorry state of American military readiness and the need to strengthen the nation's armed forces.[14]

Roosevelt received a telephone call that same day from Secretary of State Hull, who relayed a transatlantic telephone conversation he'd had with Ambassador Bullitt. Bullitt reported that French prime minister Édouard Daladier and British prime minister Neville Chamberlain were contemplating traveling to Berlin to meet with Hitler. Bullitt's information was partially correct; two days later, Chamberlain alone flew to Berlin and then traveled by car to Berchtesgaden, Hitler's mountaintop retreat, to meet with the führer. Chamberlain was desperate to find a way to avoid war, and he and the führer discussed the prospect of self-determination for the Sudeten Germans. However, the visit was inconclusive.

Among Roosevelt's ambassadors, Chamberlain's overture to Hitler elicited very different reactions. Ambassador Bullitt saw the meeting as a sign of weakness, writing to the president, "If you have enough airplanes, you don't have to go to Berchtesgaden."[15] Bullitt still hoped that representatives to an international conference might somehow find a peaceful solution. Ambassador Kennedy, in contrast to his counterpart in Paris, was very supportive of Chamberlain's outreach and continued to counsel noninvolvement on the part of the United States. Kennedy had not wavered since arriving in London. His viewpoint was reinforced after Charles Lindbergh and his wife visited him for lunch in the embassy. Lindbergh had spent the summer assessing the relative military strength of the various potential combatants and reported to Kennedy, "Germany now has the means of destroying London, Paris and Prague if she wishes." Kennedy relayed the assessment to Hull with the warning that "England and France are far too weak in the air to protect themselves."[16]

On September 22, 1938, Chamberlain met again with Hitler, this time telling the führer that Britain would accept the annexation of the Sudeten. However, Hitler had decided to raise the stakes since their last meeting and argued that Czechoslovakia should be divided up among its neighbors. The führer's demands took the British prime minister by surprise. Though none of it had been discussed with Czechoslovakian president Beneš, Chamberlain and Hitler ultimately settled on limiting Germany's military occupation to the Sudetenland. Chamberlain believed that he had negotiated an agreement to save Czechoslovakia from dismemberment, but it proved to be totally unacceptable to the Czech government. When Hitler learned that Beneš had rejected the deal, he was furious and vowed once again to destroy Czechoslovakia. While conducting a cabinet meeting, President Roosevelt received the news of Chamberlain's failed negotiations. Reading from a memo handed to him by an aide, the president announced, "Bill Bullitt just telephoned the following . . . He has just been informed . . . that Chamberlain . . . is returning to London. The news is very bad . . . It is said that Hitler wishes his troops to occupy Sudeten. Resistance and war will follow."[17]

Secretary of State Hull advised President Roosevelt to make a direct appeal to Hitler to continue negotiating. Roosevelt cabled both Hitler and Beneš with an urgent plea to settle their differences peacefully. He pointed to their obligations under the Kellogg-Briand Pact, the 1928 international agreement in which signatory states promised not to use war to resolve "disputes or conflicts of whatever nature or of whatever origin they may be."[18] Hitler responded that peace depended on the actions of the Beneš government, which had already made clear that it would not accept the German ultimatum.[19] Roosevelt immediately answered Hitler, pleading with him to restart the negotiations: "No differences are irreconcilable," but once negotiations are "broken off, reason is banished and force asserts itself. And force produces no solution for the future of humanity."[20] Meanwhile, President Beneš had little hope that any appeal to Hitler's humanity would be successful and ordered the mobilization of the country's defenses.

Hitler, enraged by the Czech government's response, prepared to address the German people—and the nations of Europe—on the growing crisis. Thirty thousand Berliners crowded the Berlin Sportpalast at 7:30 p.m. to hear Hitler speak. Millions more Germans, as well as millions of others around the world, listened on the radio. In the early part of the address, Hitler professed his desire for peace: "We gave guarantees to all Western states and have assured all countries bordering on us that Germany will respect their territorial integrity. This is not just empty talk. This is our holy will. It is not in our interest to disturb their peace. These offers on the part of Germany encountered increasing good will."

The führer then described how the nations of Europe had betrayed Germany, although he gave unconditional praise to Benito Mussolini, referring to him as the "one man who understands the despair of the German Volk [people]." Hitler referred to Il Duce as "my great friend" and praised all "he has done for us in these difficult times and how the Italian people stand with us, we shall never forget! And if there is ever an hour of equal need in Italy, then I will stand up before the German Volk and demand that it do the same."

As he reached the midpoint of his speech, Hitler addressed the situation in Czechoslovakia, declaring, "Now I demand that Herr Beneš be forced to honesty after twenty years. He will have to give over the territories on October 1." Screaming and waving his arm in the air, the führer heaped insults on the Czech prime minister:

Herr Beneš now places his last hopes in the world, and he and his diplomats do little to disguise this. They declare: "It is our only hope that Chamberlain be overthrown, that Daladier be done away with, that there are overthrows all over." They place their hope with the Soviet Union. He still believes he can escape fulfillment of his obligations. All I can say to this: "There are two men facing each other down. Over there stands Herr Beneš. And here I stand!" We are two entirely different men. While Herr Beneš danced on the world stage and hid himself there from his responsibilities, I was fulfilling my duties as a decent German soldier. And as I face this man today, I am but a soldier of my Volk.

Journalist William Shirer attended the speech, and in his diary described Hitler as "shouting and shrieking in the worst state of excitement I've ever seen him in." Shirer, who had reported for CBS News from Germany for a number of years, observed that "for the first time . . . he seemed tonight to have completely lost control of himself."[21]

President Roosevelt listened to a simultaneous translation of the address at 10:30 a.m. on the radio in his private study in the White House. At cocktails that evening, Roosevelt asked Margaret Suckley, his young cousin, "Did you hear Hitler today, his shrieks, his histrionics, and the effect on the huge audience?" Appalled by the support Hitler received from his fellow German countrymen, Roosevelt remarked, "They did not applaud, they made noises like animals."[22] At his home in Maryland, Breckinridge Long also listened with alarm to the speech. Long admired Hitler, but in his diary criticized the führer for having "made a damned fool speech today." Long thought Hitler had "his war won without a fight. But now he is near causing a fight to get what he has already won." Long called the führer "a madman" and admitted, "For the first time, I am apprehensive."[23]

Charles Lindbergh was visiting Lord and Lady Astor at Cliveden and had a different reaction. Lindbergh seized on Hitler's assertion that he was "grateful to Mr. Chamberlain for his efforts" and that "the German Volk desires nothing but peace." Lindbergh viewed those few benign phrases as symbolic of an olive branch and concluded that Hitler "seemed to leave considerable hope that war may be avoided."[24]

Listening to the speech on the radio, Ambassador Kennedy focused less on the implications for the future of Europe than on the safety of his family in the event of war. He was especially concerned that in the event of peacetime conscription his two oldest sons, Joe Jr. and Jack, were of age to be drafted into the military. He was also concerned that Rose and the younger children would be forced to leave Britain. His concerns were heightened the next morning when at breakfast he received a phone call from the British Foreign Office telling him that Sir Horace Wilson, a senior government official and close adviser to Prime Minister Chamberlain, had just concluded a meeting with Hitler. The führer told Wilson that if his ultimatum to Beneš to turn over the Sudeten had not been met by October 1, he would "smash" Czechoslovakia by "military action."[25]

Worried that Britain would become entangled in a war, and anticipating that thousands of Americans visiting or living in the United Kingdom would overrun the embassy with requests to leave the country immediately, Ambassador Kennedy called Secretary Hull and urged the State Department to prepare an evacuation plan that included sending American transport ships to Britain. Later that morning, he wrote Arthur Krock that he was "starting to think about sending Rose and the children back to America . . . Maybe to never see them again."[26]

That same day, the ambassador traveled to Buckingham Palace to personally deliver a sealed letter from President Roosevelt to King George. Kennedy did not know the contents, but the king opened it in his presence and delightedly read aloud an invitation from the president and Mrs. Roosevelt to visit the United States in 1939. His Majesty instantly realized that the visit would be a historic occasion. Kennedy was privately seething as the king told Kennedy how honored he and the queen would be to visit the United States as guests of the president and Mrs. Roosevelt. During a time of crisis, when the president should have been seeking Kennedy's advice, Roosevelt instead chose to treat his ambassador more like an errand boy. Sitting before the king, Kennedy feigned excitement over the prospect of a royal visit, but he felt humiliated.[27]

The following day, September 28, 1938, as Ambassador Kennedy prepared to leave the embassy for the Palace of Westminster, where Prime Minister Chamberlain was scheduled to deliver an address on the crisis in Czechoslovakia, an aide handed him a confidential cable from President Roosevelt, who wrote simply, "I want you to know that in these difficult days, I am proud of you."[28] Kennedy felt uplifted by the president's kind words: Perhaps he had judged the president too harshly the day before. He was unaware that Roosevelt had sent the same cable to his ambassadors in Paris, Berlin, and Prague.

As Chamberlain stood to speak, members of Parliament who had packed the House of Commons grew quiet. Chamberlain had addressed the nation the evening before in an eight-minute talk, but now covered in great detail his efforts over the past few weeks to find a solution to the Czechoslovakian crisis. The speech was a solemn chronology of Chamberlain's unsuccessful efforts to pursue peace.

Near the end of the address, just after he praised "Signor Mussolini" for his willingness to counsel Hitler to postpone any military action to "re-examine the situation and endeavor to find a peaceful settlement," Chamberlain was handed a message from Lord Halifax. After reading the note, the prime minister raised his head and said, "I have something further to tell the House. Herr Hitler has just agreed to postpone his mobilization for twenty-four hours and meet me in conference with Signor Mussolini and Signor Daladier [the French prime minister] at Munich. I need not to say what my answer will be." The hall erupted in loud applause. There was a chance that war might be avoided. Kennedy wrote in his diary, "I never was so thrilled in my life."[29]

Chamberlain flew to Munich the next day, and he, Daladier, Mussolini, and Hitler gathered at Hitler's offices in the Führerbau at 1:00 in the morning on September 30 to begin negotiations over the future of Czechoslovakia. The talks were somewhat disjointed given that Mussolini was the only one of the leaders who spoke French, German, and English and that Hitler frequently interrupted the discussion with one of his harangues. In the end, although Beneš had not been consulted, the European powers agreed to permit Germany to march into the Sudeten on October 1—just as Hitler had threatened days earlier. It was a total capitulation on behalf of England and France. Mussolini, not yet officially an ally of Hitler, wanted only to be on the winning team and was thrilled to have played a role. In a side agreement, also reached that morning, Hitler and Chamberlain signed a declaration stating their mutual "desire of our two peoples never to go to war with one another again." For the moment, the Munich Agreement, as it came to be known, had averted war.

This time when Chamberlain returned to London, he was afforded a hero's welcome. Thousands of well-wishers lined the Mall and cheered as the prime minister's black limousine sped by on the way to Buckingham Palace, where Chamberlain briefed the king and queen on the agreement. Later, as the prime minister stood on the balcony of Buckingham Palace alongside the royal couple, the crowd below roared their approval.

Returning to 10 Downing Street, Chamberlain attempted to place his mission in a historical context; he invoked Prime Minister Benjamin Disraeli's return from the Berlin Congress of 1878 after signing a peace treaty. Chamberlain declared, "My good friends, this is the second time in our history that there has come back from Germany to Downing Street peace with honor." Chamberlain then triumphantly proclaimed, "I believe it is peace for our time."[30] As would quickly become apparent, the prime minister had spoken prematurely. His optimistic assessment of the Munich Agreement would forever brand him as hopelessly naive, and worse, an appeaser of the most monstrous and terrifying dictator of the twentieth century.

In the Department of State, reaction to the Munich Agreement was mixed. Ambassador Kennedy greeted the news with excitement, remarking to Czechoslovakian diplomat Jan Masaryk, "Isn't it wonderful . . . Now I can get to Palm Beach after all."[31] Sumner Welles delivered a nationwide radio address on October 3 in which he heralded a "superb" opportunity to now establish "a new world system of law and order."[32] Welles gave Roosevelt partial credit for the agreement, noting that his letters to both Mussolini and Hitler had played a role in encouraging negotiations. Although Secretary of State Cordell Hull had advised Roosevelt to push for negotiations, he did not share Welles's perspective that the Munich Agreement signaled a breakthrough for peace in Europe. Hull didn't trust Hitler, believing that it was only a matter of time before Hitler broke his promise and invaded Czechoslovakia. As Drew Pearson reported, many in the State Department had gone "haywire" over the Munich Agreement, but "one who hasn't was Cordell Hull."[33]

The president, in typical fashion, equivocated and did not issue a formal statement from the White House. *The New York Times* reported only that Roosevelt echoed Pope Pius by offering prayers for peace. In private, the president sounded cautiously optimistic. He wrote Frederick Adams, a businessman married to his cousin Ellen W. Delano, a humorous letter, declaring, "A few days ago I wanted to kill Hitler and amputate the nose. Today, I have really rather friendly feelings for the latter and no longer wish to assassinate the Fuhrer." He adopted a more serious tone in a letter to the Canadian prime minister, Mackenzie King, who had thanked him for his role in pushing for negotiations: "I can assure you that we in the United States rejoice with you, and the world at large, that the outbreak of war was averted." Roosevelt confided to Ambassador Phillips in Rome, "I want you to know that I am not a bit upset over the final result."[34]

After the Munich Agreement, Bullitt met several times with Prime Minister Daladier and with Jean Monnet, the French financier and former deputy secretary-general of the League of Nations. The French, notwithstanding their role in the Munich Agreement, had become increasingly fearful that both their country and Britain would ultimately be drawn into a war with Germany. France had a large army and had fortified its borders along the Maginot Line in the northeast of the country, but its air force, though large, was outdated. French cities were highly vulnerable to an air attack. They were well aware of Charles Lindberg's estimate of German airpower, and it terrified them. Looking for any viable solution, Prime Minister Daladier explored with Bullitt the possibility of circumventing American neutrality laws to purchase much needed American military aircraft.

On Wednesday, October 12, Ambassador Bullitt returned to Washington, D.C. Late in the afternoon on the following day, Missy LeHand ushered him into the Oval Office. President Roosevelt warmly greeted his ambassador, though the conversation quickly turned serious, and for the next several hours, they discussed the situation in Europe. Bullitt had completely given up on the idea of rapprochement and now referred to Hitler in exactly the same terms as the president had years earlier: a "madman" who needed to be stopped at all costs. In his view, the time for negotiations and international conferences had passed. While Bullitt advocated for providing assistance to the French, he also urged the president to focus more immediately on increasing America's own airpower. Arguing that United States production at around one hundred planes per month was insufficient, Bullitt warned the president that he could no longer delay American military preparations. Bullitt's dire predictions and pessimistic outlook represented an almost complete reversal of his earlier analysis. Roosevelt listened carefully, asked a number of questions, and grew increasingly concerned.

The next morning, President Roosevelt announced at a press conference his intention to seek a $500 million supplemental appropriation for increasing American aircraft production. He also announced that he would direct the Department of State to study the possibility of removing the arms embargo from the Neutrality Act. Finally, he reported that the French prime minister's representative, Jean Monnet, would soon be visiting the United States and that he had ordered his administration to give the Frenchman full cooperation. Privately, Roosevelt told Arthur C. Murray, an unofficial representative of the British government, that Europe "could not be permitted to burn."[35] Bullitt's warning had plainly jolted the president.

On Sunday, the president, accompanied by Ambassador Bullitt, went to Hyde Park, where he engaged in another round of meetings over military preparedness with Secretary Morgenthau and Hopkins. President Roosevelt had quietly begun to put in place a group of advisers to deal with what he now viewed as an inevitable war in Europe. Although not a member of the cabinet, Ambassador Bullitt had managed to become a member of the president's inner circle and, for the moment at least, his most influential adviser on foreign policy. Harry Hopkins, whom the president would appoint as secretary of commerce in December, would oversee the effort to build up America's defenses. Based on his conversation with Bullitt, the president had decided that the first priority would be a massive enlargement of the nation's air defenses. Roosevelt wanted construction of fifteen thousand planes a year, boosting production to more than ten times the current rate. He directed Hopkins to undertake a tour of aircraft production facilities and report back immediately to him.[36]

Secretary Morgenthau objected to the measures that Bullitt outlined as too expensive, but the president had made up his mind. Morgenthau's opposition softened somewhat after Roosevelt told him that eight new airplane factories would be built in high-unemployment areas without additional cost to the government. Separately, Harry Hopkins had already met with General George Marshall, deputy chief of staff in the army and a rising star in the military, to devise a plan to use the Works Progress Administration to support the buildup. As Roosevelt explained to Morgenthau, "Hopkins could build these plants without cost to the Treasury because it would be work relief which otherwise would have to be provided in any case." It was an unusual role for Hopkins, a former social worker, but the president trusted him to get the job done. The trust turned out to be well placed; Roosevelt's confidence in Hopkins would only increase as the situation in Europe deteriorated.

24

I COULD SCARCELY BELIEVE SUCH THINGS COULD OCCUR

With its English oak paneling, gleaming silver chandeliers, and massive stone fireplace, Harvard Hall, in Boston's Harvard Club, epitomized privilege and power. Former ambassador Dodd stood at the lectern in the great hall before a room packed with lawyers, bankers, and businessmen. By the summer of 1938, it had been widely reported in the American press that a great many Jews had been arrested in Germany and thrown into concentration camps. Like too many American institutions in the 1930s, Harvard University had been slow to condemn the Nazi regime. Amid controversy, Nazi press liaison Putzi Hanfstaengl had returned to campus for his twenty-fifth reunion in 1934 and attended a cocktail party at the house of the university president, James B. Conant. The following year, the Harvard administration permitted Nazi Germany's consul general in Boston to place a wreath bearing the swastika emblem in the university chapel. Now, as he had countless times before, former ambassador Dodd warned his audience that Hitler was a megalomaniac who would plunge Europe into war. He emphasized Hitler's hatred of Jews and declared he "intends to kill them all."[1]

Many Americans were disgusted by reports of the German concentration camps, but often not disgusted enough to press for something to be done about them. Worse, there were many Americans who were not disgusted at all. There was, in fact, a strong anti-Semitic undercurrent in the American public that permeated the Department of State as well. In mid-October, a German diplomat stationed in London recounted to the German Foreign Office a conversation he had with Ambassador Kennedy, who allegedly claimed that anti-Jewish sentiment was prevalent in the United States, and that "whole segments of the population sympathized with the German attitude toward Jewry."[2] Kennedy's appraisal, given in private, was undoubtedly accurate nevertheless.

Kennedy provided a more public window into his thinking about Nazi Germany on October 19, when he was honored as the first foreigner ever to deliver the keynote address at the British Navy League's annual Trafalgar dinner. Without specific direction or any policy input from either President Roosevelt or Secretary of State Hull in the aftermath of the Munich Agreement, and seemingly unaware that the president was beginning to focus on military preparedness, Kennedy decided to use the occasion to express his admiration for Prime Minister Chamberlain and the policy of appeasement. Before a polite but skeptical audience, Kennedy stated, "It has long been a theory of mine that it is unproductive for both the democratic and dictator countries to widen the division now existing between them by emphasizing their differences, which are not self-apparent . . . The democratic and dictator countries differ ideologically, to be sure, but that should not preclude the possibility of good relations between them."[3]

Ambassador Kennedy's speech provoked criticism on both sides of the Atlantic. Many in Britain worried that in the event their country was drawn into war, Kennedy was suggesting they would have to fend for themselves. In the United States, the criticism centered more on the ambassador's appeasement of Hitler. The *New York Post* editorialized, "For [Kennedy] to propose that the United States make a friend of the man who boasts that he is out to destroy democracy, religion, and all of the other principles which free Americans hold dear . . . passes understanding." Kennedy brushed off the criticism as calumny from a "number of Jewish publishers and writers." His son Jack, now a student at Harvard, acknowledged that the Trafalgar address had been "unpopular with the Jews" but felt confident that the address had been well received "by everyone who wasn't bitterly anti-fascist."[4]

A few weeks later, the world witnessed the horror that Hitler was unleashing on Jews in Germany after Herschel Grynszpan, a seventeen-year-old Polish Jewish refugee, born in Germany and living in Paris, killed a German diplomat. Grynszpan, seeking revenge for the Nazis' deportation of his parents to Poland, marched into the German embassy in Paris and shot to death Ernst vom Rath, a third secretary in the embassy. Nazi propaganda minister Joseph Goebbels immediately seized upon the incident to whip up anti-Semitism and encourage widespread retribution. During the night of November 9 and stretching into the early morning of November 10, plainclothes Nazi hoodlums burned to the ground more than 250 synagogues, looted more than 7,000 Jewish businesses, and murdered dozens of Jews throughout Germany. Known as Kristallnacht, or the "Night of Broken Glass," the brutality of the Nazis sent shock waves throughout the world.[5]

Goebbels claimed that the violence against the Jews had been purely spontaneous. In actuality, he had played a key role in organizing the pogrom by ensuring that police and fire brigades remained idle during the rampage. Moreover, days after the violence, storm troopers rounded up more than thirty thousand Jewish men, herded them into boxcars, and sent them to concentration camps. Hitler decreed that Jews would no longer be allowed to own businesses unless non-Jews managed them. Curfews for Jews were imposed, and their travel was restricted.[6] William Dodd, the onetime Cassandra of the ambassador corps, had been right all along.

At his weekly press conference a few days later, President Roosevelt expressed outrage at the Nazi rampage, declaring that he "could scarcely believe that such things could occur in the twentieth century."[7] Roosevelt had been silent on Hitler's treatment of German Jews, but after Kristallnacht, he announced his intention to recall the U.S. ambassador, Hugh Wilson. It was a purely symbolic gesture. The Nazis no longer concerned themselves with public opinion, and it had no appreciable impact on the

Hitler government. Indeed, as Goebbels plotted the elimination of Jews from German society, a representative from the German Foreign Ministry challenged him in a meeting, suggesting that American public opinion should be taken into account. Before Goebbels could respond, Goering dismissed any consideration of the United States, calling it a "country of scoundrels" and "a gangster state." For his part, Hitler had an even more simplistic and menacing view of the United States, referring to it as part of a worldwide Jewish conspiracy.[8]

Polling in the United States showed that 94 percent of the American public disapproved of the Nazi treatment of Jews. However, the same poll revealed that 72 percent did not want to increase immigration quotas for Jews. Perhaps with this in mind, the president, who had suffered a significant defeat in the midterm elections and may have felt this was not the time to use up more of his political capital, declared that a change in the quota system "was not in contemplation."[9] Roosevelt hoped that there might be some creative alternatives to immigration and asked Undersecretary Welles to send him "any information the State Department has in regard to possible places for Jewish colonization in any part of the world." It was not clear whether the president was seeking viable alternatives for increasing Jewish immigration to the United States or, more likely, just wanted political talking points. He didn't ask for a commission to study the issue; he didn't ask Congress to hold hearings; in fact, he told Welles he did "not want any extensive memorandum—just what you happen to have on hand. I will return it to you at once after looking at it."[10]

Roosevelt sent another memorandum to Welles with a copy of a press article that criticized Ambassador Kennedy for not being especially interested in the plight of German refugees. The president attached a note for the undersecretary: "Did you see this? It is amusing."[11] Roosevelt, irritated by Kennedy's outspokenness, was content to have his ambassador in Britain receive negative press over the refugee issue. However, Kennedy's indifference to Jewish immigration didn't excuse the president's own lack of humanitarian leadership.

Convinced that Hitler could ultimately threaten the Americas, Roosevelt now focused on military preparedness and how he might augment American defenses by circumventing the neutrality laws. On the latter issue, the president believed American public opinion was shifting in his favor. Again, polling suggested that nearly two-thirds of the American people would support a boycott of German goods, though trade was limited anyway. The same poll revealed that over 90 percent of Americans believed that Hitler's territorial aspirations extended beyond Czechoslovakia. Perhaps most significantly, 60 percent of the public considered that German aggression made war more likely than peace.

In the aftermath of the Munich agreement, President Roosevelt met with one of the American heroes of World War I, retired general John J. Pershing. Before appointing Bullitt to serve in Paris, Roosevelt had asked Pershing to be the United States ambassador to France, but the general felt his advanced age prevented him from taking on such an important assignment. Still, Pershing stayed in contact with the president—he had been the first to recommend General George Marshall for high-level promotion— and Roosevelt trusted his judgment. In a long, detailed letter to the president, Pershing summarized their conversation, and laid out his recommendations for strengthening the armed forces:

> As to larger additions to our present air force, there can be no question but that it is highly advisable to have more planes available, and especially to bring about the coordination of our aeronautical industries so that they can quickly respond to tremendous increases in the production of what the Government requires . . . My concern at the moment is directed towards those requirements, or I should say essentials, in which the General Staffs of the world know that we are pathetically deficient . . . Ground forces will bear exactly the same relation to large air fleets of bombers that they do to the Navy for the protection of its bases.[12]

Roosevelt thanked Pershing for his letter and offered that he had ordered "a study made of the ammunition situation and also artillery—

especially the anti-aircraft guns." The president added that he was "having the General Staff study the ground forces that are necessarily connected with increased air operations."[13]

A few weeks later, Roosevelt sent a memorandum to the secretary of the navy, the assistant secretary of the navy, and the chief of naval operations, demanding, "Navy yards doing construction should be ordered—not requested—to put as many people to work on new ships as it is possible to use at any given time—two shifts or even three shifts where they are possible. They should be ordered to keep these people steadily on the job and not take them off for other Navy works."[14]

Germany was not the only European country that concerned Roosevelt. For many months, he had worried that American neutrality in the Spanish Civil War worked against the Loyalists, the legitimate government of Spain, and favored Franco's fascists, who were openly supported by Hitler and Mussolini.[15] Fearing the specter of a fascist alliance, Roosevelt asked his attorney general, Homer Cummings, "to study the Spanish Embargo from the legal point of view." The president, concerned about leaks to the press, added, "No written opinion seems advisable."[16]

Given the public polling, President Roosevelt may have sensed that the American people were becoming increasingly receptive to a more activist foreign policy, especially in support of the democracies fighting for their survival in Europe. However, he was acutely aware that isolationists still commanded significant influence in the United States and actually had increased their numbers in Congress during the midterm elections. Many of Roosevelt's preferred candidates had lost. While Democrats still controlled the House and the Senate, on any given issue, the president could likely not only be challenged but also defeated. It was the skillfulness of Roosevelt's leadership, in combination with the adroitness of his political mind, that allowed him to sense that while his institutional power might be waning, the American people would follow him if he could clearly define the threat and effectively communicate the challenge.

Ambassador Kennedy looked forward to returning to the United States for a two-month vacation and the opportunity to celebrate Christmas with his family in Palm Beach. Before leaving London, he wrote to Charles Lindbergh that he was "a little uncertain as to just where America is heading. I am not at all happy about the situation as it is." Kennedy expressed admiration for Chamberlain as "a man who was willing to work out a deal," but he acknowledged that "the doctrine I preached in my Navy Day speech of trying to work out something with the totalitarian states seems to be, at least temporarily, out of commission." Kennedy worried that "unless something is worked out, it is hard to tell what is going to happen to civilization."[17]

Harold Nicolson, a British member of Parliament and a critic of Chamberlain, put it more bluntly: "It has been a bad year . . . Next year will be worse."[18]

25

METHODS, SHORT OF WAR

President Roosevelt stood at the lectern in the House Chamber on January 4, 1939, and looked out at the members of Congress sitting in rows of heavy, wooden armchairs arranged in a semicircle on tiered platforms facing the Speaker's rostrum. Behind the president, a frontispiece of marble columns framed a draped American flag, ironically flanked by two bronze fasces—tied bundles of wheat—a centuries-old symbol of the power of life over death that had been appropriated by Mussolini and the fascists. Roosevelt recognized a number of his Democratic congressional supporters. He also saw a number of influential Democrats whom he had campaigned against in primaries leading up to the midterm elections; they had nonetheless won reelection. There were also many new faces; Congress now included a greatly strengthened Republican minority. In a rebuke of the New Deal and the president, the Democratic Party had lost seventy-two seats in the House of Representatives and seven seats in the Senate.

After polite applause, Roosevelt began his address on a somber note: "In reporting on the state of the nation, I have felt it necessary on previous occasions to advise the Congress of disturbance abroad and of the need of putting our own house in order in the face of storm signals from across the seas. As this Seventy-sixth Congress opens there is need for further warning. A war which threatened to envelop the world in flames has been averted; but it has become increasingly clear that world peace is not assured."[1]

It was the first State of the Union address in which President Roosevelt had prioritized foreign policy over his domestic agenda. He described the challenge in existential terms: "There comes a time in the affairs of men when they must prepare to defend, not their homes alone, but the tenets of faith and humanity on which their churches, their governments and their very civilization are founded . . . This generation will nobly save or meanly lose the last best hope on earth."[2]

The speech would be remembered as "The Methods of War" because Roosevelt made clear to Congress that he was considering various options to confront what he termed "acts of aggression against sister nations." Mindful of continuing isolationist sentiment, Roosevelt declared that there might be "methods, short of war," by which the United States could help curb the rise of fascism in Europe.[3] At the very least, the president, who had signed three neutrality laws during his second term, felt it was time to reassess their impact because "our neutrality laws may operate unevenly and unfairly—may actually give aid to an aggressor and deny it to the victim."[4]

For the most part, Congress disregarded Roosevelt's speech and ignored his warnings. Only days after the address, Senator Key Pittman of Nevada, the chairman of the Foreign Relations Committee, agreed to hold hearings on the rise of fascism in Europe, beginning with focus on Spain, where General Franco's Nationalist forces now controlled the country. However, in light of the deep divisions within the United States over the Spanish Civil War, committee members, seeing no political advantage to shining a spotlight on a foreign conflict with religious overtones, asked the chairman to postpone hearings. The president still had support for the New Deal, but many in Congress who had voted for his domestic agenda did not want to jeopardize it with an expensive diversion into the affairs of Europe. Others, whom at one time Roosevelt might have either intimidated or perhaps charmed, did not think the president would run for a third term and considered him a lame duck.

FDR and campaign manager, Louis Howe (second from the left), sitting together in Hyde Park, New York. Howe was the president's most trusted political adviser, July 11, 1932. *(Courtesy of FDR Library)*

FDR and James Roosevelt waving to a crowd as they campaign from the back of a train, 1932. *(Courtesy of Roosevelt Library)*

Ambassador Dodd is shown leaving the Palace of President Hindenburg in Berlin after presenting his credentials to the head of the Reich. According to press reports, Dodd's remarks to von Hindenburg were well received in Germany and throughout Europe. *(Courtesy of Getty Images)*

FDR celebrating his birthday at a toga party. Eleanor Roosevelt is seated over the president's right shoulder, and Louis Howe, in profile wearing a Centurion helmet, is at the right of the photo, second row from the top. Roosevelt loved a good laugh, January 30, 1934. *(Courtesy of Roosevelt Library)*

Papal Nuncio Msgr. Orsenigo, Joseph Goebbels, and Ambassador William Dodd. By June 1934, Dodd vowed to never host Nazi leadership at the U.S. Embassy, March 14, 1934. *(Courtesy of Getty Images)*

President Roosevelt prepares to deliver a fireside chat to the American people. He didn't address the gathering storm in Europe until September 1939 in his thirteenth fireside chat. *(Courtesy of Roosevelt Library)*

Hierarchy of the Nazis: Hitler, Goering, and Goebbels in Nuremburg, September 1934. *(Courtesy of Roosevelt Library)*

William Dodd was the chairman of the history department at the University of Chicago before becoming United States Ambassador to Germany. The ambassador delivers a lecture on Abraham Lincoln in front of the Carl Schurz Association in Berlin, June 14, 1935. *(Courtesy of Getty Images)*

Eleanor Roosevelt watches the president carving a turkey for the annual Thanksgiving feast in Warm Springs, Georgia, November 29, 1935. *(Courtesy of Roosevelt Library)*

Joseph P. Kennedy being sworn in Ambassador to Great Britain by Justice Stanley Reed in the White House Oval Office as President Roosevelt looks on, February 18, 1938. Roosevelt and Kennedy never trusted one another. *(Courtesy of Getty Images)*

Ambassador Joseph P. Kennedy with two of his sons, John F. Kennedy (left), later the thirty-fifth president of the United States, and Joseph Jr. (right), killed in action during WWII, in London, 1938. *(Courtesy of Getty Images)*

After leaving Vienna en route to London, Austrian neurologist Sigmund Freud, the founder of psychoanalysis, is met by Ambassador William Bullitt at the train station in Paris, June 1, 1938. *(Courtesy of Getty Images)*

Ambassador William Bullitt (left) and his private secretary, Carmel Offie, enjoy reading while aboard an ocean liner en route to the United States, circa 1938. *(Courtesy of Yale University Library)*

President Roosevelt addresses Congress on January 30, 1939: "A war which threatened to envelop the world in flames has been averted; but it has become increasingly clear that world peace is not assured." *(Courtesy of Roosevelt Library)*

President Roosevelt signing the Conscription Act, September 16, 1940. *Courtesy of Roosevelt Library)*

A woman from the Sudeten region of Czechoslovakia cries while giving the Nazi salute. Germany occupied the Sudeten on October 1, 1938. *(Courtesy of Roosevelt Library)*

U.S. Undersecretary of State and President Roosevelt's envoy to Europe, Sumner Welles, with U.S. Ambassador to Great Britain, Joseph P. Kennedy, say goodbye to First Lord of the Admiralty Winston Churchill, after paying him a visit. *(Courtesy of Getty Images)*

The President and First Lady in evening attire, 1940. Eleanor was in many ways the President's most important confidante, although their marriage was an unconventional one. *(Courtesy of Getty Images)*

Breckinridge Long was appointed Ambassador to Italy in April 1933. In 1940 President Roosevelt appointed him as assistant Secretary of State overseeing, among other things, immigration of European refugees to the United States. Long may have been the worst appointment Roosevelt made during his entire presidency. *(Courtesy of United States Holocaust Museum)*

President Roosevelt rides in a convertible with Missy LeHand and Ambassador William Bullitt. LeHand and Bullitt had at one time been romantically involved, July 22, 1940. *(Courtesy of Getty Images)*

Harry Hopkins with President Roosevelt's dog, Fala, at Hyde Park. Hopkins became President Roosevelt's most trusted adviser on foreign policy. Photograph by Margaret Stuckley (date unknown). *(Courtesy of Roosevelt Library)*

A bomb-damaged street in London, 1941. For eight months beginning in September 1940, the Luftwaffe dropped bombs on London and other strategic cities across Britain. *(Courtesy of Roosevelt Library)*

Harry Hopkins shaking hands with Minister Winston Churchill as his aide looks on, after Hopkins's visit to 10 Downing Street. Hopkins later reported to President Roosevelt on Britain's need for war materiel, June 26, 1941. (*Courtesy of Getty Images*)

President Roosevelt and Prime Minister Churchill aboard the HMS *Prince of Wales* during the Atlantic Conference in Placentia Bay, Newfoundland. Army Chief of Staff George Marshall is standing second from left, August 10, 1941. *(Courtesy of Roosevelt Library)*

President Roosevelt broadcasting from the White House to the American people on September 11, 1941: He predicts Nazi intentions to gain control of the Western Hemisphere, citing Hitler's broken promises and German invasion of European nations. The President argues that "freedom of the seas" is essential to preventing Nazi incursion into the Western Hemisphere and argues that support for Britain in their fight against Germany is critical to preserving this freedom. *(Courtesy of Roosevelt Library)*

They neither feared him nor felt compelled to support him. And there were some who simply shrugged at the prospect of a fascist Europe.

Roosevelt, however, did not give up easily. Secretary of State Hull authorized the two most important United States ambassadors, Bullitt and Kennedy, to testify before a joint hearing of the House Foreign Affairs Committee and the Senate Committee on Military Affairs on January 14, 1939. Although the hearing was closed to the public, the ambassadors' testimony was selectively leaked to the press to bolster the president's case for an increase in military expenditures. Kennedy, careful not to express his admiration for Germany, described the situation in Europe as "gloomy" and "dismal."[5] Kennedy and Bullitt had both spent time with Charles Lindbergh, and based on his estimates of Germany's military strength, they testified that German airplane production was likely greater than that of Britain and France combined. The ambassadors supported President Roosevelt's call for a $2 billion appropriation to strengthen America's armed forces and military defenses. The next morning *The New York Times* ran the headline ENVOYS VOICE FEAR OF WAR IN SPRING.[6]

Only a week later, the president's plans were dealt a severe setback when an American military plane crashed on a test flight in California. Newspapers reported that a French pilot had been pulled from the burning wreckage. The White House was forced to acknowledge that the president had allowed French pilots to train with sophisticated American airplanes, leading to rampant speculation in the press of a surreptitious pact. The training exercises had been the brainchild of Ambassador Bullitt, working with the French government.

Roosevelt summoned members of the Senate Committee on Military Affairs to the White House to assure them that training French pilots did not mean that France and the United States had a secret alliance, but he also wanted to convey that a war in Europe could negatively impact the United States. However, he slipped up when he carelessly said, "The American frontier [is] on the Rhine." One of the senators leaked the comment to the press. When a reporter asked what Roosevelt meant, the president compounded his error by claiming that he hadn't said anything of the sort—it was "a deliberate lie" made up by a "boob." Republican senator Hiram Johnson of California needled the president to the press, asking rhetorically, "Do you not think the American people have the right to know if they are down the road to war?"[7]

On the advice of Secretary of State Hull, the president reluctantly abandoned the plan to assist the French in the modernization of their air force. Although the affair damaged Roosevelt's credibility, it helped Ambassador Bullitt's reputation. The press concluded that Roosevelt's secret military training exercise with the French could only have been carried out with Ambassador Bullitt acting as the liaison. As *Newsweek* magazine reported, "The American public knew nothing of the amazing Bullitt and his one-man stop-Hitler campaign until an unscheduled California plane crash revealed that he had engineered, over the protests of War Department professionals, a deal to give France preference over the United States Army on new American-built airplane models."[8] *Time* magazine designated Ambassador Bullitt as Roosevelt's most important foreign policy adviser.

After hosting Justice Felix Frankfurter and his wife for cocktails, Franklin Roosevelt celebrated his fifty-seventh birthday on January 30 with a small dinner in the White House attended by family, friends, and a few of his closest staff. There were numerous toasts, including a humorous limerick written by Harry Hopkins—and read by him mimicking a Boston accent—that included a stanza poking fun at Ambassador Kennedy, who had returned to London.

> *Oh, Kennedy's necking with Nancy [Astor]*
> *Has tea in the Bishop's backyard*
> *The Queen is his notion of beauty*
> *Think's Chamberlain greater than God*

At 11:30 that evening, Roosevelt delivered a radio address for the birthday balls that were being held across the country to raise money in the fight to cure infantile paralysis, as poliomyelitis was called at the time. Attendees were encouraged to "dance so that others may walk."

Earlier in the day, President Roosevelt had received a telegram from Ambassador Bullitt, now back in Paris, wishing him "many happy returns." Bullitt had also sent the president a card ten days earlier in which he wrote, "I could try to tell you what it means to me to have you in the world, but I think you know . . . There is nobody like you, and I love you."[9]

That same day, four thousand miles away from Washington, in recognition of the sixth anniversary of his ascension to the chancellorship, Adolf Hitler delivered a nearly two-hour, rambling speech to the Reichstag in Berlin. As he had so many times before, Hitler railed against Jews: "It is a shameful spectacle to see how the whole democratic world is oozing sympathy for the poor tormented Jewish people, but remains hard-hearted and obdurate when it comes to helping them." Hitler maintained that war in Europe would result in "the annihilation of the Jewish race in Europe."[10] It was exactly as former ambassador Dodd had stated the previous summer in a speech at the Harvard Club in Boston when he warned of Hitler's plans to "kill them all."

26

THE LAST WELL-KNOWN MAN ABOUT WHOM THAT WAS SAID

In mid-March 1939, Hitler proceeded to consummate what he had begun months earlier in Czechoslovakia: its dismemberment and ultimate destruction as a sovereign nation. First, the führer warned the Czech president, Emil Hácha, who had succeeded Edvard Beneš, that he was prepared to intervene and forcibly annex his country. Recognizing that Czechoslovakia was less a unified country than a patchwork of ethnic enclaves, Hitler then moved to leverage the Slovak minority's desire for autonomy. On March 13, Hitler invited Slovak leader Jozef Tiso, a former Catholic priest turned politician, to Berlin and offered to support the Slovak People's Party push for independence if the party aligned itself with the National Socialist Party in Germany. The next day, Slovakia declared independence, calling itself the Slovak Republic, and Tiso sent Hitler a telegram, drafted by the Germans, requesting Nazi "protection." With the Sudeten and Slovakia now severed from Czechoslovakia, Hácha bowed to the inevitable and signed a prepared German statement handing over his country to Hitler. On March 15, German troops crossed the border into the Czech regions of Moravia and Bohemia without opposition or resistance. That evening, the swastika was raised over the Prague Castle, and Hitler announced to the world that he had established the new protectorate of Moravia and Bohemia. The Poles, the Hungarians, and the Russians would divvy up what was left of the country. Czechoslovakia had ceased to exist.[1]

Only a week later, Hitler pressured Lithuania to turn over to Germany the territory of Memel. Although Memel had once been part of Prussia, it had been annexed by Lithuania in 1923. Newspapers in Germany, controlled by the Nazis, praised Hitler's land grab, editorializing that Germany's territorial expansion should continue after Memel and recommending that Poland cede Danzig, another enclave where many German-speaking citizens resided. With the subjugation of Czechoslovakia, Hitler had shattered the illusion that he was only interested in creating a union of the German-speaking peoples across Europe. Hitler's growing German empire, and his brazen taking of Moravia and Bohemia—where the overwhelming majority of residents were not of German heritage—sparked concern and condemnation in the United States and around the world.

In Paris, Ambassador Bullitt cabled President Roosevelt, "Hitler's invasion of Czechoslovakia stunned . . . all Frenchmen." Bullitt claimed the invasion had ended "all possibility of diplomatic negotiations" and that for the French, "nothing remains but to develop as much armed force as possible, as rapidly as possible." The president refrained from public comment, instead venting privately that the British had opened the door for Hitler's aggression. The president was outraged by Hitler's perfidy but also furious at Chamberlain's pusillanimity. He told Bullitt, "I have the evening papers in front of me with headlines, 'Chamberlain washing his hands.'" Roosevelt asked Bullitt, "You know the last well-known man about whom that was said?" "Yes," Bullitt replied, "Pontius Pilate."[2]

Ambassador Kennedy was in Rome when he learned of Germany's occupation of Czechoslovakia. Sensing the threat of a wider European war, he immediately boarded an overnight train for Paris, where his wife,

Rose, was visiting for a few days. Arriving at 8:00 in the morning, and met by Carmel Offie at the station, Kennedy went to the Madeleine church and found Rose "praying with her eyes closed." Offie drove Kennedy and his wife to the ambassador's residence, where the two ambassadors had breakfast together. The usually ebullient Bullitt was downcast and discouraged, telling Kennedy that Hitler's incursion marked "the end of civilization."[3]

Ambassador Bullitt was now convinced that war with Germany was unavoidable and, on March 23, 1939, once again counseled Roosevelt to accelerate U.S. military preparations: "My guess is that by this time next year you will wish that you had an American Army of two million men ready for action." Bullitt expressed concern that Hitler could not be stopped in Europe. "The only great army on the side of decency is the French army," Bullitt wrote. He still held firm to his view that the Maginot Line was invincible and that French tanks were superior to German tanks, but he continued to worry over German air superiority, as well as Britain's lack of military preparation, claiming they "have even less of an army than we have, and it is even worse in all respects than our own." Bullitt concluded his letter to Roosevelt, writing, "The vital point, therefore, if war starts, will become the strength of the French Army . . . Americans will begin to realize that fact . . . when it is too late to create an American army and intervene in time. We ought to create that army now."[4]

The news only worsened for Roosevelt. On March 28, Franco's fascist forces in Spain, supported by both Hitler and Mussolini, seized Madrid. Tension in Europe was rising every day with the expectation that Hitler would strike again soon, almost certainly in Poland.

President Roosevelt worried that if Germany invaded Poland, France and Britain would likely declare war on Germany. Recognizing the potential need to aid western Europe's democracies, but hamstrung by the neutrality law, President Roosevelt conferred with congressional leaders on repealing it. "Well, Captain, we may as well face the facts," Vice President John Nance Garner, an isolationist, bluntly informed his boss.

"You haven't got the votes, and that's all there is to it." Sidestepping Garner and Congress, and showing a willingness to test the limits of executive power, Roosevelt asked his attorney general, Frank Murphy, about simply "ignoring" the Neutrality Act, even though, as he acknowledged, "I did sign it."[5]

27

MY MOTHER DOES NOT APPROVE OF COCKTAILS

Prime Minister Chamberlain saw that Hitler had deceived him about Czechoslovakia and humiliated him before the British people. Determined to show a new resolve, on the last day of March 1939, the prime minister addressed the House of Commons and declared that Britain would "lend the Polish government all support in their power" if "Poland were attacked."[1] Given that only weeks earlier Poland had stood by while Hitler occupied Czechoslovakia and then participated as a silent partner in its dissolution, Chamberlain's assurances seemed poorly timed. Many in Parliament wondered if Poland was worth defending.

The outrage over Hitler's territorial expansion in Europe was not shared by many influential voices in the United States. In his weekly radio address, Father Charles Coughlin claimed that the denunciations of Hitler were "raised by those who are more interested in destroying Germany than in saving democracy." Republican senator William Borah of Idaho sounded impressed by what Hitler had accomplished: "Gad, what a chance Hitler has! If he only moderates his religious and racial tolerance, he would take his place beside Charlemagne. He has taken Europe without firing a shot!"[2]

President Roosevelt recognized the prevailing isolationist sentiment in the United States and believed that while public opinion was shifting, it would not change with a speed that could match the urgency of the situation. He also confronted renewed pressure on the economic front as a recession dampened an already depressed job market. Nevertheless, Roosevelt now gave more of his time to foreign policy, focusing on Asia, where Japan's imperial army continued to ravage its neighbors, and on Europe, where war now seemed likely. Somehow the American people needed to understand that there was more at stake than improvement in the nation's economy; democracy itself was threatened. With this in mind, one of the president's first moves was to shore up America's relationship with its closest ally. For weeks, the White House and the Department of State had been working to finalize the details for the visit of Britain's King George VI and Queen Elizabeth.

Ambassador Kennedy had petitioned the Department of State for permission to return to the United States to take part in the festivities surrounding the royal visit. The department denied his request, likely on Roosevelt's instructions. The president knew Kennedy was being discussed as a potential candidate for president in 1940, and Roosevelt, yet to decide about a third term, saw no need to give the ambassador additional publicity. One of Kennedy's antagonists, Interior Secretary Harold Ickes, showed the president a copy of a British newspaper that reported Kennedy had been telling his "friends" that "the Democratic Party of the United States is a Jewish production" and that "Roosevelt will fall in 1940."[3] There is no proof that Kennedy actually made such comments, but it contributed to the president's increasingly negative view of his ambassador.

Then, too, Roosevelt believed Kennedy was completely mistaken about what was happening in Germany. The ambassador told Secretary of State Hull that he was "convinced" that Hitler didn't "want a fight." Kennedy explained to Hull that Hitler had "no money and he can't change all those people who are engaging in wartime activities without having a terrific problem."[4] However, neither Hull nor the president accepted that

Hitler's militarism and aggressive behavior in Europe could somehow be justified as a response to Germany's economic problems—as Kennedy seemed to suggest.

Interior Secretary Ickes continued to feed the president's irritation with Kennedy, relaying to him a conversation that the ambassador had with another diplomat, U.S. ambassador to Ireland John Cudahy. Ickes told Roosevelt that, according to Cudahy, Kennedy "does some pretty loud and inappropriate talking about the President. He does this before English servants, who are likely to spread the news . . . Kennedy is vulgar and coarse and highly critical in what he says about the President." Moreover, Ickes claimed that when Cudahy warned Kennedy about saying such things in front of the servants, Kennedy lashed out at him, declaring he "didn't give a damn."[5] Ickes also made Roosevelt laugh when he told him that the joke making the rounds in Parliament was that Chamberlain hoped to broaden his cabinet to make room for Kennedy.

On May 5, 1939, the day before King George VI and Queen Elizabeth were to depart for North America for their first visit, Ambassador Kennedy hosted a dinner party in their honor. Denied the opportunity to return to the United States, he and Rose decided to organize their own celebration and invited the cream of London society; Among the guests were the Duke and Duchess of Devonshire, the Duke and Duchess of Beaufort, Lord and Lady Halifax, Viscount Cranborne and his wife, and Lord and Lady Waldorf Astor.[6]

Ambassador Bullitt flew from Paris to London to attend the dinner, arriving "just after 8:00 p.m., very happy, and elegant looking, as usual," Ambassador Kennedy recorded in his diary.[7] Earlier in the spring, Rose Kennedy had crossed the English Channel to act as Bullitt's hostess at a dinner dance that he gave in honor of French president Albert Lebrun and his wife. Bullitt and Joe Kennedy had become friendly. They shared a disdain for the Department of State and an admiration for each other's political savvy, even though they increasingly disagreed over the role the United States should play in Europe.

The dinner was a stylish, sumptuous affair. Kennedy dressed in white tie and tails and Rose, in a long, satin evening gown. The London newspapers reported that King George wore the Order of the Garter, while Queen Elizabeth wore Queen Mary's Fringe Tiara, Queen Alexandra's Wedding Gift Necklace, and Queen Victoria's Fringe Brooch. The Kennedys served a dinner that was "All American," to prepare them, Joe joked, for the cooking on the other side of the Atlantic.

While Kennedy was pleased that his family's social status had never been higher, he remained deeply frustrated by what he viewed as an obstinate and bureaucratic Department of State that prevented him from influencing U.S. policy. Convinced that war still could be avoided, he decided to take matters into his own hands. Without seeking permission from the department, Ambassador Kennedy met secretly at the Berkeley Hotel with Helmuth Wohlthat, Goering's American-educated assistant who had flown to London at the invitation of James Mooney, the president of General Motors. Mooney's automobile company did a substantial amount of business in Germany, including the manufacture of trucks that would later be used against the United States during World War II. Kennedy hoped there might be some way to reach an accommodation with Germany and was especially interested in exploring whether economic ties between the United States and Germany could be deepened. "Each man made an excellent impression on the other," Mooney later wrote, "It was heartening . . . to witness the exertion of real effort to reach something constructive." Several days later, however, the *Daily Express* splashed across its front page the headline GOERING'S MYSTERY MAN IS HERE and revealed that Wohlthat had held a private meeting with the American ambassador.[8] It's not clear who leaked the story to the newspaper; perhaps the two men were spotted at the hotel together by a reporter, perhaps it was Kennedy himself, or it might have been the director of the Federal Bureau of Investigation—his informants were keeping an eye on Kennedy and reported the meeting to Director Hoover.

Kennedy's freelance diplomacy greatly irritated President Roosevelt, but the president decided not to say anything for the moment to avoid negative publicity in advance of the king and queen's visit. Prime Minister

Chamberlain, on the other hand, favorably viewed Kennedy's overtures to Germany. Only a few days after the press reports of the Wohlthat meeting, Chamberlain invited the ambassador and Rose to spend the weekend at Chequers, the palatial country house of the prime minister. The prime minister was still looking for a way to avoid conflict with Hitler but was running out of time to maneuver. He had publicly stated that Britain had no intention of isolating Germany. At the same time, Chamberlain also warned that German military intervention in Poland would bring about war.

On the evening of June 7, 1939, the king and queen of England, who began their North American tour in Canada weeks earlier, left Ontario aboard the royal train, arriving at 11:00 a.m. the next morning at Washington's Union Station. They were greeted at the station by the president and Mrs. Roosevelt. Outside, throngs of people filled the streets, hoping for a glimpse of the youthful royal couple as they were whisked off to the White House in a limousine.

According to Eleanor Roosevelt, the visit of the king and queen "was prepared for very carefully." Since the royals had visited Paris the previous year, Ambassador Bullitt sent Eleanor Roosevelt a detailed, secret memorandum recommending certain accoutrements to make them comfortable during the stay at the White House. She recalled that Bullitt "listed the furniture that should be in the rooms used by the king and queen, told me what I should have in the bathrooms and even the way the comfortables [sic] on the beds should be folded! He admonished me to have a hot-water bottle in every bed, which I did, though the heat of Washington must have made them unbearable." Eleanor would later write that she kept the memorandum as one of her "most amusing documents."

On the first evening of the royal couple's visit, the president and Mrs. Roosevelt hosted a glittering White House dinner. Guests assembled in the East Room before heading to the State Dining Room, where they feasted on calf's head soup, terrapin, peas, buttered beets, sweet-potato cones, and maple almond ice cream, all on a gold table service in use since the Madison administration. The president toasted the royal couple, remarking on the special relationship between the United States and Britain: "It is because each nation is lacking in fear of the other that we have unfortified borders between us. It is because neither of us fears aggression on the part of the other that we have entered no race of armaments the one against the other."

The following morning, the Roosevelts and the royals sailed from the navy yard on the presidential yacht down the Potomac to visit Mount Vernon. Next on the itinerary was a tour of the Fort Hunt Civilian Conservation Corps camp and a stop at Arlington National Cemetery. That evening, the British ambassador hosted the king and queen at a lavish reception at the British embassy on Massachusetts Avenue. Among the 1,400 guests were the German chargé d'affaires in Washington, Hans Thomsen, wearing "a swastika in his lapel," with his stylish wife, Bebe, on his arm.[9]

Breckinridge Long also attended the embassy party and chatted with the president's son James, who told the former ambassador that he believed his father intended to appoint Long to replace Hugh Wilson in Germany. Long, fully recovered from his stomach surgery, still admired Hitler, though he didn't approve of the führer's carving up of Czechoslovakia. Long was thrilled at the prospect of once again being an ambassador and looked forward to helping the United States establish better relations with the Third Reich.

The king and queen left for New York the following day, June 10. After visiting the British exposition at the World's Fair, they traveled from New York City by car to the president's Springwood estate in Hyde Park, New York. The president and Mrs. Roosevelt, who had arrived earlier that day on the presidential train, greeted them on the front steps. After showing the king into the living room, the president offered His Highness a cocktail, joking, "My mother does not approve of cocktails and thinks you should have a cup of tea." The king replied, "Neither does my mother," and requested a martini.[10]

During the king and queen's visit to Hyde Park, the president hosted an American-style barbecue, serving the royal couple hot dogs. Although the president's mother, Sara, was aghast at such informality, the king and queen appeared to enjoy themselves. It was exactly the image the president had hoped for. The United States and the United Kingdom shared the English language, but for the most part, Americans viewed their British cousins with skepticism as stuffy descendants of the nation that America's Founding Fathers had to battle for their independence. Roosevelt had his own reservations about the British, especially Prime Minister Chamberlain's appeasement of Hitler, but recognized that as constitutional democracies, Britain and the United States should be natural allies. He understood that if the image of Britain among Americans could be improved through the visit of the king and queen, efforts to back Britain in the event of war would be made easier.

Moreover, polling showed that the American people now favored by a small margin allowing munitions to be sent to Britain and France. Legislation, strongly supported by the president, had been introduced in the House of Representatives to amend the Neutrality Act. However, Congress remained strongly isolationist, defeating the bill before the royal visit. The president hoped the visit would increase pressure to reconsider the legislation and change the law.

At the conclusion of the royal couple's visit on June 12, Eleanor declared, "In many ways [the visit] was even more successful than [President Roosevelt] had expected." That evening the royal couple boarded the train in Poughkeepsie, taking them back to Canada. President Roosevelt waved farewell from his car parked alongside the railway station platform and shouted, "Good luck to you. All the luck in the world." As the train pulled away, the crowds who had gathered for a final peek at the king and queen spontaneously began singing "Auld Lang Syne." Eleanor recalled, "There was something incredibly moving about the scene—the river in the evening light, the voices of many people singing this old song, and the young couple waving good-bye." It was a bittersweet moment for the First Lady, who "thought of the clouds that hung over them and the worries they were going to face."[11]

While the highly publicized royal visit had undoubtedly brought Britain and the United States closer together, it did little to change Ambassador Kennedy's view that America should stay as far away as possible from the quagmire of Anglo-European affairs. The ambassador had closely followed the visit in the British newspapers and worried that it had only encouraged the view that, in the event of war, Britain could depend on the United States. As he put it to Associated Press correspondent James Reston, "A lot of people tell me that Britain is relying on two things today: One is God and the other is the United States, and recently you don't seem to have been counting too much on the Deity."[12] At a dinner party attended by the influential journalist Walter Lippmann, Kennedy was even more direct—and defeatist—declaring that war was inevitable and that Britain would be vanquished.

Even as Kennedy openly complained to his friends in the press about the burgeoning U.S. and British alliance, he felt his voice stifled by the Department of State. Not only had he been excluded from the royal visit, no one seemed to be listening to him: not the president, not Secretary of State Hull, and not even his good friend and former ally Prime Minister Chamberlain, who recognized that Hitler had gravely damaged his reputation. As Kennedy wrote to one of his journalist friends, "I am handicapped by my position, in that I cannot say what I think and I cannot resign and say what I think until at least the situation has become more quiet."[13]

Kennedy vented his frustration to Ambassador Bullitt, who promptly reported to the president, "I think I ought to tell you that Joe Kennedy phones several times a week to say that he is about to resign."[14] Bullitt liked Kennedy, and they shared some of the same frustrations about the Department of State, but they now had very different views of what America's role should be in Europe. Bullitt viewed Kennedy as a competitor and, similar to Harold Ickes, was only too happy to diminish him in the eyes of the president.

Besides sharing his dissatisfaction with Bullitt, Kennedy told his friend Arthur Krock, the *New York Times* journalist, that he wanted to resign, and Krock put it in the paper. The article described how "the young New Dealers have long ceased to approve of Mr. Kennedy." Krock went on to suggest that the only reason Ambassador Kennedy remained at his post was because the president implored him to stay for a decent interval before firing him. When Roosevelt read the story, he sent Kennedy a letter blasting Krock as "never in his whole life [having] said a really decent thing about any human being without qualifying it by some nasty dig at the end of the praise." The president called the journalist "a social parasite . . . who in his heart is a cynic who has never felt warm affection for anybody." Once again, Roosevelt worried about Kennedy's personal political agenda and feared he might do more harm at home than abroad. He ended his letter praising the ambassador as "doing a good job there" and professing "complete confidence" in him.[15] And once again, Roosevelt's flattery assuaged Kennedy—at least temporarily.

28

IT'S COME AT LAST—GOD HELP US

In the aftermath of the Munich Agreement, Winston Churchill, then a Conservative member of the British Parliament, delivered a radio address—"The Defence of Freedom and Peace"—directed at audiences in both the United States and the United Kingdom, in which he warned of the serious dangers that lay ahead if Hitler were not stopped. With palpable urgency in his voice, Churchill asked,

> We are left in no doubt where American conviction and sympathies lie; but will you wait until British freedom and independence have succumbed, and then take up the cause when it is three-quarters ruined, yourselves alone? I hear that they are saying in the United States that because England and France have failed to do their duty therefore the American people can wash their hands of the whole business. This may be the passing mood of many people, but there is no sense in it. If things have got much worse, all the more must we try to cope with them.

Churchill, the most prominent and outspoken interventionist in Britain, was convinced that the United States needed to become more involved in the defense of the European democracies. However, Prime Minister

Chamberlain did not trust Churchill. Notwithstanding growing pressure to include Churchill in his cabinet, the prime minister failed to do so until the fall of 1939 when he appointed him First Lord of the Admiralty, the same position Churchill had occupied during the First World War.

Like Chamberlain, Ambassador Kennedy held a dim view of Churchill, based not only on his politics but his character as well. Kennedy wrote to President Roosevelt on August 20, explaining Chamberlain's disdain for Churchill, saying, "[The prime minister] does not believe in the first place that he [Churchill] could deliver one-tenth as much as people think he could." Kennedy went on to disparage the outspoken Churchill as having "developed into a fine two-handed drinker [whose] judgment has never proven to be good."[1] Although he had made a fortune in the liquor industry, Kennedy abstained from drinking and considered it a weakness. But what especially worried Kennedy—and Chamberlain as well—was Churchill's belligerence toward Hitler. They feared Churchill would lead Britain into a senseless and devastating war.

President Roosevelt didn't trust the judgment of Kennedy or Chamberlain, but neither did he like Churchill, whom he knew only slightly. Back in 1918, as assistant secretary of the navy, Roosevelt first met the multitalented, yet highly controversial, British politician at a dinner in London. The president would later remark, "I have always disliked him . . . He acted like a stinker . . . lording over all of us."[2] The president would have also likely agreed with those who believed Churchill's judgment had been seriously flawed over many years. As First Lord of the Admiralty during World War I, Churchill spearheaded the ill-fated Gallipoli campaign in which Britain and France suffered upwards of 250,000 casualties during the Allied invasion of northwest Turkey. As an inexperienced Chancellor of the Exchequer in the 1920s, Churchill put Britain back onto the gold standard, a decision that many economists believed contributed to the Great Depression. More recently, he had supported King Edward VIII during the Abdication Crisis of 1936. However, Roosevelt was also aware that Churchill had a large political following in Britain. More importantly, given Churchill's inspiring radio address, the president considered Churchill to be one of the few British politicians willing to stand up to Hitler in the event of a war, which in the president's mind now seemed increasingly likely.

During the third week of August 1939, news reports chronicled Germany's military preparations for an invasion of Poland. The Associated Press (AP) reported on August 21, REICH TROOPS JAM ROUTES TO POLAND, describing how early in the morning "four of Germany's famous motorized 'super guns'"—sixteen-foot, ten-inch-caliber barrel cannons—"and an attendant ammunition train rolled through Gleiwitz" in southern Poland. The next day, another AP story reported, "Berliners who spent Sunday near the Baltic said today that train after train had rushed past them in a northeasterly direction carrying soldiers, cannons, anti-aircraft equipment, and field kitchens." That same day *The New York Times* also carried a story on Germany's mobilization of troops, describing how "at regular intervals large contingents of motorized military units left [Vienna] by way of the Danube Bridge." Ultimately, Hitler would amass 1.5 million troops along the Polish border.

Then, on August 24, the world woke up to a shocking development. Typical of headlines splashed across the front pages of newspapers was that of *The New York Times:* GERMANY AND RUSSIA SIGN 10-YEAR NON-AGGRESSION PACT; BIND EACH OTHER NOT TO AID OPPONENTS IN WAR ACTS, HITLER REBUFFS LONDON; BRITAIN AND FRANCE MOBILIZE. As *The Times* reported, German foreign minister Ribbentrop had traveled to Moscow to sign a treaty between the Soviet Union and Germany. The pact represented an important diplomatic victory for Hitler: an agreement with Stalin that if Germany attacked Poland, the Soviet Union would not join Britain and France if they chose to honor their treaty obligations to defend Poland. Based on the tepid response of the British and French to Germany's 1936 occupation of the Rhineland, its 1938 annexation of Austria, and its 1939 seizure of Czechoslovakia, Stalin calculated that the Western democracies would not stand up to Germany, and he shuddered at the prospect of the Soviet Union confronting Germany by itself. The pact meant Stalin would remain on the sidelines of a war he believed would soon engulf Europe—a war that would begin in Poland—where he also had territorial ambitions. Stalin's calculations were correct. Hitler had developed secret plans to begin the invasion of Poland on August 26. In the end, of course, the Soviet leader's gamble proved shortsighted; he failed to anticipate that any agreement with Hitler was worthless and that Germany would ultimately confront the Soviet Union.

President Roosevelt, still hoping that Italy might emerge as an honest broker to forestall a wider European conflict, sent a last-minute appeal to the king of Italy, Victor Emmanuel, on August 24, 1939. That evening, Ambassador Kennedy telephoned the White House, hoping to speak to the president. Kennedy was instead patched through to Undersecretary Sumner Welles—with the president eavesdropping on another line. Kennedy urged Welles to pressure the Poles to begin negotiations with the Nazis. When Welles responded that they were considering various options, Kennedy snapped, "I don't care how it is done, so long as something is done and done quickly." Welles then asked Kennedy if he thought the message to King Victor Emmanuel in Italy might have a positive effect. An impatient and frustrated Kennedy exploded, "The idea of addressing anything to the King of Italy who has been a nonentity for years doesn't make sense."[3] Kennedy knew that the only Italian leader who mattered was Mussolini.

Indeed, the following day Il Duce told Hitler, notwithstanding the Pact of Steel—the Italo-German alliance—Italy would not fight alongside Germany if it went to war over Poland. Hitler was irritated but knew he still had Mussolini's political support and didn't depend on Italy's military anyway. Besides, there were more significant developments for Hitler to consider; the British Parliament ratified their mutual assistance treaty with Poland. The French were equally resolute: Prime Minister Daladier telephoned Ambassador Bullitt to assure him that should Germany attack Poland, both France and England would rally at once to Poland's aid.[4]

Facing mounting opposition, Hitler hesitated, temporarily postponed the invasion, and communicated a final offer to the British: If Danzig was "returned" to Germany; he would make a proposal "to limit armaments [and] go back to peaceful pursuits." Hitler wanted Chamberlain to pressure Poland to give up its valuable port on the Baltic Sea in return for a vague proffer of peace. It smacked of Munich once again. While he waited for a response, Hitler refused to pull his troops back from the Polish border, and all of Europe remained on edge.

That evening, Prime Minister Chamberlain invited Ambassador Kennedy to join him and his top advisers in the cabinet room at 10 Downing Street. Asked for his recommendation in light of Hitler's proposal, Kennedy suggested that the prime minister work "to get [the] U.S. and other countries to get together on an economic plan that certainly would be more important to Germany than what he could possibly get out of getting anything in Poland." Kennedy argued that "to put in a billion or two now will be worth it, for if it works we will get it back and more."[5] The ambassador, who thought like the businessman he had once been, was offering a purely transactional approach to dealing with Hitler's megalomania. While his proposal was greeted with typical British politeness, it was also instantly rejected. Chamberlain, who had appeased Hitler at Munich, understood perhaps better than anyone at this point that Hitler's behavior could not be influenced by economic incentives.

While Chamberlain probed his cabinet for a response to Hitler, across the channel, Prime Minister Daladier held firm to his commitment that France would fight if Germany invaded Poland. In a message to Roosevelt on August 29, 1939, Ambassador Bullitt reiterated his confidence in the French prime minister. In part, Bullitt's esteem for Daladier derived from the prime minister's effusive praise of the ambassador, which Bullitt readily shared with the president:

> Daladier told me with tears in his eyes . . . that the recovery of France was not due to him, but to me, and added that he didn't know whether there was a God or not, but if there was and I ever faced Him, I need only say: "I stand on what I did for the decency in the world when I was Ambassador in Paris!!!!!"[6]

On the evening of August 30, Kennedy stayed later than usual at the embassy to catch up on some paperwork. In a note to Eleanor Roosevelt, scribbled at the bottom of a pro forma letter, the ambassador wrote, "We are praying that, miraculously, war may be avoided, when only a month ago everyone thought things were definitely on the upgrade."[7] At 7:00, after receiving updated news from his staff that same evening, he cabled Secretary Hull that the Poles were ready to negotiate and the Germans "have actually formulated proposals." Later that night Kennedy talked with President Roosevelt over a secure transatlantic telephone line. The president let him know that Hitler had abandoned the request for a British proposal regarding Danzig, and instead had now made sixteen separate demands of the Poles. Clearly, Hitler was not looking to negotiate a compromise.

Kennedy went to bed that night still praying that some agreement could be reached to avoid war. He remained hopeful, in part because of a recent conversation he had with his son Joe Jr., who had dined the previous week in Berlin with Unity Mitford, a pro-Nazi British socialite who hailed from one of Britain's most prominent families. Mitford had told young Kennedy, "Hitler had really great admiration for the British—they really knew how to rule."[8] Ambassador Kennedy's hopes were further buoyed on the morning of September 1, when he telephoned William Bullitt in Paris, who was convinced that "things were much better." Bullitt told Kennedy that Hitler "didn't have the guts to fight."[9] While Kennedy and Bullitt both hoped for a peaceful outcome, neither ambassador was working with current, accurate information. Their views were instead based on spotty news bulletins and the reassurances they received from high-level contacts.

Only minutes after he finished talking with Bullitt, Kennedy received startling and incontrovertible news: "[It] came with a rush, like a torrent spewing from the wires—German troops had crossed the border; German planes were bombing Polish cities, and killing civilians; the Germans were using poison gas."[10] Danzig was the first city to fall.

Missy LeHand was asleep in her third-floor bedroom in the White House when she was awakened by the loud ringing of the telephone next to her bed. She turned on her bedside lamp and glanced at her small alarm clock. It was 3:05 in the morning. Missy picked up the telephone receiver and heard the familiar voice of Bill Bullitt. She immediately sensed the tension in his voice as he explained that he had just talked to Ambassador Biddle in Warsaw; the Germans had attacked Poland. Bullitt needed to be patched through to the president at once and asked her to authorize the White House switchboard operator to wake him.

The president answered the telephone, surprisingly alert, and Bullitt reported that the German army and air force had crossed into Poland in overwhelming force and with great rapidity in what later became known as Blitzkrieg, or "lightning war." Roosevelt sounded more fatalistic than shocked. "It's come at last," he said, "God help us all."[11] He thanked Bullitt, told him to keep him apprised, and then pressed another button on his phone. He asked the White House switchboard operator to contact both Secretary Hull and Undersecretary Welles. Minutes later, he also asked Missy LeHand to contact Ambassador Kennedy in London.

After hearing the news reports of Germany's invasion, Kennedy left his residence and arrived at the embassy early in the morning. Staff immediately informed him that Prime Minister Chamberlain had sent Hitler an ultimatum to withdraw his troops from Poland by 11:00 a.m., or he would deliver an address at 11:15 to inform the British people that Britain was declaring war on Germany. Kennedy gathered staff in his office and listened to the broadcast on a small radio perched on his desk. At one point, tears welled up in the ambassador's eyes as an emotional Chamberlain declared, "Everything that I have worked for, everything that I have hoped for, everything that I have believed in during my public life has crashed in ruins."[12] Soon after the address, Kennedy telephoned 10 Downing Street, intending to leave a message of personal support for the man who in his view had performed "a great service" to "the world and especially for England." When Chamberlain heard that the ambassador was on the line, he came to the phone and thanked him for his steadfast support. His voice quaking, Chamberlain said, "We did the best we could have done but it looks as though we have failed."[13]

Ambassador Kennedy hung up the telephone and rushed off to Parliament to listen to the reaction to the prime minister's address. He had only been seated for a minute when he was told that he had "a very important phone call." As he later recorded in his diary, "I got myself a private office and was surprised and pleased to hear Missy's voice. It was sad and she told me how she was thinking of me and really was terribly sweet. [She] Asked me to call the President as he wanted to talk to me. She said how proud she was of the way I was doing this job over here and the President was too. I thanked her and said I hoped to see her soon."[14]

Kennedy reached the president, still in bed, at around 6:30 a.m. eastern standard time. Still emotional, and deeply pessimistic, Kennedy relayed that Prime Minister Chamberlain had declared war on Germany, and he despaired, "It is the end of the world . . . the end of everything."[15] Kennedy's lament echoed Bullitt, who after the German occupation of Czechoslovakia told Kennedy, "It is the end of civilization." To Roosevelt, however, such hand-wringing at a critical time only confirmed that his ambassador to London was a defeatist and no longer the right man for the job.

The streets of Washington, D.C., were dark and deserted when Secretary Hull arrived at the State Department around 3:45 a.m. Undersecretary Welles drove in from his mansion off Dupont Circle, arriving a few minutes after his boss. Other senior officials, including Assistant Secretary Moffat, gathered in the secretary's office for an emergency meeting. Dispatches came into the department that Hitler had attacked Danzig with over fifty divisions. Other reports indicated that German planes were bombing Polish cities and there were many casualties. Hull telephoned Bullitt and Kennedy, asking for their news and appraisal of the carnage. Bullitt reiterated what he had told the president the week before; in the event of war, the United States should issue an appeal to all combatants to refrain from the bombing of civilians.

Hull learned from Ambassador Phillips in Italy that Prime Minister Mussolini, fearing an Anglo-French naval and military force might retaliate against Italy, wanted to jump-start negotiations among Britain, France, and Germany. Since much of the information Hull received was incomplete—coming across the wires from various news outlets—neither the department nor the White House issued any official statement condemning the invasion. Hull and the president agreed that Bullitt's suggestion of a blanket appeal to combatants to avoid civilian casualties was a sound idea. Welles drafted the statement, and as Hull remembered, "We accordingly dispatched it."

Later that morning, President Roosevelt called a press conference to reassure the American people that Germany's invasion of Poland would not lead to American involvement in another war. *The New York Times* would later report, "He appeared to be neither exuberant nor depressed by the turn of events that kept him from his bed for all but a few hours." When asked 'Can we keep out of it?' The President cast his eyes downward for a moment as he pondered the request for comment. Then he replied: 'Only this—that I not only sincerely hope so, but I believe we can, and thus every effort will be made by the Administration to do so.'"[16]

Following the press briefing, the president convened his cabinet. Speaking in an uncharacteristically personal and reflective tone, he referred to the early-morning phone call from Ambassador Bullitt, declaring that he "had been startled by a strange feeling of familiarity." Roosevelt shared that as a young assistant secretary of the navy during World War I, the telephone beside his bed "brought me . . . tragic messages in the night." He said that he felt that after Bullitt's call, he was "picking up again an uninterrupted routine." The president then gave a more honest assessment of the challenges ahead than he had only hours earlier in his press conference: "Unless some miracle beyond our present grasp changes the hearts of men, the days ahead will be crowded days—crowded with the same problems, the same anxieties that filled to the brim those September days of 1914. For history, does, in fact, repeat."[17]

On September 3, *The New York Times* ran an a large headline in bold letters on its front page: FRANCE MOBILIZES: 8,000,000 ON CALL. Along with Great Britain, France had declared war on Germany, and the *Times* story described how the French government had called up "its armed forces, declared martial law throughout the country and ordered its parliament into special session." The reporting then lapsed into editorializing: "There is no doubt in anyone's mind that in dealing with Hitlerian Germany there is now no alternative for France than to accept the challenge which has been thrown down in Poland." But the French did not attack Germany, leading Churchill to comment, "This battle had been lost some years before," an oblique reference to France's failure to confront Germany's remilitarization after World War I.[18]

After the French and British declarations of war against Germany, American citizens living and traveling in Europe rushed to United States embassies and consulates seeking safe passage home. Undersecretary Welles asked Breckinridge Long to direct a special division being set up to support United States citizens who wanted to return home and to deal with any other unexpected emergencies caused by the outbreak of the war. Welles tapped Hugh Wilson, former ambassador to Germany, to be Long's assistant. The undersecretary also told Long what must have been already quite obvious to him: consideration of his appointment as ambassador to Germany would have to be shelved for the time being.

Long immediately set himself to the task. He made contact with each of the U.S. ambassadors in Europe, asking them to provide assessments of repatriation needs. He scoured the navy and the merchant marine to find suitable transports. He then established the procedures and length of time it would take to send ships to Europe to bring Americans back home.

Rescuing Americans from Europe became even more complicated on September 3 when the conflict spread to the Atlantic Ocean; a

German submarine torpedoed the British liner *Athenia* with fourteen hundred passengers aboard. One hundred twelve passengers, including twenty-eight Americans, lost their lives.[19] Long, acutely aware of the increasing danger from German submarines, concluded that it might take another three weeks to coordinate U.S. naval escorts for American transport ships headed for Europe. The ambassadors—with the notable exception of Kennedy—were grateful that someone in the department was focused on dealing with a rapidly deteriorating situation.

Kennedy's pique stemmed from the fact that the greatest numbers of Americans stranded in Europe were in the United Kingdom. He implored Secretary Hull to act quickly. "After all there is a war on, and it is quite conceivable that England will be bombed," he said. "If so, it is probable that Americans will be killed because there is no place in England that we can store these people and promise them immunity."[20] In the aftermath of the *Athenia* incident, Kennedy grew impatient and once again contacted the State Department to insist that ships be sent immediately. When there was no reply to his cable, Kennedy complained to the *New York Herald Tribune,* which reported that he made an expletive-filled denunciation of the Department of State's sluggish response to the crisis.[21]

Long recorded in his diary that Kennedy "has been terribly explosive," adding that the ambassador to Great Britain "seems to think that the only people needing repatriation are in the lobby of the American Embassy in London. As a matter of fact, there are 2800 in Ireland; there are many thousand in France, and there are scattered and spread hundreds of them in [countries across Europe] . . . Kennedy had been condemning everybody and criticizing everything and has antagonized most of the people in the Administration." Long thought Kennedy "was hurting himself and . . . the news stories and publicity items which went out of London with his permission, if not with his origination, indicated that he did not view the situation normally."[22]

By this point, the president felt Kennedy had become a liability and wanted to recall him. "I want to tell you something and don't pass it on to a living soul," Roosevelt said to Jim Farley, "[he sent] the silliest message to me I have ever received. It urged me to do this, that and the other thing in a frantic sort of way." But it was not just the panic that the president resented in Kennedy; he complained to Henry Morgenthau, the treasury secretary, that "Joe has been an appeaser and always will be an appeaser ... If Germany and Italy made a good peace offer tomorrow, Joe would start working on the King and his friend the Queen and from there on down to get everybody to accept it."[23]

After Germany's invasion of Poland, Ambassador Bullitt took precautions to prepare the embassy in Paris if the war came to France. He assigned all staff to one of three units—a blackout squad, a first-aid squad, and a police squad. Members of the blackout squad were posted on the roof at night to sound the alarm in case of an air raid. The police squad was responsible for assisting the many Americans who descended on the embassy; and the first-aid squad made preparations to help any American civilians or embassy personnel who might be injured during the bombing. Everyone was on a twenty-four-hour alert, including Hubert Earle, the son of former ambassador George Earle and a Harvard undergraduate, who was spending the summer working in the Paris embassy. The young man was walking home from dinner on the Rue de Rivoli on the evening of September 3, 1939, when he encountered Bullitt, who offered him a ride back to his apartment. As they passed the Hôtel des Invalides, Bullitt asked his driver to stop the car. The ambassador and the aspiring young diplomat got out and stood on the sidewalk. According to Earle, "The Ambassador lifted his gaze and pointed toward the magnificent gold dome of the structure that housed Napoleon's tomb. 'It will be a frightful thing,'" he said, "'if they bomb our beautiful Paris. I can't bear to think of that dome of the Invalides in ruins, and it seems definitely possible that when war really starts, Paris and the other great capitals of Europe may be blasted off the map.'"[24]

Although Bullitt had from time to time equivocated about Hitler's intentions, he had long felt that the outbreak of war in Europe would mean World War II. Now that war had come, the ambassador wrote to President Roosevelt that he expected "the Germans to complete soon

their destruction of Poland; then to offer peace to France and England."
Bullitt predicted, "The French and British will reject this proposal and
go on fighting. Then the Germans will turn loose on France and England their full air force with everything including gas and bacteria." In
March, Bullitt had assured the president of the invincibility of the Maginot Line, but now he hedged, "I do not exclude altogether the possibility
that Germany may be able to break the French line, but I do not believe
that this will happen." And Bullitt, who at one time had been violently
opposed to U.S. intervention in Europe, had amended his view on this as
well: "It is, of course, obvious," he said, "that if the Neutrality Act remains
in its present form, France and England will be defeated rapidly . . . By
November, the war will, in the customary manner, hibernate." Finally,
the ever ambitious Bullitt had a suggestion for the president: "If I'm still
alive, that will be about the time for you to set me to work in the United
States of America . . . You can put me in the Cabinet."[25]

One diplomat who had not been the least surprised by Germany's invasion of Poland and the outbreak of world war was William Dodd, the
former ambassador to Germany.

Dodd had maintained a busy speaking schedule during 1938, continuing to warn anyone who would listen of the Nazi threat. However, after
experiencing chronic headaches and laryngitis, the former ambassador had
checked himself into Georgetown University Hospital in January 1939.
Diagnosed with bulbar palsy, a progressive paralysis that made it difficult
for him to speak or swallow, Dodd was forced to curtail his tour. As his
ability to take food became more and more difficult, he was admitted to
Mount Sinai hospital in New York for an abdominal operation in July. But
before he underwent the operation, he contracted a life-threatening case
of bronchial pneumonia. Although Dodd's illness was barely news in the
American press, Joseph Goebbels, Hitler's minister of propaganda, learned
that the former ambassador was on the verge of death and published an
article in his Nazi newspaper, *Der Angriff,* attacking Dodd as "one of the
strangest diplomats who ever existed . . . now back among those whom he
served for 20 years—the activist war-mongering Jews."[26] When a State

Department official learned that Dodd was critically ill at Mount Sinai, he informed both the White House and the secretary of state's office. President Roosevelt and Secretary of State Hull each sent Dodd wishes for a speedy recovery. Dodd was cheered by the good wishes, especially from the president, whom he continued to idolize, and recovered sufficiently to travel to his farm, Stoneleigh, in Round Hill, Virginia on July 27.

Only weeks later, Dodd was once again confined to his bed, this time with a feeding tube, his ability to speak deteriorating by the day. The State Department counselor, Judge Moore, who had always respected the former ambassador, visited him for the last time. Moore found Dodd "in a pitiful state. He was unable to talk and had to communicate with me by using a pad and pencil, and he was unable to take any nourishment except through a stomach tube." Moore described his visit with Dodd as "one of the saddest things I have known."[27]

Notwithstanding his grave illness, Dodd continued to keep up with current events. After the Nazi invasion of Poland, in a final plea to President Roosevelt, Dodd wrote, "Hitler intends to conquer the whole world. If we do not join England and France, we shall have a hard time. All democracies must co-operate, else they, the Swiss, the Hollanders, and the Swedes and others will be annexed . . . The democracies in Europe have neglected their statesmanship. If they had co-operated on several occasions, they would have succeeded. Now it is too late."[28] The former ambassador to Germany, an acolyte of Woodrow Wilson and a promoter of the League of Nations, reluctantly conceded the time had come for America to enter a new war and to fight for the future of democracy.

29

I'M TIRED, I CAN'T TAKE IT

Charles Lindbergh stood stiffly before six microphones lined up in front of him. The celebrated though personally reclusive aviator had never before spoken on American radio. Though he professed little interest in politics, he had decided that he could not "stand by" and watch his country "pushed into war." Now, on September 15, 1939, in a room at the Carlton Hotel in Washington, D.C., he prepared to deliver a nationwide radio broadcast, covered by the three major networks, warning the American people to resist United States participation in a new world war.[1]

"If we enter fighting for democracy abroad we may end by losing it at home," Lindbergh told Americans matter-of-factly. He declared that it "was not a question on banding together to defend the white-race from invasion." They should not blame Hitler, Lindbergh explained; rather the conflict in Europe was "simply one of those age-old struggles within our own family of nations, a quarrel rising from the errors of the last war." He predicted that if the United States became involved in the war, "We are likely to lose a million men, possibly several million—the best of American youth."[2]

The following day, Ambassador Kennedy telephoned Ambassador Bullitt in Paris; Bullitt gave him an earful. Kennedy asked whether Lindbergh's broadcast would have any effect on the Neutrality Bill then being debated in Congress, and Bullitt responded that Lindbergh was a "son of a bitch," adding, "He wants to be the Fuhrer in the U.S." Bullitt told Kennedy that he didn't think that either one of them should "go to the U.S.A. for the bill," but he added, "If there is a filibuster, I am going home and will stop at nothing. You've never seen me in a fight. I'll lay that opposition low. I'll drag [Senator] Borah's name prostrate over the front page of the paper." Borah, a Democratic senator from Idaho, was perhaps the most vociferous isolationist in the United States Senate and increasingly a thorn in the side of the president. Kennedy didn't argue with Bullitt, but neither did he agree with him. In his diary, he noted that Bullitt needed "to calm down and start working for the U.S. and not acting or talking like a damned fool."[3]

Kennedy returned to the United States on December 8. He took the night train from New York to Washington, D.C., and though weary and unshaven, went immediately to the White House. Members of the press had been alerted to his visit and were at the White House gate to greet him with questions about the war. Before he entered the executive mansion, Kennedy gave an unscripted and unsolicited endorsement to a Roosevelt third term: "The problems that are going to affect the people of the United States—political, social, and economic—are already so great and becoming greater by the war that they should be handled by a man it won't take two years to educate . . . We know from what we have seen and heard that President Roosevelt's policy is to keep us out of war—and war at this time would bring to this country chaos beyond anyone's dream. This, in my opinion, overshadows any possible objection to a third term."[4] Kennedy, a shrewd political operator, wanted Roosevelt to run for an unprecedented third term because he believed he was the best person to lead the country.[5] But he also cannily framed his endorsement to reporters in a way that underscored his isolationist position and the president's previous statements about wanting to avoid war.

After the ambassador entered the White House, he was escorted to Roosevelt's bedroom. The president, still in his pajamas, was sitting up in bed, the morning papers at his side, pouring coffee from a thermos. Kennedy later recorded that the president "looked terribly tired" but, as always, Roosevelt greeted him with a warm smile. Kennedy told the president that he had just endorsed him for a third term. "No, Joe, I can't do it," the president said, "but we'll talk about that later."[6] The president wanted to hear the latest from London and was especially interested in Churchill's plan for mining Norwegian waters to disrupt German shipments of iron ore. They talked for an hour, and then Roosevelt told Kennedy he'd like to continue the conversation in the Oval Office later in the afternoon.

Kennedy left the White House and walked next door to the State Department. He dropped in on Assistant Secretary for European Affairs Jay Pierrepont Moffat, one of the few State Department officials with whom he had a good relationship. Moffat later recalled that Kennedy told him "he would prefer a key job in Washington, but lacking that, will go back in mid-January with pleasure."[7] The ambassador hadn't given up hope that he might still be appointed secretary of the treasury—in a third term.

After chatting with Moffat, Kennedy checked into a hotel, had lunch, and then returned to the White House in the afternoon. Sitting across from Roosevelt at his desk in the Oval Office, Kennedy once again told the president that the situation in Europe demanded that he run for reelection. "I'm tired, I can't take it. What I need is a year's rest," the president replied wearily. The president asked Kennedy who he thought would be the best person to succeed him in the Oval Office. When Kennedy mentioned that he had seen Cordell Hull's name floated, Roosevelt quickly disparaged the secretary's potential candidacy: "The other day, it seemed absolutely clear to me that the Russians were going to attack Finland. I was at Warm Springs and Cordell called me and said he had information—he always talks about his 'information'—that Russia was about to march [on Finland] and that we ought to prepare a statement offering to mediate. Well, Cordell didn't get the statement out until six o'clock that night . . . By that time the Russians were on their way to bomb the Finns."[8] Roosevelt liked the secretary, but didn't think he had the energy or leadership skills to be president.

Although he didn't tell Kennedy, the truth was that Roosevelt's choice to succeed him in the White House would have been his secretary of commerce, Harry Hopkins. Hopkins had helped Roosevelt create millions of jobs through his leadership of the Works Progress Administration, and the president increasingly talked to him about foreign policy as well. But Hopkins, later to be diagnosed with stomach cancer, was too sick and frail to contemplate such a massive undertaking as running for the presidency. So Roosevelt encouraged speculation of many prospective candidates, including Hull, believing that with a number of names in circulation it would be more difficult for party bosses to coalesce around one standard-bearer. It was a strategy that allowed him more time to make up his mind.

After visiting Roosevelt in the White House, Kennedy traveled to Massachusetts to visit his sons. Back in his hometown of Boston, he attended a reunion of parishioners at Our Lady of the Assumption church, where he had served as an altar boy. Asked about the possibility of America coming to the aid of Britain, the ambassador delivered an impromptu speech that was later reported by the Associated Press. Kennedy told his fellow Bostonians, "As you love America, don't let anything that comes out of any country in the world make you believe you make a situation one whit better by getting into war . . . There is no place in this fight for us. It is going to be bad enough as it is."[9] The next day Roosevelt read the remarks in the newspaper; he was tired of Kennedy's outspokenness.

As summer turned to fall, Ambassador Kennedy, now back in London, wrote repeatedly to the president, hoping to persuade him that any attempt to rescue Britain would be a fool's errand. On September 30, 1939, he told Roosevelt that the British were "more and more confused in their own minds just what they are fighting for and what they can attain if they win." Kennedy admired British resolve and determination, noting that "they will go down fighting," but quickly added, "Unfortunately, I am one who does not believe that it will do the slightest bit of good in this case." Notwithstanding his pessimism, the ambassador pleaded with the president to give his opinion "consideration" because "I live here." He referred to himself "as your friend on the job."[10]

A few days later, Kennedy followed up with another letter to the president. "There are signs of decay, if not decadence, here, both in men and institutions," the ambassador wrote. "For example, no one in power over the past dozen years has really told the English where they stand politically, economically, and financially—and they are reaping the result of that now."[11] Kennedy liked and admired Chamberlain, but he worried that his old friend had a tenuous hold on power and had made a great mistake in vowing to resist Hitler. Kennedy wrote, "The parliamentary machine is not operating to throw up reliable leaders," and wondered "whether the Chamberlain government can survive a single, serious reverse, and who is to replace the Prime Minister?" Winston Churchill had been the loudest and often the only voice warning of Hitler's insatiable desire for world domination, but notwithstanding his "prophesies in respect to Germany," Kennedy dismissed him as a possible successor to Chamberlain. Kennedy concluded, "It would not be surprising if the maelstrom of war had to cast up extra-Parliamentary leaders."[12] He didn't elaborate, but seemed to leave open the possibility of an authoritarian seizing power.

Notwithstanding Kennedy's disdain for him, Winston Churchill was enjoying a political resurrection in Britain. Writing in *The New York Times*, James Reston observed, "In the newspapers and—what is probably more important—in pubs, the people are beginning to talk about him and smile approvingly at his chip-on-the-shoulder attitude. He is the Cabinet member who gives the impression that he is getting a big kick out of fighting Adolf Hitler. He has dropped the diplomatic double talk of the Front Bench and has spoken in simple, blunt language."[13]

President Roosevelt may have had his differences with Churchill in the past, but he disagreed with Kennedy's assessment, believing the British Conservative had been clear-eyed, prescient, and resolute about the threat of Hitler in a way that no one else in Britain's government had been. Moreover, Roosevelt figured Churchill could very well become the next prime minister. With this in mind, the president quietly initiated a private correspondence with Churchill, a highly unorthodox move given that the United States was technically a neutral power, and that Churchill was not the leader of Britain. Roosevelt used Kennedy to deliver his sealed communications to Churchill. This infuriated the ambassador, who described it in his diary as "as another instance of Roosevelt's conniving mind, which never indicates he knows how to handle any organization. It's a rotten way to treat his Ambassador . . . I am disgusted."[14]

Roosevelt recognized Kennedy's ego needed to be stroked from time to time, and on October 30, he wrote his ambassador, thanking him for his "extraordinarily interesting" letters. The president, however, did take issue with Kennedy's view that there was a paucity of leadership in Britain. Roosevelt argued that "while the World War did not bring forward strong leadership in Great Britain, this war may do so, because I am inclined to think the British public has more humility than before and is slowly getting rid of the 'muddle through' attitude of the past."[15]

In contrast to Kennedy's defeatist attitude, Ambassador Bullitt adopted a more energetic and defiant tone with the president. On October 4, 1939, he wrote Roosevelt, "We are expecting the bombs to begin falling . . . in about a week, but nobody here is disturbed by the prospect." When bad weather descended on Paris for several days, Bullitt updated Roosevelt, "Everyone is expecting a major German attack the moment the present rains stop." Bullitt half jokingly told the president, "Our preparations are superb; I have converted the wine cellar in the basement of the embassy residence . . . into an abri. It is not the least bomb proof; but I have hung it in the Turkish and Bokharan embroideries that I used to have in my house on the Bosporus, and it is the last word in oriental style and comfort. Our motto is: 'We don't mind being killed, but we won't be annoyed.'"[16]

A month later, the bombs had still not fallen on Paris. Some in the press now referred to the "phony war"—a great deal of belligerent rhetoric on both sides, but no military engagement. Nonetheless, Bullitt remained convinced that it was only a matter of time before Germany attacked. He felt he had done what he could to assist the government of France in its war preparations and hoped the president would recall him to Washington to make him a member of his cabinet. Echoing Ambassador Kennedy, Bullitt began a letter on November 1 to Roosevelt by raising the issue of a third term: "Whether you like it or not you must remain President. I think you know from experience that one of the few statements I live for is Montesquieu's statement: 'A flatterer is a dangerous servant for any master.' I am not flattering when I say there is no other man in the United States who can conduct the affairs of the country with one-half as much intelligence as yourself, and there is no other man who can begin to handle the colossal problems which will arise at the end of the war." Bullitt's praise for Roosevelt was undoubtedly sincere, but it was also transparently strategic and self-serving. "As you know I have no objection to staying in France," the ambassador went on, "but I honestly believe that I may be of much more use in America . . . If you agree, the job in which I think I would be useful would be that of Secretary of War. If you do not intend to change the present set-up in the War Department, you might put me in a midship-mate, otherwise known as Secretary of the Navy." This was the second time that Bullitt had proposed the president appoint him to the cabinet. In case Roosevelt worried that Bullitt was irreplaceable in Paris, Bullitt suggested that the president consider appointing the former ambassador to Poland. "[I] believe Tony and Dora Biddle could handle the . . . job in France perfectly," he wrote. "I have introduced them to everyone from Daladier down, and they have made the most excellent impression."[17] Anthony Biddle, a fellow Philadelphian and suave millionaire, was a good friend of Bullitt's and liked by the president as well.

Though Roosevelt chose to ignore Bullitt's entreaties to return to the United States and serve in his cabinet, the ambassador remained hopeful, biding his time in Paris. After visiting the French-German border in mid-November, Bullitt reported to Secretary Hull that the ground was wet and soggy, and given the conditions, he didn't believe the Germans would launch an attack until the following March. However, in contrast to French military officials, Bullitt was increasingly concerned by the large concentrations of German troops on the borders of the Netherlands, Belgium, and Luxembourg. He worried that Germany contemplated a possible invasion soon. His colleagues in the State Department either disagreed with him or chose to ignore him. Breckinridge Long, for instance, wrote in his diary that Bullitt was wrong about Germany's war plan because such an attack "would expose the German flank."[18]

A week before Christmas 1939, Secretary Hull asked Breckinridge Long to come to his office to discuss an important matter. The two men had worked together in Democratic politics for many years. Though Hull knew Long had badly misread Mussolini, he both liked and trusted the former ambassador. Not unlike his boss, the president, the personal chemistry the secretary had with those who reported to him sometimes warped his judgment. Hull asked Long to accept the position of assistant secretary of state with responsibilities that included consular activities and the department's budget. It was a big job; Long would essentially be in control of the administration for the entire Department of State. Long told Hull he would think about it, and that night, he wrote in his diary, "I would love to be in Berlin. But I will stay here and do a work which is new to me."[19] A few days later, resigned to the fact that the president would not appoint a new ambassador to Germany anytime soon, Long accepted the assistant secretary position.

Hull was gratified, happy to have an ally and confidant close by in the department. He told Long that he had been frustrated for many years at the helm of the State Department. He contemplated retirement. According to Long, Hull told him, "There was the period when the President was thinking mostly of domestic problems and was not concentrating on any of the foreign problems." Hull resented that the president also "let a lot of people run around with authority . . . who had worked to the detriment" of his ideas.[20] The secretary was undoubtedly referring to Sumner Welles, whom the president often consulted for policy advice before asking for Hull's views. It irked Hull that Roosevelt valued Welles's advice more than his.

The year 1939 ended with an eve-of-disaster anxiety gripping the capitals of western nations. World war had erupted, but the armies of democratic Europe had yet to meet on either the battlefield or in the skies—it would later be revealed that during the last weeks of 1939, Hitler postponed attacking the Netherlands and Belgium on fourteen occasions. Only in the frigid waters of the North Atlantic, where German U-boats were making a graveyard of British and American shipping, was there evidence of an actual war. America officially remained neutral, but had attempted nevertheless to continue trade with Britain. Roosevelt was now determined that both the country and prime minister he once had disdained would not be forsaken.

Assistant Secretary Long closed out the year with a solemn albeit somewhat self-congratulatory entry to his diary:

> My desk is clean. The year's work is done. With me it has been a happy year. Good health, pleasant surroundings, additional honors, agreeable work.
>
> However much personal gratification there may be in the year passing and however personally pleasing the prospect of the New Year, it is impossible to forget the unfortunate situation of the world. Millions are on relief in our own country, war raging in the Far East—another great war spreading more and more over Europe and the high seas, economic dislocation everywhere, nations approaching bankruptcy and the moral fiber of peoples deteriorating. Bubonic plague is reported in Moscow . . .
>
> So in spite of our personal welfares the year closes in sombre [*sic*] atmosphere. In spite of the prospect of our own fortunes during the course of the New Year, including the pleasurable anticipation of a larger field and more important activity, the outlook for a normal world is non-existent. For even if there should come a cessation of hostilities the awful processes of readjustment

would follow—social disorders, retrenchment, faltering attempts at rehabilitation, distortions of commerce and industry, discouragement and fear.

My additional work may lead me into the midst of these difficulties. If it does, I trust my health will hold out and my abilities be adequate to the circumstances. And with that expression of hope the record of this year ends.[21]

Long's diary entry was uncharacteristically introspective, revealing a sensitivity and understanding of the larger challenges confronting humanity. But just as Long exhibited serious blind spots as ambassador, so, too, would the freshly minted assistant secretary exhibit other character flaws—far more serious—in his new position. Long revealed a form of rank bigotry that would cost tens of thousands of innocent lives and would forever be a stain on the Roosevelt presidency.

30

ONE MIND INSTEAD OF FOUR SEPARATE MINDS

Breckinridge Long had been anxious to see the president. At noon sharp on January 25, 1940, he entered the Oval Office for a scheduled fifteen-minute meeting. Long thanked Roosevelt for appointing him assistant secretary of state, or as he noted in his diary, for "the new expression of his confidence." During their brief meeting, Long noticed that Roosevelt, just five days short of his fifty-eighth birthday, "seemed tired and as having been suffering from the wear and tear of the strain he was constantly under." Long wrote in his diary, "He is not the fresh, rosy-cheeked Franklin Roosevelt that became President seven years ago. He has grown somewhat heavier; lines have appeared in his face; he has lost some hair and there is a great deal of gray in it." Long was quick to add, "His mind is very active, however."[1] Long's observations turned out to be an accurate diagnosis of Roosevelt's fragile health.

In early February, Ambassador Bullitt returned to Washington for a holiday. The president, who still enjoyed Ambassador Bullitt's company, invited him to dinner at the White House. As they had many times before, Bullitt, Missy LeHand, and the president enjoyed cocktails mixed by Roosevelt and then dined together in the president's study. Bullitt entertained them with his stories of life in Paris, and the president seemed to enjoy himself. Suddenly, Roosevelt slumped in his chair. LeHand immediately called for Dr. Ross McIntire, the president's personal physician. After examining the president, McIntire reported Roosevelt had suffered a minor heart attack. LeHand and Bullitt agreed not to speak of it to anyone, but it was obvious to them that the president was not a well man. He nevertheless returned to work after only a few days of rest.[2] Later in the month, Grace Tully, Roosevelt's secretary, witnessed him "occasionally nodding over his mail or dozing during dictation."[3] Finally, Roosevelt's daughter, Anna, insisted that her father be thoroughly examined by doctors at Bethesda Naval Hospital, which the president reluctantly agreed to. In March, Dr. Howard G. Bruenn reported to Dr. McIntire that the president suffered from high blood pressure and congestive heart failure. McIntire, however, misled the press, declaring that the president's health was "satisfactory."[4]

Concern within the White House over the president's physical state overshadowed the news of Ambassador Dodd's deteriorating condition. Dodd, confined to an oxygen tent at his farm in Virginia, had contracted pneumonia. On February 9, 1940, the former U.S. ambassador to Germany died with his son and daughter at his bedside.[5] In a letter to Dodd's son, Roosevelt praised the ambassador's "passion for historical truth and his rare ability to illuminate the meanings of history," and then noted somewhat formulaically, "His passing is a real loss to the nation."[6] The typewritten note was likely drafted by Grace Tully. It made no reference to the fact that Dodd had been among the earliest to warn of Hitler's evil.

Despite prodding from Ambassadors Kennedy and Bullitt and many others, President Roosevelt had given no indication that he would run for a third term. As a result, some prominent Democrats, Kennedy among them, began testing the waters. On February 12, *The Boston Post* ran the bold headline KENNEDY MAY BE A CANDIDATE, and underneath, in smaller font, STRONG MOVE TO HAVE HIM RUN FOR PRESIDENT, and below that, another subhead: AMBASSADOR REFUSES DEFINITE ANSWER. The story recounted how, vacationing at his residence in Palm Beach,

Kennedy had "maintained complete silence" about his political future, but "powerful pressure had been placed upon him to offer his candidacy." The article also noted that Kennedy's "loyalty to the president has been unswerving" and that "he would not be in public life today unless it was considered a patriotic duty."[7] While the story was not sourced, it had all the hallmarks of a trial balloon launched by Kennedy himself.

Kennedy was not the only well-known Democrat exploring a presidential run. Secretary Cordell Hull continued to be mentioned as a possible contender. Postmaster General Jim Farley, a Catholic, had filed papers to be on the ballot in the Massachusetts primary. In the early spring, Farley paid a visit to Breckinridge Long in the State Department. In his diary, Long wrote, "It is very apparent that he [Farley] thinks Cordell can be nominated and elected." Politically ambitious, Farley told Long that if Hull were nominated, he thought that he—Farley—would likely be his running mate.[8]

As political speculation swirled around possible candidates for president in 1940, Kennedy prepared to return to London. Before flying back, he stopped by the State Department one last time to visit with Assistant Secretary Moffat and to call on Ambassador Bullitt, who was still on leave from Paris. Bullitt and Kennedy had been friendly, though competitive, for as long as they had served in their respective posts in Paris and London. "I talk to Bullitt occasionally," Kennedy once wrote his wife. "His judgment is pathetic and I am afraid of his influence on F.D.R. because they think alike on many things."[9] Notwithstanding his disdain for Bullitt's judgment, the two ambassadors at one time had shared many of the same doubts about Roosevelt's openness to involvement in a European war. Now, after the events in Poland, Bullitt had changed his position on American support for England and France, and Kennedy may have wanted to better understand his colleague's shift in thinking.

Similar to Kennedy, Bullitt liked to engage the press, and as it happened, when Kennedy dropped by Bullitt's office, the ambassador was finishing an interview with Joseph Patterson, the owner and publisher of the *New York Daily News,* and one of Patterson's reporters, Doris

Fleeson. According to Bullitt, "Joe cheerfully entered the conversation and before long, he was saying that Germany would win, that everything in France and England would go to hell, and that his one interest was in saving his money for his children." As Patterson and Fleeson sat somewhat dumbfounded—not taking notes—Kennedy, using unusually strident language, disparaged the president for his ambivalent foreign policy. After the newspaper team left, Bullitt told Kennedy he had been wrong to criticize Roosevelt in front of members of the press. Bullitt's opprobrium irked Kennedy. He snapped at Bullitt, shouting that "he would say what he God-damned pleased before whom he God-damned pleased."[10]

Bullitt later recounted the incident to Secretary Ickes, no fan of Kennedy's. In his diary, Ickes wrote that Bullitt found Kennedy to be "abysmally ignorant on foreign affairs and had no grounds on which to utter such opinions. As long as he was a member of the administration he should be loyal—or at least keep his mouth shut." Bullitt told Ickes he doubted he would ever speak to Kennedy again.[11]

Bullitt also confided to Ickes that he did not want to go back to Paris. Ickes noted in his diary that Bullitt "would like a big job" in Washington, D.C. Ickes liked and respected Bullitt. Unaware that Bullitt had already raised the issue twice with Roosevelt, Ickes offered to put in a good word with the president on behalf of Bullitt for the secretary of war job.[12]

Bullitt didn't wait for Ickes's promised lobbying. In a final effort to persuade the president to appoint him to the cabinet, Bullitt sent a note to Roosevelt stating that he might "be of much more use in America during the next two years." He once again recommended that Ambassador Biddle replace him in Paris, and again suggested that he be appointed either secretary of war or secretary of the navy. As he framed it in his letter to the president, "I can promise you with my customary modesty that from my experience here, I know more about how to get ready for war than anyone except yourself." He advised the president, "The only road to salvation lies through a quadrupled production of planes in the United States." Years later, long after Roosevelt's death, Bullitt told *The New York Times* that Roosevelt only hesitated to put him in the cabinet because he could not be spared in Paris. The president needed him to stay for a few more months, but Bullitt maintained the president promised him that he would be made secretary of the navy as soon as the incumbent, Frank Knox, resigned, likely in June.[13] Whether the president actually promised Bullitt anything is not known, but the cabinet position never materialized.

Kennedy continued to vacillate between genuine admiration and bitter contempt for President Roosevelt. After returning to London, Kennedy learned that the president had decided to send Undersecretary Sumner Welles on a fact-finding mission to four European capitals, including London. During the time Kennedy had been in the United States on leave, the president had not bothered to mention Welles's upcoming trip. Once again, the ambassador felt slighted, irritated that his opinion was so lightly valued.

Roosevelt felt no obligation to include Kennedy—or any of his ambassadors—in his plans for Welles's trip. The president did not authorize the undersecretary to make any particular proposals, only to meet with all of the key players in Rome, London, Paris, and Berlin and then to advise him whether some kind of peace could yet be salvaged. As the president blithely explained to reporters at a press conference on February 9, 1940, "I have not got any idea . . . to whom he will talk to and what he will say and what they will say to him."

The decision to send Welles indicated that the president had grown tired of the increasingly contradictory advice that he was receiving from his ambassadors. Dodd had been the first ambassador to issue warnings about Hitler, although his consul, George Messersmith, was even more prescient. Bullitt had advocated for a rapprochement with Germany, but after Hitler's invasion of Poland, the ambassador became one of the most vocal supporters for American militarization. Kennedy's isolationist views reflected American public opinion, and economic considerations dominated his thinking. Assistant Secretary Long viewed the world in stark political terms and also favored isolationism; he admired Mussolini and for many years considered the Third Reich an important bulwark against Communism.

In discussing Welles's trip with the press, Roosevelt declared, "It might be a good thing to get somebody to see all of the conditions in all of the countries so that one mind would be able to cover the situation instead of getting all four separate minds reporting on separate things."[14]

Undersecretary Welles boarded an Italian ocean liner on February 17, 1940, and arrived in Naples eight days later. Mussolini had signed a treaty with Hitler but so far had maintained neutrality with Italy's neighbors. Roosevelt hoped to keep him in that position—neutral toward neighbor states and on the sidelines of any fight. Welles first met with Foreign Minister Count Galeazzo Ciano, Mussolini's son-in-law, in the grand hall of the Quirinal Palace. He described Ciano as "intelligent and frank." The next day, Welles sat down with Prime Minister Mussolini. While Welles's audience was "friendly and cordial," Il Duce made clear that Italy deserved greater respect from all the nations of Europe and that he would decide Italy's future course based on its national self-interest—even if that meant working with Hitler.[15]

Welles then traveled to Berlin where his first meeting was with Foreign Minister Ribbentrop. The two-hour meeting did not go well. Ribbentrop—sitting opposite Welles—closed his eyes and recited a litany of alleged foreign policy and trade-related transgressions on the part of the United States. Welles later described Ribbentrop to Roosevelt as having "a closed" and "a very stupid mind." He added, "I have rarely seen a man I disliked more." Next, Welles met with Rudolf Hess, deputy führer, whom he described as "of a very low order of intelligence." He also spent time with Hermann Goering. He found the Reichsmarschall to be clownish and pompous, and then commented somewhat randomly that he had "a very ugly house."

Chancellor Hitler greeted Welles at the führer's residence "very pleasantly, but with great formality." Hitler, as each of his associates had done, laid out an alternate version of history in an effort to persuade Welles that his government's intentions had been mischaracterized and Germany had been unfairly treated.[16] Hitler told the undersecretary that he was grateful for his mission and assured him that "Germany's aim, whether it must come through war, or otherwise, is a just peace." Welles left impressed by the führer, whom he described as "dignified in both speech and movement."[17]

After Berlin, Welles flew to Paris, where he was greeted by Robert Murphy, counselor of the embassy and acting ambassador in the absence of Bullitt, who was still on leave in the United States. Like Kennedy, Bullitt had not been notified by Roosevelt of Welles's mission to Europe. Murphy later recalled of Bullitt, "I knew the Ambassador felt he had an understanding with President Roosevelt which made him the principal White House adviser on European affairs." Murphy believed that Bullitt thereafter resented Welles because the undersecretary "had violated an agreed division of functions." According to Murphy, "A bitterness developed [between Welles and Bullitt] which, in my opinion, was a severe blow to American wartime policy making."[18]

Welles's reception in Paris was decidedly mixed. Members of the French government appreciated that President Roosevelt wanted peace in Europe, but a number of former French premiers and foreign ministers signed a petition urging that the United States side openly with the Allies—as Ambassador Bullitt had recommended. Welles responded as best he could, explaining that while Roosevelt was sympathetic to their cause, the president could not act alone and could only do so with the consent of the U.S. Congress.

On March 10, 1940, Welles flew across the English Channel to London where Ambassador Kennedy greeted him at the airport. Kennedy was still annoyed that Roosevelt had sent Welles to do what Kennedy felt was his job, but unlike Ambassador Bullitt, he did not blame Welles.[19] Welles was more solicitous of Kennedy than most of his colleagues in the Department of State, and the two men got along reasonably well. Over dinner the first night in London, Kennedy felt somewhat vindicated when Welles told him that Hitler "was in a mood to make a reasonable peace and the French and English somewhat in the same frame of mind."[20] But Welles revised his views a few days later after spending a late-night, three-hour session with Churchill, during which the the two men drank Johnnie Walker Red Label whiskey, and First Lord of the Admiralty chronicled Hitler's prevarications and predicted disaster if Germany were not stopped. Churchill, along with a number of members in the British Foreign Office, thought Welles naive and worried that Roosevelt was being advised by someone so obviously uninformed and ill prepared.[21] It was true that Welles was not a Europeanist—his expertise lay in Latin America—but Roosevelt trusted his judgment. Nevertheless, Churchill and his cohort need not have worried; while there is no record that the undersecretary provided President Roosevelt with any firm proposal for peace upon returning to Washington, D.C., his trip helped convince Roosevelt that the United States could no longer avoid a widening of the war in Europe. Now the president's dilemma was what to do about it.

After a relaxing vacation in Palm Beach, Ambassador Kennedy's return to London was not a happy one. Not only did he feel slighted by the president over the Welles mission, he was increasingly receiving negative press in British newspapers. He wrote his wife, Rose, "You would not believe the way public opinion in this country has turned anti-American and incidentally anti–US Ambassador Kennedy." He advised his wife not to return to London, telling her, "The things they say about me from the fact I've sent my family home because they were afraid, to the fact that I live in the country because I am being bombed etc. etc. All rotten stuff but all the favorite dinner parties at Mayfair go right to work hauling the U.S. Ambassador down."[22]

Fearful of being bombed by the Luftwaffe in his London residence, the ambassador spent an increasing amount of time commuting to London from a country house in Windsor lent to him rent-free by Horace Dodge Jr., the American automobile heir. Known as St. Leonards, the sixty-room country estate, as described by Kennedy, was "not an English type of house; it's the most modern thing you can imagine—rather big, but I think will be quite comfortable."[23] Kennedy was undoubtedly sincere about not wanting to put his wife and children in danger by returning them to an England under siege. He may also not have wanted their return to interfere with his plans to spend time, including the upcoming Easter holiday, with Clare Boothe Luce—his current paramour—at St.

Leonards. Married to publishing magnate Henry Luce, she and Kennedy had begun a romantic affair in the south of France years earlier.

Rose Kennedy heeded Joe's advice and did not return to London. A very sensible woman, she offered her husband some practical, political advice of her own:

> Joe, dear, I have a definite idea that it would be a wonderful feat if you could put over the idea that although you are against America's entering the war—still you are encouraging help to England in some way. It seems to me most people in America would be sympathetic to the idea, & it would endear you to the hearts of the British. It may be impractical, but I have felt it strongly the last two weeks.[24]

Ambassador Kennedy ignored his wife's advice. To a large extent, he chose to blame American Jews for the negative publicity, believing he had been targeted for not condemning Hitler's treatment of German Jews more vigorously. He told Rose, "Walter Lippmann is around saying he hasn't liked the U.S. Ambassador for the last 6 months. Of course the fact he is a Jew has something to do with that. It is all a little annoying but not very serious."[25]

On Friday, March 29, 1940, the German Foreign Office made public a cache of documents seized by an SS brigade from the Polish Ministry of Foreign Affairs when the German army occupied Warsaw in late September 1939. The Reich Ministry of Propaganda believed the captured documents held tremendous propaganda value that would strengthen American isolationists and place President Roosevelt in an untenable position, especially if he stood for reelection.

The documents contained correspondence and transcripts of conversations between Ambassadors Kennedy and Bullitt, as well as their communications with a number of officials in the State Department and with foreign diplomats. The letters, cables, and transcripts were supposed to be kept private. The most embarrassing of the translated documents was one purportedly authored by the Polish ambassador to the United States, Jerzy Potocki, who recounted a November 1938 conversation with Ambassador Bullitt about the coming war in Europe. Bullitt allegedly commented on the likelihood of the United States becoming involved: "Undoubtedly yes, but only after Great Britain and France make the first move!" One memorandum recorded Bullitt telling Potocki, "Feeling in the United States is so tense against Nazism and Hitlerism that there is today a psychosis among Americans similar to that before America's declaration of war on Germany in 1917."[26] Aware that the documents might be interpreted to suggest that President Roosevelt had been planning United States involvement in the war for years, Bullitt immediately issued a vigorous denial: "I have never made to anyone the statements attributed to me." Secretary of State Hull immediately backed him up as well.

The release of the documents created a brief, international media frenzy. American newspapers gave the story front-page coverage and published lengthy excerpts. *The Washington Post* described the documents as a "diplomatic sensation," the Associated Press labeled them a "paper bombshell." Secretary Hull declared, "The statements alleged have not represented in any way at any time the thought or the policy of the American government," but German propagandists argued that President Roosevelt had lied to the American people about his intention to keep America out of war.

In 1940, most Americans trusted their political leaders to tell the truth. Notwithstanding the authenticity of the documents, the denials from Bullitt and Hull rendered the impact of the release much less than the German government had hoped for. However, isolationist congressmen such as the Republican ranking member on the House Foreign Affairs Committee, Hamilton Fish III, demanded a "complete investigation" and threatened to impeach Bullitt. As Breckinridge Long noted in his diary, "The Republicans are trying to base their campaign on a fear that we will lead the country into war. We actually do not want to." Long went on to note that, as Roosevelt had hoped, "sentiment in this country is gradually changing. From 'stay out of war at any price' it is turning to 'help the Allies in every way short of war' . . . The country is now beginning to catch up with [Roosevelt]."[27]

While the publicity surrounding release of the Polish documents had little substantive impact on American public opinion, it revealed deep fissures within the Department of State. Secretary Hull had bailed out Bullitt and Kennedy, but according to Long, the secretary was "very concerned" and "has not liked the actions of either [Kennedy or Bullitt] for a long time."[28] As Long explained in his diary, "They have a custom of going over his head and talking to the president, and he has found it necessary to secure agreement with the President about his intended instructions before they are issued in order that he and the President will find themselves in perfect agreement and that the President will stand hitched." Long noted that Hull had been especially critical of Bullitt, whom he claimed "had been drinking rather freely for the last year and had been rather unorthodox in some of his conduct, not only diplomatically, but otherwise and that he feared very much that there were other things in the files which might be even more disconcerting than the present revelations."[29] In all likelihood, Hull was referring to Bullitt's legendary parties and his alleged romantic dalliances.

Secretary Hull's disdain for Bullitt meant that he and Undersecretary Welles shared a common adversary—though the two also remained suspicious of each other and had something of a strained relationship themselves. Hull believed Welles coveted the secretary of state job, observing that Welles had asked President Roosevelt several times to send him on special diplomatic missions. Hull had counseled the president against Welles's trip to Europe believing that it would sow confusion with the American public and hold out false hope for European leaders. Hull was also extremely jealous of Welles, resenting the president's obvious respect for the undersecretary's intelligence, though he, too, admired his brilliance and work ethic. As Breckinridge Long put it, Hull's problem with Welles was that the undersecretary "thinks so fast and moves so rapidly that he gets way out in front and leaves no trace of the positions he has taken or commitments he has made."[30]

Welles was certainly ambitious, but he was not entirely comfortable in the role as the president's preferred confidant and counselor, recognizing that it engendered resentment with his colleagues, especially Bullitt. (It didn't help his reputation within the Department of State when a few months later his face graced the cover of *Time* magazine.) Welles told Assistant Secretary Adolf Berle that Bullitt "hated him."[31] In truth, Bullitt simply viewed Welles as a competitor, someone whom he needed to circumvent when possible and step over when necessary.

However, Welles had other problems beyond resentment from colleagues. While Hull and Long gossiped about Bullitt's drinking, Welles also drank excessively to relieve the pressure of his job. In early May, after working in the department until after midnight, Welles and Berle walked the short distance to the Metropolitan Club, where they settled into a pair of red leather chairs on the second floor with a bottle of scotch. Welles drank four shots "in a row in quick succession" and vented his frustration to Berle, complaining that he was "furious with desire to sleep, but totally unable to do so." He predicted that Roosevelt would decline to run again and would throw his support to Hull. If Hull were elected, Welles thought he might be offered the embassy in London, but worried he would be bored and wasn't sure he could afford the high cost of entertaining in such a prominent post.[32] However, Welles was wealthy—entertainment expenses were not his real reason. His reservation about running an embassy abroad were actually related to his drinking and to unexplained absences from home that were creating a strain in his marriage.

31

CHURCHILL IS THE BEST MAN ENGLAND HAS

During the early days of May 1940, rumors swirled around Washington, D.C., that Germany was preparing to invade the Low Countries of Europe—the Netherlands, Belgium, and Luxembourg. There was also mounting speculation that Italy, which had provided aid to the fascists in Spain, might now also support Hitler militarily. After reading the cables in the State Department on May 9, Breckinridge Long acknowledged in his diary "the possibility of an immediate attack," but added, "Personally I think it is a smokescreen."[1]

The following evening, May 10, 1940, Ambassador Long attended a black-tie dinner hosted by the assistant secretary of the treasury, Basil Harris and his wife. The Belgian ambassador, Count Robert van der Straten-Ponthoz, was there and, in the middle of dinner, was called to the telephone. When he returned to the table, he leaned over Long's shoulder and whispered that General Edwin "Pa" Watson, one of the president's senior military advisers, had spoken to him on behalf of Roosevelt, telling him that the Belgian cabinet had convened an emergency session in response to reports of German troops amassing along the border. The government of Belgium feared an imminent attack by the Third Reich. As there had been a number of German troop movements along the

Belgian frontier for several weeks, all without incident, the ambassador wasn't especially concerned. He suspected it was probably just more of the same. Ambassador Long wasn't so sanguine.[2]

Long had decided before the dinner to stay the night in town instead of making the lengthy drive back to his horse farm in Maryland. He left the party about half past eleven and returned to the Mayflower Hotel where he had booked a room. Unsettled by his conversation with the Belgian ambassador, Long telephoned the Department of State to learn if there was any news and was informed Secretary Hull was in the office. Long recalled, "I spoke to him . . . he told me that he had talked with [Ambassador John] Cudahy in Brussels about eleven o'clock and that Cudahy had told him that there was much air activity and the German troops were being landed from parachutes and the air fields were being bombed. He also understood that an offensive was on against Luxembourg."[3] Long later described the urgency of the situation by noting in his diary that he was still in his tuxedo when he left his hotel room to go to the State Department.

As Long, Hull, Welles, and a few others huddled in the secretary's office, a flood of reports came across the wire: Hours earlier, in a flanking move that circumvented the French Maginot Line, German infantry, supported by paratroopers, had crossed into the Netherlands and Belgium through the Ardennes forest, taking rapid control of strategic bridges and villages. Twenty-six infantry divisions and three panzer tank divisions led the invasion. The Grand Duchy of Luxembourg had been the first to fall. In Belgium, the Germans seized the fort at Eben-Emael with its two-thousand-strong garrison, with the loss of only six German paratroopers. The Netherlands had declared war against Germany, and Belgium had requested immediate military assistance from Britain and France. The vaunted Maginot Line had proved to be nothing more than an illusion.

In London and Paris, military commanders had previously discounted the probability of invasion and were caught completely by surprise. On the heels of the attack, Parliamentarians passionately debated Britain's war policy in Westminster. A Tory backbencher, Leo Amery, denounced

Prime Minister Chamberlain by quoting Cromwell, thundering, "You have sat too long here for any good you have been doing. Depart, I say, and let us have done with you. In the name of God, go." Weary, sick, and discredited, Chamberlain, aware that he had once again underestimated Hitler, decided to step down. As the Nazis continued seizing more territory in the Low Countries, the prime minister's fellow cabinet members scrambled to find a successor who might keep their country safe.

President Roosevelt sat propped up in his bed eating his breakfast of eggs, buttered toast, and coffee and engaging in his morning ritual of scouring the daily newspapers. Roosevelt had not slept well. He had been on the telephone with Secretary Hull and Undersecretary Welles until the early-morning hours. Long recorded in his diary, "Secretary Hull went home to get some sleep, but, I stayed with Welles. I left at 5:30 in broad daylight in my evening clothes."[4] Ambassador Bullitt also had telephoned the president to confirm that the Germans had bombed more than a half dozen military bases, roads, and railway stations in France, blocking Allied troop movements.[5]

As he sipped his coffee, the president unfolded *The New York Times*. Splashed across the front page, headlines announced Germany's invasion of the Low Countries, with an accompanying article, written hours before Neville Chamberlain's resignation, predicting, as it turned out incorrectly, that the prime minister would "be saved just when it looked as though he was sure to fall." Roosevelt scanned the page: Another story reported that Belgium and the Netherlands had appealed to Britain and France for help and were informed that they "could expect all the help Britain could give them." The president was already very familiar with one story on the front page, headlined MIGHTY AIR FORCES DEMANDED BY ARMY, recounting how his War Department intended to ask for "additional funds for aircraft and air defense at this session of Congress because of what is considered the impressive demonstration of German air power in Norway and the adverse turn which the war has taken for the Allies."

President Roosevelt knew America's military capacity remained woefully inadequate. After World War I, with no mandatory military service, the readiness of the United States armed forces, with the exception of the navy, had dangerously atrophied. Both the government and the private sector had backed away from making weapons, leaving the country with virtually no munitions industry. In terms of size, the army ranked eighteenth in the world. Whereas 136 well-trained divisions had supported Germany's invasion of the Low Countries, the United States could only summon 5 fully equipped divisions. The president worried that it could take several months, perhaps even years, for the United States to muster a capable army.[6]

Later that morning, in response to the crisis in Europe, President Roosevelt presided over a meeting with his top advisers. As the sun streamed through the arched lunette windows in the Cabinet Room, the president was wheeled to his place at the center of the large mahogany table. Roosevelt began by asking Secretary Hull for a review of the incoming cable traffic from Europe. Hull's report was a litany of generalities and trivialities in the face of the seriousness of the situation—all he could offer was that Ambassador Cudahy in Belgium had cabled that the force of a bomb that fell three hundred feet from the embassy had almost knocked him down. He also noted that in Britain, the government canceled the Whitsun holiday, the long weekend celebrating the seventh weekend after Easter. Hull finished by quoting Ambassador Joseph P. Kennedy, who confirmed what was obvious to everyone: "The situation is serious."[7]

Sitting to the president's left, Secretary of Commerce Harry Hopkins, looking thin and pale, was attending his first cabinet meeting in months. After battling stomach cancer and being told that he had only months to live, Hopkins had undergone a series of blood plasma transfusions and made a miraculous recovery. At Roosevelt's invitation, he had moved into the White House, taking a room on the second floor of the residence. Having just conducted a comprehensive review of American military preparedness, Hopkins launched into a lengthy report of his findings. He was describing the steep hill the United States had to climb to achieve military readiness when an aide handed the president a note: Prime Minister Chamberlain had resigned. The new prime minister would be Winston Churchill. Roosevelt seemed relieved and confidently told his cabinet, "Churchill was the best man England had."[8]

Ambassador Kennedy attended the theater in London on May 14. After the performance, an aide notified him that Lord Beaverbrook, the newly appointed minister of aircraft production, had telephoned the embassy asking Kennedy to "come right away to the Admiralty" because Churchill wanted to see him. The prime minister was interested in Kennedy's perspective on increasing speculation that Mussolini would join Hitler's military campaign. Kennedy had been saddened by Prime Minister Chamberlain's decision to step down, and though suspicious of his successor, the ambassador was flattered to be asked to share his views. Sitting opposite Churchill discussing the affairs of Europe and Mussolini's intentions, Kennedy later recorded in his diary, "I couldn't help thinking . . . how ill-conditioned he looked and the fact that there was a tray with plenty of liquor on it alongside him, and he was drinking a scotch highball, which I felt was not the first one he had drunk that night." Kennedy wrote, "The affairs of Great Britain might be in the hands of the most dynamic individual in Great Britain but certainly not in the hands of the best judgment in Great Britain."[9]

Prime Minister Churchill may have wanted to flatter the United States ambassador in advance of a letter he sent to President Roosevelt requesting "the loan of forty or fifty of your older destroyers to bridge the gap between what we have now and the large new construction we put in hand at the beginning of the war."[10] This was not the first request for "old destroyers" that Roosevelt had received; French premier Paul Reynaud had earlier broached the idea with the president for the sale or lease of American mothballed ships.[11] Made aware of Churchill's request, Ambassador Kennedy advised Roosevelt to turn him down. By this point, however, Roosevelt almost reflexively discounted advice offered by Kennedy. In this case, the president had already made up his mind to help the Allies and directed his military advisers to study Churchill's list of urgent needs and provide Britain with whatever excess military hardware might be available.

Churchill's requests for military assistance coincided with increasingly bad news in Europe. The Netherlands had suffered tens of thousands of casualties; its army surrendered on May 15, after only four days of fighting. The news was nearly as grim in Belgium, where the Luftwaffe had bombed military installations and leveled entire villages; the Belgian army had fought bravely but had been decimated. Even more worrisome, German tanks had crashed through the French border with ease, and the French army, reputed to be one of the strongest in all of Europe, was in retreat. Premier Reynaud cabled the prime minister: "We have been defeated. We are beaten; we have lost the battle."[12] The French government was already planning its evacuation from Paris.

With the crisis in Europe deepening, on May 16, 1940, President Roosevelt addressed a joint session of Congress. His leg braces locked in place, his jaw set, Roosevelt stood at the lectern and looked out at the audience before him—and they stared back at him. This was not the confident leader who years earlier had optimistically assured the nation that better days were ahead. There were dark circles under his eyes that seemed a metaphor for a weary American economy and growing global uncertainty. The president began his address on a decidedly somber note. "These are ominous days," he said, "days whose swift and shocking developments force every neutral nation to look at its defenses in light of new factors. . . . No old defense is so strong that it requires no further strengthening and no attack is so unlikely that it may be ignored."[13]

The president used statistics passed on to him by Ambassadors Kennedy and Bullitt—inflated figures given to them by Charles Lindbergh—and declared that Germany not only had more planes than all of its opponents combined but maintained a production capacity far greater than that of its opponents. Roosevelt's voice grew stronger as he argued for dramatically increasing American production of aircraft, setting an ambitious goal of producing fifty thousand planes a year to give the United States air superiority over Germany. He also implored Congress "not to take any action which would in any way hamper or delay the delivery of American-made planes to foreign nations which have ordered them, or seek to purchase new planes." Finally, echoing the advice he had received from Ambassador Bullitt, Roosevelt asked Congress to provide additional funding to raise a modern, well-equipped army. When he finished, the entire hall erupted in loud cheers and sustained applause.[14] The leadership Roosevelt had shown in 1933 with his call to action for restoring a battered economy, he now reclaimed with a call to arms and an appeal for increased national defense.

32

MY MOTHER ALICE WHO MET A RABBIT

German panzer units continued their advance along the Somme valley, cutting off and surrounding Allied forces that had advanced into Belgium to challenge the German invasion. By May 24, 1940, the Germans had pushed the British, Belgian, and French forces back to the sea, pinning them down at Dunkirk, the seaside village on the north coast of France. From London, Ambassador Kennedy pleaded once again with President Roosevelt to sue for peace with Hitler, writing, "I think the possibility of the French considering a peace move is not beyond the realm of reason and I suspect that the Germans would be willing to make peace with both the French and British now—of course, on their own terms, but on terms that would be a great deal better than they would be if the war continues."[1] Roosevelt didn't bother to respond.

Ambassador Kennedy opined in a letter to his wife, Rose, on the British army's desperate situation. "I think the jig is up," wrote Kennedy. "The situation is more than critical. It means a terrible finish for the allies." The ambassador predicted "a dictated peace with Hitler probably getting the British navy." With German troops sacking one European city after another, Kennedy believed his gloomy forecasts over the last year had been exactly correct. He expressed an odd combination of both satisfaction and sadness: "I wish I'd been wrong."[2]

Kennedy's despair was not expressed only to his wife. He continued telling members of the British government that in his opinion Britain's days were numbered if the government refused to negotiate with Hitler. Fed up with the ambassador's pessimism, Winston Churchill finally dropped Kennedy from his circle of wartime advisers and began communicating directly with President Roosevelt, pleading with the American president to hurry the delivery of aircraft and ships. Kennedy's views had earned him the contempt of many in the British Foreign Office, one of whom described the ambassador in an internal memorandum as "a coward . . . a very foul specimen of double crosser and defeatist."[3]

On May 24, German tanks, within sight of Dunkirk, inexplicably received the order to halt. The order, as William Shirer later wrote "was the first of the German High Command's major mistakes in World War II," providing "a miraculous reprieve to the Allies, and especially the British."[4] Churchill knew the Americans could not mobilize sufficient war matériel in time to rescue the British army in France; Great Britain would have to save itself. In an audacious stroke of political and military leadership, Churchill rallied the British population and orchestrated the "miracle of Dunkirk," using every available military and civilian seaworthy vessel, nearly a thousand in all, to evacuate approximately 340,000 British and French troops.

Operation Dynamo, as it was code-named, saved the British army, but the country had paid an enormous price for its attempt to defend the army's ultimate retreat. There were over sixty thousand British casualties in the Battle of France, not to mention the abandonment of sixty-five thousand military vehicles and more than seventy-five thousand tons of ammunition.[5] And while the British army had been saved, Adolf Hitler, furious that he and his generals had missed the opportunity to crush the British military at Dunkirk, ordered the troops of the Third Reich to continue their triumphant and deadly march through France.

As German tanks rolled toward Paris in late May 1940, Ambassador Bullitt—despite having a greater arsenal of wine bottles than weapons at his disposal—was waiting for them. Adamant that he would not leave

Paris, Bullitt was holed up in the Château de Vineuil-Saint-Firmin in Chantilly, his country residence on the outskirts of the capital. The ambassador stayed in constant contact with President Roosevelt, sending telegrams and telephoning him directly. The ambassador told the president on May 28, "The Paris police have no weapons except antiquated single shot rifles." He added that he had no intention of evacuating the embassy even though "we have exactly two revolvers in this entire Mission with only 40 bullets."[6] With German forces closing in on the French capital, Bullitt wrote the president, "In case I should get blown up before I see you again, I want you to know that it has been marvelous to work for you and I thank you from the bottom of my heart for your friendship."[7]

Following his address to Congress, the president engaged in a fireside chat with the American people on May 26, 1940. Ten days earlier he had been circumspect in discussing American involvement in the European war, focusing on the need for America to rearm itself. But now he felt the political momentum had arrived when he could be openly critical of isolationists, describing the "many among us who in the past closed their eyes to events abroad because they believed . . . that what was taking place in Europe was none of our business; that no matter what happened over there, the United States could always pursue its peaceful and unique course in the world." Roosevelt declared that it was no longer possible that "hundreds of miles of salt water" made the American hemisphere immune from attack.[8]

The president also warned "today's threat of our national security is not a matter of military weapons alone. We know of new methods of attack, the Trojan horse, the fifth column that betrays a nation unprepared for treachery. Spies, saboteurs and traitors are all actors in the new strategy. With all that we must and will deal vigorously."[9] Acting on the advice of J. Edgar Hoover, who was preoccupied with the question of subversion by Nazi agents in the United States, Roosevelt directed Breckinridge Long at the State Department to tighten restrictions on immigration, which Long executed with insensitive zeal.

As historian Doris Kearns Goodwin would later explain, "Though it was absurd to believe that Jewish refugees, Hitler's principal victims, would somehow become his principal weapons against the United States, the widespread paranoia about foreigners combined with anti-Semitism to cast a net so wide that everyone except British children was caught in it."[10]

On June 3, 1940, as the British were completing their evacuation of Dunkirk, the German Luftwaffe bombed Paris and its suburbs for the first time. The city's air-raid alert was sounded at 1:18 p.m. as bombers dropped their payload in five waves of twenty-five planes each, plus one wave of thirty. A total of 1,060 bombs fell in and around Paris, destroying or damaging ninety-seven buildings and killing 254 while injuring 652, mostly civilians. United Press described the chaos in a story the next day, "For an hour the life of Paris was paralyzed by the raiding planes. Crowds hurried from the streets and offices to air-raid shelters. School children marched to underground shelters, some of them singing the national anthem. Trading was suspended on the Bourse. Subways were halted as the firing of heavy guns jarred buildings in the center of the city."[11]

To avoid antiaircraft fire, the German planes were forced to fly at a high altitude, around thirty thousand feet, which made it extremely difficult for them to locate their targets and drop bombs with any precision. Ambassador William Bullitt was attending a luncheon for high-ranking military and diplomatic guests at the French L'Armée de L'Air headquarters when suddenly he was knocked backward and momentarily blinded by plaster dust as one of the Luftwaffe's bombs fell through the ceiling less than ten feet from him. Tongue in cheek, CBS correspondent Eric Sevareid reported on the incident, "The discipline of social poise has its advantages in warfare: nobody so much as dropped his glass, and the bomb did not go off." Bullitt sent Missy LeHand the luncheon menu as a souvenir and asked her to reassure his daughter, Anne, who was in school in the States, that he remained in good health.[12] Soon thereafter, Bullitt cabled the president that he expected France to fall within the next ten days.[13]

For weeks, Bullitt had implored President Roosevelt to provide more assistance to the French. His tone became more strident and impatient as German tanks barreled toward Paris. President Roosevelt, however, would have none of it. He sent a memorandum to Undersecretary Welles, asking him to "please let Bullitt know about these 25 old PB [patrol bomber] obsolete planes. It would be silly for France to buy them . . . They only make 139 mph without bombs."[14] Days later, Roosevelt again sent a memorandum to Welles, this time on the subject of naval destroyers, asking him once again to pass on the information to Bullitt: "Our old destroyers cannot be sold as obsolete as is proven by fact."[15] Roosevelt's decision to have his views conveyed by Welles was evidence that he was tiring of Bullitt.

Ambassador Bullitt, however, refused to relent. Aware of the president's address to Congress and his fireside chat, both in support of aiding Europe's democracies, Bullitt could not understand why Roosevelt was moving so slowly in the face of the German onslaught. He again wrote the president, "At the moment words are not enough. Indeed, unaccompanied by acts they are rather sickening." Bullitt then quoted Premier Reynaud, "It [is] sad that civilization in the world should fall because a great nation with a great President could simply talk."[16] The president bristled at the arrogance and impudence of his ambassador. This time, instead of asking Welles to respond, Roosevelt wrote directly to Bullitt, lacing his reply with a heavy dose of sarcasm in an allusion to the writings of Lewis Carroll: "Such talk reminds me of my mother Alice who met a rabbit." As far as providing ships to the French, Roosevelt lashed out at Bullitt, "I cannot of course give you a list of the disposition of our ships, but if you knew you would not continue such fantasies."[17]

The president had a different set of challenges with Britain, where it was the prime minister who continuously pressed him for ships and planes, not his outspoken ambassador, Joseph Kennedy, who continued to lobby against American involvement in a war he thought unwinnable.

On June 4, 1940, Prime Minister Churchill delivered a speech in Parliament that had a number of political objectives. He felt obligated to put Britain's devastating retreat from Europe into perspective, yet simultaneously warn of a possible impending German invasion. He also needed to assure the British people that they would persevere, but at the same time prepare them for either France's defeat or, far worse, a possible accommodation with Germany. His most important goal was to fortify the collective national spirit of the British people for the terrible ordeal he knew would soon be upon them. "We shall go on to the end," Churchill said. "We shall fight in France, we shall fight on the seas and oceans, we shall fight with growing confidence and growing strength in the air, we shall defend our Island, whatever the cost may be, we shall fight on the beaches, we shall fight on the landing grounds, we shall fight in the fields and in the streets, we shall fight in the hills; we shall never surrender."[18]

Churchill's stirring words were punctuated with a final declaration clearly directed to the American people. "And even if, which I do not for a moment believe, this Island or a large part of it were subjugated and starving," Churchill said. "Then our Empire beyond the seas, armed and guarded by the British Fleet, would carry on the struggle, until, in God's good time, the New World, with all its power and might, steps forth to the rescue and the liberation of the old."[19]

While Churchill rallied the British people—and sent an unequivocal message to America—Ambassador Kennedy remained unmoved. Two days later, he wrote to Joe Jr., "If the French break—and the consensus here is they will, then I should think the finish will come quite quickly. The British, of course, will fight, but only through pride and courage. With the French out of the way and the Germans in charge of all the ports I can see nothing but slaughter ahead. I am arranging to send everybody away with the exception of about ten of us, who will stay and sleep at the chancery. I am going to try and keep this place operating as long as they leave the building standing up."[20]

Kennedy's views were well known in both the Foreign Office and at 10 Downing Street, though the ambassador now had almost no access to either. Kennedy complained about his treatment to Lord Beaverbrook,

Churchill's minister of aircraft production. Beaverbrook, a former newspaper publisher, had a nose for gossip from his newspaper days and told Kennedy that the prime minister's son, Randolph, considered the ambassador to be a potential traitor, and had turned his father against him. Kennedy seethed at such scurrilous attacks and wondered whether it was time for him to leave Great Britain and resign his post.

33

THE HAND THAT HELD THE DAGGER HAS STRUCK IT INTO THE BACK OF ITS NEIGHBOR

As German tanks rolled closer to Paris, Ambassador Bullitt traveled to Domrémy, a small village 150 miles east of Paris where Joan of Arc was born, and not far from the advancing German army. Weeks before Germany's invasion, Bullitt had committed to attend a dedication ceremony of an altar donated by a number of American churches. In a ceremony attended by only a handful of French government and church officials—villagers had been warned not to attend because a crowd might provide a target for the German Luftwaffe—Bullitt placed a white rose at the foot of a statue of Joan of Arc outside the church where she once worshipped. The ambassador then delivered a short invocation, stating, "Americans know on which side stand right, justice and Christian decency, and on which side are wrong, cruelty, and bestiality."[1] The United States remained technically neutral in the fight between Germany and France, but Bullitt made it clear which side he favored when he said, "From one end of this earth to the other, every civilized man, after his fashion, is praying for the victory of France."[2] While the ceremony was brief and the crowd was small, Bullitt's comments were reported the next day on page 3 in *The New York Times*. The Department of State had no comment.[3]

Bullitt returned to Paris just as the French government prepared to depart. On June 10, 1940, Premier Reynaud vowed in a radio address that the French would continue to fight, but neglected to repeat Georges Clemenceau's pledge in 1918 to fight *in Paris*.[4] Declaring Paris an "open city," General Maxime Weygand, France's supreme military commander, hoped that Germany would peacefully occupy the city rather than destroy it. Not waiting to find out what the Nazis had in mind, many Parisians, including Reynaud and his government ministers, made the decision to flee. Writing in *The New York Times*, P. J. Philip described the evacuation of Paris in advance of German occupation:

> The city, greatly deserted in these last weeks and days, with only rare buses and taxicabs, was still and eerie. Neighbors gathered in little knots to talk, as people do in the waiting rooms of a hospital, caught between fear and hope and clutching at every human contact for comfort.
>
> For most the great issue was whether to go or stay. Great gray trucks lined up outside public buildings showed that at least some of the public services were being evacuated. There were signs of packing everywhere. Private cars were being filled with the usual miscellaneous collection of oddments, from a birdcage to a bathtub, and usually with a mattress on the roof to do the double duty of protection in the day and a bed at night.
>
> As the day advanced the evacuation fever seemed to spread. More and more loaded trucks and cars began to drift towards the outlets of the city. At railroad stations from which any trains are still running the crowds of refugees, mostly incomers from the east and north waiting to go elsewhere, grew hour by hour and never seemed to lessen.[5]

Tens of thousands of French soldiers had already been killed by the time German tanks reached the outskirts of Paris; an estimated two million Parisians had vacated their homes in search of safety. However, Ambassador Bullitt decided that he would not abandon his post, writing

President Roosevelt, "No American ambassador in history has ever left Paris." Bullitt proposed that his friend Ambassador Anthony Biddle, the man he had previously recommended to replace him in Paris if the president should appoint Bullitt to the cabinet, be named a "special representative" to the French government. Bullitt would remain the American ambassador in Paris, but Biddle, according to Bullitt, could represent the United States wherever the new French government convened.[6]

With Hitler seemingly unstoppable, Benito Mussolini decided the time had come to choose sides. Standing on the balcony of the Palazzo Venezia, Il Duce, dressed in full military garb, hands on his hips, dramatically declared Italy's entrance into the war on the side of Germany to a cheering crowd of thousands.[7] Only days earlier, President Roosevelt had sent Il Duce a message offering to mediate between Italy and the Allies, promising to personally guarantee any agreement. However, Mussolini's son-in-law, Count Ciano, the foreign minister, told the president's ambassador, William Phillips, "It takes more than that to dissuade Mussolini. In fact, it is not that he wants to obtain this or that; what he wants is war, and, even if he were to obtain what he wants by peaceful means, he would refuse."[8]

President Roosevelt may not have been surprised by Mussolini's announcement, but he was nevertheless angered by it. He had tried for several years to flatter, to reason, to cajole, and to reassure Mussolini that Italy belonged in the company of Europe's democracies. Hours before learning of Mussolini's announcement, the president had accepted an invitation to speak at the commencement exercises at the University of Virginia the following day where his son Franklin Jr. was graduating from law school. Now, in light of the news from Italy, he decided to use the opportunity once again to warn the American people of the very dangerous situation developing in Europe by highlighting what he viewed as Mussolini's treachery.

The president and the First Lady boarded the train at Union Station in Washington, D.C., for the journey to Charlottesville, home of the university. During the three-hour trip, Roosevelt read over the draft of a speech that the Department of State had prepared for him. The president had revised it once already but was still not satisfied. He had included a sentence describing Mussolini's perfidy as "the hand that held the dagger has struck it into the back of its neighbor." Roosevelt recalled the phrase from a letter Bullitt had written him in which he said Japan had plunged "a dagger in the back" of the Soviet Union. The president thought it an apt metaphor to describe Mussolini's betrayal of France as well. However, the new draft handed to the president on the train omitted the phrase, presumably because it was viewed as too incendiary. Roosevelt discussed the omission with Eleanor, who told him, "If your conscience won't be satisfied until you put it in I would put it in." The president inserted it in longhand. Not surprisingly, the phrase made headlines when he delivered his speech at graduation. *Time* magazine called it a "fighting speech . . . more powerful and determined than any he had delivered since the war began."[9]

The former ambassador to Italy, Breckinridge Long, rarely took exception to President Roosevelt's decisions, but he objected to Roosevelt's criticism of Italy and Mussolini's decision to declare war on France. Writing in his diary, Long fretted, "If we are not very careful we are going to find ourselves the champions of a defeated cause . . . France has utterly collapsed. It may not be but a few weeks before England collapses and Hitler stands rampant across the continent of Europe."[10] Long was especially concerned about "the implications of a political nature which are pregnant with infinite possibilities." He worried that Roosevelt might have invited opposition within the Democratic Party to his nomination for a third term. He also feared that if Roosevelt "should be nominated . . . there would probably be raised by the Republicans the cry that we had tried to put the country into war; that we had jeopardized the neutrality of the United States."[11] Long, however, kept his thoughts to himself.

On June 11, 1940, Ambassador Bullitt cabled President Roosevelt: "I have talked with the Provisional Governor of Paris, who is the single government official remaining, and it may be that at a given moment I, as the only representative of the Diplomatic Corps remaining in Paris, will be obliged in the interest of public safety to take control of the City pending arrival of the German Army . . . [Prime Minister] Reynaud and [Interior Minister] Mandel just before their departures requested me to do this if necessary."[12] Bullitt viewed himself, in effect, as Paris's provisional mayor. President Roosevelt, however, was neither impressed by Bullitt's self-appointed role nor convinced that he should remain in Paris. Roosevelt immediately responded, "Strongly recommend that if all foreign chiefs of mission follow the French government to its temporary capital, you should do likewise."[13] It was the second time the president had ordered him to vacate the city. Bullitt ignored the cable and left the embassy to attend a prayer service at Notre Dame, where he was observed, head bowed as tears streamed down his cheeks, praying for the city he loved.[14]

Secretary of State Hull followed up on Roosevelt's orders to Bullitt, urging the ambassador to follow the French government to the city of Tours, where it had decamped. Hull reminded Bullitt that the French still had military bases in North Africa and encouraged him to persuade the French to fight the Germans there. But Bullitt argued that unless Roosevelt made a commitment to supply the French with armaments—and so far the president had not done so—neither he nor Roosevelt would have any credibility. He ended his cable on a personal note: "My deepest personal reason for staying in Paris is that whatever I have as character, good or bad, is based on the fact that since the age of four I have never run away from anything no matter how painful or dangerous when I thought it was my duty to take a stand. If I should leave Paris now, I would no longer be myself."[15]

A few hours later, proving that he was actually making a difference by staying in Paris, Bullitt sent a follow-up cable to Secretary Hull: "I propose to send my Military attache and my Naval attache to the German Commanding General of the forces in the Paris area to explain the situation and return with the suggestions of the German command as to methods of facilitating the orderly transition of government."[16]

With Hitler's tanks now on the outskirts of Paris, Ambassador Bullitt sent Missy LeHand a final message:

> *Dearest Lady,*
>
> *This is a last note out of Paris by the hand of the last member of my staff to leave. The telephone has been smashed by the Germans so that I cannot talk with you. The Germans are close. The Italians have declared war.*
>
> *The next days may be bad. I have nothing to say except that I am thinking of the days that we have had that have been good.*
>
> *Best, best love and thanks. Bill*[17]

It was the French army as it withdrew from Paris—not the advancing Germans—who had severed most telephone lines. Although the communications in and out of the American embassy were sporadic, a chance telephone call from the American embassy in Bern, Switzerland, opened a line for Bullitt to relay a message to the Third Reich's general staff via the American embassy in Berlin. Bullitt urgently requested the Germans recognize that "Paris has been declared an open city," thereby waiving the right to resist in exchange for a peaceful occupation.[18] The message was delivered to the acting secretary at the German ministry of foreign affairs, which agreed to a truce.

Bullitt appeared to have saved Paris from destruction, but hours later, French snipers fired on a group of German officers near the Porte Saint-Denis in the north of Paris. This enraged General Georg von Kuchler, the German army commander, who decided to order an air and artillery assault on Paris. Kuchler had demolished the Dutch city of Rotterdam only a few weeks earlier. Scheduling an attack on Paris for 8:00 the next morning, he vowed the city would be turned to rubble. Only after the French commander for the Paris area, General Henri

Dentz, was granted an emergency meeting with Kuchler and agreed to officially sign a surrender document did the German commander retract his orders for the attack.[19]

Notwithstanding the agreement, Bullitt feared that violence and mayhem might erupt at any moment. That night, he ordered embassy staff to sleep in the chancery, where he thought they would be safe.[20] As William C. Trimble, a senior aide to Bullitt remembered: "It was a beautiful night. I remember the stars and moon shining, and we were all upset, of course. I looked out about 4:00 in the morning, 5:00 maybe, because the sun was coming up, and you could see the German helmets behind the bec-de-gas, the street lights, in the Place [de La Concorde], and then more poured in, hundreds and hundreds filling the entire square."

The next morning, June 14, Bullitt made a simple entry in his diary, "Entry of Germans on Place de la Concord." Nazi soldiers unfurled giant swastika flags on the Eiffel Tower, beneath the Arc de Triomphe, and at Versailles.[21] The German high command appropriated the Hôtel de Crillon, next to the United States embassy, for its headquarters—the hotel where President Wilson resided during negotiations for the creation of the League of Nations.[22] The "City of Light" that Bullitt had so enjoyed first as a young man, and later as ambassador, was largely deserted and eerily quiet; shops and businesses closed and the remaining inhabitants cowered in their apartments and homes. Later that day, Bullitt telegraphed Secretary of State Hull, "This Embassy is the only official organization still functioning in the City of Paris except the Headquarters of the military forces, Governor and Prefecture of Police."[23]

34

I'VE TOLD YOU, ELEANOR,
YOU MUST NOT SAY THAT

F or days, the roads leading out of Paris to the south had been filled with tens of thousands of refugees. Some had cars and trucks; some were on bicycles; some pushed carts with their luggage or carried elderly relatives; most were on foot. They were tired, hungry, and thirsty. Nevertheless, they trudged on, mostly in silence, desperate to evade to the advancing German army. For those hoping to leave the war behind, their only hope was to make for the southwestern port of Bordeaux—some three hundred miles away—beyond which lay the Pyrenees and neutral Spain and Portugal.

After the fall of France, thousands of panicked refugees across Europe clamored for visas to enter the United States. Assistant Secretary Long was determined to uphold the strict immigrant quotas and visa requirements that Congress had put in place decades earlier. Moreover, Long fervently embraced President Roosevelt's warning about "a fifth column of spies and saboteurs" working on behalf of the Nazis. In his diary, he noted, "It is very apparent that the Germans are using visitors' visas to send their agents and documents through the United States and are using their Consulates in the United States as headquarters for their nationals who enter in transit permits and who are carrying confidential documents but who have not notified this Government and are not certified members of the German Foreign Service."[1] Hitler had implemented a plan to infiltrate U.S. government agencies, and there was some credible evidence to support Long's claims.

Like Roosevelt, Long was also familiar with polling that showed immigration to be extremely unpopular with the American electorate. Writing in his diary, he justified his approach as necessary to guard against the political fallout that greater immigration could have for the president's reelection. Moreover, Secretary Hull had set the tone for the department's immigration policy a year earlier. After a German ocean liner, the *St. Louis,* carrying more than nine hundred Jewish refugees, was denied permission to allow the passengers to disembark in Havana, Cuba, the ship's captain sailed off the coast of Florida, hoping for permission to enter the United States. However, Secretary of State Hull advised the president—who was busy entertaining the king and queen of England at the time—not to allow the passengers to disembark onto American soil. On Hull's orders, but with Roosevelt's awareness, a State Department telegram sent to passengers aboard the *St. Louis* stated that immigration laws required them to "await their turns on the waiting list and qualify for and obtain immigration visas before they may be admissible into the United States."[2]

On the surface, Long appeared no more bigoted than many in the Department of State; but given his mandate, he appeared willing—even eager—to channel the collective intolerance of the country. When Rabbi Stephen Wise and other Jewish leaders made it clear to Long that his narrow-minded, bureaucratic approach to immigration had dire consequences for many European Jews who faced certain death if they remained in Europe, the assistant secretary listened politely but did nothing.

Long laid out his strategy for stemming a flood of immigration in a secret memo to his colleague Adolf Berle in the State Department: "We can delay and effectively stop for a temporary period of indefinite length the number of immigrants into the United States. We could do this by simply advising our consuls to put every obstacle in the way and to require additional evidence and to resort to various administrative advices which would postpone and postpone and postpone the granting of visas."[3]

Albert Einstein, who left Germany in 1933—with the help of George Messersmith—was horrified by the restrictive approach to immigration under Long. The renowned scientist told Eleanor Roosevelt that the State Department had erected "a wall of bureaucratic measures."[4]

Nowhere was this wall more apparent than in the aftermath of surging visa requests from thousands of British who feared a German invasion following the Nazi occupation of Paris. Long wrote in his diary on June 17, "The problem of refugees is getting to be enormous . . . The English propose to take a number of refugees to Canada. Without passport requirements, which we are now working on, they could simply walk right into the United States."[5] Long viewed the potential breach of the Canadian border as not only a violation of United States law but also a potential security issue.

Two days later, Long noted in his diary that he had been asked by Secretary Hull to handle the evacuation of children out of England to the United States. He worried that there was "a lot of sentiment about it and sentimentality, but the enthusiasm is liable to wane at the end of a long period, and it would be cruel to the children and a failure to discharge our obligations if we got them in here and then failed to take care of them." He interpreted the desire to admit the British refugee children as "an enormous psychosis" on the part of the American people. "I attribute it to repressed emotion about the war," he recorded in his diary, "the chance to do something however wrong-headed it may be." Nevertheless, Long recognized that he needed to give serious consideration to the issue because "Mrs. Roosevelt is much interested."[6]

Before marrying Franklin, Eleanor lived in New York City, where she volunteered as a teacher for impoverished immigrant children at Manhattan's Rivington Street settlement house. Now, with much of Europe under Nazi control and the British living in fear of an impending invasion, she was committed to helping refugee children come to the United States. She was not alone. Polls showed that while immigration remained unpopular, Americans overwhelmingly favored evacuating as many European children as possible. As historian Doris Kearns Goodwin put it, "The refugee crisis seemed the perfect focus for Eleanor's abilities, combining her humanitarian zeal with her organizational skill."[7]

At a hastily arranged conference at New York's Gramercy Park Hotel on Lexington Avenue, a new umbrella organization, the Committee for the Care of European Children, was launched. Eleanor served as the honorary chair. Her first goal was to persuade the State Department to relax its restrictions on the granting of visas. Her second objective was to establish a network of families in the U.S. willing to care for the children once they arrived. Appearing on CBS radio, Eleanor Roosevelt argued for an administrative ruling that would permit refugee children to enter the United States as temporary visitors rather than as immigrants. "The children are not immigrants," she said. "The parents of these children will recall them once the war is over. Therefore, they should be classified as temporary visitors and not as refugees. Red tape must not be used to trip up little children on their way to safety."[8] When Long continued to obstruct the process, Eleanor decided to confront her husband.

Visiting New York City on June 19, 1940, Eleanor telephoned Franklin, who was enjoying a martini along with Harry Hopkins in the Oval Office study at the end of a long day. "He was somewhat impatient and irritated" when Eleanor raised the immigration issue, the First Lady's friend Joseph Lash recorded in his diary. The president was annoyed "that it wasn't taken for granted he was already doing all that was possible. He kept bringing up the difficulties while Mrs. Roosevelt tenaciously pointed out the possibilities. When she hung up the phone, the First Lady voiced her inability to understand what had happened to America—the traditional land of asylum, now unwilling to admit political refugees. But she would take the lists herself and send them to her friend Sumner Welles in the State Department."[9] In response to the persistent urgings of Eleanor's committee and other refugee groups, and with Welles urging him to show some flexibility, Assistant Secretary Long finally agreed to establish a special procedure to expedite the issuance of visitor visas for children. However, he continued to act at a glacial pace. Long's intransigence to assist refugee children eventually made it into the newspaper. Writing in *The Washington Post*, Joseph Alsop and Robert Kintner declared:

Those who worked for earlier admission of the English children to this country saw him [Long] use every resource of his position to obstruct their project and know he would have succeeded if the president had not rapped him smartly over the official knuckles. Those who tried to help the European political refugees heard him argue visas could not be issued to these unfortunates except in the discretion of the "independent consuls" who had received information instructions [to reject almost all visas] from Washington. Long seems to have a knack for these imbroglios.[10]

Reading the story over lunch, Eleanor confronted her husband. "Franklin," she said, "you know he's a fascist." The president looked up, somewhat irritated, and said, "I've told you, Eleanor, you must not say that." "Well, maybe I shouldn't say it," Eleanor replied, "but he is." Eleanor's inability to persuade her husband to fire Long and to admit more refugees, was, according to her son James, "the deepest regret at the end of her life."[11]

Adolf Hitler relished the irony of signing an armistice with France at the edge of the forest near Compiègne, the small French town where on November 11, 1918, Germany had surrendered to end World War I. Now, two decades later, journalist William Shirer witnessed the June 22 ceremony and recalled, "It was one of the loveliest summer days I ever remember in France. A warm June sun beat down on the stately trees—elms, oaks, cypresses, and pines—casting pleasant shadows on the wooded avenues leading to the little circular clearing."[12] The agreement established a German occupation zone in western and northern France along the Atlantic Ocean. The rest of the country was declared "free" to be governed by a collaborationist government headquartered in the small town of Vichy.

Confident that he had done what he could to ensure a modicum of safety for the residents of Paris after the Nazis occupied the city, on June 30, 1940, Ambassador Bullitt vacated the embassy and headed south. His traveling party included his trusted aide Carmel Offie, Commander

Roscoe Hillenkoetter, Counselor Robert Murphy, and his British neighbors Frances and Dudley Gilroy. They stopped in Vichy—the spa town where General Petain had established a new government in the so-called "Free Zone"—but Bullitt insisted that the layover be brief because he was anxious to leave France altogether and return to the United States. There was increasing speculation that Roosevelt would run for a third term, and Bullitt, who still aspired to a cabinet position, wanted to help with the campaign. During the visit to Vichy, an aide handed Bullitt a cable from President Roosevelt, ordering him to remain in Vichy. Bullitt tore up the message and threw it away.

After only a few days in Vichy, Bullitt and his entourage left for Spain. After a long drive along mountainous roads, they were stopped at a border crossing. Bullitt and his team handed over their passports. The Gilroys had British passports; Spain was sending British nationals back to France, where they risked imprisonment by the Nazis. Bullitt had listed the Gilroys as his personal valet and maid—working for the American mission in Paris—and therefore with diplomatic status. Dudley bowed his head and avoided eye contact with the border guards, but the elegantly dressed Frances aroused suspicion. One Spanish official commented, "She is not a maid." Carmel Offie took the border guard aside and whispered, "Of course not. Don't you understand that the ambassador has a mistress?" The Spaniard smiled and let the Gilroys pass through the border checkpoint.[13]

After reaching Barcelona, Bullitt flew to Lisbon, where he telephoned President Roosevelt. The president was surprised to learn that his ambassador to France was now in Portugal and cheerfully asked, "What are you doing in Lisbon?" Bullitt claimed communications in France had been poor for several weeks and he had never received Roosevelt's orders. The president asked Bullitt to see him when he returned.[14]

The Democrats had scheduled their 1940 convention for the middle of July. It was still unclear if President Roosevelt would stand for a third term, but party bosses worried that the Republicans, who had gathered in Philadelphia in late June, had nominated a formidable standard-bearer in political newcomer Wendell Willkie. Willkie hailed from the Midwest and became a successful corporate lawyer in New York. After practicing law, he became the CEO of a large utility. Willkie was charismatic, articulate, and combative; Harold Ickes described him as "the barefoot boy from Wall Street."[15] Roosevelt sensed Willkie—who, though an internationalist at heart, preached isolationism—would undoubtedly be a much tougher opponent than either Herbert Hoover or Alf Landon.

Because the president had not declared publicly whether he intended to run for an unprecedented third term, his supporters were casting about for alternatives. If Roosevelt didn't run, Breckinridge Long hoped that his immediate boss, Secretary Hull, might throw his hat into the ring. Hull was well liked and universally respected within the Democratic Party. But in a conversation with Supreme Court Justice Stanley Reed that revealed the depths of anti-Semitism in the United States at the time, Long learned that Hull had decided against running because his wife was Jewish, and he did "not wish to submit [her] to severe attacks."[16] Long was despondent, but a few days after his conversation with Justice Reed, Long had what he called "a very significant talk with Cordell," who put his mind to ease. The secretary told him in confidence that Roosevelt would, in fact, run again and would "be nominated by acclamation."[17] As Secretary Hull observed several years later, the fall of France had been a clarifying moment for Roosevelt. "The third term was an immediate consequence of Hitler's conquest of France and the specter of Britain standing alone between conquerors and ourselves," observed Hull. "Our dangerous position induced President Roosevelt to run for a third term."

The Democratic National Convention opened on July 15, 1940, at the Chicago Stadium with both Jim Farley, the U.S. postmaster general, and Vice President John Nance Garner contending for the nomination, and without a clear signal from President Roosevelt about a third term. Roosevelt, secluded in the White House, sought to portray himself as a leader grappling with a European war, still focused on reviving the American economy, but above all, as not consumed by politics. Harold Ickes wired the president in Washington, "This convention is bleeding. And your reputation and prestige may bleed to death with it."[18]

Still, Roosevelt remained silent. Aware that running for a third term ran against the grain of American history—many critics already referred to him as a dictator—the president, as he had confided to Hull, wanted to be nominated by a spontaneous acclamation of the delegates. The next evening, while not exactly spontaneous, Roosevelt supporters arranged for a dramatic "Draft Roosevelt" floor demonstration complete with organ music, a marching band, and confetti. On the first ballot, President Roosevelt was nominated by the delegates to run for a third term. Few had noticed that the Democratic platform had been amended, at Roosevelt's insistence, to read that the United States would "not participate in any foreign wars," except "in the case of attack."

35

I GET CONSTANT REPORTS OF HOW VALUABLE YOU ARE

mbassador Bullitt's transatlantic flight from Lisbon touched down at New York Municipal Airport on Saturday, July 20, 1940. Several newspaper reporters, anxious for his views on the escalating conflict, met him at the airport. As photographers snapped his picture, Bullitt gave an impromptu press conference, making news when he proposed that the United States recognize the Vichy government headed by the French World War I hero General Henri-Philippe Pétain. His comments were controversial because Charles de Gaulle, head of the French resistance headquartered in London, had denounced Pétain as a collaborator with the Nazis.

That afternoon, Bullitt took the train to Washington, D.C., where he dined with the president at the White House. For the first time Bullitt heard Roosevelt describe what came to be known as lend-lease, a means of circumventing the restrictions of the Neutrality Act by committing the financially strapped British to eventually return any war matériel they received from the United States.[1] "Bill, if my neighbor's house catches fire . . . and I'm watering the grass in my backyard, and I don't pass the garden hose over the fence to my neighbor, I am a fool," Roosevelt explained. "How do you think the country and the Congress would react if I should put aid to the British in the form of lending them my garden hose?"[2] Bullitt nodded and assured the president that he was doing the right thing. A few months later, after the commencement of the Nazi bombing attacks on Britain, the president would use very similar language to explain to the American public his rationale for lend-lease to Britain.

The following day, July 21, President Roosevelt held his own press conference and was asked whether Bullitt would return to France. Roosevelt sounded noncommittal, cheerfully explaining that his ambassador had earned a vacation.[3] However, the president was privately annoyed with Bullitt because he had disregarded orders to vacate Paris and to follow the French government to Vichy. Neither did Roosevelt appreciate that before checking with either himself or with Secretary of State Hull, Bullitt had publicly commented on the question of whether America should officially recognize the Vichy government. Harold Ickes, Bullitt's close friend, acknowledged that the ambassador had been "out of order in making an announcement of foreign policy which should properly have come from the State Department or from the President." Added Ickes, "I got the impression that [the president] also thinks that Bill is too quick on the trigger."[4]

In his meeting with Bullitt, the president didn't let on that he was irritated. For the moment, Roosevelt hesitated to rebuke so prominent and skilled a member of his team. He genuinely liked Bullitt and considered him not only intelligent and charming but also highly capable. He hadn't decided what role Bullitt should play in either the campaign, or in his administration should he be reelected to a third term. However, friendship with Roosevelt didn't permanently insulate anyone who, in the president's view, either carelessly or intentionally challenged his authority in a public way. Roosevelt confided to Ickes that Bullitt wanted to be named secretary of state, "but I can't do that."[5]

As the president prepared for the fall campaign, he turned his attention to the problem of his ambassador in London. When Roosevelt initially appointed Kennedy, he was happy to be sending him out of the country. But now, with the stakes so high in Europe, he considered his ambassador an obstacle to close relations with the Churchill government. The problem, however, was that Roosevelt still didn't want Kennedy back in the United States, where he might make political mischief.

After the fall of Paris, Germany seized major French seaports and naval bases, thereby giving German submarines direct access to the Atlantic. Hitler had a clear and simple strategy to defeat Britain: Sever England's maritime communications and supply lines, and then use his numerically superior air force to bomb London into submission. During the summer of 1940, the Germans carried out the first part of their strategy, sinking Allied merchant ships at a rate of ninety-eight per month and depriving Britain of much-needed supplies and war matériel. Concerned about Great Britain's ability to survive the Nazi blitzkrieg, President Roosevelt asked Major General William Donovan, a Republican and hero of World War I, to serve as his informal emissary. He instructed Donovan to travel to London to make an assessment of British resolve and capacity to wage war, but never mentioned the mission to Ambassador Kennedy.[6]

After spending several days in London meeting with British military planners and members of Churchill's inner circle, General Donovan returned to Washington, D.C., on August 3 and reported to the president and Secretary Hull that in his view the British were prepared to fight and should be given every means to do so. Donovan's report contradicted Ambassador Kennedy, who had sent yet another cable to Secretary Hull predicting that "if the British air force cannot be knocked out, then the war will drag out with the whole world continuously upset, with the final result the starvation of England and God knows what happening to the rest of Europe."[7] The ambassador didn't seem to understand that he had already lost the argument.

Following the Donovan mission, President Roosevelt had quietly authorized another special envoy, Admiral Robert Ghormley, to meet secretly with the British Admiralty to see what could be done to safeguard shipping in the Atlantic. Ordinarily, the ambassador would accompany envoys such as Donovan and Ghormley to their meetings. However, just as with the Donovan mission, the president failed to inform Kennedy of Ghormley's impending visit.

While Ghormley made his way to England, the president telephoned his ambassador. Aware that Kennedy was very unhappy, Roosevelt flattered him, telling him the Democratic Committee wanted him to come home to run the campaign that fall, but the State Department felt he was too valuable in Britain. Kennedy was not so easily taken in and sensed that Roosevelt hoped to "soft-soap" him lest he leave his London post before the election. Kennedy pushed back on Roosevelt, "I am not doing a damn thing here that amounts to anything, and my services, if they are needed, could be used to much better advantage if I were home."[8] "That's where you are all wrong," the president replied. "I get constant reports of how valuable you are to them over there and that it helps the morale of the British to have you there and they would feel they were being let down if you were to leave."[9]

On August 7, 1940, Ambassador Kennedy opened the London *Daily Herald* newspaper and learned for the first time that Admiral Ghormley had recently met not only with Prime Minister Churchill but also with the king. Kennedy was surprised to read that the negotiations on the destroyer transfer, begun in London, had been transferred to Washington where they were conducted between Churchill and Roosevelt, principally via Lord Lothian, the British ambassador to the United States.[10] Once again, Kennedy felt humiliated. Making matters worse, the article made clear that the newspaper's sources worked in the British Foreign Office. It seemed as though he was the very last to know what was happening.

Furious, Kennedy wrote to Secretary Hull predicting that the American people would interpret the Ghormley mission as evidence Roosevelt was secretly working to bring the United States into the war. "The least, it seems to me, that can be done for the American ambassador in London is to let him . . . run his own job . . . I either want to run this job or get out."[11] It was the first time Ambassador Kennedy had threatened to resign.

Next, Kennedy complained to Roosevelt about how unfair and demeaning it was that Lord Lothian, the British ambassador to the United States, had been intimately involved in the destroyers-for-bases deal but that he, the United States ambassador to Britain, had been kept in the dark. Even more insulting, the information he did receive came mainly from cables that Churchill shared with him. Kennedy was fed up: "I have been fairly active in any enterprise which I have taken up for the last twenty-five years. Frankly and honestly I do not enjoy being a dummy." Kennedy told the president that if the situation in England had not been so dire, he would have quit his post immediately. Kennedy sent another despairing note to Hull: "I am very unhappy about the whole position and of course there's always the alternative of resigning."[12] The truth was that Kennedy, a proud man, found himself in a political pickle; he had been effectively neutered in his job, but if he left his post, it would look as though he had been forced out. For the moment Roosevelt had Kennedy just where he wanted him.

As the negotiations for American ships continued, Roosevelt further ruptured the relationship with Kennedy when he asked him to personally deliver an important cable to Winston Churchill. At 10 Downing Street, Kennedy sat quietly in the prime minister's study, waiting while Churchill finished an afternoon nap. Eventually, the prime minister greeted the ambassador, who handed him the cable. Churchill read the correspondence aloud: The president intended to supply Great Britain with destroyers, torpedo boats, and a number of warplanes. In return, America would receive ninety-nine-year leases on a number of British bases, primarily in the Caribbean. Prime Minister Churchill had originally insisted that the leasing of the bases be a gift independent of the destroyers or any other aid from America, but he was nevertheless pleased with the compromise. Churchill told Kennedy, "We are going to beat this man," referring to Hitler. Kennedy smiled but was annoyed that he was learning the details of the agreement from Churchill. Kennedy later wrote in his diary, "Nothing has been said to me about it and Roosevelt's conduct in this closing phase of the negotiations was just as inconsiderate as during the entire negotiations."[13]

Notwithstanding Kennedy's pique, in early September, President Roosevelt publicly announced the agreement between the United States and Great Britain. In trading World War I vintage ships, many of which needed extensive repairs, for leases to seven air and naval bases in the Western Hemisphere, the president claimed it was the most important "reinforcement of [America's] defense . . . since the Louisiana Purchase." The agreement proved extremely popular with the American people, for even the most ardent isolationist had to acknowledge that it was a good deal for the United States.

To mark the end of summer, Secretary of the Treasury Morgenthau and his wife hosted a clambake at their estate in Peekskill, an hour due south of Hyde Park in upstate New York. President Roosevelt, Eleanor, and their family all attended. They sat on the sloping lawn, drinking beer and sipping brandy, and as twilight gave way to darkness, gathered around a bonfire to sing songs in the cool night air. "It was the kind of free, relaxed evening" that the president enjoyed, Eleanor recalled some years later. After dinner, everyone went into the house, and the president looked on with delight as the guests paired off for a square dance.[14]

Later that evening, Kennedy wired President Roosevelt and Secretary of State Hull, "There's Hell to pay here tonight!" Wave after wave of the German Luftwaffe bombed London, setting ablaze buildings, factories, and docks along the Thames. In all, 625 bombers, protected by fighter planes, carried out a massive and destructive aerial bombardment. Though Londoners took refuge in basements, underground subway stations, and bomb shelters, more than four hundred were killed and another fourteen hundred seriously injured.[15]

A few days later, the ambassador wrote to his wife, Rose, "I suppose you have been frightfully nervous reading about all the bombing . . . The last three nights in London have been simply hell." He told Rose that, the evening before, he had donned a steel helmet "and went up on the roof of the chancery and stayed there until two o'clock in the morning watching the Germans come over in relays every ten minutes and drop bombs, setting terrific fires." According to Kennedy, "You could see the dome of St. Pauls' silhouetted against a blazing inferno that the Germans kept adding to from time to time flying over and dropping more bombs."[16]

Even in Windsor, at his country house, Kennedy wasn't safe. He reported that a bomb fell about 250 yards from the house and that he had been outside looking at "searchlights and the anti-aircraft fire when we heard it coming and dove into the bushes." When fragments of the bomb were later recovered, one of them turned out to bear his initials, JPK.[17] Notwithstanding his growing reputation as an appeaser, the Luftwaffe had evidently targeted the American ambassador.

The bombing raids were relentless and punishing. Yet Kennedy, exhausted and angry, heard nothing from the Department of State, much less from President Roosevelt. On September 16, 1940, he telephoned Undersecretary Welles to complain that no one seemed to have any idea what he and his staff were going through.[18]

After two weeks of bombing every night, Germany was no closer to controlling the skies over Britain. In fact, the Luftwaffe had suffered losses that exceeded those of the Royal Air Force. The führer was forced to postpone plans for an invasion. True to his word, Churchill had no intention of negotiating with Hitler. Adding to the führer's frustration, while Germany stalled on Britain, Stalin's powerful Russian army seized Lithuania, Latvia, and Estonia.[19] Suddenly, Hitler, who had thus far met little resistance in Europe, found himself checked by Britain, competing for territory with Russia, and facing the prospect of a more assertive and engaged United States.

As the refugee crisis intensified, Assistant Secretary Breckinridge Long worked to prevent the admission of immigrants, though Eleanor Roosevelt managed to outmaneuver him in one well-publicized episode. The *Quanza,* a ship carrying 317 passengers, mostly Jewish refugees, sailed out of Lisbon bound for New York and Mexico. Some of the passengers held American visas and were permitted to disembark in New York, but

many of the Jewish refugees were denied entry, and so the ship continued its voyage to Mexico, docking in Veracruz. Though the refugees had
transit visas, for which each person had paid one hundred dollars, only a
few dozen were allowed to disembark. Forced to return to Portugal, the
ship stopped along the way to pick up coal in Norfolk, Virginia, where
the remaining 83 refugees, mostly Belgian Jews, pleaded for asylum, but
were once again denied permission to come ashore.[20] In his diary, Long
noted that Rabbi Wise and Congressman Sol Bloom, chairman of the
House Foreign Affairs Committee, and "many, many more" had pleaded
the case for the refugees, but Long contended that a grant of asylum
would be "a violation of the spirit of the law if not the letter. We have
been generous but there are limitations."[21]

After Jewish American associations appealed to Eleanor Roosevelt
about the plight of passengers aboard the *Quanza,* she spoke to her
husband and asked him to intervene. President Roosevelt dispatched
Patrick Malin, a State Department official representing the President's Advisory Council, to check the passengers' status and see if any
might be admitted. Bypassing Assistant Secretary Long, Malin designated all of the passengers as political refugees, issued them visas, and
permitted them to disembark. Long was enraged, writing in his diary
that he "remonstrated violently" over such an egregious breach of protocol. It was one of the few instances when the president ignored his
assistant secretary and adopted a humanitarian approach to Europe's
refugees. Some of the refugees later sent President Roosevelt roses
with a note reading, "With everlasting gratitude for your humane gesture, from the refugees of the SS Quanza." But one passenger had a
better understanding of what had happened: "Mrs. Roosevelt saved
my life."[22]

Eleanor Roosevelt also succeeded in assisting the evacuation of children from Britain. Thousands of American families offered to host
English children, and over the course of the war, nearly one hundred thousand children crossed the Atlantic. Ambassador Kennedy both supported
and facilitated the First Lady's efforts, but when his wife attempted to

adopt an English schoolgirl friend of their daughter Jean, the ambassador stepped in and was less than magnanimous: "I am not very much impressed with the idea of taking evacuees," Kennedy wrote Rose. "You have to assume responsibility for the child up to its 21st birthday and you have to pay all its bills." Kennedy summed up his feelings, "I think [it] will bring a lot of grief."[23]

36

YOUR BOYS ARE NOT GOING TO BE SENT INTO ANY FOREIGN WARS

The presidential campaign in the fall of 1940 took a turn in late September when Wendell Willkie anointed himself the guarantor of peace and excoriated President Roosevelt as a warmonger. Earlier in the year, Willkie had embraced American internationalism and even supported Roosevelt's call for military conscription, but now, sensing a political opening, he flayed the president, declaring, "If his promise to keep our boys out of war is no better than his promise to balance the budget they're already almost on the transports." In a speech delivered before a raucous crowd in Baltimore, the Republican nominee blasted Roosevelt: "On the basis of his past performance, with pledges to the people, if you re-elect him you may expect our entering war in April 1941." On the defensive, Roosevelt shot back, "While I am talking to you mothers and fathers, I give you one more assurance . . . I have said this before, but I shall say it again, and again, and again: Your boys are not going to be sent into any foreign wars."[1]

Willkie was gaining momentum. Though the president was a former governor of the Empire State, *The New York Times* endorsed Willkie over Roosevelt. In Boston, every major newspaper in the city opposed the president and endorsed Willkie. Indeed, in all of New England, only five small newspapers endorsed Roosevelt for a third term. It was the same throughout the country: Newspapers editorialized that historical precedent, as well as Roosevelt's record, meant that he should not be given a third term.[2]

Adolf Hitler also was following the United States presidential election. During the summer of 1940, his ambassador to the U.S., Hans Thomsen, wired his superiors in Berlin seeking funds to mount "a well-camouflaged lightning propaganda campaign" at the Republican National Convention in Philadelphia. The ambassador wanted "$60,000 to $80,000" because a Republican Congressman, whom Thomsen did not identify, was forming a committee that would publish full-page newspaper advertisements during the convention with the message "Keep America Out of War."

Republican Congressman Hamilton Fish of New York, an archenemy of President Roosevelt, headed the Committee to Keep the United States Out of Foreign Wars. While no proof ever emerged that Thomsen either received money from Berlin or gave money to Fish, the committee did publish anti-war advertisements during the Republican Convention. The text of the ads warned Republican delegates to "stop the march to war," and claimed the Democratic Party is "the interventionist and war party."[3] As historian Nicholas Wapshott has written, "Hitler . . . had his eyes on the U.S. presidential election and dearly hoped that an isolationist would win."[4] However, the führer likely would have been disappointed had Wendell Willkie won. Notwithstanding his campaign rhetoric, the Republican nominee was a committed internationalist. Willkie's foreign policy would probably have hewed closer to Roosevelt's than he was willing to acknowledge at the time.

Of course, regardless of who won the American presidency, Hitler's overriding objective was for the United States to maintain its neutrality. On September 27, 1940, he signed the Tripartite Pact in Berlin among Germany, Italy, and Japan to provide for mutual assistance should any one of the three be attacked by the United States.[5] The pact was intended, in part, as a message to America to stay out of the war. At the same time, Hitler refrained from attacking American merchant ships in the North Atlantic. According to Wapshott, Hitler had issued a "very strict order . . . not to do or say anything against the United States of America."[6] Hitler's U-boats had sunk American ships bringing supplies to Britain, but sensing America was inching closer to direct involvement in the war, he now wanted to do everything possible to steer clear of provocation.

Less than a month before the election, President Roosevelt met with Undersecretary of State Sumner Welles and Assistant Secretary Breckinridge Long in the White House. The president was in a bad mood, concerned that polls showed the presidential election to be tightening. He expressed anger at being portrayed as wanting to take the United States into war and then outlined his displeasure with the State Department. In his diary, Long remarked that Roosevelt "commented very adversely and critically" about Ambassadors Phillips, Bullitt, and Kennedy "who felt they had been so over-worked they had to come home and go on a long rest cure . . . [T]hey seemed to think that since a few bombs had missed them that they were nervous wrecks and candidates for rest cures."[7] Roosevelt was not being entirely fair to his ambassadors, given that only a few weeks earlier he had told Phillips that he "should not go back to Rome now or in the immediate future," yet he should "not resign as ambassador."[8] As for Bullitt, Roosevelt had been angry with his ambassador to France for disobeying his order to vacate Paris, but since arriving back in the United States in June, Bullitt had been traveling the country speaking on behalf of the president about the need for military preparedness. Bullitt may have once again been looking for his next job, but he was working hard to reinforce the president's message on foreign policy. The ambassador gave a highly touted speech on preparedness in his hometown of Philadelphia, described in one local editorial as "one of the great speeches of our time."[9] Another newspaper noted that "never before had a United States Ambassador . . . been presumed to talk on international affairs with such diplomatic, brutal bluntness" and speculated that "his words had been first well weighed by Mr. Roosevelt."[10]

Of course, as always, the situation with Ambassador Kennedy was of a very different nature. The mutual disdain between Ambassador Kennedy and President Roosevelt was nothing new, but it had been heightened by a spate of recent news stories and by a swirl of rumors. *The Chicago Daily News* reported that Kennedy wanted to leave his post, and on October 11, syndicated columnists Joseph Alsop and Robert Kintner speculated that Roosevelt wanted Kennedy in London "because he could do less harm there." The columnists derided Kennedy for his "gloom."[11]

Kennedy's increasingly public spat with the president worried a number of officials in the Department of State. In his diary, Long quoted Welles as saying, "Kennedy was in a very bad humor and was coming home. He would rather have orders to come, but if he did not get orders he was coming anyway and [would] resign." Welles told Long that Kennedy threatened to publicly criticize the destroyer-for-bases deal as "the worst ever."[12]

Undersecretary Welles was so concerned about Kennedy that he asked to meet with the president. As reported by Long, Welles told Roosevelt that if Kennedy returned, he might endorse Willkie. Roosevelt agreed that was a distinct possibility.[13] Their concern was well placed. Henry and Clare Boothe Luce, owners of *Time* and *Life* magazines, had endorsed Willkie, and Kennedy confided to them that he was seriously considering joining them in opposing Roosevelt's reelection. He told friends in London that he could turn out "twenty-five million Catholic voters behind Willkie to throw Roosevelt out."[14]

According to Long's diary, Welles argued Kennedy "is in a terrible blue funk about England and would give that impression here, and would advise the public probably that England was about to collapse." Again, Roosevelt agreed, but he now felt cornered by Kennedy's threat to resign, and according to Long, he "finally compromised by saying [Kennedy] could come home the latter part of the month and that he would himself send him a personal letter, which Welles was going to draft, giving him instructions about his conversation and conduct once he got here."[15]

A few days later, the president sent a cable to Kennedy, written by Welles, warning the ambassador "not to make any statements to the press on your way over, nor when you arrive in New York, until you and I have had a chance to agree upon what should be said. Please come straight through to Washington on your arrival since I will want to talk to you as soon as you get here." Roosevelt explained that "a great deal of unnecessary confusion and undesirable complications have been caused in the last few months by statements which have been made by chiefs of mission coming back to this country."[16] Roosevelt did not elaborate, but he was presumably referring to Bullitt's unauthorized public comments that the United States should recognize the Vichy government. The president understood how his tweaking Bullitt would have appealed to Kennedy. Roosevelt wanted his ambassador in a good mood when he met with him because he had a favor to ask.

Joseph Kennedy left London on October 22, 1940, after serving as ambassador to the Court of St. James's for almost two and a half years. Five days later, he disembarked from an ocean liner in New York. As had been arranged, Kennedy's first phone call was to the president. Sitting at his desk in the Oval Office, Roosevelt happened to be meeting with the Speaker of the House, Sam Rayburn, and one of the Speaker's protégés, a young congressman from Texas named Lyndon Johnson. Answering the telephone, Roosevelt was his usual cheerful self. "Ah Joe," he began, "it is so good to hear your voice." The president invited Kennedy and his wife to the White House for "a little family dinner." As Rayburn and a wide-eyed Johnson looked on, Roosevelt comically made a gesture of cutting his own throat. "I'm dying to talk to you," he told his ambassador.[17]

During the flight to Washington, Kennedy mulled over what he would say to the president. Rose Kennedy, often his best counselor, cautioned him to measure his words carefully, reminding her husband, "The President sent you, a Roman Catholic, as Ambassador to London, which probably no other President would have done . . . You would write yourself down as an ingrate in the view of many people if you resign now."[18] Rose was likely making the point for reasons other than concern for her husband's reputation: She was also reminding him of the political aspirations he had for their sons.

On October 27, 1940, Ambassador Kennedy and Rose entered the study adjoining the Oval Office to find President Roosevelt holding a cocktail shaker in one hand and reaching for a few cubes of ice with the other. Besides the Kennedys, the president had invited South Carolina senator James Byrnes and his wife, Maude, and Missy LeHand for a Sunday supper of scrambled eggs and sausages. Before dinner, as the president and his guests sipped their cocktails, the abstemious ambassador reported on the bombing of London and described his final visit with former prime minister Chamberlain. Roosevelt listened attentively, but Rose noticed that he looked "rather pale, rather ashen." At one point, Senator Byrnes suggested that the situation in Europe was volatile and that Kennedy should give a speech endorsing President Roosevelt for reelection. Kennedy let the suggestion pass without a response and ignored the senator when he repeated it a few minutes later.[19]

It was becoming evident that the ambassador had more on his mind than briefing Roosevelt on British politics or discussing a possible endorsement. Ignoring the advice Rose had given him to avoid sounding ungrateful, Kennedy laid into the president, "In the first place, I am damn sore at the way I have been treated. I feel that it is entirely unreasonable and I don't think I rate it." As the other guests ate their meals quietly, Kennedy continued, "Mr. President, as you know, I have never said anything privately in my life that I didn't say to you personally, and I have never said anything in a public interview that ever caused you the slightest embarrassment." Roosevelt offered no rebuttal to Kennedy's stream of invective and said that as far as he was concerned, Kennedy was being charitable; officious State Department bureaucrats should not have been permitted to treat old, dear friends and valued public servants like Kennedy with such callousness. Roosevelt claimed he had not been aware of their cavalier attitude, and after the election, the president promised there would be "a real housecleaning" to ensure that the most important members of the administration, like Kennedy, would never again be abused. As the evening came to a close, the president sensed that Kennedy had been somewhat mollified, and echoing Senator Byrnes, he asked Kennedy to deliver a speech endorsing his reelection. Kennedy had twice ignored Byrnes, but now the president was asking him directly. He responded, "All right, I will," and added, "but I will pay for it myself, show it to nobody in advance, and say what I wish." No sooner did he speak than Missy LeHand telephoned the Democratic National Committee to ask that their regularly scheduled weekly radio time, usually reserved for the president to address the American people, be turned over to Kennedy.[20]

Kennedy pulled the microphone close to him, saying, "Unfortunately, during this political campaign, there has arisen the charge that the President of the United States is trying to involve this country in the world war. Such a charge is false." Kennedy then personalized his support for President Roosevelt. "I have a great stake in this country, he said. "My wife and I have given nine hostages to fortune. Our children and your children are more important than anything in the world. The kind of America that they and their children will inherit is of grave concern to us all." And then Kennedy reached the peroration: "In light of these considerations, I believe that Franklin Delano Roosevelt should be reelected President of the United States."[21]

In Baltimore, Wendell Willkie claimed that Kennedy's speech confirmed the United States had no formal alliance with Great Britain, but he declared that Roosevelt nevertheless wanted to involve the United States in Britain's war with Germany. Willkie noted that in 1932, Senator Carter Glass, a former secretary of the treasury, had raised himself from his sickbed to assure the country that Roosevelt would keep his sound-money pledge. Willkie asked sardonically, "Mr. Third-Term candidate, is your pledge about peace . . . more or less sacred than the pledge you made about sound money in 1932? Are you kidding Joe Kennedy the same way you kidded Carter Glass?"[22]

As the campaign entered its final week, President Roosevelt traveled to Boston. Arriving at South Station, the president's train was met on the platform by Joseph Kennedy Jr, and by Honey Fitz-Rose Kennedy's father and a former mayor of Boston. Driven to the Boston Garden, they were joined by a smiling Ambassador Kennedy. There the president delivered his stump speech, declaring emphatically, "Your boys are not going to be sent into any foreign wars." Wendell Willkie, frustrated that the American public appeared to accept Roosevelt's claim to be an isolationist even while he prepared the country for war, complained, "That hypocritical son-of-a-bitch! This is going to beat me!"[23]

Willkie was right. On November 5 the president, Eleanor, and Franklin's mother, Sara, drove to the town hall in Hyde Park, New York, to cast their votes. That evening, as the votes were tabulated, Roosevelt breathed a sigh of relief. He received over twenty-seven million votes, to Willkie's twenty-two million votes. Once again, his margin of victory in the electoral college had been overwhelming, winning 449 out of the 531 total electoral votes.[24] A number of friends and supporters, as well as reporters and newsreel crews, had gathered that evening in the courtyard of the Springwood estate to witness the president's election for an unprecedented third term. Klieg lights illuminated Roosevelt, looking tired but happy, as he emerged from his house around midnight. After smiling and thanking his supporters, the president declared, "I don't need to tell you that we face difficult days ahead in this country."

Breckinridge Long had spent election night at his home in Maryland, sitting by the radio, listening to the returns until the election was called in Roosevelt's favor. Long, who fancied himself a shrewd political prognosticator, wrote in his diary that he had predicted Roosevelt "would win by a large majority."[25] Long, however, had fretted for many months over Roosevelt's electability given the administration's increasing military preparations and fledgling alliance with Britain. Elated by Roosevelt's victory, Long had little confidence that Roosevelt could avoid war but he remained loyal to the president, committed to his work, and politically ambitious. The former ambassador to Italy, as well as Ambassador Bullitt, had their sights set on cabinet positions during Roosevelt's third term. Ambassador Kennedy, however, had largely given up hope that he would ever be appointed Secretary of the Treasury.

37

WE WILL TALK ABOUT THAT AND THE FUTURE LATER

The day after the election, the president and Mrs. Roosevelt traveled from New York by train to Washington, D.C. After arriving at Union Station, they were driven down Pennsylvania Avenue past a cheering crowd and through the wrought iron gates to the North Portico of the White House. The only item on his schedule that day was a celebratory lunch hosted by Secretary Henry Morgenthau.

Ambassador Joseph Kennedy dropped by the White House around 12:15 p.m. He didn't have an appointment but asked asked Missy Le-Hand if the president might have a few minutes. Roosevelt agreed to see him. Kennedy entered the Oval Office, and the two old rivals shook hands. Kennedy didn't congratulate the president, but only acknowledged his victory: "Well, you've got it. I certainly don't begrudge you the next four years." With that awkward greeting, Kennedy got to the point of his visit. He wanted to resign, saying, "I told you how I feel being Ambassador without anything to do." Once again, Roosevelt tried to dissuade him. "I don't want to have to pick a new man, and you stand so well with the British, so go take a good vacation." The president thanked Kennedy for coming by thanked him for his service, and told him he had a luncheon to attend.[1]

The president received another resignation offer that day as well. William Bullitt submitted a pro forma resignation as ambassador to France, but added, "I am ready for any work you want." With Anthony Biddle now in Vichy—the president had taken Bullitt's advice and enlisted the former U.S. ambassador to Poland to represent the United States in dealings with the Petain government—and with Paris occupied by the Nazis, Bullitt was eager to take on a new challenge. Two days later, however, Bullitt received a curt reply from the president, one that he had not expected. The president did not accept Bullitt's resignation and wrote, "We will talk about that and the future later."[2] Bullitt was stunned. He believed he and the president were friends. He felt he had performed his duties as ambassador to the best of his ability, and most of the high-ranking officials in the French government credited him with saving Paris from destruction by the Germans. Upon his return to the United States, Bullitt had crisscrossed the country, giving speeches in support of Roosevelt's bid for a third term. He thought he had positioned himself well for a cabinet post. Now he didn't know what to think. Bullitt didn't blame Roosevelt. Instead, he speculated that someone in the Department of State was trying to sabotage his relationship with the president—perhaps Sumner Welles.

Assistant Secretary Breckinridge Long slept late that day, arriving at the department midmorning. In the afternoon, he went to the secretary's office to chat about the president's victory. Sumner Welles was already there, talking with the secretary. Only minutes later, Ambassador Kennedy, fresh from his meeting with the president, stopped by as well. Kennedy likely wanted to tell Secretary Hull that he planned to resign as ambassador but, seeing Welles and Long in the secretary's office, said he'd come back later. Hull told him they were just talking politics and invited Kennedy to join them. Somewhat stiffly, the ambassador sat down.

Kennedy professed happiness that Roosevelt had won, but then laid out a dark vision for the future, predicated on the "crumbling" British Empire. According to Long, Kennedy thought the United States would "have to assume a Fascist form of government here or something similar to it if we are to survive in a world of concentrated and centralized power." The ambassador also revealed, presumably for the first time, that he had twice received, but turned down, invitations from Hitler for a conference. According to Long, Kennedy went on to suggest that the United States approach Germany and Japan for "an economic collaboration."[3] It's not clear whether Kennedy used the word *collaboration,* or if it was Long's interpretation of Kennedy's remarks, but whatever the case Long couldn't think of the ambassador as an appeaser. From Long's perspective, Kennedy was simply a realist. However, as Kennedy's friend, Long advised the ambassador "not to talk to the press or to talk in a way that would scare the American people."[4]

Later in the day, Long dropped by the White House to congratulate the president. He noted in his diary, "He looks pretty well—and not as tired as one would think. He said he was going off on his yacht for a few days away from the telephone."[5]

On November 9, 1940, Neville Chamberlain died of bowel cancer. He was seventy-one years old. That same day in Boston, Ambassador Kennedy agreed to sit for an interview with three reporters, Louis Lyons of *The Boston Globe* and Charles Edmundson and Ralph Coghlan of the *St. Louis Post-Dispatch.* Perhaps distracted by the news of Chamberlain's death, the usually press-savvy ambassador failed to make it clear to the reporters whether he was speaking on or off the record. Kennedy began the interview by boasting, "I know more about the European situation than anybody else, and it's up to me to see that the country gets it." With undiplomatic bravado, the ambassador declared, "I say we're not going in. Over my dead body, I'm willing to spend all I've got to keep us out of war. We'd just be left holding the bag." Kennedy then defended the controversial Charles Lindbergh as "not so crazy either."[6] That evening, Kennedy wrote in his diary of the sorrow he felt over Chamberlain's death. He noted that he was "closer to Neville Chamberlain than . . . to anyone in England. The world and particularly England will miss his counsel . . . He really gave his life that England might live."[7]

Kennedy's interview with Lyons was excerpted the next day in *The Boston Globe.* There was an immediate uproar. Within the week, the *New York Herald Tribune* editorialized that the ambassador needed to clarify his statements—or resign. Was Kennedy suggesting that the president was deceiving the American people and taking the country to war? Was Kennedy endorsing the viewpoint of Charles Lindbergh who had suggested to make a deal with Hitler? Kennedy decided to issue a "restatement of his position," declaring that he had only wanted to convey his support "for keeping America out of war . . . Everyone has known from the beginning that I have been against American entry into the war." But President Roosevelt was furious, telling Eleanor, "I never want to see that son of a bitch again as long as I live."[8]

Two weeks later, on December 1, Kennedy stopped off in Washington on his way to Palm Beach and formally submitted his resignation to the president. Roosevelt had not forgiven Kennedy for his interview in Boston, but he kept his temper under control, continuing to believe he might need Kennedy's support in the future. The president once again thanked the ambassador for his service, asked him to stay on until a replacement was found, and then solicited his advice on a range of subjects from trade with South America to labor relations. Roosevelt had previously claimed that when Kennedy finally returned to the private sector, his influence would be significantly diminished; though the president wasn't about to entirely discount him. Roosevelt knew how to stroke the ego of his discredited and dispirited ambassador and treated Kennedy as though he still had an important voice in American foreign policy. For his part, Kennedy issued a statement saying that "[the] President was good enough to express regret over my decision, but to say that, not yet being prepared to appoint my successor, he wishes me to retain my designation as ambassador until he is prepared. But I shall not return to London in that capacity." Kennedy noted that after a short vacation, he planned to devote himself to helping "the President keep the United States out of war."[9]

On December 17, at his regular press conference, President Roosevelt outlined for the first time his plan to send aid to Great Britain. It was the beginning of his public push to make lend-lease the official policy of the United States. The next step would be congressional approval.

Joe Kennedy read the headlines about lend-lease and concluded that he had been right all along about President Roosevelt wanting to involve the United States in the European war. However, when representatives of the America First movement offered him the position of chairman and chief spokesman, Kennedy told them that he supported their cause, but was still technically an ambassador and prohibited from joining any political group. He assured them he would reassess the situation in the coming months after he returned to private life.[10]

As 1940 came to a close, the once "phony" war was now all too real. While American soldiers were not in Europe, the United States had committed itself to the defense of Britain. The Luftwaffe's London blitz had been devastating—leveling large areas of the city—but ultimately unsuccessful as Britain had neither caved nor cowered. Hitler now turned more of his attention to plan for a spring offensive against the Soviet Union; he suspended the raids over London for a time. Stalin had received specific warnings of Hitler's plans, including from the United States, but inexplicably chose to ignore them. In a final act of frustration before the end of the year, Adolf Hitler ordered one more massive aerial attack on London. For more than ten hours, German bombers dropped their payloads onto London's commercial and financial center, creating a devastating conflagration that destroyed, among other landmarks, eight churches designed by Christopher Wren and much of the medieval Guildhall, the seat of the city's municipal government. As London burned, miraculously, St. Paul's Cathedral, built in the seventeenth century and the city's tallest building, did not suffer extensive damage. Walking home early the next morning, CBS news correspondent Edward R. Murrow observed that "the windows in the West End were red with reflected fire, and the raindrops were like blood on the panes."[11]

38

HE CAN TALK TO CHURCHILL LIKE AN IOWA FARMER

C onfident that he now had a mandate from the American people, and firm in his belief that Prime Minister Churchill was alone among the world's democratic leaders capable of providing the leadership necessary to defeat Hitler, President Roosevelt was determined to provide military assistance to Great Britain. But Roosevelt worried that even if he formalized an alliance with Churchill, he did not have the right team in place in the Department of State; indeed, he no longer had ambassadors in Berlin, Rome, or any of the occupied countries of Europe. They had all been recalled. He also needed to replace Kennedy in London, and Bullitt's status had to be handled delicately.

Roosevelt moved quickly to shore up his team. He decided to keep Cordell Hull as secretary of state. Roosevelt didn't consider Hull to be either imaginative or energetic, but the secretary remained popular with his former colleagues in the Senate, and the president could count on him to be a reliable and loyal ally. However, Roosevelt needed someone more dynamic than Hull to work with European leaders, someone who would give him unvarnished advice and creative solutions, someone who would help him navigate the complicated domestic politics of military preparedness and assistance to Europe's democracies. The State

Department counselor, "Judge" Walton Moore, was well liked and wise, but he was old and ill. Undersecretary Sumner Welles might have been the person to fill the role—the president considered him highly intelligent and unquestionably loyal—but Roosevelt had heard some disturbing information about the undersecretary that gave him pause.

Shortly after his election, President Roosevelt learned of rumors that Undersecretary Welles had propositioned two male, African American porters on the presidential train the previous September. Welles had allegedly been involved in a similar incident two weeks later, while traveling to Pennsylvania for a speaking engagement in Cleveland. On both occasions, Welles reportedly had been intoxicated. The reports had all the markings of a scandal trifecta for the times: extramarital sex, homosexuality, and the possibility of interracial liaisons in an aggressively segregated society. Not only was homosexuality largely criminalized at the time, the treatment of African Americans by the white majority in the United States was another humanitarian issue the Roosevelt administration largely ignored.

The president was concerned that the press was sniffing around the story. In fact, Felix Belair, *Time* magazine's Washington bureau chief, heard about the alleged incident within twenty-four hours, likely from S. C. "Mitch" Mitchell, a porter on the presidential press car. According to Belair, "Mitch was quickly transferred to the White House, obviously to keep him quiet," a move that only aroused further speculation.

The rumors continued to spread. Senator Burton Wheeler heard about Welles's behavior from a reporter who had, in turn, reportedly heard it from Ambassador William Bullitt. Bullitt had always considered Welles a competitor and may have blamed Welles for the chill that increasingly now characterized his relationship with the president. Despite the temptation, Bullitt told Wheeler that he decided not to tell the president, for fear of "getting his legs cut off." However, the ambassador, a seasoned political operator, must have known that Roosevelt would eventually learn of the allegations.[1]

Wheeler, a Roosevelt antagonist, considered Bullitt's willingness to spread such defamatory allegations to be reprehensible, but also saw a political opportunity. With the election approaching, Wheeler and one of his colleagues in the Senate, Henrik Shipstead, a Farmer-Laborite from Minnesota, went to see Cissy Patterson, publisher of the anti–New Deal *Washington Times-Herald*. They wanted to know if the *Times-Herald* would print the story if they supplied affidavits from the porters. Patterson was no fan of the president, and such a story would certainly have damaged Roosevelt's election chances, but she considered such scandal-mongering to be sensationalism and refused to investigate the allegations, much less publish a story about them.[2]

By late November, the allegations concerning Welles had reached the desk of Judge Moore. Moore had been jealous and resentful of Welles ever since the two men had competed for the undersecretary position and Welles had bested him. Moore arranged for affidavits to be taken about the alleged incidents. To make sure that Welles loyalists in the White House, including presumably the president himself, did not discard or destroy the documents, the State Department counselor delivered copies to his friend William Bullitt.

It's not clear when President Roosevelt learned of the allegations, but on January 3, Moore, at the behest of the president, instructed FBI director J. Edgar Hoover to conduct a discreet investigation, and the director assigned the task to Edward A. Tamm, the FBI liaison with the State Department. Three weeks later, Tamm's report was on the president's desk. The FBI reported that the evidence was overwhelming that Welles had propositioned porters on two separate occasions. Welles contended that he had been drinking heavily and claimed he had been taking barbiturates to ease angina pain. Beyond that, the FBI reported, Welles remembered nothing. However, the only porter to whom a "specific" proposal had been made had died two weeks before the investigation began. There was no affidavit, therefore, from anyone "directly" propositioned, although other porters had mentioned "indirect" approaches.[3]

The president suggested somewhat unconvincingly to Director Hoover that perhaps Welles had behaved without really knowing "what he was doing." Hoover pointed out that Welles's behavior nevertheless could be criminally prosecutable in Virginia.

Roosevelt had a dilemma: He liked and trusted Welles. The Roosevelt and Welles families had been close. If the president did not wish to directly confront Welles, Hoover suggested that he find someone to travel with the undersecretary in the future to prevent a recurrence, someone mature, and not a "young man who might lend credence to the stories circulating." The president nodded in agreement. He instructed Pa Watson to assign Welles a bodyguard for future travels and told Hoover to make sure that his report did not leak. The only three copies of the FBI report were to be locked in Watson's safe.[4] Welles would remain undersecretary, but the president needed someone else to fill the role of his chief foreign policy adviser.

Early on Friday morning, January 3, 1941, Harry Hopkins was sleeping in his bedroom in the White House. Since May, Hopkins had occupied Abraham Lincoln's former study just down the hallway from the president's bedroom suite. Suddenly, the phone at the bedside rang. A bleary-eyed Hopkins answered. "Congratulations," said Steve Early, the president's press secretary.

"On what?"

"Your trip."

"What trip?" Hopkins knew Early had a mischievous sense of humor and thought this was perhaps another of his practical jokes.

"Your trip to England." Early chuckled. "The president plans to announce it at his press conference later this morning."

Hopkins had no idea what Early was talking about, but he rose, showered, dressed, and walked over to the president's office in the West Wing. There, he found the president already at his desk reviewing correspondence. "Am I going somewhere?" Hopkins asked. Roosevelt grinned and nodded. The president told Hopkins he believed there continued to be a serious dearth of communication between the United States and Britain. He wanted Hopkins to meet with Churchill and determine how the United States could best support Britain.

Roosevelt suggested Hopkins get a briefing from the State Department's Bureau of European Affairs. "I'm going right away," Hopkins said. "I'm not going to hang around here . . . I won't learn anything that way; all I need is a long talk with you."[5]

The Hopkins mission bypassed normal diplomatic channels. Hopkins held no official position, and when reporters asked the president if Hopkins was to be the next ambassador to Great Britain, Roosevelt answered, "You know Harry isn't strong enough for that job." Roosevelt told the press he was sending Hopkins to London so "that he can talk to Churchill like an Iowa farmer." Upon receiving word of Hopkins's impending visit, Winston Churchill reportedly asked, "Who?"[6]

One week later, Harry Hopkins stepped off a Pan American Airways propeller plane in London and was greeted by representatives of the British Foreign Office. The British diplomats, dressed in pinstripes and sporting bowler hats, were initially taken aback by Hopkins's rumpled suit and disheveled appearance. Churchill, however, was immediately drawn to Hopkins, admiring his optimism, lack of formality, and obvious intelligence. Churchill affectionately dubbed him "Lord Root of the Matter" for his ability to get to the heart of problems quickly.[7]

Recalling Hopkins many years later, Roosevelt speechwriter Robert Sherwood wrote:

> Hopkins naturally and easily conformed to the essential Benjamin Franklin tradition of American diplomacy, acting on the conviction that when an American representative approaches his opposite numbers in friendly countries with the standard striped-pants frigidity, the strict observance of protocol and amenities, and a studied air of lip-curling, he is not really representing America—not, at any rate, the America of which FDR was President.[8]

39

WE AMERICANS ARE VITALLY CONCERNED IN YOUR DEFENSE OF FREEDOM

On January 6, 1941, President Roosevelt stood at the lectern in the House of Representatives to deliver his eighth State of the Union address to Congress. In the president's box, Eleanor was seated next to her friend Lorena Hickok. Also seated in the box, Princess Märtha of Norway, who was smartly dressed in a black coat accented by a silver fox collar. The usually ebullient president began his speech on a somber note: "As your President, performing my constitutional duty to 'give to the Congress information of the state of the union,' I find it unhappily necessary to report that the future and safety of our country and our democracy are overwhelmingly involved in events far beyond our borders." Because American security depended on defeating the Axis, he explained, he was asking Congress for authority and funds to continue sending aid to England and other democracies fighting the Axis powers, even if these nations could no longer pay with ready cash. "Let us say to the democracies: We Americans are vitally concerned in your defense of freedom."[1]

However, Britons knew that President Roosevelt had promised many times that he would not send American troops to Europe, which by this point many viewed as essential to repelling a Nazi invasion. Moreover, they did not believe that either the president or the American people were especially concerned about their future; opinion polls consistently showed an unfavorable view of the United States. As one pollster explained it, "The percentage of unfavorable criticism of America—our friend—equals that of Italy—our enemy."[2] Clearly, Ambassador Kennedy had contributed to the negative image of the U.S. in Britain with his defeatist refrain and embrace of appeasement.

The burning question in Congress was no longer whether the United States had the right to sell arms to Britain (that was already allowed) but whether it should and how Britain would pay as its supply of dollars was vanishing. The answer embodied in lend-lease was for the American government to purchase the entire output of arms and "lend" appropriate portions of it to countries fighting the fascist dictators. The hearings in Congress during the early months of 1941 became the centerpiece of this nationwide debate.

At the behest of President Roosevelt, House majority leader John McCormack, Democrat of Massachusetts, introduced the lend-lease bill on the floor of the House on January 10, 1941. The bill was referred to the Foreign Affairs Committee, and hearings were scheduled to begin on January 21, with former ambassador Kennedy as one of the first witnesses. President Roosevelt wanted to talk with Kennedy before his appearance and invited him to the White House for an early-morning meeting on January 16.

Kennedy arrived fifteen minutes early and, instead of being ushered into the Oval Office, was taken into the president's second-floor bedroom where he found Roosevelt in his pajamas and bathrobe sitting in his wheelchair. The president was about to shave himself. There were no chairs near the basin, so Roosevelt asked Kennedy to sit on the toilet seat so he would not be talking to the president's back.

The president allowed Kennedy to once again vent his "indignation at the treatment" he had received from "the boys in the State Department" and "the President's hatchet men." The president nodded knowingly and, in an apparent attempt to establish common ground, said, "No one had received worse treatment than he [Roosevelt] had in the last eight years."[3]

Turning to the issue of lend-lease, Kennedy told the president that he had already written his opening statement. He predicted the lend-lease bill could be "forced through" but "thought it would leave a very bad taste; that it was a request for power that the American people would not grant unless they understood it better." The president washed the shaving cream from his face, once again nodded in agreement, and then "admitted that he has asked of a lot hoping to get something."[4] Then, Roosevelt turned on the charm, reminiscing about the political battles they had fought together, and promising Kennedy that once the lend-lease bill was signed into law, he intended to let the country know what extraordinary public service Kennedy had performed while in London. There were misconceptions about Kennedy's tenure as ambassador, Roosevelt said, and he promised to set the record straight.[5]

Kennedy later wrote in his diary that Roosevelt's "whole attitude was very friendly." The ambassador recalled that he told the president, "I couldn't understand why so many people were so anxious about our not being friends," and the president replied that "he paid no attention to this."[6] Roosevelt had only one objective in meeting with Kennedy: somehow persuade the ambassador to temper his upcoming testimony before Congress. Kennedy left the White House that morning once again convinced of Franklin Roosevelt's magnanimity and greatness.

While the controversial lend-lease legislation was being debated in the U.S. Congress, across the Atlantic, the president's emissary Harry Hopkins worked to understand British strategy and determine what U.S. assistance would be most helpful. At the insistence of Churchill, Hopkins traded in his bedroom in the White House for a hotel suite at Claridges; at the insistence of Churchill he was given an office at 10 Downing Street. Hopkins had planned to remain in London for two weeks, but ended up staying nearly six weeks, during which time he met with British ministers, business leaders, and military planners—and regularly with the prime minister himself. Hopkins's visit took place against the background of the German Blitz, and he witnessed firsthand the devastation of Luftwaffe bombing raids.

Hopkins remained in close contact with President Roosevelt, and in his letters and telegrams consistently praised Prime Minister Churchill's leadership and stressed the importance of delivering American aid. On January 14, 1941, he wrote:

> The people here are amazing from Churchill on down and if courage alone can win—the result will be inevitable. But they need our help desperately and I am sure you will permit nothing to stand in the way ... Churchill is the gov't in every sense of the word—he controls the grand strategy and often the details—labor trusts him—the army, navy, air force are behind him to a man. The politicians and upper crust pretend to like him. I cannot emphasize too strongly that he is the one and only person over here with whom you need to have a full meeting of the minds ... This island needs our help now Mr. President with everything we can give them.[7]

Hopkins's admiration for Churchill was on further display at a dinner organized to honor the American envoy before he returned to the United States. At the Station Hotel in Glasgow on January 17, Hopkins stood to offer a toast to the prime minister: "I suppose you wish to know what I am going to say to President Roosevelt upon my return," Hopkins said, smiling. "Well, I am going to quote you one verse from that book of books ... 'Whither thou goest, I will go; and whither thou lodgest, I will lodge: thy people shall be my people, and thy God my God.'" As Hopkins raised his glass, others at the table noticed tears streaming down the face of Churchill.[8]

Hopkins had not only grown close to the prime minister, he developed a friendship with the prime minister's wife, Clementine, whom he called "the most charming and entertaining of all the people he met."

Before his departure, King George and Queen Elizabeth, at Churchill's behest, invited Hopkins to lunch. Though committed to helping the poor and dispossessed, Hopkins also enjoyed the company of the rich and social elite. His visit to Buckingham Palace was the highlight of his stay in Britain, with the only glitch being an air-raid alert that caused the luncheon party to relocate to an underground shelter in the palace basement.

Hopkins returned to the United States on February 16, 1941, aboard Pan American's *Yankee Clipper*. Though exhausted from his trip, he reported to colleagues in the State Department that the British Foreign Office had unrealistic expectations about Roosevelt's ability to deliver lend-lease, believing that the president could quickly secure its passage in Congress and that America would then enter the war in a few months. Hopkins worried he might be partially responsible for raised expectations, aware that he likely overstated America's willingness and capacity to support the British. Nonetheless, Hopkins was satisfied with what he had accomplished during his six-week stay in London. He was confident that Churchill trusted him, a sentiment confirmed by the prime minister, who cabled Roosevelt shortly before Hopkins's departure, "It has been a great pleasure to me to make friends with Hopkins who has been a great comfort and encouragement to everyone he has met. One can easily see why he is so close to you."[9] No doubt, Hopkins, with his easygoing manner and quick grasp of the issues, proved to be a natural diplomat. Hopkins "had this marvelous ability to grow into any new situation," recalled Franklin Roosevelt Jr., "to totally dominate the details of any new situation." Now Roosevelt and Churchill, who had been skeptical of each other, both trusted Harry Hopkins.

Secretary Hull, the first witness in Lend-Lease hearings before the House Committee on Foreign Affairs on January 15, began his testimony by reading a prepared statement in support of the bill. In a somewhat plodding monotone, the secretary declared, "It has become increasingly apparent that mankind is today face to face, not with regional wars or isolated conflicts, but with an organized, ruthless and implacable movement of steadily expanding conquest." The secretary then raised the specter of war reaching American shores, maintaining that control of the high seas by law-abiding nations "is the key to the security of the Western Hemisphere." This was the core of Hull's argument: lend-lease was neither a giveaway nor a back door to America's entering the war in Europe; rather, it represented assistance to other nations as a vital part of national self-defense."[10]

The following day, it was Ambassador Kennedy's turn to testify. After meeting with President Roosevelt the previous week, the ambassador had revised his original statement. Though he continued to oppose lend-lease in its present form, arguing that the power of Congress in foreign affairs should be preserved, he supported assistance to Britain, echoing the administration's position that aid to Britain was the most effective means of avoiding war. Kennedy's attempt to offer a nuanced endorsement of lend-lease confused both opponents and supporters of the legislation and exposed him to criticism from both sides. Since Roosevelt had feared his former ambassador might adopt an isolationist tone, he was greatly relieved that Kennedy advocated American support for Great Britain. Kennedy's measured testimony helped to mitigate that of Charles Lindbergh, who appeared before the committee on January 23 and recommended the United States negotiate a separate peace with Adolf Hitler.

On January 25, 1941, former ambassador Bullitt testified. It was Bullitt's fiftieth birthday, and while the president had not offered him a new position in the administration, he remained hopeful. The committee members viewed Bullitt as both a Francophile and a longtime, staunch supporter of lend-lease. Some of the more skeptical Members pressed him on whether he had ever promised the French that they would receive assistance from the United States in case of war. Bullitt dismissed allegations of collusion with the government of France as German propaganda and read aloud into the committee's hearing record former French premier Daladier's letter to President Roosevelt from the previous year: "During the past two years when I was Prime Minister, Ambassador Bullitt always said to me that in case of a European conflict, France should make her decisions knowing that, according to the opinion of Ambassador Bullitt, the United States of America would not enter the war."[11] Bullitt went on to reinforce Hull's argument that lend-lease represented the most effective defense of America. After completing his testimony, he stood and dramatically addressed the Committee members: "The Skipper has set the course. You Representatives are the officers; we out of office are the crew. Our cargo is America!"[12] As *The New York Times* reported the next day, "Resounding applause followed."[13]

Secretary Hull and Ambassadors Kennedy and Bullitt all made helpful arguments in support of lend-lease, but those who opposed the program had not changed their minds, and it was unclear how much headway had been made with congressional skeptics. It was not until weeks later when Secretary of War Henry Stimson arranged for General George Marshall to "drop by" a negotiating session, and according to a number of senators, the general gave "a ripping speech" on lend-lease and "made a great impression." Within a matter of weeks, both houses of Congress had passed lend-lease, and on March 11, 1941, the president signed the measure into law. Shortly thereafter, the president's request for $7 billion to fund the program was approved, marking the end of the Neutrality Act and one of the most important legislative victories of Roosevelt's presidency.

In the spring of 1941, Ambassador Kennedy formally resigned his post. Roosevelt appointed John Winant, a mild-mannered former governor of New Hampshire, as United States ambassador to Britain. After the increasingly unpopular, pro-appeasement ambassador Joseph P. Kennedy, Winant's support for the British people dramatically enhanced the image of the United States. Upon landing at Bristol airport, the new ambassador declared, "I'm very glad to be here. There is no place I'd rather be at this time than in England."[14] Even though the United States Congress was still debating lend-lease and had not yet fully committed to Britain's fight, Winant's embrace of a nation that had weathered the Battle of Britain, and now confronted the prospect of a long war, cheered the British people.

Winant's popularity soared even higher when some Londoners recognized him helping victims during the horrific bombing of April 16, 1941. The ambassador had been working in his office when he "heard the scream of a bomb and massive explosion followed by the crash of breaking glass: all of his office windows had been shattered . . . On nearby Oxford Street, flames were devouring one of London's major department stores." Winant rushed from the embassy to help the victims. The following day, several newspaper articles wrote about the ambassador's courage and compassion, noting the contrast to his predecessor. As one newspaper put it, "One has often felt in the past that . . . American Ambassadors, while enjoying the freedom of the best country houses, have seen too little of the real Britain. But the sterling metal of John Winant's character will make him reach out to wider fields."[15] Winant proved just as popular with Great Britain's leadership, quickly developing close ties with King George and Prime Minister Churchill. Joe Kennedy didn't know John Winant, but he must have bristled at the unfavorable comparison. A few years later, Kennedy's daughter Kathleen—nicknamed "Kick"—who had remained in London, still seemed bitter that Winant had replaced her father, writing to her family that "I find him [Ambassador Winant] more bogus each time I see him."[16]

In the months during which Congress debated lend-lease, Hitler continued to prosecute Germany's war in Europe. In March, Hitler ordered his generals to make the necessary preparations for an attack on Russia, but first he needed to secure his southern flank. Hitler persuaded the government of Yugoslavia to join in the Tripartite Pact. However, the agreement was voided at the end of March by a popular revolt in Belgrade. Hitler was furious at the affront and vowed to destroy Yugoslavia. Delaying his planned invasion of Russia, Germany swept through the Balkans at the beginning of April and then overpowered Greece, compelling British forces to retreat to the island of Crete—where in May they were driven out. On yet another front, Hitler pushed close to the Egyptian border, effectively threatening the entire "British hold on the eastern Mediterranean."[17] The British position appeared increasingly hopeless: According to William Shirer, "[Britain's] prestige, so important in a life-and-death struggle where propaganda was so potent a weapon, especially in influencing the United States and Russia, had sunk to a new low point. But Hitler was fixated on attacking Russia, and didn't understand the strategic significance of Mediterranean to British naval power. If Hitler had pressed on in Egypt and the Middle East, he probably would've struck a fatal blow to the British Empire, as Churchill tried to relay to Roosevelt at the beginning of May."[18]

While the war spread beyond Europe, Germany continued to bomb Great Britain, striking its ports, especially Portsmouth—one of the main bases of the British fleet—but bombing as well the cities of Manchester, Liverpool, and, of course, London. German bombers attacked the capital city on a regular basis.[19] Almost half a million London residents lost their homes in just two attacks, and more than 1,200 died in attacks in April. Germany's war at sea proved to be just as devastating. In the first three weeks of May, German submarines sank twenty British merchant ships in the security zone the U.S. had established in the Atlantic.

As Hitler drew ever closer to the total domination of Europe, Secretary Hull confided to Breckinridge Long that he was "much worried about the British—thinks they are in a very bad way and are very stupid. They are alienating the French more and more by their policies—giving the French no inducement to resist German pressure—nor any reason to even be sympathetic."[20] Former ambassador Bullitt was also alarmed by Britain's impotence. However, he focused more on American leadership, increasingly exasperated by what he viewed as the president's passivity and reluctance to take bolder action. Bullitt wrote Ambassador Averell Harriman, the president's special envoy charged with coordinating lend-lease: "The President is waiting for public opinion to lead, and public opinion is waiting for a lead from the President."[21]

On May 21, 1941, 950 miles off the coast of Brazil, a German submarine intercepted the SS *Robin Moor*, a U.S.-flagged freighter carrying cargo from New York to South Africa, a member of the British Empire. After inspecting the cargo, which included automobiles, trucks, tools, and agricultural chemicals, the German commander allowed the ship's twenty-nine crewmembers and eight passengers to board lifeboats. The submarine then fired torpedoes and sank the ship. Afterward, the submarine pulled alongside one of the lifeboats, and the German commander left the stranded sailors four tins of pressed black bread and two tins of butter, explaining apologetically that he was obligated to sink the *Robin Moor* because it had been carrying war matériel to an enemy combatant.

The sinking of the SS *Robin Moor* represented the first indication that Germany was prepared to engage directly with the United States in war.

40

HISTORY HAS RECORDED WHO FIRED THE FIRST SHOT

"I have something important that I think you should see," William Bullitt said, handing President Roosevelt the dossier Counselor Judge Moore had prepared on Sumner Welles. Unaware that President Roosevelt had been briefed some months earlier on the incidents surrounding Welles's alleged promiscuous behavior, Bullitt declared that if the contents of the dossier ever leaked, it would prove deeply embarrassing for the administration. The president picked up the folder, glanced at the first page, and quickly thumbed through the rest of the document. "There is truth in the allegations," the president acknowledged, but quickly added that in his view no reputable newspaper would publish such tawdry, unproven accusations.

Bullitt argued that Welles's propositioning of male porters had occurred on more than one occasion and claimed that it was Judge Moore's "dying wish" that the undersecretary be dismissed. Bullitt was adamant: "Morale in the Department of State and the Foreign Service [is] being ruined by the knowledge that a man of the character of Welles was in control of all appointments and transfers." He pointed out that "blackmail of high government officials guilty of crimes of this nature had been used often by different powers to oblige such men to act as traitors."

Again, the president acknowledged that Bullitt's information was largely correct but said that he had seen to it that Welles would be accompanied on future trips by a bodyguard. Bullitt pointed out that the issue was not future behavior but "past crimes" and told Roosevelt that he had discussed the matter with Hull, who called Welles "worse than a murderer." The president was immovable. He agreed that solicitation was a prosecutable offense but did not think that any prosecutor would bring charges. Frustrated and irritated, Bullitt announced defiantly that while he "wanted to work on licking Hitler" and "to do all [he] could to accelerate . . . preparations for war," he would "under no circumstances" accept any position in the State Department or in the Foreign Service so long as Welles remained in office.[1]

President Roosevelt sat stone-faced. The president had enjoyed Bullitt's company in the past. He had often welcomed the ambassador's engaging letters from Moscow and Paris, although increasingly he found Bullitt's tone somewhat saccharine and too familiar. Roosevelt had been in politics for nearly three decades and was susceptible neither to being flattered—or, in this case, threatened. He picked up the telephone receiver on his desk and called his assistant, General Watson. "Pa, I don't feel well," he said. "Please cancel all appointments for the rest of the day." The president perfunctorily thanked Bullitt for dropping by, and then was wheeled from the Oval Office.[2]

Days later, Bullitt told Robert D. Murphy, his former deputy in Paris, that he would "force" Roosevelt's hand by taking the dossier to Senator H. Styles Bridges, a rabid anti-Roosevelt Republican from New Hampshire. Murphy begged him to reconsider. In the end, Bullitt didn't leak the information to Bridges, but as Murphy remembered, Bullitt "was never again given anything of substance to do." When Hull later asked Roosevelt if he should find a diplomatic post for Bullitt, the president leaned back, looked to the ceiling, and finally said, "What about Liberia. I hear that's available."[3]

As the war in Europe intensified during the summer of 1941, former ambassador Kennedy and former ambassador Bullitt continued to lend their voices to an increasingly vigorous debate over the potential involvement and role of the United States.

Kennedy accepted invitations to give commencement addresses at Oglethorpe University and Notre Dame. While he reiterated his contempt for Hitler and the Nazis, "their philosophy, their silly racism and their nightmare of world domination," Kennedy repeated in the Oglethorpe speech some of the same highly controversial language he had used in his January radio address, claiming it was "nonsense to say that an Axis victory spells ruin for us."[4] He argued that even if the British were to lose the war, the United States would survive and endure. As he put it, "From 90% to 96% of our trade is internal. We depend less on foreign markets than any great nation. If worse came to worst, we could gear ourselves to an intelligent self-constrained national economy and still enjoy a fair degree of prosperity."[5] Kennedy never addressed what Nazi rule meant for the occupied nations of Europe.

On May 27, three days after Kennedy's speech, President Roosevelt delivered his first radio address in five months. Directly contradicting Kennedy's comments about the United States persevering despite a totalitarian victory in Europe, the president predicted that Hitler's appetite for conquest would not be sated and disaster would follow.

In June 1941, Missy LeHand suddenly collapsed at a White House dinner party. Only forty-four years old, she appeared to recover, but then two weeks later suffered a paralyzing stroke. Unable to move the left side of her body, her speech severely impaired, she lay in the hospital for several weeks and then moved to Massachusetts to convalesce—never again to return to the White House. It was a bitter blow to the president, who for so long had relied on her organizational skills and companionship. Although still angry with William Bullitt for his vendetta against Undersecretary Welles, Roosevelt reached out to his former ambassador and invited him to lunch in the White House. The president's invitation was, in part, an act of friendship since both men loved Missy, but also a desire to probe Bullitt's thinking on the war in Europe. Bullitt hadn't changed his mind—he still believed it was critical for the president to show bold leadership. One of the first of the president's advisers to do so, he encouraged Roosevelt to declare war on Germany.[6]

Roosevelt's other foreign policy advisers were neither as defeatist as Kennedy nor as militant as Bullitt. Secretary Hull and some assistant secretaries, including Adolf Berle and Breckinridge Long, counseled the president to proceed with extreme caution. Both Long and Berle were longtime Anglophobes. While Berle detested Hitler, Long was more ambivalent and summed up his concern over United States support for Great Britain in his diary: "World opinion is that [the British] are licked."[7]

At daybreak, on June 22, 1941, in a stunning move that would prove to be a turning point in the war, Adolf Hitler launched Operation Barbarossa, the German invasion of the Soviet Union along a front that extended from the Artic Ocean to the Black Sea. Three army groups consisting of nearly three million German and Axis soldiers, and supported by more than three thousand tanks, poured across the Russian border. "Now the guns will be thundering," Goebbels wrote in his diary, "May God bless our weapons."[8]

Despite previous warnings given by the United States and Britain to Stalin, the Russian army was not prepared for Hitler's onslaught. The Germans destroyed a large portion of the Soviet air force on the ground. German army chief of staff General Franz Halder, who planned the invasion, gloated in his diary that the Russian army had been "tactically surprised along the entire front."[9] While Hitler publicly justified the attack, claiming Russia had repeatedly violated the Nazi-Soviet pact, President Roosevelt immediately issued a statement roundly condemning German aggression.

One week later, writing from his farm in Penllyn, Pennsylvania, former ambassador to the Soviet Union Bullitt offered the president some unsolicited advice:

The line you took when Germany attacked the Soviet Union—that of giving support to anyone (even a criminal) fighting Hitler—was, of course, sound. But the emotions aroused by the spectacle of Nazis fighting Bolsheviks were so conflicting that most people needed a lot more guidance than they got. Public opinion is now befuddled. The feeling has begun to spread that we no longer need to hurry our war preparations and that the Communists have become the friends of democracy.

I think you need to take the first opportunity—perhaps your next press conference—to point out: 1.) German attack on the Soviet Union makes it essential for us to produce [military hardware] with greater speed than ever . . . 2.) Communists in the US are just as dangerous enemies as ever.[10]

Joseph Davies, Bullitt's successor in Moscow, who had recently returned to Washington to serve as a special assistant to Secretary Hull, echoed Bullitt's recommendations, but he added that it was critical for the United States to provide aid to the Soviet Union. Davies argued that if the United States stayed on the sidelines, Stalin might make a deal with Hitler as the "lesser of two evils." Davies convinced Roosevelt that the Russian leader, while not trustworthy, was nevertheless pragmatic. The president was coming around to the view that the Soviets should be given some assistance, and though he never said so publicly, he undoubtedly knew that helping Stalin's army not only would buy time to rearm the United States but would save American lives if America entered the war.

On July 10, 1941, Hopkins and Roosevelt met with the Soviet ambassador to the United States, Constantine Oumansky, in the White House. Roosevelt pledged that the United States would do its best to provide the Soviet army with military and industrial equipment, but made it clear that Stalin needed to understand the United States also had a commitment to the British.

The following day, Roosevelt conferred at length with Harry Hopkins.

They discussed the political obstacles to extending lend-lease to the Soviet Union. Roosevelt knew he would encounter opposition from fervent anti-Communists such as Senator Harry Truman and former president Hoover, both of whom opposed providing any assistance to Russia. The president also worried about how Churchill would react and suggested Hopkins return to London for discussions with the prime minister. Lastly, the president instructed Hopkins to arrange a time and place for a meeting between himself and Churchill.

Hopkins immediately boarded a plane for London for what he knew would be a difficult mission. While in theory Churchill supported the United States providing aid to the Soviet Union, the prime minister would undoubtedly want to know how assistance to Great Britain would be impacted. Hopkins also knew Churchill would insist that any meeting between himself and Roosevelt prioritize America's entry into the war.

In London, Hopkins met with senior British government and military officials, reviewing Lend-Lease requirements and discussing overall war strategy. Hopkins also met with Prime Minister Churchill and the Soviet ambassador to Britain, Ivan Maisky, who told them that Stalin wanted Britain and the United States to open a second front by confronting the Germans in France. With Britain under siege and the memory of Dunkirk still fresh, Churchill refused to commit.

Ambassador Maisky sensed that Hopkins was sincere in his desire to help the Soviet Union and contacted Ambassador Winant to arrange a follow-up meeting. A few days later, over lunch at the U.S. embassy, Hopkins explained to Maisky that as a "non-belligerent," the United States could not open a second front but that it could help "as regards supplies." The Soviet ambassador suggested that Hopkins should travel to Moscow to meet with senior military officials to better understand what was needed. Shortly thereafter, Hopkins cabled Roosevelt, asking "whether you would think it important and useful for me to go to Moscow." From a strategic point of view, Hopkins felt it was important for the United States to encourage the Russians to keep on fighting the Germans. He told the president that he had already discussed the trip with Prime Minister Churchill, who was in accord. If the president agreed, Hopkins planned to tell Stalin that the United States was committed to "a long term supply job." Roosevelt didn't trust Stalin, and also worried that Hopkins had neither previously met the Soviet leader nor spoke a word of Russian. Nevertheless, in Roosevelt's mind, Hopkins now occupied the role that William Bullitt—who both knew Stalin and spoke fluent Russian—had for so long coveted. The former social worker had emerged as the president's most influential foreign policy adviser.

Confident he could rely on Hopkins's judgment, the president approved the Moscow trip and instructed Hopkins to leave right away. Churchill arranged for Hopkins to travel on a flying boat leaving from Scotland the next day. Before boarding a train for Scotland, Hopkins delivered a BBC broadcast affirming President Roosevelt's support for Prime Minister Churchill and the British people. Although he kept his remarks somewhat general, he sent a timely message of hope that the United States and Great Britain working together would defeat the Third Reich.

Hopkins carried a letter from Roosevelt to be hand-delivered to Stalin, stating that the purpose of his visit was to assess the Soviet Union's "most urgent requirements . . . material which can reach Russia within the next three months." President Roosevelt expressed the "great admiration all of us in the United States feel for the superb bravery displayed by the Russian people in defense of their liberty." The note also encouraged the general secretary to "treat Mr. Hopkins with the identical confidence you would feel if you were talking directly to me."[11]

General George Marshall had arranged for two U.S. military experts to accompany Hopkins to Moscow. American ambassador Laurence Steinhardt, a career diplomat who had replaced Ambassador Davies in 1939, met the three-man American delegation at the airport in Moscow and immediately drove them to Spaso House, where Hopkins, completely exhausted by the journey, went directly to bed. After only a few hours of rest, Hopkins showered, dressed, and engaged in briefings with his military advisers and with the ambassador. Steinhardt remarked to Hopkins on the historical parallels between Hitler's siege and Napoleon's in 1812. Based on his knowledge of Russian history, and his impression of Soviet leadership, Steinhardt believed the Soviets would persevere, though he hedged his prediction by noting that he had received little information about Soviet military strength.[12]

Promptly at 6:30 that evening, Hopkins, Steinhardt, and an interpreter were ushered into the general secretary's office in the Kremlin. Stalin warmly greeted the Americans, and the much-taller Hopkins would later write that his first impression of Stalin was of "a football coach's dream of a tackle."[13] Hopkins immediately assured Stalin of President Roosevelt's view "that the most important thing in the world today is to defeat Hitler and Hitlerism" and that the president was determined "to extend all possible aid to the Soviet Union at the earliest possible time." Stalin nodded solemnly and said that for international society to exist, nations must observe a "minimum moral standard." He concluded that since Hitler ignored treaty obligations and broke promises, he had "no such minimum moral standard," and therefore, the USSR and the United States were in agreement that Germany was an "anti-social force in the world" that must be destroyed. David Roll, Hopkins's biographer, has characterized Stalin's "hypocrisy as breathtaking" given his "criminal background and his instrumental role in the intentional starvation of millions of his own people, the Gulag, the purges, the nonaggression pact with the Nazis, the Katyn massacre, and countless other moral outrages."[14] Hopkins, of course, knew of the nonaggression pact that led to the destruction of Poland, but otherwise was only faintly aware of Stalin's brutality. Nevertheless, Hopkins showed obsequious admiration for the Russian's leadership qualities, and he professed great respect for Stalin's commitment to his nation's sovereignty.

Then, without "waste of word, gesture or mannerism," Hopkins later recalled, Stalin described "like an intelligent machine" the needs of the Soviet Union, including types of aircraft and the best routes for shipping supplies.[15] Later in the evening, Hopkins met with Stalin's top general,

Alexander Yakovlev. When Hopkins asked whether the Soviets needed anything in addition to the items on Stalin's list, Yakovlev replied, "I am not empowered to say whether we do or do not need tanks or anti-tank guns."[16] Hopkins quickly grasped that Stalin was not only running the government but micromanaging the war effort as well.

A few days later, on July 31, 1941, Hopkins met once again with Stalin. To build a personal relationship with the general secretary, this time Hopkins came alone. Maxim Litvinov, the former Soviet foreign minister, acted as interpreter for both men. Sitting opposite one another, Stalin launched into a lengthy "appreciation and analysis" of the war between the Soviet Union and Germany that Hopkins found both trenchant and inspiring. Stalin succeeded in persuading Hopkins that the Red Army and the Russian people, with aid from the United States and Britain, could halt the German advance on Moscow, but also made it clear that to win the war, the United States must declare war on Germany; it was, he said, "the one thing that could defeat Hitler."[17] Over the course of their nearly four-hour meeting, the Soviet leader impressed Hopkins with his "extraordinary grasp of detail" and "his capacity for clear and simple statement."[18] Hopkins, of course, was aware that Stalin had once before made a deal with Hitler, in 1939, but he thought it highly unlikely Stalin would ever again negotiate a separate peace, given the high price in blood and treasure already paid by the Soviet people. Afterward, Hopkins thanked Stalin, telling him he would make a complete report to the president.

The following day, Hopkins cabled Roosevelt, Welles, and Hull, "I feel ever so confident about this front. The morale of the population is good. There is unbounded determination to win the war."[19] Hopkins couldn't actually confirm much of what Stalin told him—like his boss, the president, he relied on his instincts and his understanding of human nature to take the measure of the Soviet leader.

In August 1941, as Washington sweltered under sustained and stifling heat, President Roosevelt announced that he was going on a fishing trip. On many occasions during his presidency, with Congress on recess,

Roosevelt had gone sailing or fishing during the late summer. Notwithstanding the worsening situation in Europe, the announcement sparked little commentary in the press.

As the presidential yacht USS *Potomac* sailed up the coast of New England, in London, Prime Minister Churchill boarded a train for Scotland. Both were bound for Newfoundland and a secret meeting arranged by Harry Hopkins, who, having completed his meetings in the Soviet Union, was once again seriously ill. Nevertheless, Hopkins joined the prime minister aboard the *HMS Prince of Wales*, a Royal Navy battleship, that crossed the Atlantic, managing to avoid German submarines prowling the dark ocean waters.

On August 4, Roosevelt boarded the Navy cruiser USS *Augusta*, which continued to sail northward. Five days later, on a cool, crisp Saturday morning, HMS *Prince of Wales* cruised slowly into Placentia Bay, a large inlet near Newfoundland. The *Augusta* was already at anchor, and as the HMS *Prince of Wales* approached, President Roosevelt, standing at the ship's railing, tipped his hat. The president stood in salute as HMS *Prince of Wales*, guns pointing to the sky, sailed slowly by. As a United States Navy band played "God Save the Queen," Roosevelt, noting the familiar melody, quipped to Hopkins, who had joined him on board the *Augusta*, "That's the best rendition of *My Country, 'Tis of Thee* I've ever heard." Afterward, the prime minister stood on his own bridge as the Royal Navy band played "The Star-Spangled Banner."[20]

It was a historic moment, infused with what a British journalist called "a touch of danger, humor, secrecy" that would "prevent the carving up of the world and the enslavement of Humanity."[21] Churchill and Roosevelt met over the next four days aboard the USS *Augusta* to discuss not only war strategy, but also to outline a postwar international system. The Atlantic Charter they drafted included eight "common principles" that the United States and Great Britain would be committed to supporting in the postwar world. Both countries agreed not to seek territorial expansion; to seek the liberalization of international trade; to establish freedom of the seas, and international labor, economic, and welfare standards. Most importantly, both the United States and Great Britain were committed to supporting the restoration of self-governments for all countries that had been occupied during the war and allowing all peoples to choose their own forms of government. This represented a total capitulation on the part of Churchill because the United Kingdom was the foremost colonial power in the world. It also represented a hugely important moment for the United States, because President Roosevelt articulated the conceptual framework for a role that America continues to play today: the leader of a rules-based liberal order that promotes global freedom and democracy.

However successful Roosevelt and Churchill were in drafting lofty goals, their meeting in the Atlantic failed to produce the desired results for either leader; the necessary encouragement for the American people to back intervention in World War II on behalf of the Allies. Notwithstanding Churchill's entreaties, the president, keenly aware that American isolationists worried more than ever about the widening conflict, would not even discuss sending American troops to Europe.

Former president Hoover invited former ambassador Kennedy to join former governor and presidential candidate Alf Landon of Kansas, President Robert Hutchins of the University of Chicago, and some ten or fifteen others, who he noted were "outside of . . . the America First group" in lending his name to the anti-intervention group. It was the second time that Kennedy had been asked to join the America First movement. Once again, he declined, noting he was "well aware of the magnificent work you have done to keep us out of war."[22] Kennedy's son Joe Jr. left Harvard before his final year of law school to join the U.S. Naval Reserve, and the former ambassador may not have wanted to create the perception that he somehow devalued his son's military service.

By the fall of 1941, Hitler, now fighting a war on two fronts, believed American lend-lease violated the United States' stated pledge of neutrality, but hoped to prevent actual U.S. military involvement in the conflict. Hitler calculated that defeat of both Britain and the Soviet Union depended on keeping American soldiers off the battlefield. However, that strategy became more complicated and more tenuous on September 4 when a German submarine patrolling in the North Atlantic, acting against orders, fired its torpedoes at the U.S. destroyer *Greer*.[23] Although the torpedoes missed, the incident highlighted the danger now confronting the United States and the need for America to defend itself.

The day after the *Greer* incident, President Roosevelt lunched with Secretary of State Hull and Harry Hopkins. Hull told the president he needed to issue a very strong statement on convoy operations and on freedom of navigation. Roosevelt asked the secretary to produce a first draft, perhaps something that could be incorporated into a longer speech. He asked to have it delivered by telegraph to Hyde Park, where he planned to spend the weekend. Hull returned to the department and huddled with his speechwriters. But when the president received Hull's draft, he was disappointed. The statement was tepid and contained no big idea or bold response. As was often the case, Hull initially took a firm stand with the president, but then retreated when it came time to propose action.

The Department of State eventually drafted four separate versions of a speech, all of which Roosevelt rejected as inadequate. Hopkins and speechwriter Sam Rosenman, using an entirely different approach, came up with the version the president finally delivered. Hopkins was responsible for much of the assertive language and inserted the paragraph, "When you see a rattlesnake poised to strike, you do not wait until he has struck before you crush him. These Nazi submarines and raiders are the rattlesnakes of the Atlantic."[24] It was the same metaphor that the president had used months earlier to describe Nazi aggression. On the evening of September 10, Hull again had second thoughts and urged Roosevelt to tone the speech down and take out all references to preemptive strike. The president refused.

At Roosevelt's insistence, the speech concluded with the words: "But let this warning be clear, from now on, if German or Italian vessels of war enter the waters the protection of which is necessary for American defense, they do so at their own peril."[25]

The president was as good as his word. One month later, on the night of October 16, 1941, the U.S. destroyer *Kearny* came to the aid of a British convoy under attack by German submarines off the coast of Iceland. The *Kearny* dropped depth charges on one of the submarines, which retaliated by torpedoing it. Eleven men of the destroyer's crew were killed, marking the first American casualties in the undeclared war with Germany. Referring to the incident involving the *Kearny* in a Navy Day speech on October 27— but failing to note that the ship had dropped depth charges before being torpedoed—Roosevelt falsely declared, "History has recorded who fired the first shot."[26]

41

A DAY THAT WILL LIVE IN INFAMY

The Japanese ambassador to the United States, Kichisaburō Nomura, and Japan's special envoy, Saburō Kurusu, sat patiently outside Secretary Hull's office, waiting to deliver an official notification from their government that due to the impasse in negotiations, it was Tokyo's intention to break off diplomatic relations with Washington. U.S. intelligence officials had intercepted the letter the day before, December 6, and showed it to President Roosevelt, who understood the letter "to mean war."[1] That same day, the president sent a telegram to Emperor Hirohito, proclaiming, "Developments are occurring in the Pacific area which threaten to deprive each of our nations and all humanity of the beneficial influence of the long peace between our two countries. These developments contain tragic possibilities . . . both Japan and the United States should agree to eliminate any form of military threat."[2]

Adolf Hitler had promised Japanese foreign minister Yōsuke Matsuoka in the spring of 1941, just before the German attack on Russia, that Germany would provide Japan mutual assistance in the event of war with the United States. Hitler's strategy hinged on his belief that Britain would not give up as long as there was the possibility that Russia and

America might come to its rescue. He would need to defeat Russia and dissuade America from entering the war.

The tensions between Japan and the United States had been rising throughout 1941, but in July, Ambassador Nomura and Secretary Hull had held a number of meetings in an effort to improve Japanese-American relations. While the talks were cordial, they made little progress because Japan continued to honor its alliance with Germany and Italy through the Tripartite Pact, and Japan insisted on economic control of Southeast Asia.[3]

During the negotiations, Japanese diplomats considered withdrawal of its military from most of China and Indochina after drawing up peace terms with the Chinese. The diplomats also agreed to adopt an independent interpretation of the Tripartite Pact, pledging not to discriminate in trade, provided other countries reciprocated. Japan's war minister, General Hideki Tojo, rejected the compromises. On July 24, 1941, the United States froze Japanese financial assets and established an embargo on steel and oil, Japan's most essential imports. At the time more than 80 percent of Japan's oil came from the United States.[4]

Japan refused to leave China but, in a final proposal on November 20, offered to withdraw its forces from southern Indochina and not to launch any attacks in Southeast Asia, provided the United States, Britain, and the Netherlands ceased aiding China and lifted their sanctions against Japan. Secretary Hull countered the Japanese proposal, declaring it must completely withdraw from China, unconditionally, and negotiate nonaggression pacts with Pacific powers.

On November 25, a Japanese carrier task force set sail for Pearl Harbor. In Washington, Secretary Hull warned the president's war council that the negotiations had stalled, and that intelligence sources indicated the possibility of Japanese surprise attacks. However, as William Shirer has written, reports by intelligence officers on "the location of the major warships of the Japanese Navy . . . listed most of them as being in home ports, including all the carriers and other warships of the task force which at that very moment had steamed to within three hundred miles of Pearl Harbor and was tuning up its bombers to take off at dawn."[5]

With Japanese ships already en route to Hawaii, Nazi foreign minister Ribbentrop told the Japanese ambassador to Germany that the Third Reich was prepared to go to war with the United States.

On the afternoon of December 7, 1941, President Roosevelt sat back in his desk chair and relaxed in an old turtleneck sweater. He and Harry Hopkins had just finished a light lunch in the Oval Office. Since it was Sunday and the White House was largely deserted, Roosevelt thought he might spend the rest of the afternoon working on his stamp collection. The president's telephone rang. A White House operator explained that Secretary of the Navy Frank Knox needed to speak with the president urgently. Roosevelt replied, "Put him on." "Mr. President," Knox said, "it looks as though the Japanese have attacked Pearl Harbor." The president paused for a moment and then simply said, "No!"[6]

Roosevelt hung up the telephone. He stared for a few moments at Hopkins in stunned silence; war had come to the United States, though not in the manner that he would have predicted. After discussing next steps with Hopkins, the president telephoned Secretary Hull in his office in the State, War, and Navy Building and told him the news. After he hung up the telephone, Hull finally showed Ambassador Nomura and Special Envoy Kurusu into his office. Standing and glaring at the Japanese diplomats, the secretary of state glanced at the official notification, declared it replete with "infamous falsehoods and distortions," and called the diplomats "bastards" and "pissants."[7]

After dismissing Nomura and Kurusu, Secretary Hull crossed Executive Avenue to the White House to meet with the president and were soon joined by Secretary of War Stimson, Secretary of the Navy Knox, and army chief of staff George Marshall. Undersecretary Sumner Welles stayed behind in his office, frantically alerting U.S. missions and allies around the world of the attack. Assistant Secretary Adolf Berle immediately ordered the confinement of Japanese diplomats and directed that the embassies of Japan, Germany, and Italy be cut off entirely from all communications. Assistant Secretary Breckinridge Long ordered U.S. ports closed as well as the borders with Canada and Mexico.[8]

When Joe Kennedy heard the news, he immediately sent Roosevelt a telegram, "Dear Mr. President. In this great crisis all Americans are with you. Name the battle post. I'm yours to command."[9]

William Bullitt, on a stopover in the Caribbean on his way to Egypt, learned of the Japanese attack from the British governor of Trinidad. In November, President Roosevelt had decided to give Bullitt another chance and appointed him his personal representative for the Near East. Bullitt retained the rank of ambassador, and the president asked him to travel to North Africa, India, Burma, and the Dutch East Indies to meet with regional leaders.[10]

Besides the U.S. ambassador to Japan, Joseph Grew, who had predicted the attack on Pearl Harbor, William Bullitt may have been one of the very few diplomats who were not completely taken by surprise. His early hope that war could be avoided was a distant memory. He had long since believed that a world war was coming and that the United States could not sit on the sidelines. He later wrote, "All democracies find it hard to face unpleasant facts and prefer to cling to happy illusions until they are hit in the head as we were at Pearl Harbor. But if democracies do not act in time . . . they are obliged finally to resort to the most costly form of defense."[11]

The following day, December 8, President Roosevelt asked Congress to declare war on Japan, delivering his iconic portrayal of December 7 as "a day that will live in infamy." As historian David Roll explained, "There had been some pressure on [Roosevelt and Hull] to have Congress declare war on Germany and Italy on December 8 when that step was taken against Japan. But they had decided to wait." President Roosevelt, along with Hull and Knox, decided that the country needed to concentrate its efforts on defeating Japan without taking on the additional burden of simultaneously fighting Italy and Germany.

The Japanese attack on the U.S. Pacific Fleet at Pearl Harbor caught Hitler as completely by surprise as it did Roosevelt. Hitler had promised

Japan that Germany would enter a war with Japan against the United States, but had not anticipated that Japan would launch a first strike. He was already preoccupied with trying to rally reluctant generals and retreating troops fighting in Russia.

However, on December 11, Hitler, in a speech before the Reichstag, declared war on the United States. The führer derided Roosevelt, claiming he had "provoked war in order to cover up the failures of the New Deal." Hitler inveighed that he "was fed up" with the attacks made by Roosevelt on him and on Nazism, his patience exhausted by the warlike acts of the U.S. Navy against German U-boats in the Atlantic.

After the führer delivered his speech, Hans Thomsen, Germany's ambassador to the United States, drove to the State Department to deliver his country's formal declaration of war. As he stepped from his black Buick sedan, he smiled and asked the attendant who greeted him, "Anybody want to buy a nice car." His wife, Bebe, told an American friend, "Leaving the United States is like leaving a second home. It is so sad! I shall come back here after the war is over. Goodbye."[12]

The timing of Hitler's declaration of war on the United States can seem hard to fathom. While he had promised to join the Empire of Japan in a war with the United States, it is likely that other factors played a role in the timing as well. Adolf Hitler despised Franklin Roosevelt and had long hated America. In addition, his underestimation of the United States and overestimation of Japan may have further fueled the timing of the declaration. He thought America's people weak and seriously underestimated its potential military capacity. He also misread Japan's military reach, believing that once the Japanese, whose navy he considered to be the most powerful in the world, disposed of the British and American fleets in the Pacific, they would help Germany by turning on Russia should Germany need it. Also, there was the matter of Hitler's insatiable thirst to be seen as the center of world power that contributed to the miscalculation. Hitler's interpreter during the negotiations leading to the Munich Agreement, Paul Schmidt, later wrote that it was the führer's "inveterate desire for prestige'" that pushed him to declare war first, in the belief that America would declare war on Germany soon.[13]

The event that Ambassadors Dodd and Bullitt had presciently predicted, the event that ambassadors Kennedy and Long had too often blindly dismissed, finally had arrived: a world war involving the United States precipitated by the murderous tyrant in Berlin and his bloody allies in Rome and Tokyo.

With determination and tenacity, Franklin Roosevelt had steered between the isolationism of the American public and the internationalism of his instincts, sifting and evaluating the conflicting reports from his designated eyes and ears in Europe at a time of great peril and uncertainty. Now the time for diplomatic maneuvering and forecasting was over. The national mission was clear and unequivocal. Now military generals would largely replace diplomats as Roosevelt's chief advisers on Europe, and he would spend significantly more time studying military maps and meeting with foreign Allied leaders than reading diplomatic cables or meeting with officials of the Department of State. The president knew the battle to save democracy would likely be large, long, and bloody. His focus was singular: From that day forward, the president explained, he would be, simply and entirely, "Dr. Win the War."

EPILOGUE

As he prepared in 1944 to run for an unprecedented fourth term, those who saw President Roosevelt speak in public noted the lines in his face and how much he had aged. His frail appearance left no doubt that the war had taken a toll on his health. His doctors warned him to cut back on his busy schedule, but he refused. He once again campaigned vigorously and won election over Republican candidate Thomas E. Dewey in November 1944. Three months later, with Harry Hopkins at his side, the president traveled to the Crimean Peninsula to attend the Yalta Conference, joined there by Stalin and Churchill. He returned to the White House completely exhausted.

In April 1945, with the allies now on the offensive, Roosevelt decided to take a brief vacation to regain his strength. As he had on so many occasions when he needed physical and mental relaxation, he traveled to the "Little White House" in Warm Springs, Georgia.

On April 12 at 1:00 p.m., Roosevelt sat in the living room of his cottage surrounded by friends and family. As he signed letters and documents, an artist stood painting his portrait at an easel nearby. The conversation was lively and the atmosphere congenial. The president turned to the artist and reminded her that they had only fifteen minutes left in the session. Suddenly, the president put his hand to his head and complained of a sharp pain. He collapsed, suffering a massive cerebral hemorrhage that ended his life in minutes. America's longest-serving president, who had led the nation through the Great Depression and World War II, died only months before the end of the war.

Former secretary of state Cordell Hull, who had retired from the Department of State after the 1944 election, received the news in Bethesda Naval Hospital, where he had been since late October recovering from treatment for tuberculosis. He issued a press statement from his hospital bed, praising Roosevelt's "inspiring vision . . . high statesmanship . . . and superb leadership."

After America's entry into World War II, President Roosevelt had asked Hull and the State Department to work on laying the groundwork for a future international organization—one that would avoid the mistakes and weaknesses of the League of Nations, yet strengthen peace and cooperation so that the world would never again confront global war. Hull and his staff spent months drafting a document that ultimately became the United Nations Charter, unveiled in mid-1943. Making good use of his prior experience in the U.S. Congress, Hull then played a critical role in galvanizing congressional support for the concept.

Before his work on the Charter, Hull had not been a particularly effective secretary of state, but in early 1944, President Roosevelt called him the "Father of the United Nations" and nominated him for the Nobel Prize for Peace. The United Nations was formally established the following year under President Truman, and Hull was honored with the Nobel Peace Prize in 1945. After suffering several strokes and heart attacks, he died in 1955.

Like Hull, Sumner Welles, issued a similarly formal, though more eloquent statement, upon learning of Roosevelt's death: "A tower has fallen. A star has set . . . Our hearts are heavy today because of the gallant leader we have lost. No man in our nation's history has done more for our country."[1]

Roosevelt had shown remarkable loyalty to some longtime friends in the Department of State, and most especially to Welles. After allegations of sexual misconduct, Welles might have become a political liability to the president in 1941, but Roosevelt chose to keep him on as undersecretary of state. However, when the allegations eventually leaked in the fall of 1943, President Roosevelt announced that he had accepted Welles's resignation "with regret," claiming that Welles was prompted to leave government service because of "his wife's poor health." The truth, however, was that Welles had been forced out of government by Secretary of State Hull and William Bullitt, both of whom had resented Welles's access to the president for many years and used the allegations in the FBI dossier against him. Rumors about Welles's alleged homosexuality had circulated in Washington, but no newspaper ever published the allegations that led to his leaving the Department. To the contrary, *Time* magazine reported that "in dropping Sumner Welles, [Hull] had dropped the chief architect of the US's Good Neighbor Policy in South America, an opponent of those who would do business with Fascists on the basis of expediency, a known and respected advocate of U.S. cooperation in international affairs."[2]

Welles continued to write books on foreign relations and became an adviser to media organizations. He died in New Jersey in 1961, survived by his third wife and several children.

Former ambassador Joseph Kennedy was far less charitable to Roosevelt in death than his former colleagues in the Department of State. He wrote his daughter Kathleen, who was still in London, "Evidently, he'd [Roosevelt] been slipping badly, and it becomes more apparent to all of us that Hopkins and the rest of them were really running this country for the last year and a half, and, if I do say so, damn near ran it into the ground." Kennedy went on to say that the president's death "was a great thing for the country," because he "had stirred up a hatred in the minds of at least half the country, and no matter whether he proposed anything good or bad." In the same letter, Kennedy's anti-Semitism surfaced once again: "The Jews are crying they've lost their greatest friend and benefactor . . They made all their bets on one man rather than on some real social improvement. Then the man dies, and their hopes for social improvement dies with him."[3] Kennedy's bitterness toward Roosevelt endured with a bizarre revisionist view of history that he privately shared with a number of people during the next several months. He insisted there would not have been a war in western Europe had not Roosevelt pressured Chamberlain to confront Hitler after the German invasion of Poland.[4]

Kennedy's enmity stemmed initially from the fact that he wanted to be secretary of the treasury but had to settle for ambassador to the Court of St. James's. President Roosevelt never completely trusted Kennedy's motives or his judgment, and the truth was that Kennedy, like Ambassador William Dodd—albeit for very different reasons—was never cut out to be an ambassador. Brash and highly opinionated, he viewed the world almost exclusively in economic terms and utterly failed to understand in a timely way the danger the Third Reich posed to the world. He had a near obsession for paving the way for his sons to achieve national elective office. For political reasons, Roosevelt tried not to alienate Kennedy, but simultaneously did everything he could to undercut him, often gratuitously. Discredited due to his support for the appeasement of Hitler, Ambassador Kennedy would never again serve in the government.

Ambassador Kennedy's oldest son, Joseph Kennedy Jr., joined the U.S. Naval Reserve in June 1941 and was later sent to Britain. He completed twenty-five bombing missions before being killed in action on August 12, 1944. When two navy priests arrived at the ambassador's house in Hyannis Port, Massachusetts, to deliver the news of Joe Jr.'s death, Kennedy stoically thanked them and then retreated to an upstairs bedroom so that his other children would not see him sobbing.[5]

Joseph Kennedy Jr. was posthumously awarded the Navy Cross. The young man, who had at one time expressed admiration Hitler, gave his life in defense of the United States—and Britain.

Out of government, Ambassador Kennedy settled in Massachusetts, where his son John, also a war hero, was elected to the House of Representatives in 1946 and to the U.S. Senate in 1952. When John Kennedy ran for president in 1960, his father used his vast fortune to help bankroll the campaign. After Senator Kennedy eked out a close

victory over Vice President Richard Nixon, the president-elect joked
that his father had told him, "I'll help you win the election, but I'll be
damned if I'm going to pay for a landslide." Though the ambassador
stayed largely on the sidelines during the campaign, he exercised enormous influence over his son's cabinet choices, including the installation
of his third son, Robert, as attorney general. Ambassador Kennedy suffered a paralyzing stroke in 1961 and died eight years later.

There is no known record of William Bullitt's reaction to the death of the
president. At the time, he was enlisted with the French army and fighting
the Nazis in Alsace under the command of General de Lattre de Tassigny.

Of all his ambassadors in Europe, Roosevelt may have been closest
to Bullitt. Roosevelt viewed Bullitt as energetic, brilliant, and highly
capable. His reporting on both Stalin and Hitler turned out to be
prescient. Although initially Bullitt had pushed for a rapprochement
between Germany and France, in 1939, he advised the president to "create an army now" because he anticipated that the United States would
eventually be drawn into the war. The following year, Bullitt saw German troops amass along its borders with the Netherlands, Luxembourg
and Belgium and correctly predicted an invasion of the Low Countries.
Many historians credit him with having saved Paris from destruction.

Bullitt, however, was politically ambitious to his own detriment. He
harbored a desire to serve in Roosevelt's cabinet as either secretary of state
or secretary of war, and he had few qualms about confronting anyone
who stood in the way of his personal advancement. Ultimately, the president tired of what he viewed as Bullitt's arrogance and insubordination.
While Bullitt amused the president, Roosevelt found Bullitt's treatment
of Undersecretary of State Sumner Welles entirely unacceptable. When
Bullitt tried to force Roosevelt to dismiss Welles from the State Department, the president recoiled and thereafter kept Bullitt at a distance.

In 1942, President Roosevelt denied Bullitt a commission in the
U.S. armed forces. A year later, Bullitt ran for mayor of Philadelphia—
without Roosevelt's endorsement—and was defeated. The following
year, Bullitt asked to see the president about a possible appointment.

However, Roosevelt had learned that Bullitt had continued to stoke the rumors of Welles's homosexuality and was infuriated by the news. When Bullitt was shown into the Oval Office, the president looked at him stone-faced and declared that he was going to "play Saint Peter." The president then leaned back, and, speaking as though Bullitt was not in the room, he mused that two men had come before him at the Pearly Gates. Welles had confessed and was admitted. Bullitt had also confessed. However, Roosevelt said, "Bill, you've tried to destroy a fellow human being . . . Get out of here and never come back."[6]

In 1946, Bullitt published a book, *The Great Globe Itself,* that was harshly critical of Roosevelt, focusing on the trust the president had placed in Stalin. In stark prose, Bullitt referred to Roosevelt, a man he had once claimed to "love," as a "weary President on the verge of thrombosis . . . who died before the actions of the Soviet government . . . forced him to admit that he had lost his gamble."[7] Out of government permanently, Bullitt continued to write articles and books about politics until his death in 1967.

Upon learning of Roosevelt's death, Breckinridge Long wrote in his diary, "I have lost a friend of long standing—nearly 30 years. True, the last few years have not seen any close personal contacts." Long then added a number of reminescences, beginning with, "His office and mine were close together in the east corridor of the 'State, War and Navy Building' in World War I," and ending with the president's reelection in 1944, when Long had sent him "a line of congratulations and received from him a friendly little note signed FDR in his own handwriting."[8]

Having fawned over Mussolini, Breckinridge Long did not distinguish himself as ambassador to Italy, yet Roosevelt brought Long back to Washington to serve in a sensitive role at the State Department and kept him there notwithstanding harsh criticism from many quarters. Long's inflexibility and gross insensitivity with regard to immigration cost the lives of many thousands of European Jews. Long was undoubtedly one of Roosevelt's worst appointments—if not the worst—during his entire presidency.

In 1943, Long testified before the House Foreign Affairs Committee and falsely claimed that the vast majority of visas granted to immigrants had been for European Jews. After the election in 1944, Long retired from the Department of State. He practiced law and pursued his interest in fox hunting and horse racing. He became a director of the Laurel Park Racecourse in Maryland and divided his time between his estates in Maryland and Palm Beach until his death in 1958.

Only days after returning from the Yalta Conference—where he had been evacuated on a stretcher—an extremely ill Harry Hopkins flew to Minnesota and checked himself into the Mayo Clinic. Charles "Chip" Bohlen, once a protégé of Bullitt's in Moscow and now a White House staffer, called Hopkins with the news of Roosevelt's death and later recalled that "there was a long silence at the other end of the phone." Although Hopkins was feeling "much better" as a result of blood transfusions given to him at the clinic, he was not a well man. Nevertheless, he decided the next morning to fly to Washington, D.C., for the funeral—and for the transition to a Truman presidency. Before boarding the plane, Hopkins telephoned his old friend and fellow speechwriter Robert Sherwood: "You and I have got something great that we can take with us all the rest of our lives . . . because we know what so many people believed about [FDR] and what made them love him. The President never let them down."[9]

Roosevelt wanted to hear different viewpoints, but he also wanted one adviser closer to him than the rest, and that individual shifted with some frequency prior to the war. He respected Secretary of State Cordell Hull, but never thought of him as either a visionary or a dynamic leader. At various points, he relied most heavily on William Bullitt, at other times it was Sumner Welles, but as the United States moved closer to war, Harry Hopkins assumed the role of chief adviser.

During World War II, Harry Hopkins accompanied President Roosevelt to every major international summit. Hopkins continued to live in the White House and saw the president more often than any other adviser, often taking meals together and socializing with him. In 1942, he married Louise Gill Macy in a White House ceremony attended by only a few close friends. Macy was a divorced, gregarious former magazine editor. At the president's insistence, the two continued to live at the White House, though they eventually moved to a town house in Georgetown in December 1943. President Truman awarded Hopkins the Distinguished Service Medal in September 1945, just four months before he died at the age of fifty-five on January 29, 1946, of cirrhosis of the liver.

Historians will continue to debate whether or not President Roosevelt should have acted earlier and done more to stop the rise of Hitler. At critical junctures during the 1930s, despite warnings from his ambassadors, he chose to remain silent in the wake of Nazi aggression. He did so when Germany remilitarized the Rhineland and, later, when he misjudged the Munich Agreement, which handed Czechoslovakia to the Nazis; in that instance, he ignored the advice of Ambassador Bullitt and continued to hope that somehow Europeans would sort out their own problems.

President Roosevelt was acutely aware for much of his presidency that any statement he made regarding concern for Europe, much less an overt action on his part, would be met by a largely isolationist public and Congress. Moreover, he continued to view his domestic agenda as paramount even as the dangers of the Nazi regime became well known. All of these factors resulted in a president reluctant to do anything publicly that might be perceived as moving America closer to war with Germany and led to his signing three neutrality bills during the 1930s.

Yet Roosevelt was instinctively an internationalist. He characterized Hitler as a "madman" as early as 1933; supported American participation in the World Court—even though he must have known it would incur the wrath of the powerful newspaper magnate William Randolph Hearst; and the president searched for ways to circumvent the Neutrality Law—eventually using his power as chief executive to make the destroyers-for-bases deal with Prime Minister Churchill. Moreover, as he monitored the rise of fascism in Germany and elsewhere, Roosevelt valued the advice of Ambassadors Dodd and Bullitt, who both warned of Hitler's militarism (though Bullitt did so much later than Dodd) and counseled engagement with Europe. Roosevelt had far less confidence in Ambassadors Kennedy and Long, who were both avowed isolationists. The president saw Kennedy as an appeaser and believed Long had badly misjudged Mussolini. Eleanor Roosevelt, in many respects the president's political conscience, and Louis Howe, his political muse, had cautioned Roosevelt about both men.

There is no doubt Roosevelt recognized that Hitler posed a threat to democracy. Here again, however, Roosevelt's thinking is difficult to discern. Despite the intensifying anti-Jewish persecution in Germany in the 1930s, he refused to condemn the Nazi government. It was not until 1938, after the violent Kristallnacht pogrom, that he issued a public statement denouncing the Nazis. Though as some critics of the president have pointed out, that statement did not contain a single explicit mention of Hitler or the Jews. William Dodd, by this point a private citizen, was the only ambassador to raise the specter of a potential Holocaust in speeches after he became a private citizen.

It's doubtful that public condemnations by the president of Hitler's treatment of Jews would have had any appreciable effect on Hitler, though it certainly would have provided greater moral leadership for the American public. And with that in mind, there is no doubt that Roosevelt could have done much more to allow for the immigration of Jewish refugees to the United States. He permitted Ambassador Long, a narrow-minded bigot and anti-Semite, to set American policy in this vital area. Roosevelt was not oblivious to the question of Hitler's evil, but he chose to focus his efforts—and spend his political capital—on military preparedness and to help America's European, democratic allies, as well as the Soviet Union. The president's reluctance to do more for European Jews will forever be the greatest failure of his presidency.

Historian Robert Dallek has written that discerning Roosevelt's view of the world is like "peering into a kaleidoscope in which a shifting array of pressures moved him from one position to another: his own ideas, domestic considerations, and foreign events, either individually or in various combinations determined [his] behavior." Ambassadors Dodd, Bullitt, Kennedy, and Long were all critical figures reflected in the Roosevelt policy kaleidoscope. So were Secretary Hull and Undersecretary Welles. In a sense, the Roosevelt presidency represents something of a historical apex for the influence of United States diplomats and their direct influence with a president—an era superseded with the creation of the National Security Council in 1947, which quickly became a key bureaucratic instrument of presidential power in foreign policy and a White House counterweight to the State Department. Though he had neither the title nor the institutional support that accompanies the position today, Harry Hopkins was America's first national security adviser.

Sometimes Roosevelt's ambassadors and State Department advisers failed to grasp the significance of important events and sometimes they gave poor advice, but they often informed the president and helped shape his thinking. In the end, of course, Franklin Roosevelt, alone, made historic decisions about American engagement and leadership in a volatile world. As he told Wendell Willkie after the election in 1940, "Some day you may well be sitting here where I am now as president of the United States . . . you'll learn what a lonely job this is."[10]

ACKNOWLEDGMENTS

I want to thank Matt Latimer and Dylan Colligan at Javelin Agency for their help in shaping the book proposal for *Watching Darkness Fall*—Matt also read a late draft and provided helpful advice. I would not have found Javelin had it not been for Jim Johnson, who connected me to Mike Berman, who connected me to Robin Sproul, who in turn connected me to Matt and Dylan.

I was fortunate to have a very good editor in Michael Flamini at St. Martin's Press. Michael knew the material well from editing previous books on this period in history; he offered constant encouragement and his comments were always on point. Michael's assistant, Hannah Phillips, could not have been more helpful. She provided especially invaluable assistance in helping to bring the parts of the book together for final publication.

Thanks to Karen Donfried and Derek Chollet, who provided office space for me at the German Marshall Fund where I spent a great deal of time reading and researching *Watching Darkness Fall*, while simultaneously writing another book on transatlantic relations.

For nearly a year, Christopher Logan served as my research assistant. Christopher not only helped me compile a massive chronology related to the book's central characters, he provided a valuable sounding board on the events of the era. With a master's degree in creative writing, he is destined to publish his own work one day.

I want to thank Phil Johnston who read an early draft. Phil has been a close friend of my family for decades. He is also on the board of the Franklin Roosevelt Library and is extraordinarily knowledgeable about our thirty-second president. John Zentay, who has helped edit my previous four books, did so once again. He read several drafts with the eye—and pen—of a meticulous lawyer. Both Douglas Frantz and Evan Thomas gave me invaluable advice on the structure of the book. I also want to thank Bob Shrum, Charles Edel, Larry Gurwin, Wick Sloane Adam Zagorin, Eric Hamburg, and David Gerken, all of whom are published authors. They read early drafts and provided useful insights.

If I had to give any advice about what to study in college, it would be that it really doesn't matter—use the time to explore. But make sure to choose your roommates carefully; two of mine, Jonathan Alter and Cliff Sloan, are not only lifelong friends but talented writers as well. Jon, a former editor at *Newsweek*, is an acclaimed presidential historian who has written biographies of Presidents Roosevelt, Obama, and, most recently, Jimmy Carter. Cliff, a former Supreme Court clerk—and my coauthor of a book on the seminal legal case *Marbury v. Madison*, is currently writing a book on the Supreme Court during World War II. They both offered helpful comments.

One of the last people to read the manuscript was a friend of mine from both prep school and college, John Campbell. I haven't seen much of John over the years: He lives in the northwest of the United States, and I live in Washington, D.C. In fact, I was soliciting him to contribute to a political campaign and mentioned in passing that I was writing a book. John kindly offered to read it. He turned out to be an extraordinarily talented editor with not only a flair for language but also a very good sense of narrative pace and historical perspective. He greatly improved the book.

Finally, I want to thank my family. Each of my three children read portions of the manuscript and made helpful contributions. My wife,

Kathleen, suggested reading the book out loud—a good method for ascertaining that the writing is clear and crisp. On long car trips up and down the East Coast, she read the manuscript aloud while I drove. She was my harshest critic, but she is always ultimately my greatest supporter. She makes both my books—and me—better.

BIBLIOGRAPHY

Abramowitz, Michael. "The Accidental Ambassador." *The American Interest,* December 19, 2013.

Abramson, Rudy. *Spanning the Century: The Life of W. Averell Harriman.* New York: William Morrow, 1992.

Adams, Henry H. *Harry Hopkins.* New York: G. P. Putnam, 1977.

Adamthwaite, Anthony P. *The Making of the Second World War.* London: Routledge, 1979.

Albright, Madeleine. *Fascism: A Warning.* New York: HarperCollins, 2018.

Alter, Jonathan. *The Defining Moment: FDR's Hundred Days and The Triumph of Hope.* New York: Simon & Schuster, 2006.

Axelrod, Alan. *Lost Destiny: Joseph Kennedy Jr. and the Doomed WWII Mission to Save London.* New York: St. Martin's, 2015.

Bailey, Fred Arthur. *William Edward Dodd: The South's Yeoman Scholar.* Charlottesville: University Press of Virginia, 1997.

Beard, Charles A. *American Foreign Policy in the Making.* New Haven, CT: Yale University Press, 1946.

Beatty, Jack. *The Rascal King: The Life and Times of James Michael Curley (1874–1958).* Reading, MA: Addison Wesley, 1992.

Berg, Scott A. *Lindbergh.* New York: Putnam, 1998.

Berle, Beatrice Bishop, and Jacobs, Travis Beal, eds. *Navigating the Rapids 1918–1971: From the Papers of Adolf A. Berle.* New York: Harcourt Brace Jovanovich, Inc., 1973.

Beschloss, Michael, R. *Kennedy and Roosevelt: The Uneasy Alliance.* New York: W. W. Norton, 1980.

Beschloss, Michael, R. *Presidents of War: The Epic Story: From 1807 to Modern Times.* New York: Crown, 2018.

Bouverie, Tim. *Appeasing Hitler: Chamberlain, Churchill and the Road to War*. London: Bodley Head, 2019.

Brinkley, David. *Washington Goes to War*. New York: Alfred A. Knopf, 1988.

Brownell, Will, and Richard N. Billings. *So Close to Greatness: A Biography of William C. Bullitt*. New York: Macmillan, 1987.

Bullitt, William C. *For the President: Personal and Secret*. Edited by Orville H. Bullitt. New York: Houghton Mifflin, 1972.

Bullock, Alan. *Hitler: A Study in Tyranny*. New York: HarperCollins, 1991 (reprint).

Burns, James MacGregor. *Roosevelt: The Lion and the Fox*. New York: Harcourt, Brace, 1956.

Chernow, Ron. *The Warburgs*. New York: Random House, 1993.

Churchill, Winston S. *The Second World War*, vol. II. Boston: Houghton Mifflin, 1953.

Cook, Blanche Wiesen. *Eleanor Roosevelt: Volume 2: 1933–1938*. New York: Viking Penguin, 1999.

Cowles, Virginia, *Looking for Trouble*. London: Faber and Faber, 2014.

Craig, Gordon A., and Felix Gilbert, eds. *The Diplomats, 1919–1939*. Princeton, NJ: Princeton University Press, 1953.

Dallek, Robert. *Democrat and Diplomat: The Life of William E. Dodd*. Oxford: Oxford University Press, 2013.

Dallek, Robert. *Franklin D. Roosevelt and American Foreign Policy, 1932–1945*. New York: Oxford University Press, 1979.

Dallek, Robert. *Franklin D. Roosevelt: A Political Life*. New York: Viking, 2017.

Davis, Kenneth S. *FDR: The New Deal Years, 1933–1937*. New York: Random House, 1979.

Davis, Kenneth S. *FDR: Into the Storm, 1937–1940*. New York: Random House, 1993.

D'Este, Carlo. *Warlord: A Life of Winston Churchill at War, 1874–1945*. New York: HarperCollins, 2008.

Dodd, Martha. *Sowing the Wind*. New York: Harcourt, Brace, 1945.

Dodd, Martha. *Through Embassy Eyes*. New York: Harcourt, Brace, 1939.

Dodd, William E. *Ambassador Dodd's Diary*. Edited by Martha Dodd. New York: Harcourt, Brace, 1941.

Downey, Kirstin. *The Woman Behind the New Deal: The Life and Legacy of Frances Perkins*. New York: Nan A. Talese, 2009.

Erbelding, Rebecca. *Rescue Board: The Untold Story of America's Efforts to Save the Jews of Europe*. New York: Doubleday, 2018.

Etkind, Alexander. *Roads Not Taken: An Intellectual Biography of William C. Bullitt*. Pittsburg: University of Pittsburg Press, 2017.

Evans, Richard J. *The Coming of the Third Reich*. New York: Penguin, 2004.

Fairweather, Nicolas. "Hitler and Hitlerism: A Man of Destiny." *Atlantic Monthly*, March 1932.

Fairweather, Nicolas. "Hitler and Hitlerism: Germany Under the Nazis." *Atlantic Monthly*, April 1932.

Farnham, Barbara Reardon. *Roosevelt and the Munich Crisis: A Study of Political Decision-Making*. Princeton, NJ: Princeton University Press, 1997.

Fleming, Thomas. *The New Dealers' War: FDR and the War Within World War II*. New York: Basic Books, 2001.

Fox, James. *Five Sisters: The Langhornes of Virginia.* New York: Simon & Schuster, 2000.

Freud, Sigmund, and William C. Bullitt. *Thomas Woodrow Wilson: A Psychological Study.* Boston: Houghton Mifflin, 1966.

Fullilove, Michael. *Rendezvous with Destiny: How Franklin D. Roosevelt and Five Extraordinary Men Took America into the War and into the World.* New York: Penguin, 1972.

Gellman, Irwin F. *Secret Affairs: Franklin Roosevelt, Cordell Hull, and Sumner Welles.* Baltimore: Johns Hopkins University Press, 1995.

Gilbert, Martin. *Kristallnacht: Prelude to Destruction.* New York: HarperCollins, 2006.

Glass, Charles. *Americans in Paris: Life and Death Under Nazi Occupation.* New York: Penguin, 2010.

Goodwin, Doris Kearns. *No Ordinary Time.* New York: Simon & Schuster, 1994.

Graham, Otis C., and Robert Wander. *Franklin Roosevelt, His Life and Times—An Encyclopedic View.* New York: Da Capo, 1980.

Gunther, John. *Roosevelt in Retrospect: A Profile in History.* New York: Harper Collins, 1950.

Hanfstaengl, Ernst. *Hitler: The Memoir of a Nazi Insider Who Turned Against the Fuhrer.* New York: Arcade Publishing, 1957.

Herzstein, Robert Edwin. *Roosevelt and Hitler: The Prelude to War.* New York: Paragon House, 1989.

Hilmes, Oliver. *Berlin 1936: Sixteen Days in August.* Translated by Jefferson Chase. New York: Other Press, 2016.

Hiltzik, Michael. *The New Deal: A Modern History.* New York: Free Press, 1957.

Hughes, Matthew, and Chris Mann. *Inside Hitler's Germany: Life Under the Third Reich.* Dulles, VA: Brassey's, 2000.

Hulen, Bertram D. *Inside the Department of State.* New York: Whittlesey House, 1939.

Hull, Cordell. *The Memoirs of Cordell Hull*, vol. 1. New York: Macmillan, 1948.

Ickes, Harold L. *The Secret Diary of Harold L. Ickes: The First Thousand Days, 1933–1936.* New York: Simon & Schuster, 1953.

Ickes, Harold L. *The Secret Diary of Harold Ickes,* vol. II. New York: Simon & Schuster, 1954.

Isherwood, Christopher. *The Berlin Stories.* New York: New Directions, 1954 (reprint).

Israel, Fred L., ed. *The War Diary of Breckinridge Long.* Lincoln: University of Nebraska Press, 1966.

Kennan, George F. *The Kennan Diaries.* Edited by Frank Costigliola. New York: W. W. Norton, 2014.

Kennedy, David M. *Freedom from Fear: The American People in Depression and War, 1929–1945.* New York: Oxford University Press, 199.

Kessler, Ronald. *Sins of the Father: Joseph P. Kennedy and the Dynasty He Founded.* New York: Warner Books, 1996.

Ketchum, Richard M. *The Borrowed Years: 1938–1941: America on the Way to War.* New York: Random House, 1989.

Klemperer, Victor. *I Will Bear Witness: A Diary of the Nazi Years, 1933–1941.* Translated by Martin Chalmers. New York: Random House, 1998.

Kotkin, Stephen. *Stalin: Waiting for Hitler, 1929–1941.* New York: Penguin, 2017

Krock, Arthur. *In the Nation: 1932–1936.* New York: McGraw-Hill, 1966.

Larsen, Eric. *In the Garden of Beasts: Love, Terror, and An American Family in Hitler's Berlin.* New York: Crown, 2011.

Lash, Joseph P. *Eleanor and Franklin.* New York: W. W. Norton, 1971.

Lash, Joseph P. *Roosevelt and Churchill, 1939–1941: The Partnership That Saved the West.* New York: W. W. Norton, 1976.

Leuchtenburg, William E. *Franklin Roosevelt and the New Deal.* New York: Harper and Row, 1963.

Lomazow, Steven, and Eric Fettman. *FDR's Deadly Secret.* New York: Public Affairs, 2009.

Manchester, William. *The Last Lion: Winston Spencer Churchill, Alone, 1932–1940.* New York: Little, Brown, 1988.

Mayers, David. *FDR's Ambassadors and the Diplomacy of Crisis.* New York: Cambridge University Press, 2013.

McConnon, Aili, and Andres McConnon. *Road to Valor: A True Story of World War II in Italy.* New York: Crown, 2013.

McIlvaine, Bill. *Harry Hopkins: President Franklin D. Roosevelt's Deputy President.* History Magazine: April, 2000. https.historynet.com/harry-hopkins-president-franklin-d-roosevelts-deputy-president.htm.

McLellan, David S., and David C. Acheson. *Among Friends: Personal Letters of Dean Acheson.* New York: Dodd, Mead, 1980.

Medoff, Rafael. *The Jews Should Keep Quiet: Franklin D. Roosevelt, Rabbi Stephen S. Wise and the Holocaust.* Philadelphia: Jewish Publication Society, 2019.

Messersmith, George. "Present Status of the Anti-Semitic Movement in Germany." German Historical Institute. September 21, 1933. http://germanhistorydocs.ghi-dc.org/.

Metcalfe, Philip. *1933.* Sag Harbor, NY: Permanent Press, 2016.

Moe, Richard. *Roosevelt's Second Act: The Election of 1940 and the Politics of War.* Oxford: Oxford University Press, 2013.

Morton, H. V. *Atlantic Meeting.* London: Methuen, 1943.

Murphy, Robert. *Diplomat Among Warriors: The Unique World of A Foreign Service Expert.* New York: Doubleday, 1964.

Nagorski, Andrew. *1941: The Year Germany Lost the War.* New York: Simon & Schuster, 2019.

Nasaw, David. *The Patriarch: The Remarkable Life and Turbulent Times of Joseph P. Kennedy.* New York: Penguin Books, 2012.

New York Times. *The Complete Front Pages: 1851–2009.* New York: Black Dog and Leventhal, 2009.

Nixon, Edgar B. *Franklin Roosevelt and Foreign Affairs,* vols. I–III. Cambridge, MA: Belknap Press, 1969.

Nowell, Elizabeth. *Thomas Wolfe: A Biography.* New York: Doubleday, 1960.

Olson, Lynne. *Citizens of London.* New York: Random House, 2010.

Overy, Richard, ed. *The New York Times Complete World War II.* New York: Black Dog and Leventhal, 2013.

Parrish, Thomas. *Roosevelt and Marshall: Partners in Politics and War.* New York: William Morrow, 1989.

Phillips, William. *The Reminiscences of William Phillips.* Oral History Collection. New York: Columbia University, 1952.

Pietrusza, David. *1932: The Rise of Hitler and FDR.* Guilford, CT: Lyons Press, 2016.

Ridley, Jasper. *Mussolini.* New York: St. Martin's, 1997.

Rippon, Anton. *Hitler's Olympics: The Story of the 1936 Nazi Games.* South Yorkshire, UK: Pen and Sword, 2006.

Roberts, Sam. "Paris Saved by a Bullitt." *Foreign Affairs,* June 2, 2015.

Roll, David L. *The Hopkins Touch: Harry Hopkins and the Forging of the Alliance to Defeat Hitler.* Oxford: Oxford University Press, 2013.

Roll, David L. *George Marshall: Defender of the Republic.* New York: Dutton Caliber, 2019.

Rolde, Neil. *Breckinridge Long.* Solon, ME: Polar Bear & Company, 2013.

Roosevelt, Eleanor. *This I Remember.* New York: Harper and Brothers, 1949.

Roosevelt, Elliott, and James Brough. *A Rendez-Vous with Destiny.* New York: G. P. Putnam, 1975.

Roosevelt, Elliott, ed. *FDR: His Personal Letters, 1928–1945,* vols. I and II. New York: Duell, Sloan and Pearce, 1950.

Roosevelt, James. *My Parents: A Differing View.* New York: Playboy Press, 1976.

Rosbottom, Ronald. *When Paris Went Dark: The City of Light Under German Occupation, 1940–1944.* London: John Murray, 2014.

Schwarz, Jordan A. *Liberal: Adolf A. Berle and the Vision of an American Era.* New York: Free Press, 1987.

Searls, Hank. *The Lost Prince: Young Joe, the Forgotten Kennedy.* New York: World Publishing, 1960.

Sherwood, Robert E. *Roosevelt and Hopkins: An Intimate Biography.* New York: Harper and Brothers, 1948.

Shirer, William L. *Berlin Diary.* New York: Knopf, 1941.

Shirer, William L. *The Rise and Fall of the Third Reich.* New York: Simon & Schuster, 1990 (reprint).

Smith, Amanda, ed. *Hostage to Fortune: The Letters of Joseph P. Kennedy.* New York: Viking, 2001.

Smith, Jean Edward. *FDR.* New York: Random House, 2007.

Smith, Kathryn. *The Gatekeeper: Missy LeHand, FDR and the Untold Story of the Partnership That Defined a Presidency.* New York: Simon & Schuster, 2016.

Solomon, Harvey. *Such Splendid Prisons: Diplomatic Detainment in America During WWII.* Lincoln: University of Nebraska/ Potomac Books, 2020.

Stacks, John F. *Scotty: James B. Reston and the Rise and Fall of American Journalism.* New York: Little, Brown, 2003.

Swift, Will. *The Kennedys Amidst the Gathering Storm.* New York: Smithsonian Books, 2008.

Toye, Richard. *Churchill's Empire: The World That Made Him and the World He Made.* New York: Henry Holt, 2010.

Wapshott, Nicholas. *The Sphinx: Franklin Roosevelt, the Isolationism and the Road to World War II.* New York: Norton, 2015.

Watt, Richard M. *Bitter Glory: Poland and Its Fate, 1918–1939.* New York: Simon & Schuster, 1979.

Weinstein, Allen, and Alexander Vassiliev. *The Haunted Wood: Soviet Espionage in America: The Stalin Era.* New York: Random House, 1999.

Weisbrode, Kenneth. *The Atlantic Century.* Cambridge, MA: Da Capo, 2009.

Welles, Benjamin. *Sumner Welles: FDR's Global Strategist.* New York: St. Martin's, 1997.

NOTES

Front Matter General

1. Gunther, p. 128.

Prologue: Happy Days Are Here Again

1. Pietrusza, p. 64.
2. Wapshott, p. 23.
3. Dallek, *Roosevelt and American Foreign Policy*, p. 19.
4. Nasaw, p. 179.
5. Ibid., p. 182.
6. Smith, J. E., p. 144.
7. Ibid., pp. 144, 145.
8. Nasaw, p. 171.
9. Alter, p. 130.
10. Brownell and Billings, pp. 128, 129.

1: This Is a Day of National Consecration

1. Graham and Wander, p. 20.
2. *New York Times*, Sunday, March 5, 1933.
3. Ibid.
4. Alter, p. 56.

2: A Small, Obscure Austrian House Painter

1. Shirer, p. 158.
2. Ibid., p. 166.

3.   Ibid., p. 159.
4.   Overy, p. 10.
5.   Fairweather, "Hitler and Hitlerism: A Man of Destiny."
6.   Ibid.
7.   Ibid.
8.   Shirer, p. 185.
9.   Roosevelt, E., *FDR*, vol. I, pp. 320, 321.
10.   Smith, K., pp. 143, 144.
11.   Nixon, *FDR and Foreign Affairs*, vol. I, p. 6.
12.   Brownell and Billings, p. 129.
13.   Ibid., p. 130.

3: The Striped-Pants Boys

1.   Hulen, pp. 15, 16.
2.   Fullilove, p. 12.
3.   Dallek, *A Political Life*, p. 3567.
4.   Weisbrode, p. 13.
5.   Alter, p. 162.
6.   Ibid.
7.   Mayers, pp. 30, 40.

4: I Want You to Go to Germany as an Ambassador

1.   Roosevelt E. *FDR*, pp. 337, 338 41.
2.   Ibid,.
3.   Beatty, p. 328.
4.   Ibid.
5.   Gellman, p. 56.
6.   Farnham, p. 53.
7.   *New York Times*, March 21, 1933, p. 1.
8.   Ibid.
9.   Erbelding, p. 10.
10.   Larson, p. 17.
11.   Metcalfe, pp. 122, 123.
12.   Dallek, *Franklin D. Roosevelt*, p. 159.
13.   Cook, p. 103.
14.   Nixon, *FDR and Foreign Affairs*, vol. I, pp. 142, 143.
15.   Dallek, *Democrat and Diplomat*, p. 43. See also Larson, p. 17.
16.   Ibid., p. 143.
17.   Larson, p. 21.
18.   Ibid., p. 27. Dallek, *Democrat and Diplomat*, p. 145.
19.   Ibid., p. 34.
20.   Ibid.
21.   Dallek, *Democrat and Diplomat*, p. 145.
22.   Metcalfe, p. 116.

5: The Vehicle Occupied by Great Caesar's Ghost

1. Rolde, p. 113.
2. Nixon, *FDR and Foreign Affairs,* vol. I, pp. 194–197.
3. McConnon and McConnon, p. 71.
4. Rolde, pp. 113, 114.
5. Nixon, *FDR and Foreign Affairs,* vol. I, pp. 194–197.
6. Ibid., pp. 542–544.
7. Roosevelt, E. *FDR,* vol. I, pp. 351–352.
8. Nixon, *FDR and Foreign Affairs,* vol. I, pp. 255–259.
9. Rolde, p. 114.
10. Larson, p. 5.
11. Ibid., p. 33.
12. Ibid., p. 45.
13. Ibid., p. 42.
14. Shirer, *The Rise and Fall of the Third Reich,* p. 208. See also, Larson, pp. 62–65.
15. Dodd to FDR, in Nixon, *FDR and Foreign Affairs,* vol. I, pp. 336, 337.
16. Ibid., pp. 328, 329.
17. FDR to Dodd, in ibid., pp. 360, 361.
18. Abramson, pp. 350, 351.
19. Ibid.
20. Nixon, *FDR and Foreign Affairs,* vol. I; Long to Roosevelt, July 17, 1933, pp. 317–320.
21. Ibid., July 8, 1933.

6: Some Changes Are in Order

1. Larson, p. 85.
2. Ibid., p. 88.
3. Ibid., p. 65.
4. Ibid., p. 62.
5. Nixon, *FDR and Foreign Affairs,* vol. I, pp. 360, 361.
6. Larson, p. 38.
7. Ibid., p. 39.
8. Ibid., p. 82.
9. Ibid, p.p. 94–97.
10. Craig and Gilbert, p. 458.
11. Ibid.
12. Etkind, p. 106.
13. Brownell and Billings, p. 128.
14. Ibid., p. 129.
15. Lash, *Eleanor and Franklin,* p. 394.
16. Smith, K., p. 144.
17. Gellman, p. 48.
18. Etkind, p. 110. See also, Bullitt, p. 39.
19. Ibid.
20. Ibid., p. 111.
21. Smith, K., p. 144.
22. Larson, p. 132.

23. Shirer, *The Rise and Fall of the Third Reich*, p. 242.
24. Ibid., p. 245.
25. Larson, p. 130. Metcalfe, pp. 159, 160. Also, Dodd, W., p. 296.
26. Ibid.
27. Ibid.
28. Metcalfe, pp. 163–165.
29. Larson, p. 150.
30. Ibid., p. 151.
31. Ibid., p. 152.
32. Dodd, W., p. 52.
33. Ibid.
34. Larson, p. 158.
35. Craig and Gilbert, p. 456. See also Dodd, W., p. 50.

7: I Wonder If You Would Try to Get the President More Interested in Foreign Affairs

1. Etkind, p. 146.
2. Brownell and Billings, p. 141.
3. Dodd, W., pp. 62, 63.
4. Kennan, pp. 86, 87.
5. Etkind, pp. 116–118.
6. Brownell and Billings, pp. 143, 144.
7. Nixon, *FDR and Foreign Affairs*, vol. I, pp. 516, 517.
8. Long to David Lawrence, Long papers, box 104, August 9, 1933.
9. Israel, p. xviii, September 16, 1933.
10. Nixon, *FDR and Foreign Affairs*, vol. I., pp. 394, 395.
11. Gunther, p. 299.

8: I Am Much Too Fond of You All

1. Smith, A., p. 127.
2. Ibid.
3. Ibid., p. 118.
4. Ibid., p. 120.
5. Ibid.
6. Ibid., p. 127.
7. Nixon, *FDR and Foreign Affairs*, vol. I, pp. 507–509.
8. Roosevelt, E., *FDR*, pp. 379, 380.
9. Larson, p. 241.
10. Shirer, *The Rise and Fall of The Third Reich*, p. 213. See also Larson, p. 209.
11. Ibid.
12. Etkind, p. 146.
13. Smith, K., p. 147.
14. Ibid., p. 125.
15. Ibid., p. 148.
16. Nixon, *FDR and Foreign Affairs*, vol. II, pp. 100, 101.
17. Bullitt, p. 83.
18. Nixon, *FDR and Foreign Affairs*, vol. II, pp. 47, 48.

9: Just Think What the Career Boys Will Say!

1. Dodd, W., pp. 84, 85.
2. Larson, pp. 232–234.
3. Dodd, W., pp. 88, 19.
4. Ibid., p. 326.
5. Dodd, W., pp. 90, 91.
6. Ibid.
7. Nixon, *FDR and Foreign Affairs,* vol. II, pp. 34, 35.
8. Larson, p. 245.
9. Nixon, *FDR and Foreign Affairs,* vol. II, pp. 35, 36.
10. Smith, p. 120.
11. Larson, p. 167.
12. Ibid., p. 168.
13. Ibid., p. 166.
14. Gunther, p. 23.
15. McIlvaine, Harry Hopkins, History Magazine, April, 2000.
16. Lash, *Eleanor and Franklin,* p. 571.
17. Dodd, W., p. 94.

10: Ambassador Long Was Swell to Us

1. Smith, A., p. 132.
2. Ibid., p. 130.
3. Ibid., p. 131.
4. Ibid., p. 133.
5. Larson, p. 292. See also, Dodd, W., p. 115.
6. Larson, p. 284.
7. Shirer, p. 218.
8. Ibid., p. 219.
9. Dodd, W., p. 115.

11: Downhearted About Europe

1. *New York Times,* July 1, 1934, p. 1.
2. Shirer, p. 222.
3. Larson, p. 328.
4. Ibid., p. 331.
5. Ibid., pp. 332, 333.
6. Ibid., p. 329.
7. Roosevelt, E., *FDR,* pp. 412, 413.
8. Shirer, p. 279.
9. Ibid., p. 226.
10. Nixon, *FDR and Foreign Affairs,* vol. II, pp. 180, 181.
11. Ibid.

12: What a Mess It All Is!

1. Ibid., p. 208.
2. Ibid.
3. Roosevelt, E., *FDR*, p. 450.
4. Dodd, W., pp. 210, 211.
5. Ibid., p. 214.
6. Ibid., p. 214; see March 15, 1935.
7. Ibid., pp. 236, 237.
8. Ibid., p. 216; see February 23, 1935. See also Larson, p. 360.
9. Nixon, *FDR and Foreign Affairs*, vol. II, pp. 387–389.
10. Nixon, *FDR and Foreign Affairs*, vol. II, pp. 426–429.
11. Craig and Gilbert, p. 452.
12. Roosevelt, E., *FDR*, p. 475.
13. Bullitt, p. 110.
14. Larson, p. 340.
15. Nixon, *FDR and Foreign Affairs*, vol. II, pp. 486–489.
16. Roosevelt, E., *FDR*, p. 480.

13: Without Doubt the Most Hair-Trigger Times

1. In analyzing the Ethiopian situation—his assessment of the French and British strategies were largely accurate—Long's only failure, a significant one, was that he seemed to approve of Italy's possible invasion of Ethiopia, and gave little thought to the potential subjugation of a defenseless country.
2. Nixon, *FDR and Foreign Affairs*, vol. II, pp. 437, 438.
3. Ibid.
4. Shirer, *Rise and Fall of the Third Reich*, pp. 284, 285.
5. Nixon, *FDR and Foreign Affairs*, vol. II, pp. 455, 456. See also Dodd, W., pp. 344, 345.
6. Ibid., pp. 588–590.
7. Ibid.
8. Manchester, p. 70.
9. Nixon, *FDR and Foreign Affairs*, pp. 553, 554.
10. Ibid.
11. Dodd, W., p. 239.
12. Martha Dodd also had affairs with both high-ranking Nazis and Communists—one of whom, a Russian diplomat, was ultimately killed by Stalin.
13. Nowell, p. 272.
14. Nixon, *FDR and Foreign Affairs*, vol. II, p. 480.

14: If Men Were Christian, There Would Be No War

1. Watt, p. 133.
2. Dodd, W., p. 244.
3. Ibid., p. 245.
4. Nixon, *FDR and Foreign Affairs*, vol. II, pp. 525–530.
5. Ibid., p. 529.

6.   Roosevelt, E., *FDR*, pp. 446, 447.
7.   Ibid., pp. 530, 531.
8.   Ibid.

15: Hypnotized by Mussolini

1.   Ridley, p. 269.
2.   Roosevelt and Brough, p. 130.
3.   *New York Times,* October 5, 1935, p. 1.
4.   Nixon, *FDR and Foreign Affairs,* vol. III, p. 44.
5.   Ibid., p. 28.
6.   Israel, pp. xxii, xxiii.
7.   Nixon, *FDR and Foreign Affairs,* vol. III, pp. 114, 115.
8.   Ibid., pp. 54, 55.
9.   FDR, *Letters,* pp. 530, 531.
10. Cook, p. 242. See also, Ickes, *The Secret Diary,* vol. I, p. 494.
11. Dodd, W., p. 291.

16: Pack Up Your Furniture, the Dog, and the Servant

1.   Davis, *FDR: The New Deal Years,* p. 593.
2.   Gellman, p. 124.
3.   Ibid., p. 122.
4.   Rolde, p. 120.
5.   Roosevelt, E., *FDR,* pp. 543, 544.
6.   Ibid.
7.   Dodd, W., pp. 300, 301.
8.   Ibid., p. 242.
9.   Ibid., p. 278.
10. Ibid., p. 309.
11. Ibid., p. 301.
12. Larson, p. 341.
13. Dodd, W., p. 291.
14. Ibid., p. 276.
15. Gellman, p. 101.
16. Roosevelt and Brough, p. 121.
17. Roosevelt, E., *FDR,* pp. 560, 561.
18. Dodd, W., pp. 308–310.
19. Bullitt, pp. 157, 158.
20. Shirer, p. 293.
21. Dodd, W., p. 333.
22. Rolde, p. 123.
23. Roosevelt, E., *FDR,* p. 583.
24. Brownell and Billings, pp. 185, 186.
25. Shirer, p. 295.
26. Roosevelt, E., *FDR,* vol. 1, pp. 585, 586.
27. Burns, p. 271.

28. Nixon, *FDR and Foreign Affairs,* vol. III, p. 337.
29. Ibid.
30. Ickes, Diary, pp. 625–627.

17: I Hate War

1.   Dodd, W., p. 343.
2.   Shirer, p. 233.
3.   Hilmes, pp. 239, 240.
4.   Dodd, W., p. 342.
5.   Nowell, p. 328.
6.   Nixon, *FDR and Foreign Affairs,* p. 389.
7.   Smith, K., p. 190.
8.   Ibid.
9.   Ibid.
10. Roosevelt, J., p. 107.
11. Brownell and Billings, p. 186.
12. Beard, p. 173.
13. Roosevelt, E., *FDR,* p. 611.
14. Etkind, p. 56.
15. Roosevelt, E., *FDR,* p. 611.
16. Nixon, *FDR and Foreign Affairs,* vol. III, pp. 424, 425.
17. Rolde, p. 125. Nixon, *FDR and Foreign Affairs,* vol. III, p. 343.
18. Nixon, *FDR and Foreign Affairs,* vol. III, p. 343.
19. Ibid.
20. Ibid., pp. 452–454, incl. fnt. 3.
21. Bullitt, pp. 179, 180.

18: I Still Don't Like the European Outlook

1.   Bullitt, pp. 176, 177.
2.   Smith, K., p. 194.
3.   Bullitt, pp. 176, 177.
4.   Glass, p. 14.
5.   Bullitt, p. 177.
6.   Smith, K., p. 194.
7.   Burns, p. 288.
8.   Davis, pp. 652, 653.
9.   Cook, p. 470.
10. Ibid.
11. Bullitt, pp. 194, 195.
12. Ibid., p. 195.
13. Ibid., p. 196.
14. Dodd, W., pp. 371, 372.
15. Larson, p. 342.
16. Bullitt, pp. 200–202.
17. Ibid.

18. Roosevelt and Brough, p. 152.
19. Burns, p. 296.

19: What a Grand Fight It Is Going to Be!

1. Roosevelt and Brough, p. 153.
2. Burns, p. 292.
3. Beard, p. 177.
4. Burns, p. 298.
5. Rolde, p. 127.
6. Ibid.
7. Roosevelt and Brough, pp. 178, 179.
8. Gellman, pp. 122, 123.
9. Lash, p. 571.
10. McLellan and Acheson, p. 12.
11. Dodd, W., pp. 94 (May 24, 1934), 422 (June 30, 1937).
12. Ibid., pp. 408, 409.
13. Ibid.
14. Craig and Gilbert, p. 456.
15. Gellman, p. 154.
16. Craig and Gilbert, p. 452.
17. Ibid., pp. 452, 453.
18. Larson, pp. 344, 345.
19. Craig and Gilbert, p. 453.
20. Ibid.
21. Roosevelt, J., p. 208.
22. Ibid.

20: Joe, Just Look at Your Legs

1. Ridley, p. 285.
2. Shirer, p. 301.
3. Roosevelt and Brough, p. 182.
4. Goodwin, p. 22.
5. Gellman, p. 149.
6. Beschloss, *Roosevelt and Kennedy*, p. 154.
7. Ibid.
8. Larson, p. 346.
9. Dodd, W., pp. 428, 429.
10. Larson, p. 346.
11. Ibid., p. 344.
12. Ibid., p. 347.
13. Dodd, W., p. 430.
14. Bullitt, pp. 232–233.
15. Ibid., p. 233.
16. Ibid., pp. 234, 235.
17. Ibid., p. 235.

18. Ibid., pp. 237, 238.
19. Larson, p. 347.
20. Dodd, W., pp. 433, 434.
21. Gunther, p. 132.
22. Nasaw, p. 273.
23. Swift, pp. 5, 6.
24. Manchester, pp. 242, 243.
25. Wapshott, p. 47.
26. Nasaw, p. 276.
27. Dodd, W., pp. 445–447.
28. Ibid., p. 445.
29. Ibid.
30. Ibid., pp. 446, 447.
31. Roosevelt and Brough, p. 190.

21: Everybody Down the Line Will Be Sent to Siam

1. Beschloss, *Roosevelt and Kennedy*, p. 159.
2. Swift, pp. 16–18.
3. Beschloss, *Roosevelt and Kennedy*, p. 164.
4. Ibid., p. 159. See also, *Life*, April 11, 1938.
5. Smith, A., pp. 202, 203.
6. Larson, p. 349.
7. Ibid., pp. 348–350.
8. Leuchtenburg, p. 276.
9. Roosevelt, E., *FDR*, vol. II, pp. 743, 744.
10. Larson, p. 356.
11. For a detailed description of the meeting, see Shirer, pp. 325–330.
12. Ibid., pp. 337–341.
13. Rolde, p. 131.
14. Farnham, p. 76.
15. Shirer, *Rise and Fall of the Third Reich*, p. 353.
16. Etkind, p. 81.
17. Ibid., p. 82.

22: May God . . . Prove That You Are Wrong

1. Swift, p. 39.
2. Nasaw, p. 293.
3. Ibid., pp. 294, 295.
4. Kessler, p. 159.
5. Dallek, *FDR and American Foreign Policy*, p. 161.
6. Nasaw, p. 302.
7. Bullitt, p. 254. See also, Ickes, *Secret Diary*, vol. 2, p. 381.
8. Nasaw, p. 303.
9. Roosevelt, E., *FDR*, p. 786.
10. Nasaw, p. 306.
11. Larson, p. 349.

12. Davis, p. 312.
13. Smith, A., p. 259.
14. Davis, pp. 365, 366.
15. Bullitt, p. 271.
16. Ibid.
17. Downey, pp. 288–290.
18. Ibid.
19. Wapshott, p. 82.
20. Bullitt, p. 273.
21. Ibid., pp. 269–271.
22. Ibid.
23. Ibid.
24. Ibid., p. 272.
25. Roosevelt, E., *FDR*, pp. 740, 741.

23: Resistance and War Will Follow

1. Nasaw, p. 328.
2. Beschloss, *Kennedy and Roosevelt*, p. 175.
3. Ibid.
4. Roosevelt, E., *FDR*, p. 809.
5. Nasaw, p. 331.
6. Ibid., p. 333.
7. Ibid.
8. Adamthwaite, p. 176.
9. Roosevelt, E., *FDR*, pp. 790, 791. For a more complete discussion of Wilson's tenure as ambassador, see also Mayers, pp. 52–57.
10. Ibid.
11. Wapshott, p. 86.
12. Cowles, p. 147.
13. Ibid.
14. Davis, p. 327.
15. Brownell and Billings, p. 221.
16. Wapshott, pp. 88, 89.
17. Brownell and Billings, pp. 221, 222.
18. Overy, p. 20. *New York Times,* September 26, 1938.
19. Shirer, p. 400.
20. Overy, p. 20. *New York Times,* "Roosevelt Makes Appeal, September 27, 1938.
21. Shirer, *Berlin Diary,* September 26, 1938, p. 410.
22. Wapshott, p. 92.
23. Rolde, p. 132.
24. Wapshott, p. 92.
25. Swift, p. 95.
26. Wapshott, p. 92.
27. Swift, p. 95.
28. Ibid., p. 96.
29. Ibid., pp. 96, 97.
30. Ibid., p. 99.

31. Cook, pp. 543, 544.
32. Welles, p. 212.
33. Ibid.
34. Leuchtenburg, p. 285. See also Roosevelt, E., *FDR*, vol. II, pp. 813, 814, 818.
35. Browning and Billings, p. 324.
36. Ibid., p. 325.

24: I Could Scarcely Believe Such Things Could Occur

1. Larson, pp. 351, 352.
2. Mayers, pp. 62, 63.
3. Swift, pp. 104–106.
4. Wapshott, p. 96.
5. Shirer, *Rise and Fall of the Third Reich*, p. 430.
6. Ibid., p. 435. See also Gilbert, pp. 26–29.
7. Swift, pp. 111, 112. See also Wapshott, p. 96.
8. Shirer, p. 433.
9. Swift, p. 112.
10. Roosevelt, E., *FDR*, vol. I, p. 830.
11. Ibid., p. 829.
12. Ibid., p. 837.
13. Ibid., p. 838.
14. Ibid., p. 843.
15. Ibid., p. 297.
16. Ibid., pp. 832, 833.
17. Smith, A., p. 305.
18. Swift, p. 126.

25: Methods, Short of War

1. Wapshott, p. 112.
2. Ibid.
3. Swift, p. 129.
4. Roosevelt, E., *FDR*, p. 849.
5. Swift, p. 130.
6. *New York Times*, January 15, 1939.
7. Leuchtenberg, p. 287.
8. Brownell and Billings, p. 229.
9. Ibid.
10. Swift, p. 132.

26: The Last Well-Known Man About Whom That Was Said

1. Shirer, pp. 442, 443.
2. Smith, A., p. 321.
3. Ibid.
4. Bullitt, p. 333.
5. Smith, J. E., p. 388.

27: My Mother Does Not Approve of Cocktails

1. Shirer, p. 465.
2. Leuchtenburg, p. 287.
3. Beschloss, *Kennedy and Roosevelt*, p. 187.
4. Ibid., p. 186.
5. Wapshott, p. 131.
6. Swift, p. 160.
7. Ibid.
8. Ibid., p. 158.
9. Solomon, p. 49.
10. Wapshott, p. 129.
11. Ibid., pp. 130, 131.
12. Ibid., p. 166.
13. Smith, A., p. 335.
14. Bullitt, p. 356.
15. Swift, p. 178.

28: It's Come at Last—God Help Us

1. Ibid., p. 176.
2. Olson, p. 9.
3. Beschloss, *Kennedy and Roosevelt*, p. 189.
4. Bullitt, p. 360.
5. Nasaw, p. 402.
6. Brownell and Billings, p. 238.
7. Beschloss, *Kennedy and Roosevelt,* p. 190.
8. Nasaw, p. 404.
9. Axelrod, p. 18.
10. Swift, p. 188.
11. Wapshott, p. 133.
12. Ibid., p. 134.
13. Smith, A., pp. 365–367.
14. Ibid.
15. Wapshott, p. 134.
16. Overy, p. 35. Felix Belair Jr., "Roosevelt Pledge: He Promises Efforts to Keep U.S. Out of War—Thinks It Can be Done," *New York Times,* September 2, 1939, p. 1.
17. Smith, J. E., p. 435.
18. Shirer, *Rise and Fall of the Third Reich*, p. 635.
19. Ibid., p. 622.
20. Nasaw, p. 408.
21. Ibid., p. 409.
22. Israel, p. 10.
23. Beschloss, *Kennedy and Roosevelt*, p. 191.
24. Browning and Billings, p. 239.
25. Bullitt, p. 369.
26. Larson, p. 353.
27. Gellman, p. 159.
28. Dallek, *Democrat and Diplomat*, p. 230.

29: I'm Tired, I Can't Take It

1. Berg, p. 397.
2. Frank L. Kluckhohn, "Lindbergh Urges We Shun War," *New York Times*, September 9, 1939. See also Wapshott, p. 143.
3. Smith, A., pp. 378, 379.
4. Beschloss, *Kennedy and Roosevelt*, p. 198.
5. Browning and Billings, p. 243.
6. Beschloss, *Kennedy and Roosevelt*, p. 199.
7. Nasaw, p. 430.
8. Beschloss, *Kennedy and Roosevelt*, pp. 199, 200.
9. Ibid., pp. 200, 201.
10. Smith, A., p. 384.
11. Ibid., p. 385.
12. Ibid.
13. Overy, p. 61. James B. Reston, "Churchill Awakens Britons," *New York Times*, October 3, 1939.
14. Ibid., pp. 392, 393.
15. Roosevelt, E., *FDR,* vol. II, p. 950.
16. Browning and Billings, p. 243.
17. Ibid.
18. Israel, p. 35.
19. Ibid., pp. 41, 42.
20. Ibid., pp. 45, 46.
21. Ibid., pp. 48, 49.

30: One Mind Instead of Four Separate Minds

1. Israel, p. 56.
2. Moe, p. 173.
3. Dallek, *Franklin D. Roosevelt*, p. 550.
4. Lomazow and Fettman, p. 106.
5. Dallek, *Democrat and Diplomat,* p. 251.
6. Larson, p. 354.
7. Beschloss, *Kennedy and Roosevelt*, p. 202.
8. Israel, p. 79.
9. Beschloss, *Kennedy and Roosevelt*, pp. 203, 204. Ickes, *Diary,* p. 300.
10. Ibid., pp. 203, 204.
11. Ickes, *Diary,* p. 300.
12. Etkind, p. 194.
13. Bullitt, letter to the editor, *New York Times*, February 19, 1948.
14. Dallek, *Franklin D. Roosevelt*, p. 368.
15. Shirer, *Rise and Fall of the Third Reich*, pp. 686–688. See also, Welles, pp. 244–257, and David, pp. 523–527.
16. Shrirer, *Rise and Fall of the Third Reich*, pp. 686–688.
17. Ibid.
18. Murphy, p. 35.
19. Beschloss, *Kennedy and Roosevelt*, p. 204.

20. Wapshott, p. 164.
21. Ibid., p. 163.
22. Nasaw, p. 434.
23. Wapshott, p. 150.
24. Nasaw, p. 434.
25. Ibid.
26. "Salient Excerpts From the White Book Issued by German Foreign Office," *New York Times*, March 30, 1940, p. 4.
27. Israel, p. 86.
28. Ibid., pp. 73, 74.
29. Ibid.
30. Ibid., p. 67.
31. Welles, pp. 259, 260.
32. Berle, p. 311.

31: Churchill Is the Best Man England Has

1. Ibid., p. 85.
2. Israel, pp. 88, 89.
3. Ibid.
4. Ibid. Long's skepticism was shared by others in the Department of State, due in part to the fact that the Netherlands had remained neutral in World War I, and the Germans had respected their neutrality at the time. The Dutch assumed the Germans would respect their neutrality once again.
5. Goodwin, p. 17.
6. Ibid., p. 23.
7. Ibid., p. 25.
8. Ibid., pp. 31–33.
9. Nasaw, p. 441.
10. Ibid., p. 458.
11. Roosevelt, E., *FDR*, p. 1036.
12. Roberts, p. 12.
13. Goodwin, pp. 40, 41.
14. Ibid., pp. 43, 44.

32: My Mother Alice Who Met a Rabbit

1. Beschloss, *Kennedy and Roosevelt*, p. 206.
2. Smith, A., p. 432.
3. Nasaw, p. 431.
4. Shirer, *Rise and Fall of the Third Reich*, pp. 728, 729.
5. Wapshott, p. 175. See also, Shirer, *Rise and Fall of the Third Reich*, p. 735.
6. Goodwin, p. 62. See also, Bullitt, p. 416.
7. Ibid.
8. Wapshott, pp. 174, 175.
9. Goodwin, pp. 103, 104.
10. Ibid. p. 103.
11. United Press International, June 3, 1940.

12. Smith, K., p. 223.
13. Wapshott, p. 174.
14. Roosevelt, E., *FDR,* p. 1029.
15. Ibid., p. 1036.
16. Bullitt, p. 446.
17. Nixon, *FDR and Foreign Affairs,* vol. III, pp. 14, 15.
18. Churchill, p. 118.
19. Ibid.
20. Nasaw, p. 450.

33: The Hand That Held the Dagger Has Struck It into the Back of Its Neighbor

1.   *Foreign Affairs,* June 2, 2015, pp. 16, 17.
2.   Ibid.
3.   *New York Times,* June 13, 1939, p. 3.
4.   *Foreign Affairs,* June 2, 2015, pp. 16, 17.
5.   Overy, pp. 107, 108. "Many Flee Paris But Hope Persists," *New York Times,* June 10, 1940.
6.   Welles, p. 260.
7.   Nasaw, p. 451.
8.   Leuchtenburg, p. 302.
9.   Goodwin, pp. 67–69.
10. Leuchtenberg, p. 303, fnt. 11.
11. Israel, pp. 104, 105.
12. Glass, p. 15.
13. Welles, p. 261.
14. Glass, pp. 15, 16.
15. Ibid.
16. Bullitt, p. 467.
17. Smith, K., p. 223.
18. Glass, p. 16.
19. Ibid., p. 17.
20. *Foreign Affairs,* June 2, 2015, p. 19.
21. Shirer, p. 738.
22. *Foreign Affairs,* June 2, 2015, p. 23.
23. Glass, p. 150.

34: I've Told You, Eleanor, You Must Not Say That

1.   Israel, p. 114.
2.   Amy B. Wang, "A Ship Full of Refugees Fleeing the Nazis Once Begged the U.S. for Entry. They Were Turned Back," *Washington Post,* January 29, 2017.
3.   Goodwin, p. 173.
4.   Lash, *Eleanor and Franklin,* p. 636.
5.   Israel, p. 108.
6.   Ibid., pp. 109, 110. See also Goodwin, pp. 99, 100.
7.   Goodwin, pp. 99, 100.
8.   Ibid.

9. Ibid., pp. 103, 104.
10. "The Bureaucrats Are Pouting," *Washington Post,* November 25, 1940.
11. Goodwin, p. 176.
12. Shirer, *Rise and Fall of the Third Reich,* pp. 741, 742.
13. Glass, p. 105.
14. Welles, p. 262.
15. Moe, pp. 274, 275.
16. Israel, p. 118.
17. Ibid., pp. 199, 120.
18. Leuchtenburg, p. 316.

35: I Get Constant Reports of How Valuable You Are

1. Smith, K., p. 230.
2. Ibid.
3. Brownell and Billings, pp. 266, 267.
4. Smith, K., p. 231.
5. Ibid.
6. Nasaw, p. 449.
7. Ibid., p. 461.
8. Smith, A., p. 463.
9. Swift, p. 265.
10. Ibid., pp. 271, 272.
11. Ibid.
12. Smith, A., p. 463.
13. Wapshott, pp. 193, 194. See also, Smith, A., p. 464.
14. Goodwin, p. 151.
15. Shirer, *Rise and Fall of the Third Reich,* p. 780.
16. Smith, A., p. 466.
17. Ibid.
18. Swift, pp. 280, 281.
19. Shirer, *Rise and Fall of the Third Reich,* p. 794.
20. Goodwin, p. 174.
21. Rolde, p. 164.
22. Goodwin, p. 174.
23. Wapshott, pp. 200, 201.

36: Your Boys Are Not Going to Be Sent into Any Foreign Wars

1. Leuchtenburg, p. 320.
2. Gunther, p. 134.
3. Solomon, pp. 71, 72.
4. Wapshott, p. 164.
5. Shirer, *Rise and Fall of the Third Reich,* p. 803.
6. Wapshott, p. 165.
7. Israel, pp. 141, 142.
8. Roosevelt, E., *FDR,* p. 1066.
9. Bullitt, p. 510.

10. Ibid., p. 500.
11. Nasaw, p. 481.
12. Ibid., p. 482.
13. Ibid., pp. 481, 482.
14. Smith, K., pp. 234, 235.
15. Israel, pp. 141, 142.
16. Welles, p. 263. See also Nasaw, p. 482.
17. Beschloss, pp. 215, 216.
18. Ibid., p. 216.
19. Ibid., pp. 217, 218.
20. Ibid.
21. Ibid., pp. 219, 220.
22. Beard, p. 309.
23. Beschloss, *Kennedy and Roosevelt*, p. 221.
24. Nasaw, p. 496.
25. Israel, p. 146.
    37: We Will Talk About That and the Future Later

37: We Will Talk About That and the Future Later

1. Smith, A., p. 491.
2. Welles, p. 271.
3. Leuchtenburg, p. 303, fnt. 11. Also, Israel, p. 148.
4. Ibid.
5. Israel, p. 148.
6. Wapshott, pp. 231, 232.
7. Smith, A., p. 493.
8. Swift, p. 294.
9. Nasaw, p. 504.
10. Wapshott, pp. 251, 252.
11. Olson, p. 52.

38: He Can Talk to Churchill Like an Iowa Farmer

1. Welles, pp. 273–274.
2. Ibid., pp. 271–273.
3. Ibid.
4. Ibid., p. 274.
5. Adams, p. 199.
6. Ibid.
7. Ibid., p. 200.
8. Sherwood, p. 255.

39: We Americans Are Vitally Concerned in Your Defense of Freedom

1. Goodwin, p. 201.
2. Olson, p. 12.
3. Smith, A., pp. 524–529.
4. Ibid., p. 525.

5. Ibid.
6. Ibid., p. 529.
7. Roll, *The Hopkins Touch,* p. 88.
8. Fullilove, p. 135.
9. Ibid., p. 98.
10. Testimony of Secretary of State Cordell Hull, hearing before the Committee on Foreign Affairs, 77th Congress, 1st session on H.R. 1776.
11. Bullitt, pp. 407, 408.
12. Ibid., pp. 510, 511.
13. Ibid.
14. Olson, p. 5.
15. Ibid., p. 24.
16. Smith, A., p. 633.
17. Shirer, p. 827.
18. Ibid.
19. Bullitt, p. 519.
20. Israel, p. 175.
21. Olson, p. 88.

40: History Has Recorded Who Fired the First Shot

1. Bullitt, pp. 512–514.
2. Welles, pp. 278, 279.
3. Ibid.
4. Nasaw, p. 360.
5. Ibid., p. 359.
6. Bullitt, pp. 517, 518.
7. Olson, p. 90.
8. Goodwin, p. 253
9. Shirer, *Rise and Fall of the Third Reich,* p. 852.
10. Bullitt, pp. 522, 523.
11. Roll, *The Hopkins Touch,* p. 122.
12. Ibid., pp. 122, 126.
13. Ibid., p. 126.
14. Ibid., p. 127.
15. Ibid., p. 128.
16. Ibid., p. 128.
17. Ibid., p. 133.
18. Ibid., p. 132.
19. Ibid., p. 131.
20. Morton, pp. 12–15.
21. Ibid., p. 62.
22. Nasaw, p. 531.
23. Shirer, *Rise and Fall of the Third Reich,* p. 883.
24. Adams, p. 253.
25. Ibid.
26. Shirer, *Rise and Fall of the Third Reich,* p. 883, see footnote.

41: A Day That Will Live in Infamy

1. Brinkley, p. 86.
2. John G. Reid, Louis E. Gates, and Ralph R. Goodwin, eds. *Foreign Relations,* vol. iv (Washington, D.C.: U.S. Government Printing Office, 1941), p. 724.
3. Shirer, p. 884.
4. Ibid., p. 885.
5. Ibid., p. 892.
6. Gunther, p. 319.
7. Brinkley, p. 87. See also Welles, p. 314.
8. Welles, p. 314.
9. Smith, A., p. 533.
10. Etkind, p. 206. See also Bullitt, pp. 528, 529.
11. Bullitt, pp. 528, 529.
12. Brinkley, p. 93.
13. Shirer, *Rise and Fall of the Third Reich,* pp. 895, 89.

Epilogue

1. Gellman, p. 276.
2. *Time,* "One More Scalp," September 6, 1943.
3. Smith, A., pp. 616–618.
4. Nasaw, p. 579.
5. Ibid., pp. 570, 571.
6. Welles, p. 345.
7. Brownell and Billings, pp. 306, 307.
8. Rolde, pp. 260, 261.
9. Roll, *The Hopkins Touch,* p. 381.
10. Sherwood, p. 3.

INDEX